Quality Early Learning

HUMAN DEVELOPMENT PERSPECTIVES

Quality Early Learning

Nurturing Children's Potential

Edited by Magdalena Bendini and
Amanda E. Devercelli

WORLD BANK GROUP

ISBN (paper): 978-1-4648-1795-3
ISBN (electronic): 978-1-4648-1796-0
DOI: 10.1596/978-1-4648-1795-3

Cover illustration: © Robert Neubecker c/o theispot. Used with permission of Robert Neubecker c/o theispot. Further permission required for reuse.
Cover design and interior graphics: Melina Rose Yingling, World Bank.

Library of Congress Control Number: 2021922754

Human Development Perspectives

The books in this series address main and emerging development issues of a global/regional nature through original research and findings in the areas of education, gender, health, nutrition, population, and social protection and jobs. The series is aimed at policy makers and area experts and is overseen by the Human Development Practice Group Chief Economist.

Previous titles in this series

All books in the Human Development Perspectives series are available at https://openknowledge.worldbank.org/handle/10986/2161.

Contents

Boxes

Figures

Photographs

Tables

Foreword

Quality early childhood education (ECE) is one of the most important investments societies can make to help children build strong foundations that will support a lifetime of learning. Young children have enormous capacity to learn during their early years; we must nurture and harness this capacity and ensure children's early years are filled with high-quality, playful learning experiences.

We know from decades of evidence from around the world that high-quality ECE can help children develop the cognitive and socioemotional skills, executive function, and motivation that will help them succeed in school and beyond. When children enter primary school without strong foundations, they are likely to struggle much more to achieve their potential.

School is one of the most important spaces for equalizing opportunities. Quality ECE is a powerful tool to address inequality early in the child's development process. It can reduce the gap in foundational skills between children from poorer homes and their more affluent peers, which is often stark by age three and widens as children progress through the school system—unless children receive the right stimulation.

Yet, despite the overwhelming evidence of the value of ECE, today too many children either do not have access to ECE or are enrolled in ECE that is not of good enough quality to unlock their potential. Access to ECE has increased dramatically in the past decade, and today 62 percent of children are enrolled in ECE worldwide. This is good progress, but it is insufficient. Just 20 percent of children in low-income countries are enrolled, and we know that within countries there are great inequalities by socioeconomic status, disability, geographic location, and other factors that affect access to ECE of reasonable quality.

Even when children are enrolled in ECE, many of them are not learning or having as positive an early learning experience as they could because of low levels of quality. The expansion of ECE in recent decades has not, unfortunately, been consistently accompanied by investments to ensure quality. We have seen what happens when we expand access to education without ensuring quality. Schooling has been divorced from learning, and we are living with the results of this failure to ensure children's learning environments are high quality. An estimated 53 percent of 10-year-old children in low- and middle-income countries are unable to read and understand a short text; this "learning poverty" begins early, which means our efforts to address it must also begin early.[1] As countries expand access to ECE, it is imperative that they also ensure that children are in quality early learning environments from an early age.

The COVID-19 (coronavirus) pandemic is exacerbating the learning crisis, with predictions that learning poverty may rise to around 70 percent in the aftermath of the pandemic. The youngest children have been hit particularly hard, with access to learning opportunities limited at home and a host of deprivations that will affect their development, including increased poverty rates and food insecurity, reduced access to basic health care, and increased levels of stress and violence in homes. As countries seek to build back better from the pandemic they will face pressure and resource constraints, but we cannot let this lead to reduced resources for ECE.

World Bank investments respond to demand from countries. In the past five years, our portfolio of ECE investments has doubled from US$550 million to more than US$1 billion, and over this time we increased the share of ECE funding within our education portfolio from 5 percent to 11 percent. But still we know there is more to be done, and we are committed to working closely with client countries to ensure all children have access to quality ECE.

This volume brings together some of the foremost academics and implementation experts in the field of early learning and child development to share the evidence on different aspects of quality ECE and guidance for implementation. Each chapter focuses on a specific topic with a review of evidence and practical and feasible ideas to guide implementation in low- and middle-income countries. We hope this volume will assure readers that actionable and evidence-based strategies are available to deliver quality ECE at scale.

Quality ECE is essential to unlocking the potential within each child; it is also a compelling investment for systems and will be imperative if we are to address the global learning crisis. But it is not easy. We need to be honest that, although investments in ECE have enormous potential, expansion in access without ensuring quality will not lead to more learning. There is a common misconception that educational services for young children can be provided cheaply, that the teachers in ECE tend to be younger, or that not much experience or expertise is required to be a good ECE teacher and hence teachers could be hired at a lower cost. That is wrong. The child's experience will depend mostly on interactions with the teacher, and the teacher's influence on the child's development process compels us to bring the most talented professionals to that task.

Many countries have a unique window of opportunity right now to establish quality and equitable ECE while access is still relatively low, and to build systems that can ensure quality as ECE access grows. Getting this right early—both in the early years of children's lives and in the early years of setting up an ECE system—is easier than fixing problems later. Our children deserve high-quality, playful early learning experiences, and our education systems need to offer children high-quality early learning if we hope to produce capable and confident learners ready to face the challenges ahead. The task is urgent. Too many three-, four-, and five-year-olds are already there. Waiting.

Jaime Saavedra
Global Director, Education Global Practice
The World Bank

Note

1. Learning poverty means being unable to read and understand a simple text by age 10. This indicator brings together schooling and learning indicators: it begins with the share of children who have not achieved minimum reading proficiency (as measured in schools) and is adjusted by the proportion of children who are out of school (and are assumed not able to read proficiently). For more on this indicator, see the World Bank's 2019 report *Ending Learning Poverty: What Will It Take?*

Acknowledgments

This volume was edited by Magdalena Bendini and Amanda E. Devercelli, with the support of a core team comprising Elaine Ding, Melissa Kelly, Adelle Pushparatnam, and Medhanit Solomon Tekle. The team is deeply grateful to the authors who contributed to writing this volume: Cynthia Adlerstein, Violeta Arancibia, Juan Barón, Alejandra Cortázar, Caitlin M. Dermody, Sharon Lynn Kagan, Carrie Lau, Emma Pearson, Benjamin Piper, Nirmala Rao, Kristin Shutts, Iram Siraj, Yasmin Sitabkhan, Elizabeth Spelke, and David Whitebread. Funding for this work came from the World Bank's Early Learning Partnership Trust Fund, with support from the LEGO Foundation. The team appreciates the support and guidance provided by World Bank management and, in particular, from Jaime Saavedra, Global Director, Education Global Practice, and Omar Arias, Practice Manager, Global Knowledge and Innovation, Education Global Practice.

A number of World Bank colleagues served as peer reviewers and provided insightful comments and feedback: Melissa Adelman, Enrique Alasino, Samer Al-Samarrai, Diego Luna Bazaldua, Frances Beaton-Day, Tara Béteille, Ingrid Bjerke, Florencia Lopez Boo, Cristóbal Cobo, Michael Crawford, David Evans, Deon Filmer, Ariel Fiszbein, Ning Fu, Marcela Gutierrez Bernal, Amer Hasan, Alaka Holla, Peter Holland, Ella Humphry, Ines Kudo, Renata Lemos, Victoria Levin, Oni Lusk-Stover, Deborah Newitter Mikesell, Ezequiel Molina, Sophie Naudeau, Samira Nikaein Towfighian, Owen Ozier, Shawn Powers, Manal Bakur Quota, Halsey

Rogers, Shwetlena Sabarwal, Alonso Sanchez, Indhira Vanessa Santos, Tigran Shmis, Sergio Venegas Marin, and Tracy Wilichowksi.

The team thanks the advisory panel members, M. Caridad Araujo, Rukmini Banerji, Yasabu Berkneh, Margaret Burchinal, Harris Iskandar, Katherine Merseth King, Slinde Tove Mogstad, Peter Muzawazi, Amina Mwitu, Martin Woodhead, and Hirozaku Yoshikawa.

Sherrie Brown and Paul Gallagher edited the volume. Honora Mara served as the proofreader, and Melina Rose Yingling designed the cover and graphics. The team thanks Amy Lynn Grossman, Jewel McFadden, and their colleagues in the World Bank's formal Publishing Program.

In memory of Dr. David Whitebread, whose great intellect, playful spirit, unique expertise, and generous approach to scholarship have influenced the way millions of children learn and play. His work and life will continue to inspire us all.

About the Contributors

Cynthia Adlerstein is an assistant professor in the Faculty of Education at the Pontifical Catholic University of Chile. Her current research interests include modeling early childhood learning environments, enabling children's lived citizenship, and professional development in early childhood education for educational justice. She has published articles, chapters, policy briefs, research reports, and two books that frame these topics. Her research is grounded in interdisciplinary projects that combine mixed-methods and participatory approaches. Her recent work includes a longitudinal research and development effort into how Chile's MAFA—Physical Learning Environments Modeling System—improves early childhood education quality and children's learning outcomes. She also published a regional study supported by the United Nations Educational, Scientific and Cultural Organization on the state of early childhood teachers in Latin America, concentrating on the need to systematize data on professional conditions and promote systemic policy design based on solid local evidence. Cynthia currently combines the research agenda with teaching and training early childhood education professionals and postgraduate researchers. She holds a PhD in social sciences from FLACSO Argentina.

Violeta Arancibia is a psychologist and professor in the School of Psychology at the Pontifical Catholic University of Chile, mainly in the areas of educational psychology, talented education, and public policies for teachers. She has held numerous positions, including academic director (vice-dean) of the Faculty of Social Sciences at the Pontifical Catholic University of Chile, visiting professor at Stanford University, visiting scholar at Harvard University, and visiting professor at Radboud University. She founded and was director of the Center for Studies and Talent Development until 2011. In that year she became director of the Center for Improvement, Experimentation and Pedagogical Research at the Ministry of Education of Chile, where she was responsible for the design and implementation of policies in initial teacher training, teacher evaluation, and continuing education. She was named one of "The 100 women leaders of the Bicentenario in Chile." She has consulted for the World Bank as a specialist in education and teacher policies in projects in Armenia, the Dominican Republic, Ecuador, El Salvador, Haiti, Kuwait, Madagascar, Mexico, Mozambique, Nicaragua, Pakistan, Paraguay, and Peru. Violeta holds PhDs from the Pontifical Catholic University of Chile and the University of Wales.

Juan Barón is a senior economist in the South Asia Region of the Education Global Practice at the World Bank and the co-lead for the Management Capacity and Service Delivery Thematic Group. In his work supporting analytical and lending activities, he applies quantitative and qualitative research methods, including impact evaluations, to a range of topics on labor, gender, education economics, and others. He has published on multiple areas of education and economics. Juan has led the preparation of education projects in several regions and has attempted to bring analytical insights and new data collection methods more directly to the implementation support of World Bank operations, including in components with an early childhood education focus. He has been based in Haiti and Pakistan. He currently works as part of the Pakistan education team. Before his current role, Juan worked for the Latin America and the Caribbean Region of the World Bank's Global Education Practice, the East Africa Poverty unit, and the Central Bank of Colombia. Juan holds a PhD in economics from the Australian National University, which was supported by a scholarship from the Central Bank of Colombia.

Magdalena Bendini is a senior economist in the Latin America and the Caribbean Region of the Education Global Practice at the World Bank. In this role, she leads large-scale early childhood projects with the governments of El Salvador and Honduras. She has been studying and working on issues related to human development and poverty for the past 15 years at the World Bank, the Organisation for Economic Co-operation and Development, the United Nations Development Programme, and other international organizations. Her recent work has focused primarily on early childhood development as well as the development of skills over the life cycle. Magdalena was a core team member of the *World Development Report 2018: Learning to Realize Education's Promise* and contributed to the World Bank's Skills for Africa regional study. She also worked at the Center for

Universal Education at the Brookings Institution on the Skills for a Changing World project. She holds a PhD in public policy from the University of Maryland.

Alejandra Cortázar is an investigator at the Center for Studies in Early Childhood. She has worked as a researcher and consultant on issues of early childhood development, early education, and early childhood social policies for the United Nations Children's Fund, the World Bank, the Inter-American Dialogue, and specialized academic and research centers in Chile and elsewhere. She is a former member of the board of directors of the Education Quality Agency of Chile and a member of the board of the Educational Opportunity Association Foundation. Alejandra holds a PhD in education with a focus on public policy in initial education and a master's degree in developmental psychology from Teachers College, Columbia University.

Caitlin M. Dermody is a policy and research specialist at the Collaborative for Academic, Social, and Emotional Learning (CASEL). In this role she supports the policy and research efforts of the Collaborating States Initiative (CSI). Caitlin specializes in the developmental nature of social and emotional learning (SEL), early childhood education and care, and systemic SEL policy at the state and federal levels. Caitlin has acted as a state policy consultant to support the development of key publications and resources for the CSI. Before joining CASEL, she served as research assistant to Sharon Lynn Kagan at the National Center for Children and Families at Teachers College, Columbia University. Caitlin has also served as an intern at the Brookings Institution and the Yale Center for Emotional Intelligence. Her research focuses on systems of early childhood education and care, social and emotional learning, and policies that affect young children and families. Caitlin holds a master's degree in child development and education from the University of Oxford and a bachelor's degree in sociology and education studies from Yale University.

Amanda E. Devercelli is the World Bank's global lead for early childhood development (ECD), where she works across the institution to expand and improve investments in ECD, ensure delivery of high-quality operational and analytical work, and build capacity of its staff and clients. Amanda launched the World Bank's Early Learning Partnership in 2012, a US$60 million fund that has generated more than US$2 billion in funding to scale up high-quality ECD services worldwide. Amanda has led operational and analytical work across different regions and published on a range of topics, including childcare, measuring early childhood outcomes, and systems approaches to scale ECD. Before joining the World Bank, Amanda worked with community-based schools in Kenya and Peru and with several international civil society organizations in the field of international development. She has a master's degree from the Harvard Graduate School of Education and was awarded the Reynolds Fellowship in Social Enterprise from the Harvard Kennedy School of Government.

Elaine Ding is an analyst in the World Bank's Education Global Practice. Her work focuses mainly on early childhood development, teacher professional development, and early grade reading. She was part of the team that launched the Education Practice's Global Learning Target and accompanying Literacy Policy Package. Previously, Elaine supported work on human development projects in the East Asia and Pacific and the Middle East and North Africa Regions. Before joining the World Bank, she was a primary school teacher in Washington, DC. Elaine holds a master's degree from Harvard University and a bachelor's degree from Georgetown University.

Sharon Lynn Kagan is the Virginia and Leonard Marx Professor of Early Childhood and Family Policy; codirector of the National Center for Children and Families at Teachers College, Columbia University; and adjunct professor at Yale University's Child Study Center. She has helped shape early childhood practice and policies throughout the United States and has worked with UNICEF, the World Bank, and the Inter-American Development Bank in 75 countries. Sharon is a Fulbright Scholar, an elected Fellow of the American Educational Research Association, and a member of the National Academy of Education, as well as the author of 250 articles and 18 books. She is recognized for her path-breaking practical and theoretical work on early childhood systems, school readiness, standards and assessments, and advancing the development of the field of early childhood policy. She is the only woman in US history to have earned three of the country's most prestigious educational awards: the Distinguished Service Award from the Council of Chief State School Officers, the James Bryant Conant Award for Lifetime Service to Education from the Education Commission of the States, and the Harold W. McGraw, Jr. Prize in Education. Sharon holds a master's degree in liberal arts from Johns Hopkins University and a PhD in education from Teacher's College, Columbia University.

Melissa Kelly is a consultant in the World Bank's Global Knowledge and Innovation unit of the Education Global Practice. In this role, she supports capacity building of the Early Years Fellows, World Bank teams, and policy makers worldwide as well as implementation of early childhood projects in Central America and Southern Africa. She has focused on parenting and early learning programs across education, health, and social protection sectors. Melissa has held several leadership roles in early childhood, including as former chair of the Asia-Pacific Regional Network for Early Childhood. Her previous roles include director of program strategy and ECD senior advisor at ChildFund International and ECD specialist and Mozambique ECD program manager at Save the Children. Melissa holds a master's degree in international educational development from Teachers College, Columbia University.

Carrie Lau is an assistant professor in the Faculty of Education at the University of Hong Kong. Her research focuses on early childhood development and education, particularly in second language development and early childhood education policy. Her work embraces a bioecological approach to understanding the relationship between individuals and their contexts. Her research has examined home, school, and policy influences on early learning and development. Recent publications address the home learning environment and development of English as a second language, early education policy and child development, and stunting and early stimulation in the Asia-Pacific region. Carrie holds a PhD in early childhood education from the University of Hong Kong, an EdM in human development and psychology from the Harvard Graduate School of Education, and a BA in child development from Tufts University.

Emma Pearson is a senior lecturer, director of internationalization, and director of the Early Childhood Education Master of Arts Program at the University of Sheffield. She is also an associate professor in the College of Education at United Arab Emirates University. Emma is interested in understanding and highlighting the role of families and communities in supporting young children's education and well-being, particularly in marginalized and low-resource communities. Her work involves critical examination of ways in which globalized early childhood policy and practice are responsive to the unique lives and realities of families and communities across diverse contexts. She is a consulting editor for the journal *Child Development*. Emma has been a regular consultant to international organizations for more than 10 years, including UNICEF, UNESCO, the Asia-Pacific Regional Network for Early Childhood, and the Organisation Mondiale pour l'Education Préscolaire. She has taught at universities in Australia; Brunei Darussalam; and Hong Kong SAR, China. Emma holds a PhD from the University of Hong Kong.

Benjamin Piper is director of Global Education for the Bill & Melinda Gates Foundation and is based in Ethiopia. In this role he supports grantees focused on improving foundational literacy and numeracy in low- and middle-income countries. He was previously senior director, Africa Education, for RTI International, where he provided support to large-scale education projects across Asia, the Middle East, and Sub-Saharan Africa. Benjamin also served as the chief of party of the Kenyan national literacy program called Tusome, the set of randomized controlled trials in Kenya called PRIMR, and the National Tablets Programme. He was the principal investigator for Learning at Scale, a multicountry study of highly effective large-scale education programs and an external evaluation of programs increasing playful pedagogy at large scale with funding from the LEGO Foundation. He was also the principal investigator for Science of Teaching, an effort funded by the Gates Foundation to increase knowledge about the technical details of how to improve pedagogy at large scale. He has lived in East Africa since 2007. He has a doctorate in international education from Harvard Graduate School of Education and master's degrees in international education policy and school leadership from Harvard Graduate School of Education and Furman University, respectively.

Adelle Pushparatnam is an education specialist in the World Bank's Global Knowledge and Innovation unit of the Education Global Practice. She leads the Bank's work on measurement in early childhood and the measurement and improvement of teaching practices. Adelle engages in the Bank's work in the areas of socioemotional skills and inclusive education. Before joining the Bank, Adelle worked with children with autism, in both home and school settings. She also worked with Camfed, an international nonprofit organization that focuses on girls' education and young women's empowerment in Africa. Adelle holds a PhD in psychology with a focus on early childhood development and an MPhil in psychology from the University of Cambridge. She has a BSc in psychology from the University of Oregon, with minors in special education and business administration.

Nirmala Rao is the Serena H C Yang Professor in Early Childhood Development and Education, chair professor of Child Development and Education, and director of the Consortium for Research on Early Childhood Development and Education, Faculty of Education at, the University of Hong Kong. She is a developmental and chartered (educational) psychologist by training and has conducted research on early childhood development and education in Asian cultural contexts. This work has focused on the development of psychometrically robust and culturally sensitive measures of both early childhood development and the quality of early childhood education, early educational policy in the Asia-Pacific region, evaluation of early childhood programs, and culture, policy, and pedagogy in the early years. Nirmala has published widely, serves on the editorial board for premier scholarly journals, participated in high-level international meetings, written advocacy materials, and undertaken consultancies for international organizations. She has received awards for both research and teaching. She has also had significant administrative leadership roles in the Faculty of Education and at the Graduate School of the University of Hong Kong. Nirmala holds a PhD from Tulane University.

Kristin Shutts is a professor of psychology at the University of Wisconsin-Madison. She is the lab director and principal investigator for the Social Kids Lab at the Waisman Center, an institute focused on advancing knowledge of human development, developmental disabilities, and neurodegenerative diseases. Kristin studies how children apprehend their social world, and she is particularly interested in the development of social categories and intergroup biases in early childhood. She is an elected fellow of the Association for Psychological Science and serves on the editorial boards of several journals (*Child Development, Cognition*, and the *Journal of Cognition and Development*). Kristin holds a PhD in developmental psychology from Harvard University.

Iram Siraj is a professor of child development and education, Department of Education at the University of Oxford. Iram has codirected a number of influential studies on preschool provision, effective pedagogy, curriculum, and leadership. Her current studies include research into the impact of evidence-based professional development, effective environments for learning, and use of research tools to promote language and mathematics in the early years across preschool and elementary education. She has authored more than 250 publications, including three widely used rating scales that measure the quality of environments and pedagogy in early childhood education and care and promote child outcomes in the cognitive (ECERS-E 4th edition, 2010), social-emotional (SSTEW, 2015), and physical (MOVERS, 2017) domains. Iram has worked for and provided advice to UNESCO, UNICEF, the World Bank, the Organisation for Economic Co-operation and Development (OECD), the Bernard Van Leer and the Aga Khan Foundations, and has supported policy work internationally with the OECD, governments, and universities. She was awarded an OBE for her service to early childhood education and care in the Queen's honors in 2015. Iram holds a master's degree in history from Essex University and a PhD in education from the University of Warwick.

Yasmin Sitabkhan is a senior mathematics education researcher with RTI International's International Education Division. With more than two decades of experience in education, she provides technical expertise in mathematics and reading instruction, focused on early childhood through grade three, to projects around the world, including in Sub-Saharan Africa, South and Central Asia, North Africa, and Central and South America. Yasmin designs, analyzes, and disseminates results from various mixed-methods research studies to governments and donors worldwide.

Her interests build on her experiences as a classroom teacher, focusing on research regarding culture and cognition, teacher training and support, and classroom instruction. In her current role, Yasmin supports the Okuu Keremet! (Learning is Awesome) program in the Kyrgyz Republic, the Uzbekistan Education for Excellence Program, and the LEGO Foundation's Learning through Play initiative. She holds a PhD in development of mathematics and sciences from the University of California, Berkeley.

Elizabeth Spelke is the Marshall L. Berkman Professor of Psychology at Harvard University and an investigator at the National Science Foundation–MIT Center for Brains, Minds and Machines. Her laboratory focuses on the sources of uniquely human cognitive capacities, especially young children's prodigious capacities for fast and flexible learning. She studies these capacities by investigating their origins and growth in human infants and children, by considering human cognition in relation to the capacities of diverse nonhuman animals, by comparing the capacities of humans from diverse cultures, and then by collaborating with neuroscientists, computational cognitive scientists, and economists to probe how and why children learn. The core of Elizabeth's research uses behavioral methods and laboratory-based tasks to investigate the concepts and reasoning of infants, children, and adults. Her newest work asks whether children's fast and flexible learning can be illuminated by, and contribute to, research in artificial intelligence, and whether insights into children's learning can both inform, and grow from, research evaluating measures to enhance the education and development of children worldwide. Elizabeth holds a PhD in psychology from Cornell University.

David Whitebread was an influential academic and researcher in developmental cognitive psychology and early childhood education, based at the University of Cambridge Faculty of Education. David brought his experience of 12 years as a primary school teacher into this work. He was internationally recognized as a leading authority in the understanding of self-regulation and metacognition in young children, with early research in these areas relating to problem-solving and reasoning, mathematical strategies, and road safety skills. David's later research focused on the early development of play and playfulness in young children, and the role of language and self-regulation in supporting these important aspects of development. With generous support from the LEGO Foundation, he founded the research center for Play in Education, Development and Learning in the Faculty of Education, which he oversaw until his retirement in 2017. David was widely published in academic journals and wrote or edited a number of books, including *Teaching and Learning in the Early Years* (4th edition, 2015, Routledge) and *The SAGE Handbook of Developmental Psychology and Early Childhood Education* (2019, SAGE).

Abbreviations

BSM	boundary spanning mechanism
CENDI	Centro de Desarrollo Infantil del Frente Popular y Libertad (Childhood Development Center of the Popular Front "Land and Freedom"), Mexico
ECD	early childhood development
ECE	early childhood education
ECEC	early childhood education and care
FCV	fragility, conflict, or violence
HIC	high-income country
LMICs	low- and middle-income countries
MAFA	Modelamiente de Ambientes Físicos de Aprendizaje (Physical Learning Environments Modeling System), Chile
MOPS	Management and Organization Practice Survey
NGO	nongovernmental organization
OECD	Organisation for Economic Co-operation and Development
PD	professional development
QAF	Quality Assurance Framework
SABER-ECD	Systems Approach to Better Education Results–Early Childhood Development
SBM	school-based management

All dollar amounts are US dollars unless otherwise indicated.

Overview

From Evidence to Effective Policies: How to Invest in Early Childhood Education to Nurture Children's Potential

INTRODUCTION

The world is facing a learning crisis: an estimated 53 percent of 10-year-old children living in low- and middle-income countries (LMICs) are unable to read and understand a short text (World Bank 2019). The COVID-19 (coronavirus) pandemic is exacerbating this learning crisis; it is estimated that, without targeted strategies to mitigate the effects of school closures, economic shocks, and learning loss, the existing "learning poverty"[1] may rise to 63 percent in the aftermath of the pandemic (World Bank 2020b).

Learning poverty starts early in many children's lives. Even before the pandemic, an estimated 43 percent of the world's under-five population—almost 250 million children—were at risk of not reaching their developmental potential due to the debilitating effects of poverty and malnutrition (Black et al. 2017). In addition to being disproportionately exposed to negative health and economic shocks, children from disadvantaged families tend

This section was written by Magdalena Bendini, Amanda E. Devercelli, Elaine Ding, Melissa Kelly, and Adelle Pushparatnam.

1

to have more limited access to early stimulation, early learning programs, and learning materials at home and in their communities (McCoy et al. 2018). These children enter school without the preparation they need to succeed, and enter classrooms that are often overcrowded and of low quality. The lack of school readiness locks many children into a cycle of underperformance, grade repetition, and, eventually, dropout. It also leads to substantial waste of education systems' limited resources.[2]

Early childhood education (ECE) programs designed to meet the needs of young children are an essential component of a comprehensive package of interventions children need during early childhood.[3] Quality ECE[4] can help tackle learning poverty by building human capital and setting children on higher developmental trajectories. ECE programs are rapidly expanding around the world, presenting an opportunity to address early learning gaps that undermine children's ability to thrive in school. But, as evidenced by the current learning crisis, in spite of near universal enrollment rates in primary education, increased access may not lead to more learning.[5] As access to ECE expands, countries must ensure that expanded access is predicated upon parallel investments in quality to promote child learning.

In this volume, *quality ECE* refers to *center-based education services for children ages three to six that nurture children's potential and promote early learning*. While there is no universal threshold for "enough" quality, key investments to improve children's learning outcomes include improving the capacity of the ECE workforce (both educators and leaders), providing age-appropriate pedagogy and curriculum, and ensuring safe and stimulating learning spaces. Increasingly, evidence suggests that, for investments in ECE to be effective, program quality—the quality of classroom interactions and environment—should be at least higher than the quality of care and stimulation that children would experience in the absence of the program (either at home or at an alternative program) (Cascio and Schanzenbach 2014).

This volume provides actionable and evidence-based strategies for the delivery of quality ECE at scale. Chapters 1 through 6 synthesize evidence on key factors and strategies for effective ECE service delivery that leads to child learning,[6] and discuss how these strategies can be put into practice in LMICs. This overview provides guidance on how to prioritize investments in ECE to ensure quality, beginning with a review of the evidence on the promise of ECE and current challenges to realize its potential, followed by a discussion on ways that governments can sequence investments and implement recommendations from the volume's chapters so that access is expanded with sufficient quality to promote early learning. The overview's closing section discusses key complementary investments in the home environment and other factors that influence early learning outside of school.

The overview highlights three key points:

1. *Expansion of access to ECE must be balanced with efforts to ensure and improve quality.* ECE improves learning outcomes and productivity later in life, but only when it is of sufficient quality. To ensure that investments in ECE lead to improved learning, the scale of ECE expansion should not exceed the speed at which a minimum level of quality can be ensured.
2. *Investments that lead to more learning for children should be prioritized first.* Key investments to boost quality in the classroom—including improving the capacity of the existing stock of the ECE workforce, adopting age-appropriate pedagogy, and ensuring safe and stimulating learning spaces—need not be very expensive or complex to be effective.
3. *Systems that deliver quality early learning at scale are built intentionally and progressively.* Building such systems takes time and multiple investments, requires planning, and entails a focus on promoting early learning.

INVESTING IN QUALITY ECE TO TACKLE LEARNING POVERTY AND BUILD HUMAN CAPITAL

The Promise of ECE

Quality ECE can harness children's natural ability and motivation to learn, and foster cognitive and socioemotional skills, executive function, and motivation (Duncan and Magnuson 2013; Rao et al. 2014). Learning is sequential and cumulative (Knudsen 2004), and a strong foundation paves the way for a virtuous cycle of skill acquisition and productivity throughout life (Cunha and Heckman 2007).

Quality ECE is a powerful tool with which to address early disadvantages and inequality. In rich and poor countries alike, disadvantaged children benefit most from quality ECE. Compared with their wealthier peers, children from low-income families who experience quality ECE achieve greater gains across developmental domains, including in cognitive and socioemotional skills (see, for example, Britto et al. 2016; Burchinal et al. 2015; Holla et al. 2021; Rao et al. 2017; Yoshikawa et al. 2013). For example, in a low-income community in the United States, the HighScope Perry Preschool Project enrolled children into a high-quality ECE program, leading to higher educational attainment, increased earnings, better health outcomes, and lower crime rates for program participants four decades later (Heckman et al. 2010).

ECE is a cost-effective way to improve learning for children,[7] with impacts extending over the life course for children, their families, and societies. Beyond improvements in learning outcomes during ECE (Holla et al. 2021), investments in ECE increase the productivity of investments in other education levels (Cunha and Heckman 2007; Johnson and Jackson 2019). At primary levels, children who have attended ECE demonstrate higher attendance and better achievement, and are less likely to repeat, drop out, or require remedial or special education (Berlinski and Schady 2015; Naudeau et al. 2011). Quality early learning opportunities also lead to increased perseverance in school, higher education attainment, and improved health and labor market outcomes (Chetty et al. 2010; OECD 2017; Schweinhart et al. 2005). Children who benefit from quality ECE are more likely to vote and less likely to commit crimes (Currie 2001; Magnuson, Ruhm, and Waldfogel 2007; Schweinhart et al. 2005; Sondheimer and Green 2010; World Bank 2018b). The availability of high-quality ECE can also generate strong positive spillovers, including increased participation of older siblings in school (Martinez, Naudeau, and Pereira 2012) and of mothers in the labor force (Berlinski and Galiani 2007; Evans, Jakiela, and Knauer 2021).

Challenges to Realizing Quality ECE

Despite the documented high rates of return for quality ECE, access remains insufficient and unequal. Global enrollment rates in ECE nearly doubled between 2000 and 2019, from 33 percent to 62 percent, with the most dramatic increases occurring in lower- and upper-middle-income countries (figure O.1). South Asia (the region that boasts the largest under-eight population), for example, more than tripled ECE enrollment in the past two decades, expanding coverage from 17 percent to 62 percent (UIS 2019). Yet, while 62 percent of children are now enrolled in ECE worldwide, just 20 percent of those enrolled are in low-income countries (UIS 2020). Within countries, substantial variation exists based on socioeconomic status, geographic location, and other factors, with children from low socioeconomic status having the lowest access to ECE (McCoy et al. 2018). In low-income countries, for example, rich children are eight times more likely to attend ECE programs than their poor peers (UNICEF 2019). Other marginalized groups, including ethnic and racial minorities, refugees, and displaced children, may be denied access to ECE (as they are other levels of education).

Deep underfunding undermines ECE's potential. The expansion of ECE has not been consistently accompanied by investments designed to ensure

Figure O.1 Early Childhood Education Enrollment, 1970–2019

a. By region

b. By country-income level

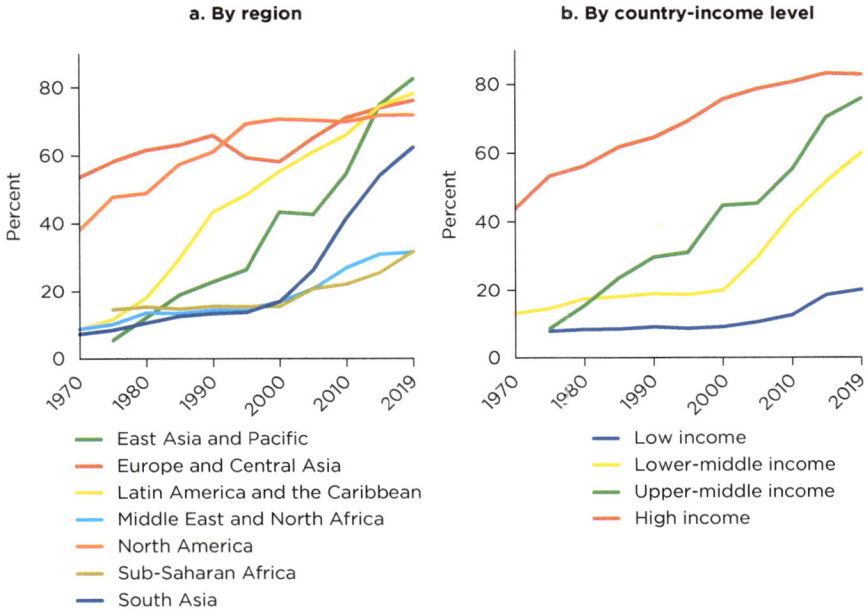

East Asia and Pacific
Europe and Central Asia
Latin America and the Caribbean
Middle East and North Africa
North America
Sub-Saharan Africa
South Asia

Low income
Lower-middle income
Upper-middle income
High income

Source: UIS 2020.

quality in service provision (World Bank 2018b). Data on financing are limited for many countries, but available data show that, although domestic public financing for ECE has increased since the early 2000s, it remains critically low, especially in low-income countries. Available figures for 2017 suggest that an average of 6.6 percent of domestic education budgets globally were allocated to ECE, with 40 percent of countries with data spending less than 2 percent (UNICEF 2019). Moreover, given that both ECE access and quality are correlated with families' socioeconomic status, limited public financing can exacerbate early learning gaps.

Even within the current low levels of investment, there is scope to improve the way in which ECE is delivered. For instance, in many countries, ECE expansion has occurred without a comprehensive and coherent systems approach. The absence of effective policy, institutional arrangements, financing plans, and regulatory and quality assurance frameworks has led to fragmented expansion and inadequate quality (UNICEF 2019;

World Bank 2013). The institutional arrangements for ECE vary across countries, and efforts to scale access are often hampered by lack of clear mandates and failure to plan expansion within a broader education systems approach. Some countries deliver ECE services through early childhood education and care systems, others through national or local education systems, and still others rely on a combination of the two.[8] Even when included in the larger education system, ECE often falls outside the official structure of primary education in public school systems (UIS 2019), limiting alignment across education levels and potentially leading to informal arrangements regarding workforce development and school leadership and management. Coordination between the institutions responsible for ECE and other sectors that support broader child development through nutrition, health, or other interventions is difficult in the absence of clear regulatory and policy frameworks (see chapter 6). Although many countries have policies on paper that lay out mechanisms for coordination or quality assurance systems, too often these written documents are not implemented due to weak implementation capacity or planning (Neuman and Devercelli 2013).

Numerous other challenges inhibit the delivery of quality ECE. Although similar to those confronted in primary education, in ECE these challenges are often linked to and exacerbated by the lack of a coherent systems approach to delivering ECE (see chapter 6). For instance, many LMICs lack learning or teaching standards for ECE. Structural standards (for example, for infrastructure)[9] are more common, but often hard to comply with, particularly by ECE centers operated by the community or other nonstate actors who may lack the necessary resources (see chapter 4). Beyond standards, information on adopted pedagogical approaches and their alignment with ECE learning environments is limited (see chapters 2 and 3). Countries often do not have an approved ECE curriculum available for teachers to use, and, even when they do, the content is often overly difficult, focused on skills more appropriate for primary school–age children, divorced from local context (not in a language that children understand, for example), or delivered through rote memorization (see chapter 2). ECE leaders often lack the specific knowledge and skills needed to support educators and to manage their centers or classes effectively to promote quality (see chapter 5).

The need for educators with specialized ECE training poses a key challenge in delivering quality ECE in LMICs. ECE educators must have the skills and tools to provide differentiated instruction and foster a supportive and inclusive classroom environment for all learners (see chapter 3). Yet entry and training requirements (as well as training opportunities) for ECE teachers are often the lowest in education systems.[10] Even with low entry requirements, just 44 percent of ECE teachers in low-income countries have received at least the minimum pre- and in-service training required for teaching at the ECE level in their country, compared with 72 percent of primary teachers (OECD 2018). ECE educators tend to receive lower remuneration, experience worse working conditions, and have lower prestige and even less support than their primary education counterparts.[11] These factors contribute to high staff turnover in ECE centers compared with primary and secondary education institutions (Neumann and Devercelli 2013), which not only is detrimental to children's development but also results in severe inefficiencies in service provision (Oberhuemer, Schreyer, and Neuman 2010; OECD 2006).[12]

The nonstate sector is playing a crucial role in expanding access to ECE in many countries, filling gaps in the public sector, including limited financial resources, infrastructure, and human resources to expand access to universal ECE. Nonstate provision, which is highly diverse,[13] now accounts for about 37 percent of global preschool provision and has increased since 2010, both in total numbers (reflecting the overall growth in preschool enrollment) and as a percentage of total enrollment (figure O.2). Comparable cross-country data with which to draw conclusions regarding the quality of nonstate provision vis-à-vis the quality of public provision are not available. However, high degrees of informality and unregistered providers in many countries necessitate increased governmental engagement with the private sector to regulate and ensure quality. Moreover, the

Figure O.2   Increasing Enrollment in Private Preschool, 2000–19

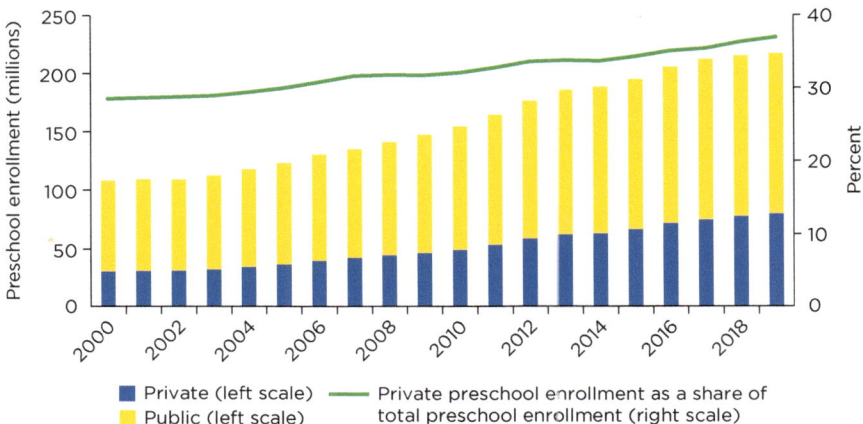

Legend:
- Private (left scale)
- Public (left scale)
- Private preschool enrollment as a share of total preschool enrollment (right scale)

Source: World Bank using UIS 2020 indicators.

potential for expansion of some nonstate models may be limited by management capacity and the fragmentation of service provision, reinforcing the need for an effective public system to engage with nonstate providers.

In sum, more and better investments are needed to make the most of ECE's enormous potential and avoid repeating the same mistakes that led to the global learning crisis in primary education. Expanding access to ECE without sufficient quality constitutes an inefficient use of limited resources that may bring about negligible or even detrimental effects on learning (Britto, Yoshikawa, and Boller 2011; Howes et al. 2008). Although more resources and a systems approach are essential to ensuring the long-term stability and quality of ECE provision at scale, more child learning can be achieved if investment decisions are informed by the growing body of evidence on how to improve the effectiveness of ECE to nurture children's ability to learn. In the face of resource and capacity constraints, further exacerbated by the COVID-19 pandemic, the most essential aspects of ECE should be prioritized first for ECE to expand effectively and promote learning for all children.

PROGRESSIVELY BUILDING SUSTAINABLE QUALITY ECE

The rich body of knowledge synthesized in this volume and past experiences from countries around the world suggest that successful policy and program implementation to build high-quality ECE systems should be grounded on promoting child learning above other potential imperatives. Resources are always limited; thus, systems face trade-offs not only between the breadth and quality of coverage, but also across crucial elements of quality, and between short- and longer-term goals. For example, as ECE systems expand, they carry substantial infrastructure and other major recurrent costs, such as teacher salaries. These costs often make up a large percentage of ministry of education budgets, limiting resources for investment in curricula, materials, professional development, and other needs; conversely, an immediate need for learning materials may hold up investments in monitoring systems that help ensure the quality of ECE over time. As governments assess how much can be achieved in the short, medium, and long run, they should take care to consistently allocate resources toward promoting learning in ECE classrooms along the way. This section discusses ways to prioritize, sequence, and implement recommendations from the volume's chapters to progressively build sustainable quality ECE at scale.

Balancing the Quantity and Quality of ECE

The recent expansion of access to ECE has the potential to lift many children's early learning trajectories. But overly ambitious targets and plans risk instilling pressure to scale quickly without ensuring quality. Quality can be harder to achieve at scale and often decreases as systems expand. A rapidly growing ECE system can challenge existing quality assurance efforts given that standards may be harder to uphold at scale without strong focus on and investment in quality. For example, the provision of suitable spaces to meet growing ECE supply can be challenging, and, in many places, expansion has been completed in the absence of ensuring minimum safety standards. Systems that have rapidly increased coverage have also struggled to secure the necessary workforce to meet growing service provision. Confronted with the challenge of identifying and training staff, some systems have made hiring and training requirements more flexible without adequately investing in the preparation of and support for those without qualifications, thus compromising the quality of their ECE workforce (Pardo and Adlerstein 2016).

The challenges and opportunities that countries face to improve conditions for child learning depend to some extent on countries' quality and coverage starting points, which, as documented earlier in this overview, vary widely across LMICs.[14] The pace at which countries expand access to ECE and the pace and sequence of investments to improve quality also vary significantly, reflecting what is already in place as well as the political will, momentum, and finance for ECE that define countries' possibility frontiers. Together, these factors determine a country's pathway to improving access to quality ECE.

Figure O.3 presents a highly stylized snapshot of starting points, with nascent ECE systems reaching a small fraction of the population with limited quality on one end of the spectrum (lower-left quadrant), and more established ECE systems reaching a significant percentage of children and providing quality services that promote learning on the other (upper-right quadrant). In addition to starting points, figure O.3 presents a few illustrative pathways toward quality early learning. Although the figure represents an abstraction of the very diverse, complex, and typically nonlinear trajectories countries follow on the path to expanding ECE, it helps illustrate how prioritization and sequencing of key investments to promote child learning at scale may vary by countries' starting points, possibilities, and aspirations.

Pathway 1 in figure O.3 is illustrative of Ethiopia's efforts to rapidly expand coverage from 5 percent in 2010 to 80 percent by 2021, while building quality. Pathway 2 reflects a more gradual process of consolidation of resources, learning, and budget expansion, such as the approach

Figure O.3 Pathways to scaling quality and access

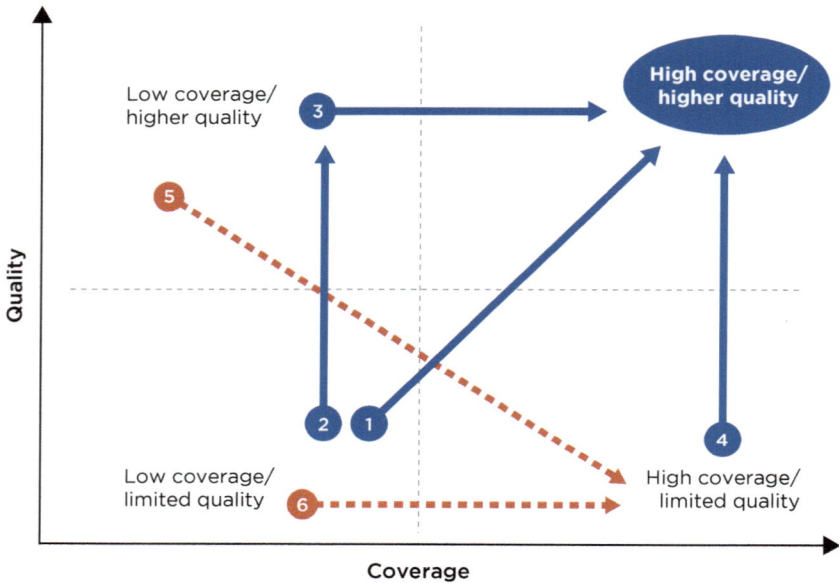

Source: Original figure for this publication.

embraced by Bhutan, which created scalable foundations for quality through national child development standards, and built the curriculum implementation and operational guidelines based on these standards before expanding coverage. Pathway 3 also depicts the gradual process of increasing access while maintaining quality (in Norway, for example). Finally, pathway 4 represents the trajectory to quality ECE for countries that already have moderate to high ECE coverage and are focusing investments on improving quality. In Kenya, for example, where ECE enrollment was about 76 percent in 2016, the government has undertaken a number of efforts in recent years to improve quality, including creating a Directorate for Early Childhood Development and Education within the Ministry of Education, devising National Quality Standards for Early Childhood Development and Education, and undertaking a decentralization effort that shifted some responsibility for service delivery and quality assurance to the county level.

It is critical to emphasize that countries should not expand ECE beyond the point at which a minimum level of quality can be guaranteed. The risk of doing so (as illustrated in pathways 5 and 6 in blue in figure O.3) is that the additional resources allocated to ECE may not lead to desired improvements in the foundational skills children require to succeed in school. While working to expand access to ECE, countries must take care to ensure ECE services are of sufficient quality to promote child learning. Many countries have a unique window of opportunity now to establish quality ECE while access is still relatively low. In the face of limited resources and difficult trade-offs, an accurate assessment of existing ECE coverage and quality should help determine which ECE investments are tackled first (as discussed below in this section) and inform expansion strategies.

Strategies for the expansion of quality early learning should prioritize children from disadvantaged families from the start. Although providing quality ECE to the most disadvantaged children can present more challenges, it can produce the greatest returns to investment because children from disadvantaged families benefit the most from quality ECE (Cascio 2015; Yoshikawa et al. 2013). Moreover, a growing body of evidence suggests that even marginal improvements in access to learning opportunities provided by ECE programs are effective at boosting learning in very disadvantaged settings (for example, see Ganimian, Muralidharan, and Walters 2021; Martinez, Naudeau, and Pereira 2017), suggesting that prioritizing access to ECE for children from low socioeconomic status can be highly cost-effective.

Access to quality early learning for children from disadvantaged families can be achieved through varying strategies. For example, Ethiopia's O-Class expanded access to ECE to children living in rural and remote areas in the four states that the government classified as emerging regions (based on development indicators), and to those from poorer backgrounds. The government is also working to roll out a two-year program to address further social and gender equity concerns. Countries with more established ECE systems can also increase efforts to achieve universal access. In Norway, where 97 percent of three-to-five-year-olds attend kindergarten services, state grants to kindergartens and nationwide subsidy schemes continue to ensure that low-income families pay a maximum of 6 percent of their income for a place in kindergarten (Engel et al. 2018). The program also extended hours in 2015 in response to working families' needs. In Hong Kong SAR, China, where 100 percent of children access services, the Free Quality Kindergarten Education scheme provides an annual flat-rate subsidy in the form of a voucher that can cover up to 100 percent of school fees, as well as a fixed amount for school-related expenses (Wong and Rao 2015).

Governments should consider whether and how strategies to leverage the nonstate sector can help tackle inequality. For example, if there is sufficient private provision of quality ECE for families that can afford it, governments can focus limited public resources on families most in need. Governments could also offer incentives for the nonstate sector to provide quality ECE to vulnerable populations, including learners with disabilities, girls, ethnic and racial minorities, and refugees or displaced persons, among others. Regardless of the specific strategy, ensuring consistently sufficient quality across service providers is essential, and two-tier quality systems that undermine vulnerable children's opportunities should be avoided.

Leveraging the nonstate sector to expand access to quality ECE involves governments engaging with local providers, setting realistic standards that

---

BOX 0.1

Gradually Upskilling the Workforce: The Case of Hong Kong SAR, China

The development of the regulated early childhood education (ECE) sector in Hong Kong SAR, China, was a response to the challenges that proliferated during the massive expansion of private ECE access. Enrollment in private unregulated ECE services grew twelvefold between 1951 and 1979, and this explosion of ECE demand resulted in a private ECE sector increasingly defined by poor service delivery, an untrained workforce, and high child-to-adult ratios.

In response to growing public pressures to offer more (and better) ECE, the government released an official policy on preprimary services in 1981, setting stringent targets for the upgrading of ECE quality in decades to come. This policy targeted ECE teacher training in particular and articulated the goal of certifying 45 percent of teachers and 100 percent of principals in five years and reaching 90 percent of teachers by 1992. This same document also made recommendations for minimum standards related to space, materials, equipment, and child-to-adult ratios in kindergarten classrooms.

One of the biggest investments in the ECE sector came through policies and financing focused on teacher professional development. Beginning in the mid-1990s, the government allocated 163 million Hong Kong dollars (HK$) over four years to provide professional training to kindergarten teachers, created certificates of ECE for in-service teachers, and implemented a government-subsidy scheme that allowed kindergartens to increase pay for trained teachers without needing to substantially increase parental fees. These measures to enact defined standards for classroom quality required an eightfold increase in government expenditure for kindergarten

continued next page

Box O.1 (*continued*)

education in 10 years, from HK$81.5 million in 1990/91 to HK$608 million in 1999/2000.

The entire education system underwent another full-scale reform in 2000, which again raised the workforce requirements for ECE teachers, introduced performance indicators that set standards for the ECE sector, and put in place a trial quality assurance mechanism. It also advanced a systems-thinking approach, reorganizing childcare centers for children three years and younger under the remit of the social welfare department, and putting kindergartens under the jurisdiction of the education department. The program also extended hours in 2015 in response to working families' needs.

Source: Wong and Rao 2015.

encourage registration, and safeguarding quality assurance (see, for example, box O.1 on Hong Kong SAR, China). Governments should map out local providers and design strategies that make the most of different providers' profiles. A critical issue facing governments is how to encourage nonstate ECE centers' registration. Often, quality standards—for example, physical space per child or playground requirements in urban areas—discourage or preclude providers from registering. To increase registration rates, which is critical to ensuring governments can fulfill their quality assurance role, quality standards should be feasible while still ensuring children's safety. The Jamaica Early Childhood Commission offers a practical approach, whereby centers must meet three basic requirements to register and are then given guidance and support to improve over time to achieve higher levels of quality. It is critical that the state maintains responsibility for quality assurance and has systems in place to ensure quality across nonstate and public sector provision.

Prioritizing Investments to Boost Child Learning while Building Quality ECE at Scale

Quality ECE is built progressively, requiring simultaneous investments across the range of ECE elements over time. Although evidence from systemwide interventions on programs' cost-effectiveness is still limited, a growing body of studies points to some key investments to improve children's learning outcomes. Such interventions include improving ECE educators' capacity, as well as age-appropriate pedagogical approaches to support learning and promote nurturing, responsive, and stimulating

BOX O.2

Children Learn Best in the Language They Understand

Children learn more and are more likely to stay in school if they are first taught in a language that they speak and understand. Yet an estimated 37 percent of students in low- and middle-income countries are required to learn in a different language, putting them at a significant disadvantage throughout their school life and limiting their learning potential. Children affected by language policies are often disadvantaged in other ways—for example, they tend to be in the bottom 40 percent of the socioeconomic scale and live in more remote areas. Of the 20 countries with the highest rates of learning poverty globally, 12 use instructional languages that few of their students understand when they start primary school, indicating that language of instruction is one of the most important reasons many countries have very low learning levels.

When children are first taught in a language that they speak and understand, they learn more, are better prepared to learn other languages, are able to learn other subjects such as math and science, are more likely to stay in school, and enjoy a school experience appropriate to their culture and local circumstances. Moreover, learning in the first language lays the strongest foundation for learning in a second language later on in school. Effective language-of-instruction policies are a cost-effective way to boost children's learning and school progression so that public funds can be allocated to other strategies to improve access and quality.

The World Bank policy approach to language of instruction is guided by five principles:

1. Teach children in their first language starting with early childhood education services through at least the first six years of primary schooling.
2. Use a student's first language for instruction in academic subjects beyond reading and writing.
3. If students are to learn a second language in primary school, introduce it as a foreign language with an initial focus on oral language skills.
4. Continue first language instruction even after a second language becomes the principal language of instruction.
5. Continuously plan, develop, adapt, and improve the implementation of language-of-instruction policies, in line with country contexts and educational goals.

Source: Crawford and Marin 2021.

classroom interactions (Egert, Fukkink, and Eckhardt 2018; Perlman et al. 2016; von Suchodoletz et al. 2017; Wolf et al. 2019; Yoshikawa et al. 2013) in a language that children understand (box O.2). There is also growing evidence that the effectiveness of interventions that improve children's learning hinges on the coherence of curricula, pedagogy, and teacher professional development (Pianta et al. 2017; Weiland et al. 2018). Interventions that enable rich classroom interactions through safe and stimulating learning spaces, as well as manageable child-to-teacher ratios and group sizes, also facilitate child learning (von Suchodoletz et al. 2017; Yoshikawa et al. 2013).

While working toward long-term objectives, countries should ensure that short- to medium-term ECE policies and services are grounded in the knowledge of what and how young children learn (chapter 1) and achieve a minimum level of quality that benefits children enrolled today (figure O.4). Whereas some of the earlier evidence on the effectiveness of ECE comes from intensive pilot programs in high-income countries that were very expensive,[15] growing evidence from LMIC settings points to considerably less expensive and less complex ECE interventions that improve key elements of classroom quality and promote learning gains, especially in settings where the quality of service provision is low and children's exposure to stimulating learning opportunities is limited.

Figure O.4 Prioritizing Investment to Boost Child Learning while Building Quality ECE at Scale

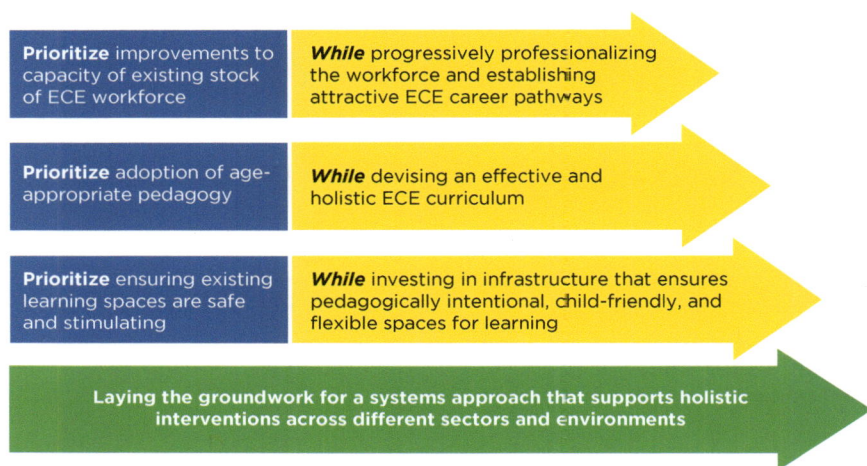

Prioritize improvements to capacity of existing stock of ECE workforce

While progressively professionalizing the workforce and establishing attractive ECE career pathways

Prioritize adoption of age-appropriate pedagogy

While devising an effective and holistic ECE curriculum

Prioritize ensuring existing learning spaces are safe and stimulating

While investing in infrastructure that ensures pedagogically intentional, child-friendly, and flexible spaces for learning

Laying the groundwork for a systems approach that supports holistic interventions across different sectors and environments

Source: Original figure for this publication.
Note: ECE = early childhood education.

To sustainably expand effective ECE, countries starting with limited quality should prioritize improving educators' capacity to support learning in ECE classrooms while gradually investing to professionalize the ECE workforce. The quality of the workforce is one of the best predictors of educationally rich interactions in ECE classrooms (Phillips et al. 2017). Building an effective ECE workforce is an involved, lengthy, and costly endeavor, particularly in systems in which resources and capacity are constrained (see chapters 3 and 5 on educators and leaders, respectively). While incrementally building practical preservice training and establishing attractive ECE career pathways, countries with limited quality should prioritize investments to develop in-service training and continuous professional development approaches that equip educators with an adequate level of content to foster early learning in ECE classrooms. Strategies for ongoing support and professional development, including communities of practice and organizational mentoring, can be effective complements to improving teacher competencies.[16] Countries with low ECE coverage and limited ability to rapidly train a high-quality workforce should set qualification requirements that are feasible in the short term while building in opportunities to improve workforce capacity over time (chapter 3).

Interventions to boost the capacity of ECE educators to support child learning need not be very expensive or complex. For example, in BRAC Play Labs in Bangladesh, Play Lab leaders are given short preservice trainings over a period of a few weeks, focused on fundamentals to lead the center, such as room organization, setting up timetables, and basic pedagogical skills, as well as supplementary monthly training through dedicated in-service training days. Community members and parents in this program assist with preparing materials and/or maintaining classroom spaces. This intervention costs US$81 per child per year over the two-year program and has led to improved teaching practices and child development outcomes (Whitebread and Yesmin 2021). In Ghana, the National Nursery Teacher Training Center conducts a five-day in-service preprimary training followed by refresher courses at regular intervals. The approach focuses on experiential learning to help educators understand and apply age-appropriate, play-based approaches in the classroom. Initial findings from an impact evaluation indicate that regular in-service training and ongoing professional development could yield significant positive impacts on teaching and classroom quality, as well as teacher motivation (Wolf et al. 2019). The total cost of implementing the program, including the time value of participants and trainers and direct budgetary expenditures, is US$16 per child (Wolf et al. 2017).

Developing effective curricula that foster early learning takes considerable time and effort (chapter 2).[17] To maximize learning in the short run, countries with no curriculum or one that needs to be updated can prioritize the adoption of age-appropriate pedagogy and associated guides and learning materials, while an effective curriculum is devised. For example, Bhutan prioritized the development of guidelines for curriculum implementation to orient teachers to their role in the classroom. Bhutan's 2018 Curriculum Implementation Guide includes information on child development, setting up the physical learning environment, relational pedagogy, classroom management, and child assessment, and provides learning activities organized by weekly themes. Beyond adopting a pedagogy, ensuring its alignment with educators' in-service training is crucial. In settings where capacity is very low, pedagogical tools and lesson plans can be an additional source to guide educators in the classroom in the short run (see chapter 2). The Tayari preschool program that ran in Kenya from 2014 to 2018 cost an average of US$15 per child per year for an intervention arm that included teacher training, classroom instructional support, learner workbooks, teachers' guides, and other instructional materials (APHRC 2018).

In contexts of fragility, conflict, and violence, effective pedagogy is even more important to provide structure and build supportive relationships between children and teachers while engaging regularly with parents and caregivers (see box O.3). For example, the Little Ripples program in Chad works with Darfuri refugee teachers in camps to implement a curriculum focused on play-based learning, positive socio-emotional and behavioral management, and a mindfulness component for children and teachers to create a calm space. In the program, children made strong improvements in emergent literacy and number skills while caregivers reported decreases in externalizing behaviors, such as kicking, biting, and hitting, coupled with increases in positive prosocial behaviors (Bouchane et al. 2018).

While building ECE infrastructure, countries with limited quality should prioritize conditioning existing spaces for early learning to be safe, accessible, and stimulating. Children do not require fancy ECE infrastructure or materials to learn, even if they can benefit from it (see box O.4 for a more detailed discussion of technology use in ECE). They need settings that allow for exploration and engagement with others and the surrounding environment, both indoors and outdoors. Countries with higher coverage can prioritize investments to improve existing learning spaces so that they are pedagogically intentional and facilitate children's learning. The toys and materials in the classroom should be familiar to students and support a culturally relevant and inclusive learning environment (see chapter 4). Cushions, rugs, and mats can all be deployed easily to enable spatial flexibility and support focused behavior—and are all relatively low-cost elements. According to Wright, Mannathoko, and Pasic (2009), the average cost of converting a standard classroom into a

BOX O.3

Early Childhood Education in Contexts of Fragility, Conflict, and Violence

By the end of 2018, 415 million children worldwide were living in conflict-affected areas, with 149 million living in high-conflict areas. Some 31 million, or 50 percent, of the world's forcibly displaced were children. It is estimated that half of the world's poor and two-thirds of the extreme poor will live in situations of fragility, conflict, or violence (FCV) by 2030. In these environments, child development is more likely to be impeded by toxic stress and service disruption. This is compounded by the fact that access to education is already severely compromised in FCV contexts, and early learning is in particular— fewer than 10 percent of children in FCV contexts receive some kind of early childhood education (ECE).

For children living in these contexts, quality ECE can be a protective factor, offering opportunities to learn and play, feel safe, and access other essential services such as nutrition and links to health services. While children are attending ECE, parents' time can also be freed up for income generation or other activities necessary for the household to survive. ECE interventions implemented at the local level can help restore the social contract and develop community trust, and can also play a role in mitigating local conflicts. Because "fancy" infrastructure is not necessarily required, ECE expansion is ideal for community-driven development.

Though ECE in fragile environments may be delivered in unique settings or under unique pressure, the principles described in the chapters in this volume are still relevant, chief among them the importance of a caring and capable ECE educator, the importance of pedagogy, opportunities to play and to learn through play, and the identification of flexible ways to use available spaces to facilitate learning. Some programs have deliberately integrated curriculum around managing the effects of trauma and conflict mitigation. Additionally, ECE in fragile settings should have a specific focus on primary caregivers and other adults because they can mitigate the negative effects of trauma and provide care and stimulation even in the absence of formal structures and when families are on the move.

Sources: GCPEA 2018; UIS 2020; UNICEF 2019.

BOX O.4

Technology

Technology is being increasingly used to expand access to learning resources in children's school and home environments. Evidence from a range of contexts indicates that high-quality educational content delivered via television can promote better developmental outcomes. Several studies of interactive audio instruction have demonstrated that it can be an effective and low-cost mechanism for delivering early learning to remote areas and to support teachers with training. Although still limited, emerging evidence also suggests that educational apps can boost preschoolers' learning outcomes. Technology can also be used to reach parents, for example, by using mobile apps or text messaging to deliver information about effective parenting practices and the importance of early childhood education. During the COVID-19 (coronavirus) pandemic in particular, there have been increased efforts to broadcast educational content targeted at both caregivers and young children through radio, television, text messaging, mobile apps, loudspeakers, and online platforms, sometimes accompanied by print materials, to support learning continuity. Technology can also be used to foster more inclusive early childhood classroom environments. In particular, assistive technologies, such as screen readers, audio books, or mobility aids, can support learners with physical disabilities or hearing and auditory impairments.

Several considerations need to be taken into account regarding the use of technology in quality early learning programs. First, young children benefit most from quality in-person interactions (chapter 1), and there are concerns about the developmental effects of too much exposure to screen time. Technology should not be used as a substitute for social interaction, and there are safety considerations, such as data privacy and cybersecurity. The COVID-19 pandemic has exposed the digital divide that disproportionately affects poor communities' access to learning opportunities. Policy makers should balance investments in connectivity and age-appropriate digital technology with investments in teacher professional development and parental support to address the above considerations and ensure equity and the resilience of the early childhood education system.

Sources: Borzekowski 2018; Dore et al. 2019; GEEAP 2020; Griffith et al. 2019; Hassinger-Das et al. 2020; Kearney and Levine 2019; Madigan et al. 2019; Mares and Pan 2013; Mateo Diaz et al. 2020; Richards and Calvert 2017; Saavedra Chanduvi, Aedo Inostroza, and Arias Diaz 2020; World Bank 2020c; Wright et al. 2001.

stimulating learning environment in Kenya is US$25. Bangladesh's Early Years Preschool Program offers children an additional year of ECE by utilizing existing government ECE classrooms in two shifts, allowing for relatively rapid deployment and significant cost savings (Spier et al. 2019).

Building Quality Early Learning Systems Intentionally and Progressively

While ensuring minimum conditions for learning are in place, countries should invest in laying the groundwork for a systems approach to achieve sustainable quality early learning at scale. A systems approach to ECE may also facilitate coordination with other services that support early learning, such as health and social protection (see chapter 6). Building systems that deliver quality early learning takes time, planning, and multiple investments. Country planning requires an honest assessment of the current status and key challenges for ECE, a review of available resources (human, financial, and systemwide), and an articulation of objectives to expand access to quality ECE in the short, medium, and long run (see, for example, box O.5 on Norway's universalization of ECE). Importantly, achieving sustainable, quality early learning at scale requires a resourced national ECE plan and dedicated financial commitments.

Building a quality early learning system entails a focus on results. A key step in this process is devising developmentally and culturally appropriate learning standards that create shared expectations for what children should be learning in ECE, as well as process and structural quality standards. Learning and quality standards should be agreed on in-country and include stakeholder engagement with local authorities and community members to ensure they are realistic and locally relevant. Also crucial are the definition and establishment of a regulatory framework for sustainable implementation of standards, including monitoring compliance. When accompanied by the necessary resources to sustain their implementation, these regulatory frameworks can help improve service delivery conditions across public and nonstate sector ECE providers (see chapters 4 and 5).

Monitoring and quality assurance efforts can help countries learn what works in the local context, identify implementation bottlenecks to improving child learning (which can be helpful to fine-tune interventions and policy), and define which investments to prioritize and which to deploy over time, informing learning feedback loops that help guide the growth of the ECE system toward quality early learning at scale (figure O.5).

Countries should prioritize investments in data systems that capture child learning and quality of learning environments, as well as in strengthening monitoring and quality assurance systems to ensure up-to-date

BOX O.5

Public Pressure for Expanded Childcare and the Gradual Universalization of ECE in Norway

Norway's state early childhood education (ECE) sector grew out of mounting public pressure to provide childcare The country began by providing federal subsidies to formal childcare programs in 1962, followed by a formal survey to determine the state of childcare options and the demand for formal childcare. The survey found that 35 percent of mothers with three-to-six-year-olds stated a need for formal childcare but there was only 5 percent childcare coverage nationwide. The same survey found that, of those who used out-of-home care on a regular basis, more than 85 percent relied on informal and unregulated arrangements.

Norway defined its first set of ECE sector objectives in its 1972 Kindergarten White Paper. The document proposed radical changes to public childcare policies, setting out universal childcare—with a focus on children with special needs—as an explicit goal over the policy cycle. The government set out to quadruple the number of childcare spaces within the first decade and then passed the Kindergarten Act in 1975 to regulate kindergartens.

The development of Norwegian ECE policy has been an iterative process spanning many decades. After introducing the first Kindergarten Act in 1975, the government defined a phased effort to expand and publicly finance access. Shortly thereafter, Norway introduced the aim of publicly subsidizing universal access to high-quality ECE in the same decade and then focused on establishing federal regulations for quality of care, including establishing teacher requirements, a national curriculum, and a universal framework for early childhood education and care provision. In 2005, Norway instituted a new Kindergarten Act, incorporating strict regulations for how ECE centers would be staffed and operated and introducing a five-year recruitment initiative as well as new regulations for kindergarten teacher education. This was accompanied by new goals and standards, with the Directorate for Education and Training issuing national guidelines on inspection to help municipalities and county governors' offices fulfill their monitoring roles. Since 1975, progression toward universal access has occurred incrementally, with parental fees charged for ECE decreasing correspondingly. ECE enrollment in Norway stands at 97 percent as of 2018, with grants to kindergartens continuing to ensure that low-income families pay a maximum of 6 percent of their income for a place in kindergarten (Engel et al. 2018).

Sources: Engel et al. 2018; UIS 2020.

information is available for decision-making. Appropriate instruments are needed for monitoring learning and quality standards. In the medium to longer term, these standards, along with the identified monitoring instruments, contribute to the establishment of a monitoring or information system to track ECE implementation, cost-effectiveness, service provision, and child outcomes. An effective monitoring or information system also includes mechanisms for access to, and use of, data across a wide range of stakeholders to create learning feedback loops.

Clear goals are key to the design and implementation of monitoring and quality assurance efforts. Child outcome assessments have a variety of purposes (see, for example, table 1A.1 in Clarke and Luna-Bazaldua 2021), and different instruments are designed accordingly. For example, an assessment used by teachers in the classroom to inform instruction looks different from one used to monitor child outcomes at the population level, and from a screening or diagnostic tool designed to identify children with developmental delays or disabilities. To ensure that the resulting data are fit for purpose, the selected instruments must align with the intended goal of the assessment. In addition, care must be taken to ensure that instruments are used only for their intended purposes. Stakeholders must be clear on the purposes of the assessments and safeguards in place to ensure that assessments are not misused to, for example, exclude children from the education system.

Figure O.5 Problem-Driven Iterative Adaptation Drives Successful Policy Implementation

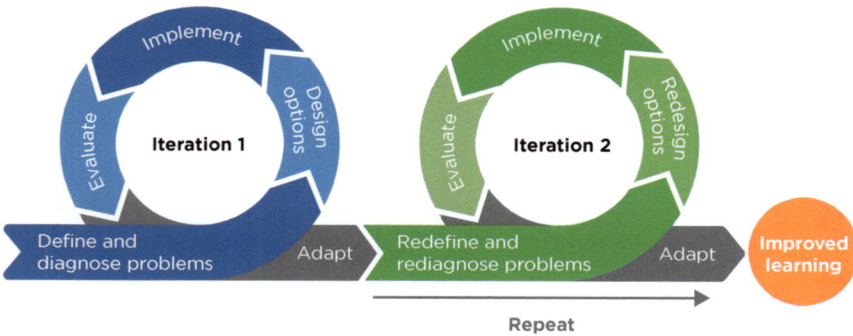

Source: Adapted from Andrews, Pritchett, and Woolcock 2017 in World Bank 2018b.

INVESTMENTS BEYOND ECE THAT PROMOTE EARLY LEARNING

A number of factors outside the ECE setting play a crucial role in shaping children's developmental trajectories (Britto, Yoshikawa, and Boller 2011). Although the bulk of this volume focuses on the quality of classroom-based early learning and its effects on children's development, factors such as parental engagement, learning resources at home, and learning resources in the community greatly influence children's learning. These factors are important in and of themselves, but also interact with the quality of ECE in affecting learning outcomes. For example, quality early learning in a classroom setting can mitigate some of the effects of a poor home learning environment, and likewise a rich home learning environment can complement the effects of quality ECE (Anders et al. 2012; McDonald Connor et al. 2005; Melhuish et al. 2008; Votruba-Drzal et al. 2013).

The COVID-19 pandemic has shed new light on the crucial role that the home and community environments play in young children's learning (box O.6). During the pandemic, learning has suffered greatly because of school closures (Azevedo et al. 2020), especially during children's early years when the in-person interactions and relationships matter most (Lopez Boo, Behrman, and Vasquez 2020). As such, early learning interventions that target home and community environments play an important role in promoting resilience and equity while improving learning outcomes for all children.

The quality of parent-child interactions from the earliest years greatly influences children's learning outcomes. As chapter 1 discusses, parents and caregivers are key decision-makers and stakeholders in their children's education. Their beliefs about the purpose of ECE and how children should learn can affect the uptake and design of ECE programs (Wolf et al. 2019). Taken together, these factors highlight the need for interventions to empower parents to make evidence-based decisions about their children's early learning, to help parents improve the quality of their parenting practices and interactions with children at home, and to increase parent involvement with the formal learning environment. These interventions are effective at both changing parents' behaviors and improving child outcomes in LMICs (Barrera-Osorio et al. 2020; Britto et al. 2015; Jeong, Pitchik, and Yousafzai 2018). Design considerations and specific pathways to impact vary by local context, and more research is necessary on variations in caregiving beliefs and practices (Kabay, Wolf, and Yoshikawa 2017;

BOX O.6

The COVID-19 Pandemic and Early Childhood Education

The COVID-19 (coronavirus) pandemic has dramatically affected children's lives and access to learning. Young children have been and will continue to be particularly vulnerable during the COVID-19 pandemic and recovery. This vulnerability stems from several issues, including the developmental period of their life and relatively narrow window in which to intervene before primary school entry, the need for caregivers to engage with and support young children's learning at home, limited access to education technology or physical learning materials in many homes, and decisions by some countries to prioritize virtual learning for older children rather than younger children.

To avoid the loss of these learning opportunities, countries had to act quickly during the crisis to reach children, and adjustments to programs will be necessary during the recovery phase to reflect the lost learning opportunities that will affect many children for years to come. System-level issues will also need to be addressed because many countries are expected to now experience even more overenrollment in early childhood education (ECE) or early primary grades as a result of the lost time when some children could not enroll.

Although countries are striving to provide distance learning programs for six-to-eight-year-olds, programs for four-to-five-year-olds are less common. There are bright spots though. In Colombia, the Instituto Colombiano de Bienestar Familiar launched the Mis Manos te Enseñan (My Hands Teach You) program to provide pregnant women and young children with information, activity kits, phone calls, and other support to promote children's development. In North Macedonia, the government created a TV classroom and the Eduino digital platform aimed at enhancing the learning of ECE and primary school children. The World Bank also supported the government in securing the rights to *Sesame Street*, a television program that provides critical early education to children, which airs on three national television stations and reaches an estimated 250,000 children daily. In addition, the government has partnered with the World Bank on the Read@Home initiative, a new effort to get reading, learning, and play materials into homes, targeting families that are unlikely to be reached with many of the remote learning approaches being rolled out by ministries of education in the context of the COVID-19 pandemic. In North Macedonia, Read@Home will reach all children ages three to twelve from the country's poorest 10 percent of households. Each child receives a package of four picture books in his or her native tongue with accompanying questions and activities for each book,

continued next page

Box O.6 *(continued)*

along with suggestions to help parents read with their children and ideas to play together.

In the medium term, the economic downturn caused by the impacts of COVID-19 may reduce both the demand for schooling and the supply of quality schooling because of reduced household income and public fiscal constraints. In many countries, ECE typically receives fewer budget resources than older grades. Government budgets for ECE may be reduced and, within individual families, the choice may be made to prioritize limited education funding for older children instead of younger children.

The costs of the pandemic will be felt long into the future of young children's lives. A recent study by the Inter-American Development Bank (Lopez-Boo, Behrman, and Vasquez 2020) simulated the cost of ECE program closures in 140 countries due to the COVID-19 pandemic. To estimate the cost of ECE closures, the team simulated future earnings forgone when the children become adults as percentages of GDP due to declines in ECE participation net of ECE program costs. The study finds that closure of ECE programs for 12 months will cost 5.9 percent of GDP of lower-middle-income countries and 2.4 percent of GDP of low-income countries (the relatively smaller cost to low-income countries reflects the low enrollment of children in ECE before the pandemic).

As countries consider how to respond to the challenge of delivering quality early learning opportunities in the COVID-19 context, the following policy and programming recommendations may be helpful:

- Ensure ECE is included within ministry of education programming for distance learning, including the development of quality content and support for dissemination.
- Engage with and support parents with ideas, information, and materials to encourage their children's learning, including learning through play and early stimulation via phone, television, radio, direct outreach, and material delivery such as storybooks in languages that families understand. Level the playing field in access to resources, particularly in rural areas, for poorer households, and where caregivers are not literate.
- Ensure ECE is part of reenrollment campaigns.
- Plan for potential overenrollment in preprimary or early grades of primary where disrupted school years or repetition may result in surges in young children's enrollment and potential overcrowding in preprimary and early primary grades.

Sources: Kelly 2021; Kim et al 2020; Lopez-Boo, Behrman, and Vasquez 2020; Naceva, Galevski, and Kelly 2020; World Bank 2020a.

Pence and Marfo 2008; Wadende, Oburu, and Morara 2016) to ensure ECE can be underpinned by a clear understanding of local norms, values, and expectations.

The quantity and quality of learning resources available at home influence the quality of children's early learning. For example, consistent with the evidence in chapters 1, 2, and 4, a study covering 35 low-, middle-, and high-income countries found that having at least one children's book at home almost doubled the likelihood of the child being on track for literacy and numeracy, controlling for variables such as maternal education and wealth index quintile, children's age, and area of residence (Manu et al. 2019). However, many children are growing up in homes without these learning resources. It is important to note that interventions involving the distribution of learning materials to the home have the most impact when parents and caregivers are provided with ongoing support to use these materials to promote their children's development (Knauer et al. 2020; Saavedra Chanduvi, Aedo Inostroza, and Arias Diaz 2020). This has become even more critical during the COVID-19 pandemic as parents have been asked to take on additional roles to support young children's learning continuity at home (box O.6).

Beyond the home, learning spaces and resources should expand to include the wider community. Public learning spaces supplement the school and home learning environments by increasing the resources available to all children. For instance, an intervention in rural Mongolia showed that access to mobile book and toy libraries greatly expanded the learning resources that children had access to and had a positive effect on children's development (World Bank 2017). Similarly, thoughtfully designed playgrounds with a focus on nature and neighborhood green spaces also have positive effects on child outcomes (Carr and Luken 2014; Flouri, Midouhas, and Joshi 2014). Taking a step further, recent efforts have married the science of learning with urban planning and placemaking, turning to less commonly considered public spaces, such as bus stops and grocery stores, as chances to embed learning opportunities for children (Bustamante et al. 2019; Hadani and Vey 2020).

Efforts to improve early learning should be complemented with efforts to improve other crucial aspects of child development such as health, nutrition, child protection, and social protection. When supporting parents' and other caregivers' efforts to promote children's development in the early years, it is important to treat child development holistically (Richter et al. 2017). Indeed, children's healthy development is a key determinant of their learning, both in early childhood and beyond.

For example, nutrition and health interventions, such as micronutrient supplementation, have positive effects on children's learning outcomes (Galasso and Wagstaff 2019; Richter et al. 2017). Child protection interventions can reduce the incidence of child maltreatment (Mikton and Butchart 2009), and cash transfer programs can alleviate household constraints, and thus also have a positive effect on child outcomes (Nandi et al. 2017). In Indonesia, for example, various government entities and nongovernmental organizations work together to run parent education programs that cover many areas of the country. The Ministry of Health disseminates information on immunization, health, and safety practices; and district health offices offer classes taught by paraprofessionals and other specialized professionals to parent groups (Tomlinson and Andina 2015). The Ministry of Education and Culture provides grants to preschool programs that submit successful proposals to create parent education programs, and programs that receive the grant must require that parents bring their children and interact with them during class (World Bank 2018a).

Many children in LMICs are exposed to multiple risk factors that cannot be addressed by a single intervention, and, as such, multifactor or multisectoral interventions are needed. Adding a parental support intervention to a cash-transfer program can have potentially additive effects on child development outcomes because together they boost both household income and parent education on child development (Fernald et al. 2017). For example, in the Head Start program in the United States, the combination of multiple program components, including parental involvement, health checkups, nutritious meals, and early learning services, contributed to improving children's socioemotional, cognitive, and physical development. Moreover, participating children were 93 percent less likely to be removed from their home environment and placed into foster care (Aikens et al. 2013; Klein, Fries, and Emmons 2017; Lee et al. 2013; US Department of Health and Human Services 2010). Another benefit of adopting a multisectoral approach is the expansion of the number of existing platforms, such as community-based programs and social safety nets, that can be leveraged to reach the most vulnerable and hard-to-reach populations in an effective and sustainable way. For example, Peru's Primero la Infancia (Childhood First) strategy includes integrated packages of services for pregnant women and children zero to five years across health, education, and social services sectors—such as prenatal visits, home visiting for parental support and nutrition, cash transfers, and preschool—some of which are universal and others that are targeted on the basis of need (Peru, Ministry of Social Development and Inclusion 2016).

CONCLUSION

The expansion of ECE across LMICs presents an opportunity for countries to address learning poverty and inequality and build human capital for the future. Access to ECE has expanded dramatically across all regions and income levels in the past 20 years and is accelerating rapidly. This investment in ECE offers great promise for learning—there is no other time in life during which the brain is as sensitive to learning opportunities, with the potential for investments to yield a lifetime of benefits.

ECE leads to learning if it is of sufficient quality; the pace of ECE expansion, therefore, must be conditioned on the speed at which a minimum level of quality can be ensured. The rapid scale-up of ECE access in LMICs over the past decades has shown that quality can be harder to achieve at scale, and that quality can decrease as systems expand. For investments in ECE to yield returns, the expansion of ECE must be carried out with a strong focus on, and associated investments in, quality to foster child learning. At best, increasing access without due emphasis on quality is an inefficient use of limited resources; at worst, it can undermine children's developmental outcomes. Thus, access to ECE should expand only to the point at which quality can be ensured.

Many countries have a unique window of opportunity now to establish quality ECE while access is still relatively low and to build systems that can ensure quality as ECE access grows. Getting this right early—both in the early years of children's lives and in the early years of setting up an ECE system—is easier than fixing problems later. Countries' strategies for the expansion of quality ECE should prioritize children from disadvantaged households from the start, and, as countries' coverage rates climb higher, specialized approaches to reach the most vulnerable children who remain excluded can be introduced to better support their learning.

Countries should prioritize investments that promote child learning. Efforts to expand ECE should balance a strong focus on a minimum level of quality across different elements of ECE with a long-term plan to achieve sustainable quality early learning at scale. Countries should concurrently work on the articulation of long-term system objectives and ECE strategy, while prioritizing short-run investments to boost quality in the classroom, including improving the capacity of the existing stock of ECE workforce, adopting age-appropriate pedagogy, and ensuring safe and stimulating learning spaces. To be effective, interventions to boost child learning need not be very expensive or complex, but they need to be grounded in the knowledge of what and how young children learn.

Although countries' experiences vary, building systems that deliver quality early learning takes time and planning, multiple investments, and many adjustments through iteration and adaptation. National planning and goals that are clear and feasible are necessary for more effective and equitable use of ECE investments in the short, medium, and long run. Information systems can help countries diagnose conditions on the ground and identify bottlenecks to improving child learning, which can be helpful to adapting interventions and policy through learning feedback loops, as well as defining which investments to prioritize and which to deploy over time. Achieving sustainable, quality early learning at scale requires sufficient public resources, deployed to the range of ECE elements discussed in this volume, prioritizing a minimum level of quality across elements, while creating a long-term plan to improve over time.

ECE is not enough on its own to promote early learning. Complementary investments in the home environment and in other factors that influence early learning outside of school, especially for the most disadvantaged children, are needed. Policies to boost quality early learning in ECE should be accompanied by programs that support parents and caregivers, as well as programs that address holistic child development across health, nutrition, and protection. By strengthening and engaging with the many systems that affect young children beyond the formal learning environment, education systems can be more effective, equitable, and resilient in delivering quality in the early years.

ANNEX OA: NONSTATE SECTOR ENGAGEMENT IN ECE

The nonstate sector comprises a range of different actors engaged in direct service provision and in ancillary services, including for-profit ECE centers (formal and informal), nongovernmental organizations, faith-based providers, community-based models, parent cooperatives, and employer-supported programs (table OA.1).

Enrollment in ECE nonstate providers varies by region (figure OA.1), though in many countries official figures likely understate the scope because of high degrees of informality and unregistered providers. Provision of ECE by low-cost private providers is increasing in urban areas. For example, a survey of 4,407 working poor families across eight cities in India found that 90 percent of their four- and five-year-olds attended ECE at an affordable private school (Irfan et al. 2017). In rural, harder to reach areas, market conditions are less conducive to low-cost private providers; however, many community and nongovernmental organization groups provide preschool services (for example, the Aga Khan Foundation Madrasa Resource Center community preschool program, which operates in Kenya, Tanzania, and Uganda, or BRAC Play Labs operating in Bangladesh and Tanzania).

Table OA.1 Typograph of Nonstate Sector

Type of provider	Description
Formal for-profit providers	• Privately managed preschools; range from high-end to low-cost services • Often single providers, some chains • Stand-alone or attached to a primary school
Informal for-profit providers	• Privately managed preschools; range from high-end to low-cost services • Often single providers, some chains • Stand-alone or attached to a primary school
Community-based models	• Community-managed, usually with NGO or government support • Stand-alone or attached to a primary school • *Often overlaps with faith-based or NGO providers*
Faith-based providers	• Some affiliation with a religious institution or faith • *Often overlaps with community-based providers*
NGO providers	• NGO-supported or NGO-managed services • *Often overlaps with community-based or faith-based providers*
Parent cooperatives	• Focus on parental ownership and contributions • Can be facilitated by movements and policies or occur organically
Employer-supported programs	• Often with an intention to provide parents with childcare • Various models include onsite childcare (established or contracted), partnerships with other companies, reserved places, or subsidies

Source: Devercelli and Beaton-Day 2020.
Note: NGO = nongovernmental organization.

Figure OA.1 Percentage of Preschool-Age Children by Type of Enrollment, 2019

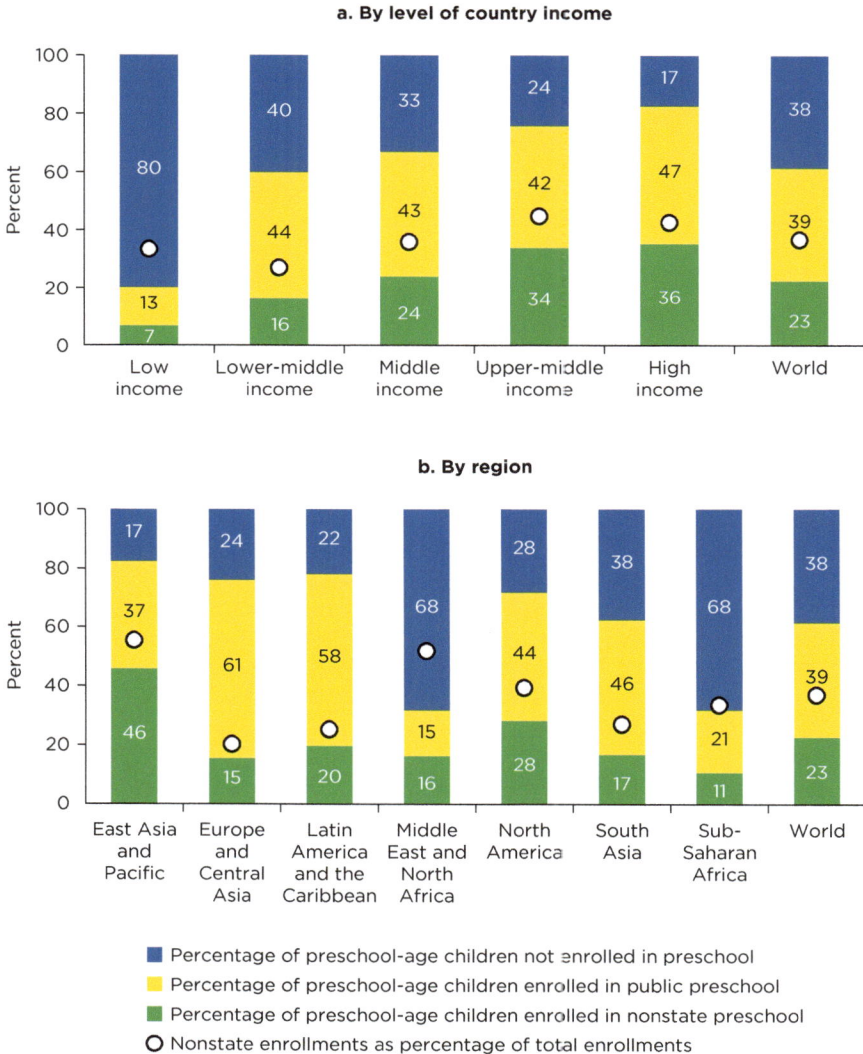

a. By level of country income

b. By region

■ Percentage of preschool-age children not enrolled in preschool
■ Percentage of preschool-age children enrolled in public preschool
■ Percentage of preschool-age children enrolled in nonstate preschool
○ Nonstate enrollments as percentage of total enrollments

Source: World Bank analysis using UIS 2020 indicators.

NOTES

1. Learning poverty means being unable to read and understand a simple text by age 10. This indicator brings together schooling and learning indicators: it begins with the share of children who have not achieved minimum reading proficiency (as measured in schools) and is adjusted by the proportion of children who are out of school (and are assumed not able to read proficiently) (World Bank 2019).
2. For instance, in nearly 40 LMICs, grade 1 enrollment rates are 30 percent greater than the number of grade 1–age children, largely because of repetition in grade 1 (Crouch and Merseth 2017).
3. Other crucial interventions to support human capital development during early childhood include health, nutrition, and protection from stress.
4. ECE includes center-based programs delivered at preschools, kindergartens, nursery schools, and community centers. These programs can be public, private, or community based and can range from one year right before the start of primary school to three years starting at age three.
5. Motivated by the Millennium Development Goals, in the past two decades many countries rapidly expanded enrollment in basic education. However, this expansion came with stagnation or reduction in learning outcomes because systems were not equipped to receive new entrants and ensure quality (World Bank 2018b).
6. In this volume, *learning* encompasses holistic child development and well-being, which are necessary conditions for learning.
7. In its Smart Buys report, the Global Education Evidence Advisory Panel, cohosted by the World Bank and the United Kingdom's Foreign, Commonwealth and Development Office, endorsed ECE as a Good Buy given that there is good evidence that these interventions are cost-effective (GEEAP 2020).
8. Provision of ECE varies greatly around the world. In countries where ECE is the purview of more than one system, sometimes services are split by children's age, with the early childhood education and care system providing services for younger children (for example, three-to-four-year-olds), while the year immediately before primary school (five-to-six-year-olds) is provided by the local education system. In other cases, both systems deliver services for children three to six years old in parallel.
9. The literature on ECE typically distinguishes between "structural" and "process" dimensions of quality. Structural quality encompasses quality of physical and other basic elements of the classroom that are easily and objectively quantifiable, such as infrastructure, materials, and play items, as well as standards related to staff-to-child ratios and group size, among others. Structural features can influence process quality and accelerate and support learning. Process quality relates to children's everyday experiences and involves the social, emotional, and instructional aspects of children's classroom experience, including the daily interactions that children have with their teachers,

peers, and environment (Vandell et al. 2010). Yet these dimensions of quality ECE are difficult to measure, are less visible to decision-makers, and can be difficult to improve—which may help explain why country strategies to improve the quality of ECE often focus too narrowly on inputs or structural aspects of ECE settings (for example, infrastructure, service standards).

10. Information from the Systems Approach for Better Education Results–Early Childhood Development (SABER-ECD) database ; https://saber.worldbank.org /index.cfm?indx=8&pd=6&sub=0).

11. Information from SABER-ECD database.

12. These ECE workforce challenges are seen against the backdrop of a severe shortage of ECE teachers worldwide. LMICs are home to 60 percent of the world's ECE-age children but have only 32 percent of all ECE teachers (UNICEF 2019). To meet the Sustainable Development Goal target of universal ECE coverage by 2030, the world will need 9.3 million new ECE teachers, 90 percent of whom will be needed in LMICs (UNICEF 2019).

13. See annex OA for more details on nonstate ECE provision.

14. Systemwide ECE quality is hard to quantify given limited data on its key outcome: child learning outcomes. Though imperfect, early-grade learning outcome indicators could shed some light on the level of quality of ECE service provision, especially in countries with high ECE coverage. For example, the Early Grade Reading Assessment (EGRA) measures oral fluency and basic literacy skills among second and third graders. Although scores do not capture the isolated impacts of ECE and may not have been administered in a child's mother tongue or first language, EGRA indicators such as the ability to read a single word are reflective of the effectiveness of the education system in the early years. For example, in Liberia, where net enrollment in preprimary is 59 percent, more than 30 percent of second graders still cannot read a single word, and in Kenya, where gross enrollment in preprimary is 78 percent, 23 percent of grade 1 students still cannot read a single word.

15. For example, the Perry Preschool Program's cost was approximately US$13,780 per child per school year (in 2017 dollars).

16. See chapter 3 for a detailed discussion and examples of the strategies highlighted here.

17. Curricula constitute the basis of what and how young children are taught, and pedagogy is the basis for how educators organize and facilitate the educational experience in ECE classrooms. Effective ECE curricula are culturally informed and evidence based and foster emergent literacy and early mathematics skills, along with physical and socioemotional development, in a language that children understand (see box C.2). For example, counting blocks is a more effective way to build children's understanding of numbers than asking them to solve the equation $2 + 2 = 4$. Effective pedagogy helps children represent and communicate their ideas and engage their naturally playful ways of exploring the world, and it provides an appropriate mix of cognitive challenge and opportunity for self-regulation. See chapter 2 for a discussion of effective curricula and pedagogy.

REFERENCES

Aikens, Nikki, Ashley Kopack Klein, Louisa Tarullo, and Jerry West. 2013. "Getting Ready for Kindergarten: Children's Progress During Head Start." FACES 2009 Report, OPRE Report 2013-21a, Office of Planning, Research and Evaluation, Administration for Children and Families, US Department of Health and Human Services, Washington, DC. https://eric.ed.gov/?id=ED580354.

Anders, Yvonne, Hans-Günther Rossbach, Sabine Weinert, Susanne Ebert, Susanne Kuger, Simone Lehrl, and Jutta von Maurice. 2012. "Home and Preschool Learning Environments and Their Relations to the Development of Early Numeracy Skills." *Early Childhood Research Quarterly* 27 (2): 231–44. https://doi.org/10.1016/j.ecresq.2011.08.003.

Andrews, Matt, Lant Pritchett, and Michael Woolcock. 2017. *Building State Capability: Evidence, Analysis, Action.* Oxford, UK: Oxford University Press. https://library.oapen.org/bitstream/id/bb540dab-9bbb-45ea-8ef1-4843b24dd432/624551.pdf.

APHRC (African Population and Health Research Center). 2018. *Impact Evaluation of Tayari School Readiness Program in Kenya: Endline Report.* Nairobi: APHRC. https://aphrc.org/wp-content/uploads/2019/07/Impact_Evaluation_ECDE_Tayari-long-report.pdf.

Azevedo, João Pedro, Amer Hasan, Diana Goldemberg, Syedah Aroob Iqbal, and Koen Geven. 2020. "Simulating the Potential Impacts of COVID-19 School Closures on Schooling and Learning Outcomes: A Set of Global Estimates." Policy Research Working Paper 9284, World Bank, Washington, DC. https://openknowledge.worldbank.org/handle/10986/33945.

Barrera-Osorio, Felipe, Paul Gertler, Nozomi Nakajima, and Harry Anthony Patrinos. 2020. "Promoting Parental Involvement in Schools: Evidence from Two Randomized Experiments." Policy Research Working Paper 9462, World Bank, Washington, DC. https://openknowledge.worldbank.org/handle/10986/34729.

Berlinski, Samuel, and Sebastian Galiani. 2007. "The Effect of a Large Expansion of Pre-Primary School Facilities on Preschool Attendance and Maternal Employment." *Labour Economics* 14 (3): 665–80. https://doi.org/10.1016/j.labeco.2007.01.003.

Berlinski, Samuel, and Norbert Schady. 2015. "More Bang for the Buck: Investing in Early Childhood Development." In *The Early Years: Child Well-Being and the Role of Public Policy*, edited by Samuel Berlinski and Norbert Schady, 148–78. New York: Palgrave Macmillan. https://doi.org/10.1057/9781137536495_6.

Black, Maureen M., Susan P. Walker, Lia C. H. Fernald, Christopher T. Andersen, Ann M. DiGirolamo, Chunling Lu, Dana C. McCoy, et al. 2017. "Early Childhood Development Coming of Age: Science through the Life Course." *Lancet* 389 (10064): 77–90. https://doi.org/10.1016/S0140-6736(16)31389-7.

Borzekowski, Dina. 2018. "A Quasi-Experiment Examining the Impact of Educational Cartoons on Tanzanian Children." *Journal of Applied Developmental Psychology* 54: 53–59.

Bouchane, Kathleen, Hirokazu Yoshikawa, Katie Maeve Murphy, and Joan Lombardi. 2018. "Early Childhood Development and Early Learning for Children in Crisis and Conflict." Paper commissioned for the 2019 Global

Education Monitoring Report *Migration, Displacement and Education: Building Bridges, Not Walls*, United Nations Educational, Scientific and Cultural Organization, Paris. https://unesdoc.unesco.org/ark:/48223/pf0000266072.

Britto, Pia Rebello, Stephen J. Lye, Kerrie Proulx, Aisha K. Yousafzai, Stephen G. Matthews, Tyler Vaivada, Rafael Perez-Escamilla, et al. 2016. "Nurturing Care: Promoting Early Childhood Development." *Lancet* 389 (10064): 91–102. https://doi.org/10.1016/S0140-6736(16)31390-3.

Britto, Pia Rebello, L. Angelica Ponguta, Chin Reyes, and Romilla Karnati. 2015. *A Systematic Review of Parenting Programmes for Young Children in Low- and Middle-Income Countries*. New York: United Nations Children's Fund. https://sites.unicef.org/earlychildhood/files/P_Shanker_final__Systematic_Review_of_Parenting_ECD_Dec_15_copy.pdf.

Britto, Pia Rebello, Hirokazu Yoshikawa, and Kimberly Boller. 2011. "Quality of Early Childhood Development Programs in Global Contexts: Rationale for Investment, Conceptual Framework and Implications for Equity." *Social Policy Report* 25 (2): 3–23. https://eric.ed.gov/?id=ED519240.

Burchinal, Margaret, Katherine Magnuson, Douglas Powell, and Sandra Soliday Hong. 2015. "Early Childcare and Education." In *Handbook of Child Psychology and Developmental Science*, edited by Richard M. Lerner, 1–45. Hoboken, NJ: John Wiley & Sons, Inc. https://doi.org/10.1002/9781118963418.childpsy406.

Bustamante, Andres S., Brenna Hassinger-Das, Kathy Hirsh-Pasek, and Roberta M. Golinkoff. 2019. "Learning Landscapes: Where the Science of Learning Meets Architectural Design." *Child Development Perspectives* 13 (1): 34–40. https://doi.org/10.1111/cdep.12309.

Carr, Victoria, and Eleanor Luken. 2014. "Playscapes: A Pedagogical Paradigm for Play and Learning." *International Journal of Play* 3 (1): 69–83. https://doi.org/10.1080/21594937.2013.871965.

Cascio, Elizabeth. 2015. "The Promises and Pitfalls of Universal Early Education." *IZA World of Labor*. https://doi.org/10.15185/izawol.116.

Cascio, Elizabeth U., and Diane W. Schanzenbach. 2014. "Proposal 1: Expanding Preschool Access for Disadvantaged Children." In *Policies to Address Poverty in America*, edited by Melissa Kearney and Benjamin Harris. Washington, DC: Brookings.

Chetty, Raj, John N. Friedman, Nathaniel Hilger, Emmanuel Saez, Diane Whitmore Schanzenbach, and Danny Yagan. 2010. "How Does Your Kindergarten Classroom Affect Your Earnings? Evidence from Project STAR." Working Paper 16381, National Bureau of Economic Research, Cambridge, MA. https://doi.org/10.3386/w16381.

Clarke, Marguerite, and Diego Luna-Bazaldua. 2021. *Primer on Large-Scale Assessments of Educational Achievement*. National Assessments of Educational Achievement series. Washington, DC: World Bank. https://openknowledge.worldbank.org/handle/10986/35494.

Crawford, Michael F., and Sergio Venegas Marin. 2021. *Loud and Clear: Effective Language of Instruction Policies for Learning*. Washington, DC: World Bank Group. http://documents.worldbank.org/curated/en/517851626203470278/Loud-and-Clear-Effective-Language-of-Instruction-Policies-For-Learning.

Crouch, Luis, and Katherine A. Merseth. 2017. "Stumbling at the First Step: Efficiency Implications of Poor Performance in the Foundational First Five Years." *PROSPECTS* 47 (3): 175–96. https://doi.org/10.1007/s11125-017-9401-1.

Cunha, Flavio, and James Heckman. 2007. "The Technology of Skill Formation." *American Economic Review* 97 (2): 31–47.

Currie, Janet. 2001."Early Childhood Education Programs." *Journal of Economic Perspectives* 15 (2): 213–38. https://doi.org/10.1257/jep.15.2.213.

Devercelli, A., and F. Beaton-Day. 2020. *Better Jobs and Brighter Futures: Investing in Childcare to Build Human Capital*. Washington, DC: World Bank.

Dore, Rebecca A., Marcia Shirilla, Emily Hopkins, Molly Collins, Molly Scott, Jacob Schatz, Jessica Lawson-Adams, et al. 2019. "Education in the App Store: Using a Mobile Game to Support U.S. Preschoolers' Vocabulary Learning." *Journal of Children and Media* 13 (4): 452–71. https://doi.org/10.1080/17482798.2019.1650788.

Duncan, Greg J., and Katherine Magnuson. 2013. "Investing in Preschool Programs." *Journal of Economic Perspectives* 27 (2): 109–32.

Egert, Franziska, Ruben G. Fukkink, and Andrea G. Eckhardt. 2018. "Impact of In-Service Professional Development Programs for Early Childhood Teachers on Quality Ratings and Child Outcomes: A Meta-Analysis." *Review of Educational Research* 88 (3): 401–33. https://doi.org/10.3102/0034654317751918.

Engel, Arno, W. Steven Barnett, Yvonne Anders, and Miho Taguma. 2018. *Norway. Early Childhood Education and Care Policy Review*. Paris: OECD Publishing. http://www.oecd.org/education/Early-Childhood-Education-and-Care-Policy-Review-Norway.pdf.

Evans, D. K., P. Jakiela, and H. A. Knauer. 2021. "The Impact of Early Childhood Interventions on Mothers." *Science* 372 (6544): 794–96.

Fernald, Lia C. H., Rose M. C. Kagawa, Heather A. Knauer, Lourdes Schnaas, Armando Garcia Guerra, and Lynnette M. Neufeld. 2017. "Promoting Child Development through Group-Based Parent Support within a Cash Transfer Program: Experimental Effects on Children's Outcomes." *Developmental Psychology* 53 (2): 222–36. https://doi.org/10.1037/dev0000185.

Flouri, Eirini, Emily Midouhas, and Heather Joshi. 2014. "The Role of Urban Neighbourhood Green Space in Children's Emotional and Behavioural Resilience." *Journal of Environmental Psychology* 40 (December): 179–86. https://doi.org/10.1016/j.jenvp.2014.06.007.

Galasso, Emanuela, and Adam Wagstaff. 2019. "The Aggregate Income Losses from Childhood Stunting and the Returns to a Nutrition Intervention Aimed at Reducing Stunting." *Economics and Human Biology* 34 (August): 225–38. https://doi.org/10.1016/j.ehb.2019.01.010.

Ganimian, Alejandro J., Karthik Muralidharan, and Christopher R. Walters. 2021. "Augmenting State Capacity for Child Development: Experimental Evidence from India." Working Paper 28780, National Bureau of Economic Research, Cambridge, MA. https://doi.org/10.3386/w28780.

GCPEA (Global Coalition to Protect Education from Attack). 2018. *Education under Attack 2018*. New York: GCPEA.

GEEAP (Global Education Evidence Advisory Panel). 2020. *Cost-Effective Approaches to Improve Global Learning: What Does Recent Evidence Tell Us Are "Smart Buys" for*

Improving Learning in Low- and Middle-Income Countries? Washington, DC: World Bank. https://documents1.worldbank.org/curated/en/719211603835247448 /pdf/Cost-Effective-Approaches-to-Improve-Global-Learning-What-Does -Recent-Evidence-Tell-Us-Are-Smart-Buys-for-Improving-Learning-in-Low -and-Middle-Income-Countries.pdf.

Griffith, Shayl F., Katherine G. Hanson, Benjamin Rolon-Arroyo, and David H. Arnold. 2019. "Promoting Early Achievement in Low-Income Preschoolers in the United States with Educational Apps." *Journal of Children and Media* 13 (3): 328–44. https://doi.org/10.1080/17482798.2019.1613246.

Hadani, Helen, and Jennifer Vey. 2020. *Scaling Playful Learning: How Cities Can Reimagine Public Spaces to Support Children and Families*. Washington, DC: Brookings Institution. https://www.brookings.edu/wp-content/uploads/2020 /09/Scaling-Playful-Learning_Hadani-Vey_Final.pdf.

Hassinger-Das, Brenna, Sarah Brennan, Rebecca A. Dore, Roberta Michnick Golinkoff, and Kathy Hirsh-Pasek. 2020. "Children and Screens." *Annual Review of Developmental Psychology* 2 (1): 69–92. https://doi.org/10.1146/annure v-devpsych-060320-095612.

Heckman, James J., Seong Hyeok Moon, Rodrigo Pinto, Peter A. Savelyev, and Adam Yavitz. 2010. "The Rate of Return to the HighScope Perry Preschool Program." *Journal of Public Economics* 94 (1): 114–28. https://doi.org/10.1016/j .jpubeco.2009.11.001.

Holla, Alaka, Magdalena Bendini, Lelys Dinarte, and Iva Trako. 2021. "Is Investment in Preprimary Education Too Low? Lessons from (Quasi) Experimental Evidence across Countries." Policy Research Working Paper 9723, World Bank, Washington, DC.

Howes, Carollee, Margaret Burchinal, Robert Pianta, Donna Bryant, Diane Early, Richard Clifford, and Oscar Barbarin. 2008. "Erratum to 'Ready to Learn? Children's Pre-Academic Achievement in Pre-Kindergarten Programs.'" *Early Childhood Research Quarterly* 23 (3): 429–30. https://doi.org/10.1016/j .ecresq.2008.08.001.

Irfan, Ahmed, Ashish Karamchandani, Akshay Kohli, and Vikram Jain. 2017. "The Preschool Promise: The Opportunity to Transform Learning Outcomes for India's Working Poor." FSG Mumbai. https://www.fsg.org/publications /preschool-promise.

Jeong, Joshua, Helen O. Pitchik, and Aisha K. Yousafzai. 2018. "Stimulation Interventions and Parenting in Low- and Middle-Income Countries: A Meta-Analysis." *Pediatrics* 141 (4): e20173510. https://doi.org/10.1542/peds.2017-3510.

Johnson, R. C., and C. K. Jackson. 2019. "Reducing Inequality through Dynamic Complementarity: Evidence from Head Start and Public School Spending." *American Economic Journal: Economic Policy* 11 (4): 310–49.

Kabay, Sarah, Sharon Wolf, and Hirokazu Yoshikawa. 2017. "'So That His Mind Will Open': Parental Perceptions of Early Childhood Education in Urbanizing Ghana." *International Journal of Educational Development* 57 (November): 44–53. https://doi.org/10.1016/j.ijedudev.2017.08.013.

Kearney, Melissa S., and Phillip B. Levine. 2019. "Early Childhood Education by Television: Lessons from Sesame Street." *American Economic Journal: Applied Economics* 11 (1): 318–50.

Kelly, Melissa. 2021. "Early Learning Partnership Case Studies." Unpublished, World Bank, Washington, DC.

Kim, Janice, Mesele Araya, Chanie Ejigu, Belay Hagos, Pauline Rose, and Tassew Woldehanna. 2020. "The Implications of COVID-19 on Early Learning Continuity in Ethiopia: Perspectives of Parents and Caregivers." Research and Policy Paper 20/11, REAL Centre, University of Cambridge, Cambridge, UK. https://www.educ.cam.ac.uk/centres/real/publications/Covid-19%20and%20Early%20Years%20Education%20in%20Ethiopia.pdf.

Klein, Sacha, Lauren Fries, and Mary M. Emmons. 2017. "Early Care and Education Arrangements and Young Children's Risk of Foster Placement: Findings from a National Child Welfare Sample." *Children and Youth Services Review* 83 (2017): 168–78. https://www.sciencedirect.com/science/article/pii/S0190740917303195.

Knauer, Heather A., Pamela Jakiela, Owen Ozier, Frances Aboud, and Lia C. H. Fernald. 2020. "Enhancing Young Children's Language Acquisition through Parent-Child Book-Sharing: A Randomized Trial in Rural Kenya." *Early Childhood Research Quarterly* 50: 179–90. https://doi.org/10.1016/j.ecresq.2019.01.002.

Knudsen, E. I. 2004. "Sensitive Periods in the Development of the Brain and Behavior." *Journal of Cognitive Neuroscience* 16 (8): 1412–25. https://doi.org/10.1162/0898929042304796.

Lee, RaeHyuck, Fuhua Zhai, Wen-Jui Han, Jeanne Brooks-Gunn, and Jane Waldfogel. 2013. "Head Start and Children's Nutrition, Weight, and Health Care Receipt." *Early Childhood Research Quarterly* 28 (4). https://www.ncbi.nlm.nih.gov/pmc/articles/PMC3810984/.

Lopez Boo, Florencia, Jere R. Behrman, and Claudia Vazquez. 2020. *Economic Costs of Preprimary Program Reductions due to COVID-19 Pandemic.* Washington, DC: Inter-American Development Bank. https://publications.iadb.org/publications/english/document/Economic-Costs-of-Preprimary-Program-Reductions-due-to-COVID-19-Pandemic.pdf.

Madigan, Sheri, Dillon Browne, Nicole Racine, Camille Mori, and Suzanne Tough. 2019. "Association between Screen Time and Children's Performance on a Developmental Screening Test." *JAMA Pediatrics* 173 (3): 244–50. https://doi.org/10.1001/jamapediatrics.2018.5056.

Magnuson, Katherine A., Christopher Ruhm, and Jane Waldfogel. 2007. "Does Prekindergarten Improve School Preparation and Performance?" *Economics of Education Review* 26 (1): 33–51. https://doi.org/10.1016/j.econedurev.2005.09.008.

Manu, Alexander, Fernanda Ewerling, Aluisio J. D. Barros, and Cesar G. Victora. 2019. "Association between Availability of Children's Book and the Literacy-Numeracy Skills of Children Aged 36 to 59 Months: Secondary Analysis of the UNICEF Multiple-Indicator Cluster Surveys Covering 35 Countries." *Journal of Global Health* 9 (1): 010403. https://doi.org/10.7189/jogh.09.010403.

Mares, Marie-Louise, and Zhongdang Pan. 2013. "Effects of Sesame Street: A Meta-Analysis of Children's Learning in 15 Countries." *Journal of Applied Developmental Psychology* 34 (3): 140–51. https://doi.org/10.1016/j.appdev.2013.01.001.

Martinez, Sebastian, Sophie Naudeau, and Vitor Pereira. 2012. "The Promise of Preschool in Africa: A Randomized Impact Evaluation of Early Childhood

Development in Rural Africa." International Initiative for Impact Evaluation, New Delhi.

Martinez, Sebastian, Sophie Naudeau, and Vitor Pereira. 2017. "Preschool and Child Development under Extreme Poverty: Evidence from a Randomized Experiment in Rural Mozambique." Policy Research Working Paper 8290, World Bank, Washington, DC. https://openknowledge.worldbank.org /handle/10986/29112.

Mateo Díaz, Mercedes, Laura Becerra Luna, Juan Manuel Hernández-Agramonte, Florencia López Boo, Marcelo Pérez Alfaro, and Alejandro Vasquez Echeverria. 2020. *Nudging Parents to Increase Preschool Attendance in Uruguay.* Washington, DC: Inter-American Development Bank. https://publications.iadb.org/publications /english/document/Nudging-Parents-to-Improve-Preschool-Attendance-in-Uruguay.pdf.

McCoy, D. C., C. Salhi, H. Yoshikawa, M. Black, P. Britto, and G. Fink. 2018. "Home- and Center-Based Learning Opportunities for Preschoolers in Low- and Middle-Income Countries." *Children and Youth Services Review* 88: 44–56.

McDonald Connor, Carol, Seung-Hee Son, Annemarie H. Hindman, and Frederick J. Morrison. 2005. "Teacher Qualifications, Classroom Practices, Family Characteristics, and Preschool Experience: Complex Effects on First Graders' Vocabulary and Early Reading Outcomes." *Journal of School Psychology* 43 (4): 343–75. https://doi.org/10.1016/j.jsp.2005.06.001.

Melhuish, Edward C., Mai B. Phan, Kathy Sylva, Pam Sammons, Iram Siraj-Blatchford, and Brenda Taggart. 2008. "Effects of the Home Learning Environment and Preschool Center Experience upon Literacy and Numeracy Development in Early Primary School." *Journal of Social Issues* 64 (1): 95–114. https://doi.org/10.1111/j.1540-4560.2008.00550.x.

Mikton, Christopher, and Alexander Butchart. 2009. "Child Maltreatment Prevention: A Systematic Review of Reviews." *Bulletin of the World Health Organization* 87 (5): 353–61. https://doi.org/10.2471/BLT.08.057075.

Naceva, Bojana, Martin Galevski, and Melissa Kelly. 2020. "Read@Home: Effective Partnerships to Reach Vulnerable Children in North Macedonia." *Education for Global Development* (blog), December 17, 2020. https://blogs.worldbank.org /education/readhome-effective-partnerships-reach-vulnerable-children-north -macedonia#:~:text=In%20its%20first%20roll%20out,national%20 social%20safety%20net%20program.

Nandi, Arindam, Sonia Bhalotra, Anil B. Deolalikar, and Ramanan Laxminarayan. 2017. "The Human Capital and Productivity Benefits of Early Childhood Nutritional Interventions." In *Disease Control Priorities, Third Edition (Volume 8): Child and Adolescent Health and Development,* edited by Donald A. P. Bundy, Nilanthi de Silva, Susan Horton, Dean T. Jamison, and George C. Patton. Washington, DC: World Bank. https://doi.org/10.1596/978-1-4648-0423-6.

Naudeau, Sophie, Naoko Kataoka, Alexandria Valerio, Michelle Neuman, and Leslie Kennedy Elder. 2011. *Investing in Young Children: An Early Childhood Development Guide for Policy Dialogue and Project Preparation.* Washington, DC: World Bank. https://openknowledge.worldbank.org/handle/10986/2525.

Neuman, Michelle J., and Amanda E. Devercelli. 2013. "What Matters Most for Early Childhood Development: A Framework Paper." Systems Approach for Better

Education Results (SABER) Working Paper Series 5, World Bank, Washington, DC. https://openknowledge.worldbank.org/handle/10986/20174.

Oberhuemer, Pamela, Inge Schreyer, and Michelle J. Neuman. 2010. *Professionals in Early Childhood Education and Care Systems: European Profiles and Perspectives*. Opladen, Germany: Verlag Barbara Budrich. https://doi.org/10.2307/j.ctvddznx2.

OECD (Organisation for Economic Co-operation and Development). 2006. *Starting Strong II: Early Childhood Education and Care*. Paris: OECD Publishing. http://www.oecd.org/education/school/startingstrongiiearlychildhoodeducationandcare.htm.

OECD (Organisation for Economic Co-operation and Development). 2017. *Starting Strong 2017: Key OECD Indicators on Early Childhood Education and Care*. Paris: OECD Publishing. http://www.oecd.org/education/starting-strong-2017-97892 64276116-en.htm.

OECD (Organisation for Economic Co-operation and Development). 2018. *Starting Strong: Engaging Young Children*. Paris: OECD Publishing. https://www.oecd -ilibrary.org/docserver/9789264085145-en.pdf?expires=1613074080&id=id& accname=guest&checksum=3321CC7CA46E6DE7910C49116DECE74C.

Pardo, Marcela, and Cynthia Adlerstein. 2016. "Estado del arte y criterios orientadores para la elaboración de políticas de formación y desarrollo profesional de docentes de primera infancia en América Latina y el Caribe." Chile: United Nations Educational, Scientific and Cultural Organization. https://unesdoc .unesco.org/ark:/48223/pf0000245157.

Pence, Alan R., and Kofi Marfo. 2008. "Early Childhood Development in Africa: Interrogating Constraints of Prevailing Knowledge Bases." *International Journal of Psychology* 43 (2): 78–87. https://doi.org/10.1080/00207590701859143.

Perlman, Michal, Olesya Falenchuk, Brooke Fletcher, Evelyn McMullen, Joseph Beyene, and Prakesh S. Shah. 2016. "A Systematic Review and Meta-Analysis of a Measure of Staff/Child Interaction Quality (the Classroom Assessment Scoring System) in Early Childhood Education and Care Settings and Child Outcomes." Edited by Jacobus P. van Wouwe. *PLOS ONE* 11 (12): e0167660. https://doi.org/10.1371/journal.pone.0167660.

Peru, Ministry of Social Development and Inclusion. 2016. Aprueban los Lineamientos "Primero la Infancia," en el marco de la Política de desarrollo e inclusión social DECRETO SUPREMO N° 010-2016-MIDIS. http://www.midis .gob.pe/wp-content/uploads/2019/08/DS_N_010-2016-MIDISv2.pdf.

Phillips, Deborah A., Mark W. Lipsey, Kenneth A. Dodge, Ron Haskins, Daphna Bassok, Margaret R. Burchinal, Greg J. Duncan, Mark Dynarski, Katherine A. Magnuson, and Christina Weiland. 2017. "Puzzling It Out: The Current State of Scientific Knowledge on Pre-Kindergarten Effects. A Consensus Statement." Brookings, Washington, DC. https://www.brookings.edu/research /puzzling-it-out-the-current-state-of-scientific-knowledge-on-pre-kindergarten -effects/.

Pianta, Robert, Bridget Hamre, Jason Downer, Margaret Burchinal, Amanda Williford, Jennifer LoCasale-Crouch, Carollee Howes, Karen La Paro, and Catherine Scott-Little. 2017. "Early Childhood Professional Development: Coaching and Coursework Effects on Indicators of Children's School

Readiness." *Early Education and Development* 28 (8): 956–75. https://doi.org/10.1080/10409289.2017.1319783.

Rao, Nirmala, Jin Sun, Eva Chen, and Patrick Ip. 2017. "Effectiveness of Early Childhood Interventions in Promoting Cognitive Development in Developing Countries: A Systematic Review and Meta-Analysis." *Hong Kong Journal of Paediatrics* 22 (1): 14–25. http://www.hkjpaed.org/pdf/2017;22;14-25.pdf.

Rao, Nirmala, Jin Sun, Jessie M. S. Wong, Brendan Weekes, Patrick Ip, Sheldon Shaeffer, Mary Young, Mark Bray, Eva Chen, and Diana Lee. 2014. *Early Childhood Development and Cognitive Development in Developing Countries: A Rigorous Literature Review*. London: Department for International Development. http://eppi.ioe.ac.uk/cms/Portals/0/PDF%20reviews%20and%20summaries/ECD%202014%20Rao%20report.pdf?ver=2014-10-02-145634-017.

Richards, Melissa N., and Sandra L. Calvert. 2017. "Media Characters, Parasocial Relationships, and the Social Aspects of Children's Learning across Media Platforms." In *Media Exposure during Infancy and Early Childhood*, edited by Rachel Barr and Deborah Nichols Linebarger, 141–63. Cham: Springer International Publishing. https://doi.org/10.1007/978-3-319-45102-2_9.

Richter, Linda M., Bernadette Daelmans, Joan Lombardi, Jody Heymann, Florencia Lopez Boo, Jere R. Behrman, Chunling Lu, et al. 2017. "Investing in the Foundation of Sustainable Development: Pathways to Scale Up for Early Childhood Development." *Lancet* 389 (10064): 103–18. https://doi.org/10.1016/S0140-6736(16)31698-1.

Saavedra Chanduvi, Jaime, Mario Cristian Aedo Inostroza, and Omar S. Arias Diaz. 2020. *Realizing the Future of Learning: From Learning Poverty to Learning for Everyone, Everywhere*. Washington, DC: World Bank. http://documents.worldbank.org/curated/en/250981606928190510/Realizing-the-Future-of-Learning-From-Learning-Poverty-to-Learning-for-Everyone-Everywhere.

Schweinhart, L. J., J. Montie, Z. Xiang, W. S. Barnett, C. R. Belfield, and M. Nores. 2005. *Lifetime Effects: The High/Scope Perry Preschool Study through Age 40*. Ypsilanti, MI: High/Scope Press.

Sondheimer, Rachel Milstein, and Donald P. Green. 2010. "Using Experiments to Estimate the Effects of Education on Voter Turnout." *American Journal of Political Science* 54 (1): 174–89. https://doi.org/10.1111/j.1540-5907.2009.00425.x.

Spier, Elizabeth, Kevin Kamto, Adria Molotsky, Azizur Rahman, Najmul Hossain, Zannatun Nahar, and Hosneara Khondker. 2019. *Bangladesh Early Years Preschool Program Impact Evaluation Midline Results*. Washington, DC: American Institutes for Research; London: Save the Children. https://idela-network.org/resource/bangladesh-early-years-preschool-program-impact-evaluation-midline-results/.

Tomlinson, Heather Biggar, and Syifa Andina. 2015. *Parenting Education in Indonesia: Review and Recommendations to Strengthen Programs and Systems*. Washington, DC: World Bank. https://doi.org/10.1596/978-1-4648-0621-6.

UIS (United Nations Educational, Scientific and Cultural Organization Institute for Statistics). 2019. Education (database). http://data.uis.unesco.org/.

UIS (United Nations Educational, Scientific and Cultural Organization Institute for Statistics). 2020. Education (database). http://data.uis.unesco.org/.

UNICEF (United Nations Children's Fund). 2019. *A World Ready to Learn.* New York: UNICEF. https://data.unicef.org/resources/a-world-ready-to-learn-report/.

US Department of Health and Human Services. 2010. *Head Start Impact Study. Final Report.* Washington, DC: US Department of Health and Human Services, Administration for Children and Families.

Vandell, Deborah Lowe, Jay Belsky, Margaret Burchinal, Laurence Steinberg, Nathan Vandergrift, and NICHD Early Child Care Research Network. 2010. "Do Effects of Early Child Care Extend to Age 15 Years? Results from the NICHD Study of Early Child Care and Youth Development: Age 15 Follow-Up." *Child Development* 81 (3): 737–56. https://doi.org/10.1111/j.1467-8624.2010.01431.x.

von Suchodoletz, Antje, D. Susie Lee, Bharanthy Premachandra, and Hirokazu Yoshikawa. 2017. "Associations among Quality Indicators in Early Childhood Education and Care (ECEC) and Relations with Child Development and Learning: A Meta-Analysis." Background document to "Engaging Young Children: Lessons from Research about Quality in Early Childhood Education and Care." OECD Publishing, Paris. http://www.oecd.org/education/school/ECEC-meta-analysis-studies.pdf.

Votruba-Drzal, Elizabeth, Rebekah Levine Coley, Amanda S. Koury, and Portia Miller. 2013. "Center-Based Child Care and Cognitive Skills Development: Importance of Timing and Household Resources." *Journal of Educational Psychology* 105 (3): 821–38. https://doi.org/10.1037/a0032951.

Wadende, Pamela, Paul O. Oburu, and Abel Morara. 2016. "African Indigenous Care-Giving Practices: Stimulating Early Childhood Development and Education in Kenya." *South African Journal of Childhood Education* 6 (2): 7. https://doi.org/10.4102/sajce.v6i2.446.

Weiland, Christina, Meghan McCormick, Shira Mattera, Michelle Maier, and Pamela Morris. 2018. "Preschool Curricula and Professional Development Features for Getting to High-Quality Implementation at Scale: A Comparative Review across Five Trials." *AERA Open* 4 (1): 233285841875773. https://doi.org/10.1177/2332858418757735.

Whitebread, David, and S. Yesmin. 2021. "Factors Contributing to the Effectiveness of Preschool PlayLabs in Bangladesh, Tanzania and Uganda." Paper presented at the European Early Childhood Educational Research (EECERA) Conference, Zagreb, August 29–September 21.

Wolf, Sharon, J. Lawrence Aber, Jere R. Behrman, and Edward Tsinigo. 2019. "Experimental Impacts of the 'Quality Preschool for Ghana' Interventions on Teacher Professional Well-Being, Classroom Quality, and Children's School Readiness." *Journal of Research on Educational Effectiveness* 12 (1): 10–37. https://doi.org/10.1080/19345747.2018.1517199.

Wolf, Sharon, Edward Tsinigo, Jere R. Behrman, Laurence J. Aber, and Alix Bonarget. 2017. "Developing and Testing Supply- and Demand-Side Interventions to Improve Kindergarten Educational Quality in Ghana." World Bank Group, Washington, DC.

Wong, Jessie M. S., and Nirmala Rao. 2015. "The Evolution of Early Childhood Education Policy in Hong Kong." *International Journal of Child Care and Education Policy* 9 (1): 3. https://doi.org/10.1007/s40723-015-0006-y.

World Bank. 2013. "Republic of Uzbekistan—Improving Early Childhood Care and Education." World Bank Group, Washington, DC.

World Bank. 2017. "Pre-Primary Education in Mongolia: Access, Quality of Service Delivery, & Child Development Outcomes." World Bank, Washington, DC. http://documents1.worldbank.org/curated/en/481101490364915103/pdf/113752-WP-PUBLIC-P152905-QualityJanWithExecMarchclean.pdf.

World Bank. 2018a. *Growing Smarter: Learning and Equitable Development in East Asia and Pacific. World Bank East Asia and Pacific Regional Report.* Washington, DC: World Bank. https://openknowledge.worldbank.org/handle/10986/29365.

World Bank. 2018b. *World Development Report 2018: Learning to Realize Education's Promise.* Washington, DC: World Bank. https://openknowledge.worldbank.org/handle/10986/28340.

World Bank. 2019. *Ending Learning Poverty: What Will It Take?* Washington, DC: World Bank. https://openknowledge.worldbank.org/handle/10986/32553.

World Bank. 2020a. "15 Ways to Support Young Children and Their Families in the COVID-19 Response." World Bank, Washington, DC. https://openknowledge.worldbank.org/handle/10986/33646.

World Bank. 2020b. "How Countries Are Using Edtech (Including Online Learning, Radio, Television, Texting) to Support Access to Remote Learning during the COVID-19 Pandemic." World Bank, Washington, DC. https://www.worldbank.org/en/topic/edutech/brief/how-countries-are-using-edtech-to-support-remote-learning-during-the-covid-19-pandemic.

World Bank. 2020c. *Roadmap for Safer and Resilient Schools: Guidance Note 2.* Washington, DC: World Bank. https://openknowledge.worldbank.org/handle/10986/33840.

Wright, C. A., C. Mannathoko, and M. Pasic. 2009. *Child-Friendly Schools.* New York: United Nations Children's Fund.

Wright, John C., Aletha C. Huston, Kimberlee C. Murphy, Michelle St. Peters, Marites Pinon, Ronda Scantlin, and Jennifer Kotler. 2001. "The Relations of Early Television Viewing to School Readiness and Vocabulary of Children from Low-Income Families: The Early Window Project." *Child Development* 72 (5): 1347–66. https://doi.org/10.1111/1467-8624.t01-1-00352.

Yoshikawa, Hirokazu, Christina Weiland, Jeanne Brooks-Gunn, Margaret R. Burchinal, Linda M. Espinosa, William T. Gormley, Jens Ludwig, Katherine A. Magnuson, Deborah Phillips, and Martha J. Zaslow. 2013. "Investing in Our Future: The Evidence Base on Preschool Education." Society for Research in Child Development, Washington, DC. https://eric.ed.gov/?id=ED579818.

1

Learning in the Early Years

OVERVIEW

Children are born to learn, and they are the most capable learners on the planet. Children's early learning opportunities build foundations for future learning and impact their capacity to reach their full potential. This chapter describes five areas of core knowledge that children gain in the first eight years of life, including learning about (1) places, (2) numbers, (3) objects, (4) people's actions and goals, and (5) social interactions, communication, and language. Understanding these five areas can help us tap into the innate ability of children to learn quickly and prodigiously well before they enter primary school. This chapter also examines the learning skills and tools that help young children learn, including executive functions, imagination, metacognition, and motivation. Finally, the chapter discusses factors that promote and hinder early learning. Taken together, this knowledge and understanding can inform policies that promote quality early childhood education and nurture children's potential to learn well.

INTRODUCTION

Children are born to learn. They learn faster, more flexibly, and more economically than any machine, and they generalize their learning to new situations far more effectively than the smartest products of contemporary computer science (Lake et al. 2017). Children's prodigious learning testifies both to their biological predisposition to learn by

This chapter was written by Elizabeth Spelke and Kristin Shutts.

exploring the world and by engaging with others, and to their exceedingly smart and adaptable capacity for exploration and discovery. This capacity sets young children up for a lifetime of gaining and using knowledge—a critical condition for successful and productive lives in all contemporary countries and cultures.

This chapter provides an overview of children's learning in the first eight years of life. Because children's learning builds on what they already know, and on the ways in which they gain further knowledge, understanding what young children know and how they learn is key to designing and providing effective early childhood education (ECE). Later chapters elaborate on the content presented here and connect this content to information regarding curricula, pedagogy, teacher training, learning environments, school management, and a systems approach to ECE. As with the other chapters in this book, the content of this chapter is informed by empirical research from diverse fields. In cases in which research has yet to produce clear conclusions, limitations and suggestions for further research are noted.

In recent decades, insights into children's learning have come primarily from studies in developmental cognitive science, a field of research that combines methods and findings from diverse disciplines including psychology, anthropology, linguistics, organismic and molecular biology, neuroscience, economics, computer science, and education. Conclusions from this field are informed by laboratory experiments probing the cognitive capacities of young children, together with experiments on model animals and machines, probing the brain systems by which children learn and the computations by which their knowledge grows. In addition, an understanding of children's learning benefits from field research in children's homes and schools using randomized controlled experiments and other empirical methods to evaluate interventions that aim to enhance children's learning in the environments and at the time scales over which their learning proceeds.

This research shows that learning in the early years provides the foundations for later learning. Learning is possible at all ages, and every child can benefit from a good education, but older children will advance more easily in later grades if they achieve a firm foundation for learning during the early years. The basic science of young children's learning sheds light on the conditions that allow all children to build that foundation, regardless of their nationality, culture, or material and social advantages or disadvantages. It does not directly translate into recipes for school curricula, but its findings are a rich source of ideas for improving education worldwide. These ideas, in turn, can be evaluated by implementing them in randomly selected schools and comparing their impacts on children's learning and development relative to the standard curriculum implemented under otherwise comparable conditions. In this way, research on children's learning provides information that is critical for educators and policy makers alike.

This chapter begins by reviewing research on children's prodigious learning capacities. Next, it focuses on five areas of core knowledge in which young children learn rapidly and spontaneously, developing a foundation for later learning in school: (1) places, (2) numbers, (3) objects, (4) people's actions and goals, and (5) social relationships, communication, and language. After introducing these core areas of knowledge, the chapter turns to evidence concerning the more general cognitive skills and predispositions that support children's learning across diverse content areas, including executive functions that regulate attention and action planning, imagination, their capacity for metacognition, and their motivation to learn. Finally, the chapter considers factors that promote and hinder young children's learning and highlights important questions for further research.

CHILDREN ARE BORN TO LEARN

From birth, children perceive their environment and start to learn about it, especially by looking and listening. Like animals that must move from birth and avoid predators, newborn infants perceive depth, movement, and objects. Like animals that must learn critical features of their environment from birth—for example, the location of their nest (Gallistel 1990), the approximate size of their social group (Rugani. Regolin, and Vallortigara 2010), and the appearance and behavior of their family members (Sugita 2008) and of objects (Chiandetti and Vallortigara 2011; Wood 2013)— newborn infants perceive the extended surface layout (Slater, Mattock, and Brown 1990), the approximate number of objects in an array (Izard et al. 2009), faces (Mondloch et al. 1999), patterns of biological motion (Simion Regolin, and Bulf 2008), and vocalizations (Vouloumanos and Werker 2007).

Infants not only perceive objects, places, and people from birth but also begin learning about these entities. In some cases, learning even starts before birth, as evidenced by the ability of newborn infants to detect, orient to, and identify the sounds of their native language when they first hear them outside the womb (Mehler et al. 1988), sounds that their auditory system has detected over the last months of gestation. But learning accelerates after birth as infants become immersed in the natural and social world. In the first few months of life, infants begin to distinguish human faces from those of other species (Di Giorgio et al. 2012; Heron-Delaney, Wirth, and Pascalis 2011) and to recognize their caregivers (Burnham 1993; Pascalis et al. 1995). Well before they begin to speak, infants learn to distinguish the vowels and consonants of their native language from those of foreign languages (Kuhl 2004; Werker 1989), to parse the speech stream into words (Saffran, Aslin, and Newport 1996), to discover the structure of phrases (Shi, Werker, and Cutler 2006), and to connect the most frequent words they hear to the things and events that speakers refer to (Bergelson and Swingley 2012).

From birth, moreover, infants' learning is propelled by their inherent curiosity and sociality. Infants are naturally predisposed to explore their environment by looking, listening, and acting so they can learn about the world around them (Fantz 1964; Stahl and Feigenson 2015). Right from the start, infants are oriented to people who engage with them (Farroni et al. 2002; Meltzoff and Moore 1977; Meltzoff et al. 2018), and they learn things from others before they can do those things themselves (Liu et al. 2019; Skerry, Carey, and Spelke 2013). Infants are particularly interested in, and good at learning from and about, those who use infant-directed speech (Fernald 1985) or song (Mehr, Song, and Spelke 2016; Mehr and Spelke 2018) and those who speak and behave like the members of their families (Kinzler, Dupoux, and Spelke 2007; Liberman, Woodward, and Kinzler 2017). By the end of the first year, infants become interested in sharing what they know with others (Meltzoff 2007; Tomasello et al. 2005).

Infants' inherent interest in exploring and learning both from and about their environment continues into childhood and beyond. In addition to these early tendencies to learn from other people and to be curious about the world, young children have been found to be especially gifted learners in a number of specific areas of knowledge. Because all children's learning in school ultimately builds on the knowledge that they have gained in these core areas, the chapter turns next to this evidence.

Key Takeaways

- Children are the most capable learners on earth.
- Children's learning in the early years sets the stage for lifelong learning.

FIVE CORE KNOWLEDGE AREAS

Children possess a small number of cognitive and brain systems that help them identify and think about specific aspects of the world, such as places, things, and people. These *core knowledge areas* (also known as *core knowledge systems*) are evident in human infants, are shared by other animals, function throughout life, and are common to people living in diverse cultures. Each core knowledge area also has been tracked into the brains of animals and human adults, children, and infants, where it activates specific regions of the cerebral cortex. Thus, developmental scientists can identify common core areas across different individuals, at different ages, and living in different cultures. As scientists from diverse disciplines have studied the properties of these areas, their studies have revealed at least five distinct core knowledge areas that are central to all children's learning. This section discusses these five areas.

Learning about Places

Beginning in infancy, children are sensitive to the structure of the places that surround them. Toddlers use that structure to learn about the environments that they explore and the paths that will take them from one place to another. Both in school and out, children also use that structure to learn the diverse spatial symbols—from pictures to maps to written texts—that introduce children to worlds beyond their immediate experience, including faraway places, long-extinct animals, myths, and microorganisms.

Infants do not begin to master walking until the end of the first year. Nevertheless, infants possess the functional brain systems that underlie navigation, spatial memory, and action planning in humans and other animals (Spelke and Lee 2012). Using these systems, infants represent locations where objects are hidden in an extended spatial layout (Newcombe and Huttenlocher 2000), the paths that agents travel (Gergely et al. 1995), and the locations that are their goals (Hamlin, Hallinan, and Woodward 2008; Liu and Spelke 2017). Once they can crawl and walk, toddlers use geometry to navigate between environmental locations (Landau, Gleitman, and Spelke 1981), as do other animals (for review, see Gallistel 1990). These and other findings provide evidence of a dedicated cognitive system by which humans and other animals represent where we are within the environment through which we travel.

The mechanisms that give rise to these representations are among the best-understood cognitive mechanisms in all of neuroscience (O'Keefe 2014). These mechanisms not only support children's learning about their immediate environment but also are fundamental to young children's learning of spatial symbols such as pictures (DeLoache et al. 1998), maps (Shusterman, Lee, and Spelke 2008; Uttal 2000), scale models (DeLoache 2000), and number lines: the simplest mathematical symbols (Dehaene 2011; Siegler and Opfer 2003). Children's early spatial representations allow them not only to learn about symbols like pictures and maps but also to learn *from* them. As early as age two, children can learn the location of a hidden object from its location in a picture (Suddendorf 2003). By age two-and-a-half, they learn from its location in a purely abstract, geometric map (Winkler-Rhoades, Carey, and Spelke 2013). Using rulers, a form of number lines, children begin to master measurement. Other spatial symbols support children's learning of the alphabet (which may begin as early as two-to-three years) and their rapid decoding of letter sequences, a skill that is essential for learning to read (Dehaene 2009). Most fundamentally, studies of the hippocampus, an ancient cortical structure that is a central locus for spatial representation, reveal its fundamental role not only in navigation but also in conscious memory of past events (Squire et al. 2010), action planning (Pfeiffer and Foster 2013), and thought, imagination, and invention (Gupta et al. 2010; Ullman et al. 2017).

These early spatial abilities are malleable, and activities that exercise them have been shown to enhance children's learning in school. For example, children's abilities to navigate by maps and to perceive geometric structure in pictures is enhanced by practice: When five-year-old children practice these tasks for four months, their spatial abilities are improved, not only when they are tested during the first three months that follow the practice but also when they are tested a full year later, with no intervening opportunities for additional practice or rehearsal (Dillon et al. 2017). Moreover, when children exercise these abilities in contexts that encourage learning of mathematical language and symbols, children show both immediate and enduring gains in school math learning (Dean et al. 2021; Dillon et al. 2017; Lauer and Lourenco 2016; Newcombe 2010; Wai, Lubinski, and Benbow 2009). Young children's biologically based spatial abilities are resources that should be nourished over the preschool and early school years, both to enhance their intuitive understanding of the world and to enhance their readiness for learning in school.

Key Takeaways

- Early spatial abilities support children's learning about their immediate environment, as well as learning about spatial symbols such as pictures, maps, scale models, the alphabet, and number lines.
- Young children's spatial abilities can be nourished to enhance school readiness.

Learning about Numbers

Infants and children are sensitive to numbers: the relative magnitudes of different sets of objects, the relative frequencies of different events, and the transformations in number that occur as objects or events are combined. Building on this sensitivity, children learn both to choose among sets of objects, to predict the outcomes of events, and to decipher the operations at the center of primary school mathematics.

Humans and other animals have a dedicated system for representing approximate numbers of objects and events: Which bushes in the environment provide the most berries? Which open fields are most often attacked by predators (Carey 2009; Gallistel 1990)? This system is present and functional in newborn infants (Coubart et al. 2014; de Hevia et al. 2014; Izard et al. 2009), and it sharpens progressively over infancy and childhood (Halberda and Feigenson 2008; Starr and Brannon 2015). This system is often thought to figure in children's learning of the statistical properties of the environment (O'Grady and Xu 2020), learning that is critical for predicting future events (Gershman 2017). Finally, it is known to support operations of arithmetic: infants and preschool children can compare two dot arrays based on numerosity (Xu and Spelke 2000), they can relate increases in numerosity to increases in line length (Rugani and de Hevia 2017), and they can add two arrays of dots and compare the sum to a third array (Barth et al. 2005; Barth et al. 2006; Gilmore, McCarthy, and Spelke 2010). In all these respects, children's abilities resemble those that adults use to estimate numerosity without counting (Barth, Kanwisher, and Spelke 2003; Dehaene 2011; Halberda et al. 2012; Hyde and Spelke 2009).

Like their intuitive representations of places, children's intuitive representations of number support their learning of numerical symbols, including the number words that children begin to recite at age two (Szkudlarek and Brannon 2017) but take years to master (Wynn 1990), the Arabic symbols that many children throughout the world master by age four or five (Dillon et al. 2017), and the operations of formal arithmetic that children are taught in primary school (Gilmore, McCarthy, and Spelke 2007; Halberda, Mazzocco, and Feigenson 2008). The acuity of children's perception of numbers—how finely they can distinguish two sets on the basis of their numerosities—is associated with formal mathematical abilities throughout life (Chen and Li 2014; Halberda et al. 2012). Indeed, regions of the brain that are activated during tests of numerical ability (also known as numerical acuity) performed on young children also are activated when professional mathematicians reason about difficult problems in their field (Amalric and Dehaene 2016). In kindergarten children, the ability to add two arrays of dots and compare the sum to a third array, when tested near the start of the school year, predicts children's learning of school math as assessed by the teacher at the end of that year (Gilmore, McCarthy, and Spelke 2010). Once children learn both number words and Arabic notation, they can use these symbols to perform symbolic arithmetic with approximate precision before they are taught any arithmetic algorithms in school (Gilmore, McCarthy, and Spelke 2007, 2010). All these findings suggest that intuitive conceptions of numbers, arising in infancy, serve as guideposts for children's learning of school mathematics.

Further studies show that children's approximate numerical acuity improves with experience. Among Amazonian children who begin their formal education at variable ages, approximate numerical acuity is better predicted by amount of schooling than by chronological age (Piazza et al. 2013). Moreover, both lab and field studies show that activities exercising intuitive, approximate number abilities produce short-term (zero to three months) enhancement in performance of symbolic arithmetic (Dillon et al. 2017; Hyde, Khanum, and Spelke 2014; Khanum et al. 2016; Park et al. 2016). When these activities occur in contexts that foster spatial language and introduce spatial symbols, they produce more enduring enhancements to children's school math learning (Dean et al. 2021). Young children's inherent numerical abilities are resources to be nourished in early childhood.

Key Takeaways

- From infancy, children's intuitive conception of numbers provides guideposts for their learning of mathematics at school.
- The right activities to exercise that intuitive ability can produce lasting improvements in mathematical learning at school.

Learning about Objects

At birth, children detect objects and follow their motions, and they use objects to guide their developing understanding of mechanical events and their engagement with the technologies of their culture. Early knowledge of objects guides not only children's developing understanding of the physical world but also their understanding of numbers and arithmetic.

It is often said that the world of an infant is a "buzzing, blooming confusion" of sensory-motor experience, a view first articulated by William James. Jean Piaget argued instead that infants' sensory-motor experience is organized from the start, and he rightly noted that children's knowledge of objects grows by leaps and bounds over the first two years of life. Piaget believed, however, that infants begin with no knowledge of objects, space, or causality. Contrary to the views of James and Piaget, research on human infants, together with research on newborn animals of other species, provides evidence that infants organize their sensory world into objects from the start. They perceive depth (Adolph, Kaplan, and Kretch 2021; Gibson and Walk 1960), and they use depth relations to perceive where one object ends and the next begins (for example, the boundary between their ball and the hand of a parent who holds it), the solid shape of an opaque object whose back is not in view (Kellman 1984), and even the continued existence and solidity of an object that moves partly or wholly out of view behind another object (Baillargeon 1986; Valenza et al. 2006) or is obscured by darkness (Clifton et al. 1991). Newborn infants are prepared to learn how objects move when they are and are not stably supported, and what happens when objects fall, collide, or disappear behind other objects. From birth, infant animals perceive objects, recognize objects that are partly or fully hidden, and reason about objects' motions and interactions (Chiandetti and Vallortigara 2011; Regolin and Vallortigara 1995), as do young human infants (for reviews, see Baillargeon 1993; Carey 2009; Kellman and Arterberry 2006), providing evidence that abilities are present at the onset of experience of the visible world.

From these beginnings, infants rapidly learn about specific kinds of objects and their behavior through their active exploration (Schulz 2012; Stahl and Feigenson 2015; Téglás et al. 2011; Ullman et al. 2017). Infants and preschool-age children learn rapidly to recognize and categorize the objects around them by their characteristic forms and functions for human action (for review, see Rakison and Oakes 2003). Over early childhood, they learn to manipulate spoons and hammers (Keen 2011), plan multistep actions that allow them to rake in an object that is out of reach (Claxton, Keen, and McCarty 2003), stack a pile of blocks into a tower that does not fall (Chen et al. 2010), and infer the hidden properties of an object, such as its weight, from its interactions with other objects (Ullman et al. 2017).

Children use their abilities to track objects to infer how the number of objects in a set changes when a single new object is added or taken away from the set (Izard, Streri, and Spelke 2014), an important milestone for the development of the number concepts used in counting and in primary school arithmetic (Carey 2009). Preschool children also use their abilities to categorize objects by their forms and functions to extend their number concepts and develop an intuitive understanding of exact arithmetic, for example, an understanding that two dogs and two cats combine to form a set of four pets (Rosenberg and Feigenson 2013). Finally, the next section shows that young children use their knowledge of inanimate objects to enhance their understanding of people and their actions, intentions, and goals.

Key Takeaways

- Early knowledge of objects guides children's developing understanding of the physical world, including the numbers, arithmetic, tools, and technologies of their culture.
- Fostering knowledge of objects helps children navigate the world and enhances numeracy.

Learning about People's Actions and Goals

By three months of age, infants are sensitive to people's actions and goals, and their emerging understanding of the actions of others serves as a foundation for the development of their own motor skills and for their understanding of people's intentions and their mental states.

From birth, newborn infants distinguish animate from inanimate objects (Meltzoff and Moore 1977) as do other animals (Mascalzoni, Regolin, and Vallortigara 2010). Young infants perceive the bodies and actions of people from their movements (Bertenthal and Pinto 1994) and infer the goals and intentions that guide those actions (Luo and Johnson 2009). Before infants can pick up and manipulate objects, they understand that other people cause their own motions and, by moving, cause changes in the objects that they manipulate (Liu et al. 2019). As infants become able to act intentionally on objects themselves and come to understand the actions of others, their causal knowledge grows (Muentener and Schulz 2014). Moreover, infants attribute goals and intentions to other people who engage in these actions, and they infer, by observing others' actions, what objects and events the people value (Liu et al. 2017; Woodward 1998).

Over the preschool years, children's understanding of their own and other people's actions and intentions grows extensively. They come to view other people as capable of action planning, of opening a box, for example, not out of a simple desire to see a box with an open lid, but out of a desire to access the object that the box contains (Piaget 1954; Sommerville and Woodward 2005). They also come to view other people's actions not as direct responses to the external environment but as guided by their beliefs about the environment: if a person expresses a desire for an object and a belief that it lies inside a given box, children come to expect the person to search for the object inside that box, even if they themselves know that the object lies in a different location (Wellman 2014; Wimmer and Perner 1983). Children's own action planning, and their reasoning about their own mental states, develops hand in hand with their understanding of the actions and mental states of others (Comalli et al. 2016). These developments are critical foundations for children's school readiness, because children's learning from teachers depends on their abilities to understand what the teachers intend to convey to them.

Beginning in infancy and continuing through the preschool years, young children also evaluate other people on the basis of their actions. Young infants prefer individuals who take action to help (rather than hinder) others (Hamlin et al. 2013). Further, both toddlers and preschool-age children discriminate against individuals whose actions violate social norms— including those who act in ways that are unkind, unfair, or unconventional (Hamlin et al. 2011; Hardecker et al. 2016; Yang et al. 2018). Toddlers and older children also are sensitive to others' mental states when evaluating their actions; they distinguish between intentionally versus unintentionally helpful and harmful actions (Dunfield and Kuhlmeier 2010; Vaish, Carpenter, and Tomasello 2010; Woo et al. 2017). Naturalistic studies confirm that children evaluate others on the basis of their actions: children who are more prosocial tend to be more popular among peers than children who exhibit fewer prosocial tendencies (Greener 2000; Paulus 2017).

Key Takeaways

- Children's emerging understanding of people's actions and goals serves as a foundation for the development of children's own motor skills and for their understanding of people's intentions and mental states.
- Children's deepening understanding of their own and other people's actions and intentions helps children relate to others and prepares them for school.

Learning about Social Interactions, Communication, and Language

Children are sensitive to people's social relationships, communication, language, and mental states—the foundation for socially guided learning that is central to the development of children's knowledge, skills, and values, both at home and in school.

From birth, infants are interested in other people: they are drawn to look at faces (Valenza et al. 1996), to attend to voices over other sounds (Vouloumanos and Werker 2007), and to gestures over other actions (Goldin-Meadow 2005; Petitto et al. 2004). Infants also are predisposed to imitate other people's sounds and gestures (Mampe et al. 2009; Meltzoff and Moore 1977; Meltzoff et al. 2018), as are other animals (Ferrari et al. 2006; Myowa-Yamakoshi et al. 2004). Infants begin to learn the sounds and words of their language by listening to the speech of others (see the section titled "Children Are Born to Learn"). As early as three months of age, infants learn by observing the actions of the people around them (Liu, Brooks, and Spelke 2019).

Learning from others accelerates in the second year. First, children begin to exhibit a remarkable, species-specific capacity to learn language from language. Although birds and border collies can learn to associate spoken words to objects (Pepperberg 1990; Pilley and Hinzmann 2014), toddlers can learn the meanings of new words in the absence of the objects they refer to, simply by observing two people in conversation (Yuan and Fisher 2009). Moreover, toddlers use other people's speech to learn about the world: they infer a change in the state of the world simply by hearing a person's report of that change (Ganea et al. 2007). These changes usher in a period in which children rapidly gain competence at learning from others by evaluating their competence and social appropriateness as informers (see the section titled "Young Children's Learning Skills and Tools").

Rich evidence suggests that all these developments are modulated by children's social and language experience. Advances in children's reasoning about knowledge and ignorance are predicted by individual differences in the language that children hear at home (Devine and Hughes 2018). Even children's learning to categorize objects—a skill that is critical for tool use—and their learning of number words and symbols—learning that is critical to their readiness for learning school mathematics—are predicted best by the number of nouns in children's language (Negen and Sarnecka 2012; Smith 2003). Analyses of recordings of the language that is spoken directly to children at home, or spoken to others within children's hearing, reveal that children's vocabulary, in turn, is predicted by the number of conversational exchanges children participate in or observe (Romeo et al. 2018; Wang et al. 2020).

Research in developmental cognitive neuroscience reveals rich interactions between social cognitive development, language development, learning to use symbols, and learning to read (Dehaene 2009). Early capacities for language and action planning, propelled by predispositions to learn from social others, enable literate adults to engage in rapid learning of new writing systems (Lake et al. 2017), and they prepare children who live in homes with books and family members who read with them for learning to read and write in primary school (Castles, Rastle, and Nation 2018; Duursma, Augustyn, and Zuckerman 2008).

Alphabets are symbol systems used by people to communicate information in a manner that endures over time and distances. To master an alphabetic writing system, children must recruit and orchestrate multiple abilities that begin to emerge in infancy, including their language learning, their sensitivity to spatial patterns and symbols, and especially their capacities to make sense of the actions and discern the intentions of the people who communicate with them. As children accomplish these tasks, their minds and brains undergo qualitative changes that foster the development of this critical cognitive skill (Dehaene 2009).

The skill that children gain when they learn to read comes to enhance their learning in all areas of knowledge, for the experience of reading increases children's vocabulary, speech, writing, and, of course, their knowledge of the world (Castles, Rastle, and Nation 2018).

Key Takeaways

- Children's early sensitivity to social relationships, communication, language, and mental states helps them learn both about and from other people in their social worlds.
- Stimulating environments promote language and literacy development, which are key for school readiness and enhance learning across all areas of knowledge.

YOUNG CHILDREN'S LEARNING SKILLS AND TOOLS

Children's learning in all areas of core knowledge depends on an arsenal of general learning skills and tools that support children's engagement with and learning about the world. Children's learning depends on a host of executive functions that regulate their attention and action planning. It depends on their powers of imagination that guide their play and their simulations of actual or possible events. It depends on their capacity for metacognition, especially their understanding of what they and others do and do not know and how their knowledge and skills can grow. And it depends on the ways in which children's learning environments cultivate their inherent motivation to learn. These skills and tools can be enhanced by the experiences that homes and preschools can provide. This section focuses on these general cognitive skills, which are most relevant to children's ability to thrive and learn in school.

Executive Functions: Focusing Attention, Planning, and Memory

Executive functions are critical for children to learn effectively and accomplish goals. Children need to be able to focus their attention, plan, remember what has gone before, and switch flexibly from one activity to the next. The cognitive skills underlying these abilities are collectively called executive functions. Researchers have identified three fundamental executive functions that support children's learning: inhibition (for example, resisting impulses, ignoring distractions), working memory (for example, keeping information in mind, playing with ideas), and cognitive flexibility (for example, changing tasks, adjusting to change) (for reviews, see Best and Miller 2010; Carlson, Zelazo, and Faja 2013; Diamond 2013; Miyake et al. 2000).

Better executive function skills are positively related to school readiness and school performance, as well as later life outcomes such as career success (for review, see Diamond 2013). They critically underlie the ability to plan sequences of actions—both overt actions and mental ones—that are central to all school activities, from performing mental calculations to writing a paragraph. Indeed, researchers have found links between executive function skills and children's learning in the core areas of knowledge reviewed in the previous section. Children with better executive function skills perform better on measures probing their mathematical skills (Bull, Espy, and Wiebe 2008; Clark, Pritchard, and Woodward 2010; Cragg and Gilmore 2014; Prager, Sera, and Carlson 2016), social reasoning (Eisenberg et al. 2004; Perner and Lang 1999; Sabbagh et al. 2006), and language abilities (Blair and Razza 2007; Follmer 2018).

Executive functions are apparent from birth (Dehaene-Lambertz and Spelke 2015) but undergo rapid improvement during early childhood (for review, see Carlson, Zelazo, and Faja 2013). This growth is supported by brain maturation, including a part of the brain, called the prefrontal cortex, that is active even before birth. Executive function skills improve naturally as children grow, but some research also indicates that executive functions can be improved through direct skill training (for example, some working memory computer games; Aksayli, Sala, and Gobet 2019) or through curricula that emphasize executive functions skill building (for example, training teachers in helping children improve self-regulation skills; Watts et al. 2018).

However, it is important to recognize that available evidence suggests that executive function training effects are sometimes narrow (for example, children improve on the trained task or skill but not on other skills; Aksayli, Sala, and Gobet 2019) or inconsistent across measures (for example, Watts et al. 2018; for review and discussion, see Nesbitt and Farran 2021). Further, a recent large-scale, longitudinal, field-based randomized controlled trial revealed that one of the most comprehensive curricula seeking to build young children's executive function skills ("Tools of the Mind") is not effective (Nesbitt and Farran 2021). At this point, it is not clear which interventions are most effective for engendering meaningful improvements in young children's executive functions.

Key Takeaways

- Executive functions help children focus their attention, plan, and remember.
- Children with better executive function skills perform better on measures probing their mathematical skills, social reasoning, and language abilities.
- It is widely believed that executive functions are malleable, but thus far efforts to improve children's self-control, working memory, and cognitive flexibility have proved to be less successful than efforts to enhance children's knowledge and skills in specific cognitive domains.

Imagination: Boosting Learning and Communication Skills

Research on mental simulation underscores the importance of play and other activities that stimulate children's imagination in ECE. Mental simulations support children's insights, discoveries, and creativity. They play an important role in children's learning because they allow children to manipulate and rehearse ideas that have been introduced to them, thereby enhancing learning and memory for material (Allen, Smith, and Tenenbaum 2020; Piaget 1952). They also support children's insights, discoveries, and creativity by allowing them to represent in their minds possible objects or activities that they have never witnessed, and indeed that do not yet exist (Harris 2000; Liu et al. 2019; Piaget 1952). And they allow children to learn about activities that are too hazardous to be performed directly (for example, when a child simulates a new way to get home from school).

Imagination refers to the ability to simulate, and therefore experience, events that one is not currently perceiving, including events from the distant past, events that might happen in the future, and events that could have happened but did not. Research on children's imagination or pretend play underscores the value of mental simulation for children's learning in a variety of areas of knowledge. Pretending gives children the opportunity to practice expressing themselves and communicating with others (thus facilitating social and language development) (for review, see Singer, Golinkoff, and Hirsh-Pasek 2006). Further, the intensity, quality, and complexity of children's pretense is correlated with children's perspective-taking abilities (Lillard and Kavanaugh 2014; Taylor and Carlson 1997)—perhaps because it allows children to practice different roles (for example, parent, teacher, student).

Research in cognitive science, neuroscience, and computational sciences has revealed that processes of mental simulation are ubiquitous in animals (for review, see Foster 2017) and human adults (for example, Liu et al. 2019). Most mental simulations occur unconsciously, at far greater speeds than the actual events that are simulated—at least 10 times faster in studies measuring simulation activity in human adults, who report no awareness of the simulations that they perform over the course of learning a new, demanding task (Liu et al. 2019).[1] Building on research with rats, recent work reveals brain processes in human adults that simulate experiences of nonspatial sequential learning tasks as well as tasks of navigation and action planning, and that these simulations aid adults' performance (Schuck and Niv 2019). To date, no experiments in cognitive neuroscience have measured these simulation processes in human infants and young children. Because infant brains are active both during sleep and at rest, beginning before birth (for review, see Dehaene-Lambertz and Spelke 2015), and because spontaneous activity in fetal brains importantly influences the strength of synaptic connections in the visual system (Katz and Shatz 1996), the role of simulation processes in children's learning is a fruitful area for future study.

Key Takeaways

- Imagination, or pretend play, supports insight, discovery, and creativity in children.
- Pretending provides children with an opportunity to express themselves and communicate with others.
- Pretense elicits processes of mental simulation. Although simulation processes have not been studied systematically in children, they enhance learning and memory in adults and other animals, consistent with the value of pretense and imagination in children's learning.

Metacognition: Learning to Learn

Knowing what you know, what you do not know, and how to extend your knowledge and use it more effectively are critical tools for learning at all ages (Chatzipanteli, Grammatikopoulos, and Gregoriadis 2014; Dunlosky and Metcalfe 2008). These metacognitive abilities can motivate learners to return to or explore material they have not mastered, and to move on from material they have already mastered and build on their knowledge in productive ways (Flavell 1979; Metcalfe 2009).

Research suggests that even infants can track and communicate about their own uncertainty in some circumstances (Goupil and Kouider 2016; Goupil, Romand-Monnier, and Kouider 2016), but preschool children are able to reflect on and articulate their own states of knowledge and ignorance more clearly (Ghetti, Hembacher, and Coughlin 2013). In one study (Cherney 2003), for example, three-year-old children's use of terms connoting uncertainty (for example, "guess," "think") versus certainty (for example, "know," "forget") was related to their performance on a spatial memory task. Children who said they "knew" where a reward was, for example, were more likely to locate the reward than those who said they "thought" it was in a particular place. Both by this assessment and on other tasks, children's metacognitive abilities improve markedly between three and five years of age (Ghetti, Hembacher, and Coughlin 2013).

Metacognition improves after the preschool years as well (Lyons and Zelazo 2011). For example, children in one study (O'Leary and Sloutsky 2017) were asked to decide which of two gray boxes contained more dots. When asked how well they thought they performed on the task, five-year-old children tended to overestimate their performance, but seven-year-old children did not. Moreover, five-year-old children continued to overestimate their performance even when they received clear feedback throughout the task about their performance (a happy face appeared when they made a correct choice and a sad face appeared when they did not). These findings suggest that children—especially at young ages—may need help tracking their knowledge and performance in classrooms.

Metacognition supports children's success in school (for example, Bryce, Whitebread, and Szücs 2015) and can be improved through direct skills training programs (Dignath, Buettner, and Langfeldt 2008). Teachers can also enhance children's learning from classroom instruction by encouraging children to engage in metacognitive thinking, for example, by asking children questions about their strategies and knowledge (such as "How did you know that would work?") (Grammer, Coffman, and Ornstein 2013).

Research with older children provides evidence that metacognition can have downsides: if children decide that they are simply not talented in some areas of core knowledge, they may decrease rather than increase their efforts to learn in those areas (Dweck 2008). Young children are less apt to exhibit this counterproductive mindset, however, and curricula emphasizing "growth mindsets" about intelligence, that is, the idea that intelligence and learning, like physical strength and athletic skill, can be increased through effort, improve older children's persistence and academic performance under some conditions (Dweck and Yeager 2019; Yeager et al. 2019), though not others (Sisk et al. 2018). Fortunately, young children appear to use their metacognitive abilities primarily to guide their learning, and they seek to learn skills and material they have not yet mastered. There are other motivational patterns that do vary across children and bear on what and when they learn, as addressed in the next section.

Key Takeaways

- Metacognition, or knowing what you know, what you do not know, and how to extend your knowledge and use it more effectively, is critical for learning at all ages.
- Metacognitive abilities can motivate learners to return to or explore material they have not mastered, and to move on from material they have already mastered.
- Children's metacognitive abilities improve markedly between three and five years of age.

Motivation: A Key Driver for Learning

Children are naturally curious and ready to learn both on their own and from other people (see the sections titled "Children Are Born to Learn" and "Five Core Knowledge Areas"), but individual differences in motivation to learn are also evident in childhood. Three motivational constructs of particular relevance in educational settings are *interest* (engagement with materials and activities), *persistence* (the tendency to continue working on a task even when it is difficult or results in performance mistakes), and *trust* between teachers and learners.

Research with young children reveals individual differences in levels of both interest and persistence. High levels of interest and persistence predict better academic and social achievement in school. Further, both interest and persistence are correlated with parental behaviors (Martin, Ryan, and Brooks-Gunn 2013; Neitzel, Alexander, and Johnson 2019). For example, in one longitudinal study, more supportive parenting (such as noticing and responding appropriately to children's signals) on the part of mothers of one-year-old children predicted higher interest and persistence on novel laboratory tasks at three years of age, which in turn predicted better performance on academic skills assessments in kindergarten (Martin, Ryan, and Brooks-Gunn 2013).

Outside the parent-child context, the behaviors of other adults also affect children's motivation. For example, laboratory studies reveal that infants and toddlers will work harder to solve a problem after observing an adult expend significant energy solving a (different) problem (Leonard, Lee, and

Schulz 2017). Further, toddlers and young children persist more on difficult tasks when adults use language that emphasizes the children's actions rather than their abilities (Cimpian et al. 2007; Lucca, Horton, and Sommerville 2019). For example, in one study (Cimpian et al. 2007), researchers asked four-year-old children to role-play scenarios in which they drew a picture of an object (for example, an apple) and then heard the teacher say either "You are a good drawer" or "You did a good job drawing." Then, children role-played drawing another picture and making a mistake (for example leaving ears off a cat). Children who had previously heard the statement that focused on their ability were less interested in drawing another picture in the future compared with children who had previously heard the statement that focused on their activity.

To be motivated to learn the material and skills presented to them in school, children must trust those who seek to teach them (Corriveau and Winters 2019). In this context, it is particularly important to recognize that much of what children are taught early in their education can seem arbitrary to them. For example, in the late preschool and early school years, children are introduced to letters that combine to form the words, phrases, and texts that they will use in reading, and to numerals that combine to form the numbers, arithmetic algorithms, and equations that they will use in solving problems in mathematics. These symbols have apparently arbitrary properties: the letter is pronounced differently in different contexts (consider the h in "hat," "the," and "night"), and the same numerals convey different numbers in different arrangements (consider the 1 and 2 in "12" and "21"). Letters and numbers therefore do not represent entities in the same manner as do pictures, which can depict the same entities in different arrangements. Children, moreover, will not appreciate why letters and numbers combine as they do until they become skilled readers and arithmetic calculators. As a consequence, many of the actions of ECE teachers, and many of the tasks they set for children, occur for reasons that children cannot yet understand. To learn what they need to know in school, children must trust that their teachers' requests and demonstrations will prove to be worthwhile.

As reviewed previously (in the "Five Core Knowledge Areas" section), young children are remarkably good at learning from others—even when the basis for a teacher's actions is opaque (Csibra and Gergely 2009; Király, Csibra, and Gergely 2013). However, laboratory research shows that young children are especially motivated to trust information provided by adults who have previously demonstrated effective actions (Birch, Akmal, and Frampton 2010) as well as those who have provided accurate information in the past (Harris 2017). For example, when given the opportunity to accept or request new information from someone who has previously displayed knowledge (versus ignorance) about what different objects are called, young children favor knowledgeable adults (Jaswal and Neely 2006; Koenig and

Harris 2005). Children are also more likely to remember information that is conveyed by competent and trusted adults (Sabbagh and Shafman 2009).

Children also tend to trust adults who are members of their own sociocultural group. For example, from infancy. children attend more to those who speak with an accent that matches the children's home community (Kinzler, Dupoux, and Spelke 2007), and preschool-age children favor information conveyed by adults who speak their language with their community's native accent (Kinzler, Corriveau, and Harris 2011). By four to seven years of age, children are also more trusting of information provided by those who match their own racial group membership (Chen, Corriveau, and Harris 2013).

Taken together, the results from laboratory studies suggest that children in ECE will learn best from teachers who are highly knowledgeable about the material they teach and those whose social identities align with children's homes and local communities (Corriveau and Winters 2019). Accordingly, research on children's educational outcomes reveals that students benefit from having teachers who are members of their own sociocultural group. For example, in the United States, having just one Black teacher before third grade significantly increases Black students' persistence and motivation in later grades and their likelihood of graduating from high school (Gershenson et al. 2021). Having a teacher who shares children's social identity may increase children's trust in their teacher and the information the teacher provides—but further research is necessary to pinpoint mechanisms underlying the benefits of sociocultural convergence between teachers and students.

Key Takeaways

- Children's motivation to learn varies depending on their level of interest and persistence, as well as the trust between teachers and learners.
- High levels of interest and persistence predict better academic and social achievement in school.
- Children learn best from competent, knowledgeable, and confident adults. They tend to trust adults whose language, culture, and interests are similar to those of the people in the child's social world.

WHAT PROMOTES AND HINDERS CHILDREN'S LEARNING?

The capacities and motivational patterns described in previous sections guide the learning of children in all cultures, across all socioeconomic levels. Further, gender differences in cognitive abilities are largely absent (Hyde 2005; Spelke 2005). The nurturance of these abilities and motivations therefore provides a good target for ECE programs worldwide. However, context does matter for learning. As reviewed in the previous section, features of teachers (for example, their knowledge levels, their sociocultural identities and practices) affect children's trust in the information that teachers provide. Adequate sleep and nutrition, as well as positive attention from trusted adults, are critical for learning. Freedom from prejudice and stereotyping are also important. However, many children face adversity, living and learning in conditions that can hold them back from achieving their full potential. In particular, children who experience adversity face challenges that can affect the extent to which they are apt to benefit from what others try to teach them, even though their basic aptitude for learning is as high as that of other children. When designed to meet the needs of young children, high-quality ECE programs can protect early learning trajectories (Walker et al. 2011). The following discussion describes a few factors that can hinder learning and some ways in which ECE can counter them.

Malnourishment, Insufficient Sleep, and Neglect

Inadequate nutrition and sleep, as well as neglect by caregivers, can negatively affect children's ability to learn and succeed in school (Bick and Nelson 2016; Dewald et al. 2010; Grantham-McGregor et al. 2007; Jyoti, Frongillo, and Jones 2005; McLaughlin, Sheridan, and Lambert 2014; Smith and Pollak 2020; Winicki and Jemison 2003). However, these negative influences can be at least partially addressed in schools: First, some studies reveal positive effects of school-delivered meals and snacks on children's learning and academic outcomes (for example, Aurino et al. 2018; Chakraborty and Jayaraman 2019). Second, classroom naps have been shown to boost young children's learning by enhancing their memory for information presented during the school day (Kurdziel, Duclos, and Spencer 2013). Third, when ECE educators who provide emotional warmth, sensitivity, and responsiveness are available, children can develop a secure attachment relationship with them (Fuhs, Farran, and Nesbitt 2013), which in turn can promote the growth of self-reliance, the capacity for emotional regulation, and the emergence and course of social competence, among other things (Sroufe 2005). ECE programs can also promote children's emotional security through consistency in the behavior and expectations of educators who establish clear and consistent routines for children (Williford, Carter, and Pianta 2016).

Social Biases

Young children detect and care about social categories and social group memberships—including those based on ethnicity, race, gender, and class (Rhodes and Baron 2019; Shutts 2015; Shutts et al. 2016; Skinner and Meltzoff 2019). Unfortunately, children's sensitivity to social grouping—and to societal stereotypes—can lead them to think and behave in ways that are unfair and unkind in the classroom. Children from stigmatized groups commonly experience negative treatment on the basis of their group membership (for example, negative stereotyping, teasing, and social exclusion), and such experiences are associated with poorer academic outcomes (for example, Levy et al. 2016; Wong, Eccles, and Sameroff 2003). Research on effective strategies for identifying and addressing social biases—in particular, strategies that produce robust, long-term decreases in biases—in school is sorely needed.

Key Takeaways

- To fulfill their learning potential, children need adequate sleep and nutrition, positive social relationships with adults they trust, and freedom from prejudice and stereotyping.
- ECE can address negative factors that hinder learning.

CONCLUSION AND AREAS FOR FUTURE RESEARCH

The cognitive capacities reviewed in this chapter emerge in infancy and function throughout life. They are possessed by all children, and they can be harnessed to foster children's learning in all countries and cultures. To realize this promise, however, ECE must be sensitive to children's current level of understanding; take place in settings that address children's needs for food, rest, and a safe, predictable environment; and engender children's trust in those who teach them.

Young children explore and learn rapidly and spontaneously by building on five core areas of knowledge. Children are primed to learn by understanding places, numbers, objects, people, and relationships. We can support their predisposition to learn by enhancing the development of four key sets of skills, from executive functions and imagination to metacognition and motivation to learn. Together, this knowledge can be harnessed to establish solid foundations for quality early learning for children everywhere.

Despite how much the understanding of what and how young children learn has grown in recent decades, many open questions remain, providing a road map for future investigation. For example, because children learn by building on what they already know, how can insights from the science of learning be translated into effective early school curricula? Efforts to develop effective curricula for preschool children are hindered by the absence of systematic evaluations of specific curricular practices at this level. Nevertheless, research investigating the long-term impacts of preschools on children's school learning make it clear that curricula matter: randomized controlled experiments that test and compare the effectiveness of different curricula for enhancing preschool children's learning can reveal the strengths and weaknesses of different preschool curricula.

Field testing of educational curricula may be criticized for producing findings that may not generalize to populations and cultures beyond where the curriculum is tested, both because children in different cultures come to school with different experiences and expectations and because schools in different countries may have different educational goals for their children. The latter differences have diminished, however, given the importance of educating children to contribute to the global economy, and educational goals are easier to measure, thanks to the advent of international evaluations of students' achievement in different countries. Although children in different cultures do vary in their experiences, cultural variations are not likely to exert prominent effects on curricular interventions that are based on findings from studies of early cognitive development. The cognitive capacities reviewed in this chapter emerge in infancy and continue to function throughout life. They are possessed by all children, and they foster children's learning in all countries and cultures and at all economic levels. This research also can be harnessed to support the development of curricula, pedagogy, and learning environments, as well as to inform teacher and school management training.

Because children learn from people they trust and people from their communities, how can learning environments be created that bridge to children's homes and communities and that foster that trust? Many school systems use sports, music, and art to bridge cultural divides within the school and enlist children in activities with common goals. However, systematic studies have not measured the impacts of such activities on children's learning of the primary school curriculum: learning to read, to communicate effectively, to calculate, to measure, and to reason about the physical world, the living world, and the social and cultural environment. For example, one review of experiments evaluating effects of music training on children's school-relevant skills finds no consistent evidence that music training benefits young children's academic performance (Mehr 2015).

An alternative strategy is to introduce games with academic content into preschool and primary school classrooms as a complement to the regular academic curriculum. Recent experiments have evaluated one set of curricula for preschool, kindergarten, and first grade children consisting of games with numerical and spatial content, played socially by groups of children, led by local community members (Dillon et al. 2017) or by the regular kindergarten or first grade teacher (Dean et al. 2021; see also Clements et al. 2011; Griffin and Case 1997). The games aimed to foster children's social and communicative skills of teaching to and learning from others, as well as skills of numerical and spatial cognition. The curriculum involved no specific teaching of arithmetic, but the two best-performing curricula included both instruction in and play with spatial symbols and with numerals and their combinations. As noted in the section "Young Children's Learning Skills and Tools," these symbols and combinations follow rules that preschool children are not yet in a position to understand. When children are challenged to learn these rules in a social, game context, however, they may be motivated to master them, thereby gaining skill in an enjoyable group activity and taking the first steps in mastering these symbol systems. These curricula showed positive effects on children's numerical and geometrical reasoning, both on an immediate posttest (Dillon et al. 2017) and on tests conducted one year later (Dean et al. 2021). Because most of the children had completed the first year of primary school at the latter time point, the games may have helped both to build children's knowledge of mathematical symbols in preschool and to enhance their trust in the primary school teachers who delivered their subsequent instruction in formal mathematics.

Because productive learning happens both inside and outside school, how can adults who care for children (for example, parents, preschool teachers, primary school teachers, social workers, health care professionals) become involved in activities that promote young children's learning and healthy development and that ready them, cognitively and motivationally, for formal learning in school? Studies in developmental cognitive science suggest a wealth of activities that children might share with their siblings and family members, and that might enhance their cognitive development either at home or in preschools. In the coming years, more programs to develop, implement, and evaluate these activities in preschool and early primary school settings would be welcome. This research will be especially valuable if the curricula that it evaluates target abilities and propensities that emerge early in the preschool years, building on capacities that are shared by all children. Specific curricula that build on children's universal capacities for understanding the world, exploring, and learning may or may not prove to be effective in the field: their effectiveness must be tested in systematic field experiments. If curricula building on universal capacities are found to be successful in one culture, however, they are likely to be effective for children in other cultures as well. Research that implements and evaluates both home-based and preschool-based activities to enhance young children's reading readiness, math readiness, executive function, metacognitive skills, persistence, and trust in teachers promises to provide valuable information on how to better prepare all the world's children for the transition to school (for example, Mackey et al. 2011).

See table 1.1 for a review of the key takeaways in this chapter.

Table 1.1   Chapter 1: Summary of Key Takeaways

Children are born to learn

- Children are the most capable learners on earth.
- Children's learning in the early years sets the stage for lifelong learning.

Learning about places

- Early spatial abilities support children's learning about their immediate environment, as well as spatial symbols such as pictures, maps, scale models, and number lines.
- Young children's spatial abilities can be nourished to enhance school readiness.

Learning about numbers

- From infancy, children's intuitive conception of numbers provides guideposts for their learning of mathematics at school.
- The right activities to exercise that intuitive ability can produce lasting improvements in mathematical learning at school.

Learning about objects

- Early knowledge of objects guides children's developing understanding of the physical world, including the numbers, arithmetic, tools, and technologies of their culture.
- Fostering knowledge of objects helps children navigate the world and enhances numeracy.

Learning about people's actions and goals

- Children's emerging understanding of people's actions and goals serves as a foundation for the development of children's own motor skills and for their understanding of people's intentions and mental states.
- Children's deepening understanding of their own and other people's actions and intentions helps children relate to others and prepares them for school.

Learning about social interactions, communication, and language

- Children's early sensitivity to social relationships, communication, language, and mental states helps them learn both about and from other people in their social worlds.
- Stimulating environments promote language and literacy development, which are key for school readiness and enhance learning across all areas of knowledge.

continued next page

Table 1.1 (*continued*)

Executive functions: Focusing attention, planning, and memory

- Executive functions help children focus their attention, plan, and remember.
- Children with better executive function skills perform better on measures probing their mathematical skills, social reasoning, and language abilities.
- It is widely believed that executive functions are malleable, but efforts to improve children's self-control, working memory, and cognitive flexibility have proved to be less successful than efforts to enhance children's knowledge and skills in specific cognitive domains.

Imagination: Boosting learning and communication skills

- Imagination, or pretend play, supports insight, discovery, and creativity in children.
- Pretending provides children with an opportunity to express themselves and communicate with others.
- Pretense elicits processes of mental simulation. Although simulation processes have not been studied systematically in children, they enhance learning and memory in adults and other animals, consistent with the value of pretense and imagination in children's learning.

Metacognition: Learning to learn

- Metacognition, or knowing what you know, what you do not know, and how to extend your knowledge and use it more effectively, is critical for learning at all ages.
- Metacognitive abilities can motivate learners to return to or explore material they have not mastered, and to move on from material they have already mastered.
- Children's metacognitive abilities improve markedly between three and five years of age.

Motivation: A key driver for learning

- Children's motivation to learn varies depending on their level of interest and persistence, as well as the trust between teachers and learners.
- High levels of interest and persistence predict better academic and social achievement in school.
- Children learn best from competent, knowledgeable, and confident adults. They tend to trust adults whose language, culture, and interests are similar to those of the people in the child's social world.

What promotes and hinders children's learning?

- To fulfill their learning potential, children need adequate sleep and nutrition, positive social relationships with adults they trust, and freedom from prejudice and stereotyping.
- ECE can address negative factors that hinder learning.

Source: Original table for this publication.
Note: ECE = early childhood education.

NOTE

1. Striking demonstrations of the role of mental simulation in learning, memory, and invention come from experimental research with rodents. For example, researchers have found that, when a rat completes spatial navigation tasks (that is, mazes), different cells in the hippocampus fire as the rat changes its location (O'Keefe and Nadel 1978). Interestingly, the same hippocampal neurons also fire after rats complete the maze (and do so in the same order; Gupta et al. 2010). This so-called replay at rest is critical to supporting rats' learning and memory; when neuronal replay is blocked during the rest period, rats' learning is impaired (Girardeau et al. 2009). But simulations are not simply faithful replays of a rat's past experience: rats also simulate paths through the environment that they have never taken because barriers stood in their way (Gupta et al. 2010; Ólafsdóttir et al. 2015). In this respect, rats' simulations resemble those of toddlers at play (for example, Leslie 1987).

REFERENCES

Adolph, K. E., B. E. Kaplan, and K. S. Kretch. 2021. "Infants on the Edge: Beyond the Visual Cliff." In *Developmental Psychology: Revisiting the Classic Studies,* 2nd ed., edited by A. Slater and P. Quinn, 551–72. London: SAGE Publications.

Aksayli, N. D., G. Sala, and F. Gobet. 2019. "The Cognitive and Academic Benefits of Cogmed: A Meta-Analysis." *Educational Research Review* 27: 229–43.

Allen, K., K. Smith, and J. Tenenbaum. 2020. "Rapid Trial-and-Error Learning with Simulation Supports Flexible Tool Use and Physical Reasoning." *Proceedings of the National Academy of Sciences* 117 (47): 29302–10.

Amalric, M., and S. Dehaene. 2016. "Origins of the Brain Networks for Advanced Mathematics in Expert Mathematicians." *Proceedings of the National Academy of Sciences* 113 (18): 4909–17.

Aurino, E., A. Gelli, C. Adamba, I. Osei-Akoto, and H. Alderman. 2018. "Food for Thought? Experimental Evidence on the Learning Impacts of a Large-Scale School Feeding Program in Ghana." Discussion Paper 01782, International Food Policy Research Institute, Washington, DC.

Baillargeon, R. 1986. "Representing the Existence and the Location of Hidden Objects: Object Permanence in 6-and 8-Month-Old Infants." *Cognition* 23 (1): 21–41.

Baillargeon, R. 1993. "The Object Concept Revisited: New Direction in the Investigation of Infants' Physical Knowledge." In *Visual Perception and Cognition in Infancy,* edited by C. Granrud, 265–315. Mahwah, NJ: Lawrence Erlbaum Associates, Inc.

Barth, H., N. Kanwisher, and E. Spelke. 2003. "The Construction of Large Number Representations in Adults." *Cognition* 86 (3): 201–21.

Barth, H., K. La Mont, J. Lipton, S. Dehaene, N. Kanwisher, and E. Spelke. 2006. "Non-Symbolic Arithmetic in Adults and Young Children." *Cognition* 98 (3): 199–222.

Barth, H., K. La Mont, J. Lipton, and E. S. Spelke. 2005. "Abstract Number and Arithmetic in Preschool Children." *Proceedings of the National Academy of Sciences* 102 (39): 14116–21.

Bergelson, E., and D. Swingley. 2012. "At 6–9 Months, Human Infants Know the Meanings of Many Common Nouns." *Proceedings of the National Academy of Sciences* 109 (9): 3253–58.

Bertenthal, B. I., and J. Pinto. 1994. "Global Processing of Biological Motions." *Psychological Science* 5 (4): 221–25.

Best, J. R., and P. H. Miller. 2010. "A Developmental Perspective on Executive Function." *Child Development* 81 (6): 1641–60.

Bick, J., and C. A. Nelson. 2016. "Early Adverse Experiences and the Developing Brain." *Neuropsychopharmacology* 41 (1): 177–96.

Birch, S. A. J., N. Akmal, and K. L. Frampton. 2010. "Two-Year-Olds Are Vigilant of Others' Nonverbal Cues to Credibility." *Developmental Science* 13: 363–69.

Blair, C., and R. P. Razza. 2007. "Relating Effortful Control, Executive Function, and False Belief Understanding to Emerging Math and Literacy Ability in Kindergarten." *Child Development* 78 (2): 647–63.

Bryce, D., D. Whitebread, and D. Szücs. 2015. "The Relationships among Executive Functions, Metacognitive Skills and Educational Achievement in 5 and 7 Year-Old Children." *Metacognition and Learning* 10 (2): 181–98.

Bull, R., K. A. Espy, and S. A. Wiebe. 2008. "Short-Term Memory, Working Memory, and Executive Functioning in Preschoolers: Longitudinal Predictors of Mathematical Achievement at Age 7 Years." *Developmental Neuropsychology* 33 (3): 205–28.

Burnham, D. 1993. "Visual Recognition of Mother by Young Infants: Facilitation by Speech." *Perception* 22 (10): 1133–53.

Carey, S. 2009. *The Origin of Concepts.* New York: Oxford University Press.

Carlson, S. M., P. D. Zelazo, and S. Faja. 2013. "Executive Function." In *Oxford Library of Psychology. The Oxford Handbook of Developmental Psychology (Vol. 1): Body and Mind,* edited by P. D. Zelazo, 706–43. Oxford: Oxford University Press.

Castles, A., K. Rastle, and K. Nation. 2018. "Ending the Reading Wars: Reading Acquisition from Novice to Expert." *Psychological Science in the Public Interest* 19: 5–51.

Chakraborty, T., and R. Jayaraman. 2019. "School Feeding and Learning Achievement: Evidence from India's Midday Meal Program." *Journal of Development Economics* 139: 249–65.

Chatzipanteli, A., V. Grammatikopoulos, and A. Gregoriadis. 2014. "Development and Evaluation of Metacognition in Early Childhood Education." *Early Child Development and Care* 184: 1223–32.

Chen, E. E., K. H. Corriveau, and P. L. Harris. 2013. "Children Trust a Consensus Composed of Outgroup Members—But Do Not Retain That Trust." *Child Development* 84 (1): 269–82.

Chen, Q., and J. Li. 2014. "Association between Individual Differences in Non-Symbolic Number Acuity and Math Performance: A Meta-Analysis." *Acta Psychologica* 148: 163–72.

Chen, Y. P., R. Keen, K. Rosander, and C. von Hofsten. 2010. "Movement Planning Reflects Skill Level and Age Changes in Toddlers." *Child Development* 81 (6): 1846–58.

Cherney, I. 2003. "Young Children's Spontaneous Utterances of Mental Terms and the Accuracy of their Memory Behaviors: A Different Methodological Approach." *Infant and Child Development* 12: 89–105.

Chiandetti, C., and G. Vallortigara. 2011. "Intuitive Physical Reasoning about Occluded Objects by Inexperienced Chicks." *Proceedings of the Royal Society B: Biological Sciences* 278 (1718): 2621–27.

Cimpian, A., H. M. C. Arce, E. M. Markman, and C. S. Dweck. 2007. "Subtle Linguistic Cues Affect Children's Motivation." *Psychological Science* 18 (4): 314–16.

Clark, C., V. E. Pritchard, and L. J. Woodward. 2010. "Preschool Executive Functioning Abilities Predict Early Mathematics Achievement." *Developmental Psychology* 46 (5): 1176–91.

Claxton, L. J., R. Keen, and M. E. McCarty. 2003. "Evidence of Motor Planning in Infant Reaching Behavior." *Psychological Science* 14 (4): 354–56.

Clements, D. H., J. Sarama, M. E. Spitler, A. A. Lange, and C. B. Wolfe. 2011. "Mathematics Learned by Young Children in an Intervention Based on Learning Trajectories: A Large-Scale Cluster Randomized Trial." *Journal for Research in Mathematics Education* 42 (2): 127–66.

Clifton, R. K., P. Rochat, R. Y. Litovsky, and E. E. Perris. 1991. "Object Representation Guides Infants' Reaching in the Dark." *Journal of Experimental Psychology: Human Perception and Performance* 17 (2): 323–29.

Comalli, D. M., R. Keen, E. S. Abraham, V. J. Foo, M.-H. Lee, and K. E. Adolph. 2016. "The Development of Tool Use: Planning for End-State Comfort." *Developmental Psychology* 52 (11): 1878–92.

Corriveau, K. H., and M. A. Winters. 2019. "Trusting Your Teacher: Implications for Policy." *Policy Insights from the Behavioral and Brain Sciences* 6 (2): 123–29.

Coubart, A., V. Izard, E. S. Spelke, J. Marie, and A. Streri. 2014. "Dissociation between Small and Large Numerosities in Newborn Infants." *Developmental Science* 17 (1): 11–22.

Cragg, L., and C. Gilmore. 2014. "Skills Underlying Mathematics: The Role of Executive Function in the Development of Mathematics Proficiency." *Trends in Neuroscience and Education* 3 (2): 63–68.

Csibra, G., and G. Gergely. 2009. "Natural Pedagogy." *Trends in Cognitive Sciences* 13 (4): 148–53.

Dean, J. T., H. Kannan, M. R. Dillon, E. Duflo, and E. S. Spelke. 2021. "Combining Symbols with Intuitive Material in Number and Geometry Games Durably Enhances Poor Children's Learning of First Grade Mathematics." Unpublished, Abdul Latif Jameel Poverty Action Lab (J-PAL) South Asia, New Delhi, India.

Dehaene, S. 2009. *Reading in the Brain.* New York: Penguin Viking.

Dehaene, S. 2011. *The Number Sense: How the Mind Creates Mathematics,* 2nd edition. New York: Oxford University Press.

Dehaene-Lambertz, G., and E. S. Spelke. 2015. "The Infancy of the Human Brain." *Neuron* 88 (1): 93–109.

de Hevia, M. D., V. Izard, A. Coubart, E. S. Spelke, and A. Streri. 2014. "Representations of Space, Time, and Number in Neonates." *Proceedings of the National Academy of Sciences* 111 (13): 4809–13.

DeLoache, J. S. 2000. "Dual Representation and Young Children's Use of Scale Models." *Child Development* 71 (2): 329–38.

DeLoache, J. S., S. L. Pierroutsakos, D. H. Uttal, K. S. Rosengren, and A. Gottlieb. 1998. "Grasping the Nature of Pictures." *Psychological Science* 9 (3): 205–10.

Devine, R. T., and C. Hughes. 2018. "Family Correlates of False Belief Understanding in Early Childhood: A Meta-Analysis." *Child Development* 89 (3): 971–87.

Dewald, J. F., A. M. Meijer, F. J. Oort, G. A. Kerkhof, and S. M. Bögels. 2010. "The Influence of Sleep Quality, Sleep Duration and Sleepiness on School Performance in Children and Adolescents: A Meta-Analytic Review." *Sleep Medicine Reviews* 14 (3): 179–89.

Diamond, A. 2013. "Executive Functions." *Annual Review of Psychology* 64: 135–68.

Di Giorgio, E., I. Leo, O. Pascalis, and F. Simion. 2012. "Is the Face-Perception System Human-Specific at Birth?" *Developmental Psychology* 48 (4): 1083–90.

Dignath, C., G. Buettner, and H. P. Langfeldt. 2008. "How Can Primary School Students Learn Self-Regulated Learning Strategies Most Effectively?: A Meta-Analysis on Self-Regulation Training Programmes." *Educational Research Review* 3 (2): 101–29.

Dillon, M. R., H. Kannan, J. T. Dean, E. S. Spelke, and E. Duflo. 2017. "Cognitive Science in the Field: A Preschool Intervention Durably Enhances Intuitive but Not Formal Mathematics." *Science* 357 (6346): 47–55.

Dunfield, K. A., and V. A. Kuhlmeier. 2010. "Intention-Mediated Selective Helping in Infancy." *Psychological Science* 21 (4): 523–27.

Dunlosky, J., and J. Metcalfe. 2008. *Metacognition.* Thousand Oaks, CA: SAGE Publications.

Duursma, E., M. Augustyn, and B. Zuckerman. 2008. "Reading Aloud to Children: The Evidence." *Archives of Disease in Childhood* 93: 554–57.

Dweck, C. S. 2008. *Mindset: The New Psychology of Success.* New York: Random House Digital, Inc.

Dweck, C. S., and D. S. Yeager. 2019. "Mindsets: A View from Two Eras." *Perspectives on Psychological Science* 14 (3): 481–96.

Eisenberg, N., C. L. Smith, A. Sadovsky, and T. L. Spinrad. 2004. "Effortful Control: Relations with Emotion Regulation, Adjustment, and Socialization in Childhood." In *Handbook of Self-Regulation: Research, Theory, and Applications,* edited by R. F. Baumeister and K. D. Vohs, 259–82. New York: Guilford.

Fantz, R. L. 1964. "Visual Experience in Infants: Decreased Attention to Familiar Patterns Relative to Novel Ones." *Science* 146 (3644): 668–70.

Farroni, T., G. Csibra, F. Simion, and M. H. Johnson. 2002. "Eye Contact Detection in Humans from Birth." *Proceedings of the National Academy of Sciences* 99 (14): 9602–05.

Fernald, A. 1985. "Four-Month-Old Infants Prefer to Listen to Motherese." *Infant Behavior and Development* 8 (2): 181–95.

Ferrari, P. F., E. Visalberghi, A. Paukner, L. Fogassi, A. Ruggiero, and S. J. Suomi. 2006. "Neonatal Imitation in Rhesus Macaques." *PLOS Biology* 4 (9): e302.

Flavell, J. H. 1979. "Metacognition and Cognitive Monitoring: A New Area of Cognitive-Developmental Inquiry." *American Psychologist* 34 (10): 906–11.

Follmer, D. J. 2018. "Executive Function and Reading Comprehension: A Meta-Analytic Review." *Educational Psychologist* 53 (1): 42–60.

Foster D. J. 2017. "Replay Comes of Age." *Annual Review of Neuroscience* 40: 581–602.

Fuhs, M. W., D. C. Farran, and K. T. Nesbitt. 2013. "Preschool Classroom Processes as Predictors of Children's Cognitive Self-Regulation Skills Development." *School Psychology Quarterly* 28 (4): 347–59.

Gallistel, C. R. 1990. *The Organization of Learning*. Cambridge, MA: MIT Press.

Ganea, P. A., K. Shutts, E. S. Spelke, and J. S. DeLoache. 2007. "Thinking of Things Unseen: Infants' Use of Language to Update Mental Representations." *Psychological Science* 18 (8): 734–39.

Gergely, G., Z. Nádasdy, G. Csibra, and S. Bíró. 1995. "Taking the Intentional Stance at 12 Months of Age." *Cognition* 56 (2): 165–93.

Gershenson, S., C. M. D. Hart, J. Hyman, C. Lindsay, and N. W. Papageorge. 2021. "The Long-Run Impacts of Same-Race Teachers." Working Paper 25254, National Bureau of Economic Research, Cambridge, MA. https://www.nber .org/papers/w25254.

Gershman, S. J. 2017. "Predicting the Past, Remembering the Future." *Current Opinion in Behavioral Sciences* 17: 7–13.

Ghetti, S., E. Hembacher, and C. A. Coughlin. 2013. "Feeling Uncertain and Acting on It during the Preschool Years: A Metacognitive Approach." *Child Development Perspectives* 7 (3): 160–65.

Gibson, E. J., and R. D. Walk. 1960. "The 'Visual Cliff.'" *Scientific American* 202 (4): 64–71.

Gilmore, C. K., S. E. McCarthy, and E. S. Spelke. 2007. "Symbolic Arithmetic Knowledge without Instruction." *Nature* 447 (7144): 589–91.

Gilmore, C. K., S. E. McCarthy, and E. S. Spelke. 2010. "Non-Symbolic Arithmetic Abilities and Mathematics Achievement in the First Year of Formal Schooling." *Cognition* 115 (3): 394–406.

Girardeau, G., K. Benchenane, S. Wiener, G. Buzsáki, and M. B. Zugaro. 2009. "Selective Suppression of Hippocampal Ripples Impairs Spatial Memory." *Nature Neuroscience* 12: 1222–23.

Goldin-Meadow, S. 2005. *The Resilience of Language: What Gesture Creation in Deaf Children Can Tell Us about How All Children Learn Language*. New York: Psychology Press.

Goupil, L., and S. Kouider. 2016. "Behavioral and Neural Indices of Metacognitive Sensitivity in Preverbal Infants." *Current Biology* 26 (22): 3038–45.

Goupil, L., M. Romand-Monnier, and S. Kouider. 2016. "Infants Ask for Help When They Know They Don't Know." *Proceedings of the National Academy of Sciences* 113 (13): 3492–96.

Grammer, J., J. L. Coffman, and P. Ornstein. 2013. "The Effect of Teachers' Memory Relevant Language on Children's Strategy Use and Knowledge." *Child Development* 84 (6): 1989–2002.

Grantham-McGregor, S., Y. B. Cheung, S. Cueto, P. Glewwe, L. Richter, B. Strupp, and International Child Development Steering Group. 2007. "Developmental Potential in the First 5 Years for Children in Developing Countries." *Lancet* 369 (9555): 60–70.

Greener, S. H. 2000. "Peer Assessment of Children's Prosocial Behaviour." *Journal of Moral Education* 29 (1): 47–60.

Griffin, S., and R. Case. 1997. "Re-Thinking the Primary School Math Curriculum: An Approach Based on Cognitive Science." *Issues in Education* 4 (1): 1–51.

Gupta, A. S., A. A. Matthijs, D. S. Touretzky, and A. D. Redish. 2010. "Hippocampal Replay Is Not a Simple Function of Experience." *Neuron* 65 (5): 695–705.

Halberda, J., and L. Feigenson. 2008. "Developmental Change in the Acuity of the 'Number Sense': The Approximate Number System in 3-, 4-, 5-, and 6-Year-Olds and Adults." *Developmental Psychology* 44 (5): 1457–65.

Halberda, J., R. Ly, J. B. Wilmer, D. Q. Naiman, and L. Germine. 2012. "Number Sense across the Lifespan as Revealed by a Massive Internet-Based Sample." *Proceedings of the National Academy of Sciences* 109 (28): 11116–20.

Halberda, J., M. M. Mazzocco, and L. Feigenson. 2008. "Individual Differences in Non-Verbal Number Acuity Correlate with Maths Achievement." *Nature* 455 (7213): 665–68.

Hamlin, J. K., E. V. Hallinan, and A. L. Woodward. 2008. "Do as I Do: 7-Month-Old Infants Selectively Reproduce Others' Goals." *Developmental Science* 11 (4): 487–94.

Hamlin, J. K., T. Ullman, J. Tenenbaum, N. Goodman, and C. Baker. 2013. "The Mentalistic Basis of Core Social Cognition: Experiments in Preverbal Infants and a Computational Model." *Developmental Science* 16 (2): 209–26.

Hamlin, J. K., K. Wynn, P. Bloom, and N. Mahajan. 2011. "How Infants and Toddlers React to Antisocial Others." *Proceedings of the National Academy of Sciences* 108 (50): 19931–36.

Hardecker, S., M. F. H. Schmidt, M. Roden, and M. Tomasello. 2016. "Young Children's Behavioral and Emotional Responses to Different Social Norm Violations." *Journal of Experimental Child Psychology* 150: 364–79.

Harris, P. L. 2000. *The Work of the Imagination*. Oxford: Blackwell.

Harris, P. L. 2017. "Trust." *Developmental Science* 10 (1): 135–38.

Heron-Delaney, M., S. Wirth, and O. Pascalis. 2011. "Infants' Knowledge of Their Own Species." *Philosophical Transactions of the Royal Society of London. Series B, Biological Sciences* 366 (1571): 1753–63.

Hyde, D. C., S. Khanum, and E. S. Spelke. 2014. "Brief Non-Symbolic, Approximate Number Practice Enhances Subsequent Exact Symbolic Arithmetic in Children." *Cognition* 131 (1): 92–107.

Hyde, D. C., and E. S. Spelke. 2009. "All Numbers Are Not Equal: An Electrophysiological Investigation of Small and Large Number Representations." *Journal of Cognitive Neuroscience* 21 (6): 1039–53.

Hyde, J. S. 2005. "The Gender Similarities Hypothesis." *American Psychologist* 60 (6): 581–92.

Izard, V., C. Sann, E. S. Spelke, and A. Streri. 2009. "Newborn Infants Perceive Abstract Numbers." *Proceedings of the National Academy of Sciences* 106 (25): 10382–85.

Izard, V., A. Streri, and E. S. Spelke. 2014. "Toward Exact Number: Young Children Use One-to-One Correspondence to Measure Set Identity but Not Numerical Equality." *Cognitive Psychology* 72: 27–53.

Jaswal, V. K., and L. A. Neely. 2006. "Adults Don't Always Know Best: Preschoolers Use Past Reliability over Age When Learning New Words." *Psychological Science* 17 (9): 757–58.

Jyoti, D. F., E. A. Frongillo, and S. J. Jones. 2005. "Food Insecurity Affects School Children's Academic Performance, Weight Gain, and Social Skills." *Journal of Nutrition* 135 (12): 2831–39.

Katz, L. C., and C. J. Shatz. 1996. "Synaptic Activity and the Construction of Cortical Circuits." *Science* 274 (5290): 1133–38.

Keen, R. 2011. "The Development of Problem Solving in Young Children: A Critical Cognitive Skill." *Annual Review of Psychology* 62: 1–21.

Kellman, P. J. 1984. "Perception of Three-Dimensional Form by Human Infants." *Perception and Psychophysics* 36 (4): 353–58.

Kellman, P. J., and M. E. Arterberry. 2006. "Perceptual Development." In *The Handbook of Child Psychology: Cognition, Perception, and Language,* 6th ed., edited by D. Kuhn and R. S. Siegler, 109–60. Hoboken, NJ: Wiley.

Khanum, S., R. Hanif, E. S. Spelke, I. Berteletti, and D. C. Hyde. 2016. "Effects of Non-Symbolic Approximate Number Practice on Symbolic Numerical Abilities in Pakistani Children." *PLOS ONE* 11 (10): e0164436.

Kinzler, K. D., K. H. Corriveau, and P. L. Harris. 2011. "Children's Selective Trust in Native-Accented Speakers." *Developmental Science* 14 (1): 106–11.

Kinzler, K. D., E. Dupoux, and E. S. Spelke. 2007. "The Native Language of Social Cognition." *Proceedings of the National Academy of Sciences* 104 (30): 12577–80.

Király, I., G., Csibra, and G. Gergely. 2013. "Beyond Rational Imitation: Learning Arbitrary Means Actions from Communicative Demonstrations." *Journal of Experimental Child Psychology* 116 (2): 471–86.

Koenig, M. A., and P. L. Harris. 2005. "Preschoolers Mistrust Ignorant and Inaccurate Speakers." *Child Development* 76 (6): 1261–77.

Kuhl, P. K. 2004. "Early Language Acquisition: Cracking the Speech Code." *Nature Reviews Neuroscience* 5 (11): 831–43.

Kurdziel, L., K. Duclos, and R. M. Spencer. 2013. "Sleep Spindles in Midday Naps Enhance Learning in Preschool Children." *Proceedings of the National Academy of Sciences* 110 (43): 17267–72.

Lake, B. M., T. D. Ullman, J. B. Tenenbaum, and S. J. Gershman. 2017. "Building Machines That Learn and Think Like People." *Behavioral and Brain Sciences* 40: e253.

Landau, B., H. Gleitman, and E. Spelke. 1981. "Spatial Knowledge and Geometric Representation in a Child Blind from Birth." *Science* 213 (4513): 1275–78.

Lauer, J. E., and S. F. Lourenco. 2016. "Spatial Processing in Infancy Predicts Both Spatial and Mathematical Aptitude in Childhood." *Psychological Science* 27 (10): 1291–98.

Leonard, J. A., Y. Lee, and L. E. Schulz. 2017. "Infants Make More Attempts to Achieve a Goal When They See Adults Persist." *Science* 357 (6357): 1290–94.

Leslie, A. M. 1987. "Pretense and Representation: The Origins of 'Theory of Mind.'" *Psychological Review* 94 (4): 412–26.

Levy, D. J., J. A. Heissel, J. A. Richeson, and E. K. Adam. 2016. "Psychological and Biological Responses to Race-Based Social Stress as Pathways to Disparities in Educational Outcomes." *American Psychologist* 71 (6): 455–73.

Liberman, Z., A. L. Woodward, and K. D. Kinzler. 2017. "The Origins of Social Categorization." *Trends in Cognitive Sciences* 21 (7): 556–68.

Lillard, A. S., and R. D. Kavanaugh. 2014. "The Contribution of Symbolic Skills to the Development of an Explicit Theory of Mind." *Child Development* 85 (4): 1535–51.

Liu, S., N. B. Brooks, and E. S. Spelke. 2019. "Origins of the Concepts Cause, Cost, and Goal in Prereaching Infants." *Proceedings of the National Academy of Sciences* 116 (36): 17747–52.

Liu, S., and E. S. Spelke. 2017. "Six-Month-Old Infants Expect Agents to Minimize the Cost of Their Actions." *Cognition* 160: 35–42.

Liu, S., T. D. Ullman, J. B. Tenenbaum, and E. S. Spelke. 2017. "Ten-Month-Old Infants Infer the Value of Goals from the Costs of Actions." *Science* 358 (6366): 1038–41.

Liu, Y., R. J. Dolan, Z. Kurth-Nelson, and T. E. J. Behrens 2019. "Human Replay Spontaneously Reorganizes Experience." *Cell* 178 (3): 640–52.

Lucca, K., R. Horton, and J. A. Sommerville. 2019. "Keep Trying!: Parental Language Predicts Infants' Persistence." *Cognition* 193: 104025.

Luo, Y., and S. C. Johnson. 2009. "Recognizing the Role of Perception in Action at 6 Months." *Developmental Science* 12 (1): 142–49.

Lyons, K. E., and P. D. Zelazo. 2011. "Monitoring, Metacognition, and Executive Function: Elucidating the Role of Self-Reflection in the Development of Self-Regulation." *Advances in Child Development and Behavior* 40: 379–412.

Mackey, A. P., S. S. Hill, S. I. Stone, and S. A. Bunge 2011. "Differential Effects of Reasoning and Speed Training in Children." *Developmental Science* 14 (3): 582–90.

Mampe, B., A. D. Friederici, A. Christophe, and K. Wermke. 2009. "Newborns' Cry Melody Is Shaped by Their Native Language." *Current Biology* 19 (23): 1994–97.

Martin, A., R. M. Ryan, and J. Brooks-Gunn. 2013. "Longitudinal Associations among Interest, Persistence, Supportive Parenting, and Achievement in Early Childhood." *Early Childhood Research Quarterly* 28 (4): 658–67.

Mascalzoni, E., L. Regolin, and G. Vallortigara. 2010. "Innate Sensitivity for Self-Propelled Causal Agency in Newly Hatched Chicks." *Proceedings of the National Academy of Sciences* 107 (9): 4483–85.

McLaughlin, K. A., M. A. Sheridan, and H. K. Lambert. 2014. "Childhood Adversity and Neural Development: Deprivation and Threat as Distinct Dimensions of Early Experience." *Neuroscience and Biobehavioral Reviews* 47: 578–91. https://doi.org/10.1016/j.neubiorev.2014.10.012.

Mehler, J., P. Jusczyk, G. Lambertz, N. Halsted, J. Bertoncini, and C. Amiel-Tison. 1988. "A Precursor of Language Acquisition in Young Infants." *Cognition* 29 (2): 143–78.

Mehr, S. A. 2015. "Miscommunication of Science: Music Cognition Research in the Popular Press." *Frontiers in Psychology* 6: 988.

Mehr, S. A., and E. S. Spelke. 2018. "Shared Musical Knowledge in 11-Month-Old Infants." *Developmental Science* 21 (2): e12542.

Mehr, S. A., L. A. Song, and E. S. Spelke. 2016. "For 5-Month-Old Infants, Melodies Are Social." *Psychological Science* 27 (4): 486–501.

Meltzoff, A. N. 2007. "'Like Me': A Foundation for Social Cognition." *Developmental Science* 10: 126–134.

Meltzoff, A. N., and M. K. Moore. 1977. "Imitation of Facial and Manual Gestures by Human Neonates." *Science* 198: 75–78.

Meltzoff, A. N., L. Murray, E. Simpson, M. Heimann, E Nagy, J. Nadel, E. J. Pedersen, et al. 2018. "Re-examination of Oostenbroek et al. 2016: Evidence for Neonatal Imitation of Tongue Protrusion." *Developmental Science* 21 (4): e12609.

Metcalfe, J. 2009. "Metacognitive Judgments and Control of Study." *Current Directions in Psychological Science* 18 (3): 159–63.

Miyake, A., N. P. Friedman, M. J. Emerson, A. H. Witzki, A. Howerter, and T. D. Wager. 2000. "The Unity and Diversity of Executive Functions and Their Contributions to Complex 'Frontal Lobe' Tasks: A Latent Variable Analysis." *Cognitive Psychology* 41 (1): 49–100.

Mondloch, C. J., T. L. Lewis, D. R. Budreau, D. Maurer, J. L. Dannemiller, B. R. Stephens, and K. A. Kleiner-Gathercoal. 1999. "Face Perception during Early Infancy." *Psychological Science* 10 (5): 419–22.

Muentener, P., and L. Schulz. 2014. "Toddlers Infer Unobserved Causes for Spontaneous Events." *Frontiers in Psychology* 5: 1–9.

Myowa-Yamakoshi, M., M. Tomonaga, M. Tanaka, and T. Matsuzawa. 2004. "Imitation in Neonatal Chimpanzees (*Pan troglodytes*)." *Developmental Science* 7 (4): 437–42.

Negen, J., and B. W. Sarnecka. 2012. "Number-Concept Acquisition and General Vocabulary Development." *Child Development* 83 (6): 2019–27.

Neitzel, C. L., J. M. Alexander, and K. E. Johnson. 2019. "The Emergence of Children's Interest Orientations during Early Childhood: When Predisposition Meets Opportunity." *Learning, Culture and Social Interaction* 23: 100271.

Nesbitt, K. T., and D. C. Farran. 2021. "Effects of Prekindergarten Curricula: *Tools of the Mind* as a Case Study." *Monographs of the Society for Research in Child Development* 86 (1).

Newcombe, N. S. 2010. "Picture This: Increasing Math and Science Learning by Improving Spatial Thinking." *American Educator* 34 (2): 29–35.

Newcombe, N. S., and J. Huttenlocher. 2000. *Making Space: The Development of Spatial Representation and Reasoning*. Cambridge, MA: MIT Press.

O'Grady, S., and F. Xu. 2020. "The Development of Non-Symbolic Probability Judgments in Children." *Child Development* 91 (3): 784–98.

O'Keefe, J. 2014. "Spatial Cells in the Hippocampal Formation." Nobel Lecture, December 4, 2014. https://www.nobelprize.org/uploads/2018/06/okeefe -lecture.pdf.

O'Keefe, J., and L. Nadel. 1978. *The Hippocampus as a Cognitive Map*. New York: Oxford University Press.

Ólafsdóttir, H. F., C. Barry, A. B. Saleem, D. Hassabis, and H. J. Spiers. 2015. "Hippocampal Place Cells Construct Reward Related Sequences through Unexplored Space." *eLife* 4: e06063.

O'Leary, A. P., and V. M. Sloutsky. 2017. "Carving Metacognition at Its Joints: Protracted Development of Component Processes." *Child Development* 88 (3): 1015–32.

Park, J., V. Bermudez, R. C. Roberts, and E. M. Brannon. 2016. "Non-Symbolic Approximate Arithmetic Training Improves Math Performance in Preschoolers." *Journal of Experimental Child Psychology* 152: 278–93.

Pascalis, O., S. de Schonen, J. Morton, C. Deruelle, and M. Fabre-Grenet. 1995. "Mother's Face Recognition by Neonates: A Replication and an Extension." *Infant Behavior and Development* 18 (1): 79–85.

Paulus, M. 2017. "How to Dax? Preschool Children's Prosocial Behavior, But Not Their Social Norm Enforcement, Relates to Their Peer Status." *Frontiers in Psychology* 8: 1779.

Pepperberg, I. M. 1990. "Cognition in an African Gray Parrot (*Psittacus erithacus*): Further Evidence for Comprehension of Categories and Labels." *Journal of Comparative Psychology* 104 (1): 41–52.

Perner, J., and B. Lang. 1999. "Development of Theory of Mind and Executive Control." *Trends in Cognitive Sciences* 3: 337–44.

Pettito, L. A., S. Holowka, L. Sergio, B. Levy, and D. Ostry. 2004. "Baby Hands That Move to the Rhythm of Language: Hearing Babies Acquiring Sign Languages Babble Silently on the Hands." *Cognition* 9: 43–73.

Pfeiffer, B. E., and D. J. Foster. 2013. "Hippocampal Place-Cell Sequences Depict Future Paths to Remembered Goals." *Nature* 497 (7447): 74–79.

Piaget, J. 1952. *Play, Dreams and Imitation in Childhood.* New York: W. W. Norton and Co.

Piaget, J. 1954. *The Construction of Reality in the Child.* Translated by M. Cook. New York: Basic Books.

Piazza, M., P. Pica, V. Izard, E. S. Spelke, and S. Dehaene. 2013. "Education Enhances the Acuity of the Nonverbal Approximate Number System." *Psychological Science* 24 (6): 1037–43.

Pilley, J. W., and H. Hinzmann. 2014. *Chaser: Unlocking the Genius of the Dog Who Knows 1000 Words.* Boston: Mariner Books.

Prager, E. O., M. D. Sera, and S. M. Carlson. 2016. "Executive Function and Magnitude Skills in Preschool Children." *Journal of Experimental Child Psychology* 147: 126–39.

Rakison, D. H., and L. M. Oakes, eds. 2003. *Early Category and Concept Development: Making Sense of the Blooming, Buzzing Confusion.* Oxford: Oxford University Press.

Regolin, L., and G. Vallortigara. 1995. "Perception of Partly Occluded Objects by Young Chicks." *Perception and Psychophysics* 57 (7): 971–76.

Rhodes, M., and A. Baron. 2019. "The Development of Social Categorization." *Annual Review of Developmental Psychology* 1: 359–86.

Romeo, R. R., J. A. Leonard, S. T. Robinson, M. R. West, A. P. Mackey, M. L. Rowe, and J. D. Gabrieli. 2018. "Beyond the 30-Million-Word Gap: Children's Conversational Exposure Is Associated with Language-Related Brain Function." *Psychological Science* 29 (5): 700–10.

Rosenberg, R. D., and L. Feigenson. 2013. "Infants Hierarchically Organize Memory Representations." *Developmental Science* 16 (4): 610–21.

Rugani, R., and M. D. de Hevia. 2017. "Number-Space Associations without Language: Evidence from Preverbal Human Infants and Non-Human Animal Species." *Psychonomic Bulletin and Review* 24 (2): 352–69.

Rugani, R., L. Regolin, and G. Vallortigara. 2010. "Imprinted Numbers: Newborn Chicks' Sensitivity to Number vs. Continuous Extent of Objects They Have Been Reared With." *Developmental Science* 13: 790-97.

Sabbagh, M. A., and D. Shafman. 2009. "How Children Block Learning from Ignorant Speakers." *Cognition* 112 (3): 41522.

Sabbagh, M. A., F. Xu, S. M. Carlson, L. J. Moses, and K. Lee. 2006. "The Development of Executive Functioning and Theory of Mind. A Comparison of Chinese and U.S. Preschoolers." *Psychological Science* 17 (1): 74–81.

Saffran, J. R., R. N. Aslin, and E. L. Newport. 1996. "Statistical Learning by 8-Month-Old Infants." *Science* 274 (5294): 1926–28.

Schuck, N. W., and Y. Niv. 2019. "Sequential Replay of Nonspatial Task States in the Human Hippocampus." *Science* 364: eaaw5181.

Schulz, L. 2012. "The Origins of Inquiry: Inductive Inference and Exploration in Early Childhood." *Trends in Cognitive Sciences* 16 (7): 382–89.

Shi, R., J. F. Werker, and A. Cutler. 2006. "Recognition and Representation of Function Words in English-Learning Infants." *Infancy* 10 (2): 187–98.

Shusterman, A., S. Ah Lee, and E. S. Spelke. 2008. "Young Children's Spontaneous Use of Geometry in Maps." *Developmental Science* 11 (2): F1–F7.

Shutts, K. 2015. "Young Children's Preferences: Gender, Race, and Social Status." *Child Development Perspectives* 9 (4): 262–66.

Shutts, K., E. L. Brey, L. A. Dornbusch, N. Slywotzky, and K. R. Olson. 2016. "Children Use Wealth Cues to Evaluate Others." *PLOS ONE* 11 (3): e0149360.

Siegler, R. S., and J. E. Opfer. 2003. "The Development of Numerical Estimation: Evidence for Multiple Representations of Numerical Quantity." *Psychological Science* 14 (3): 237–50.

Simion, F., L. Regolin, and H. Bulf. 2008. "A Predisposition for Biological Motion in the Newborn Baby." *Proceedings of the National Academy of Sciences* 105 (2): 809–13.

Singer, D., R. M. Golinkoff, and K. Hirsh-Pasek, eds. 2006. *Play=Learning: How Play Motivates and Enhances Children's Cognitive and Social-Emotional Growth.* New York: Oxford University Press.

Sisk, V. F., A. P. Burgoyne, J. Sun, J. L. Butler, and B. N. Macnamara. 2018. "To What Extent and under Which Circumstances Are Growth Mind-Sets Important to Academic Achievement? Two Meta-Analyses." *Psychological Science* 29 (4): 549–71.

Skerry, A. E., S. E. Carey, and E. S. Spelke. 2013. "First-Person Action Experience Reveals Sensitivity to Action Efficiency in Prereaching Infants." *Proceedings of the National Academy of Sciences* 110 (46): 18728–33.

Skinner, A. L., and A. N. Meltzoff. 2019. "Childhood Experiences and Intergroup Biases among Children." *Social Issues and Policy Review* 13 (1): 211–40.

Slater, A., A. Mattock, and E. Brown. 1990. "Size Constancy at Birth: Newborn Infants' Responses to Retinal and Real Size." *Journal of Experimental Child Psychology* 49: 314–22.

Smith, K. E., and S. D. Pollak. 2020. "Rethinking Concepts and Categories for Understanding the Neurodevelopmental Effects of Childhood Adversity." *Perspectives on Psychological Science* 1745691620920725.

Smith, L. B. 2003. "Learning to Recognize Objects." *Psychological Science* 14 (3): 244–50.

Sommerville, J. A., and A. L. Woodward. 2005. "Pulling out the Intentional Structure of Action: The Relation between Action Processing and Action Production in Infancy." *Cognition* 95 (1): 1–30.

Sroufe, L. A. 2005. "Attachment and Development: A Prospective, Longitudinal Study from Birth to Adulthood." *Attachment and Human Development* 7 (4): 349–67.

Spelke, E. S. 2005. "Sex Differences in Intrinsic Aptitude for Mathematics and Science?: A Critical Review." *American Psychologist* 60 (9): 950–58.

Spelke, E. S., and S. A. Lee. 2012. "Core Systems of Geometry in Animal Minds." *Philosophical Transactions of the Royal Society B: Biological Sciences* 367 (1603): 2784–93.

Squire, L. R., A. S. van der Horst, S. G. McDuff, J. C. Frascino, R. O. Hopkins, and K. N. Mauldin. 2010. "Role of the Hippocampus in Remembering the Past and

Imagining the Future." *Proceedings of the National Academy of Sciences* 107 (44): 19044–48.

Stahl, A. E., and L. Feigenson. 2015. "Observing the Unexpected Enhances Infants' Learning and Exploration." *Science* 348 (6230): 91–94.

Starr, A., and E. M. Brannon. 2015. "Evolutionary and Developmental Continuities in Numerical Cognition." *Mathematical Cognition and Learning* 1: 123–44.

Suddendorf, T. 2003. "Early Representational Insight: Twenty-Four-Month-Olds Can Use a Photo to Find an Object in the World." *Child Development* 74 (3): 896–904.

Sugita, Y. 2008. "Face Perception in Monkeys Reared with No Exposure to Faces." *Proceedings of the National Academy of Sciences* 105 (1): 394–98.

Szkudlarek, E., and E. M. Brannon. 2017. "Does the Approximate Number System Serve as a Foundation for Symbolic Mathematics?" *Language Learning and Development* 13 (2): 171–90.

Taylor, M., and S. M. Carlson. 1997. "The Relation between Individual Differences in Fantasy and Theory of Mind." *Child Development* 68 (3): 436–55.

Téglás, E., E. Vul, V. Girotto, M. Gonzalez, J. B. Tenenbaum, and L. L. Bonatti. 2011. "Pure Reasoning in 12-Month-Old Infants as Probabilistic Inference." *Science* 332 (6033): 1054–59.

Tomasello, M., M. Carpenter, J. Call, T. Behne, and H. Moll. 2005. "Understanding and Sharing Intentions: The Origins of Cultural Cognition." *Behavioral and Brain Sciences* 28 (5): 675–735.

Ullman, T. D., E. S. Spelke, P. Battaglia, and J. B. Tenenbaum. 2017. "Mind Games: Game Engines as an Architecture for Intuitive Physics." *Trends in Cognitive Sciences* 21 (9): 649–65.

Uttal, D. H. 2000. "Seeing the Big Picture: Map Use and the Development of Spatial Cognition." *Developmental Science* 3 (3): 247–86.

Vaish, A., M. Carpenter, and M. Tomasello. 2010. "Young Children Selectively Avoid Helping People with Harmful Intentions." *Child Development* 81 (6): 1661–69.

Valenza, E., I. Leo, L. Gava, and F. Simion. 2006. "Perceptual Completion in Newborn Human Infants." *Child Development* 77 (6): 1810–21.

Valenza, E., F. Simion, V. M. Cassia, and C. Umilta. 1996. "Face Preferences at Birth." *Journal of Experimental Psychology: Human Perception and Performance* 22 (4): 892–903.

Vouloumanos, A., and J. F. Werker. 2007. "Listening to Language at Birth: Evidence for a Bias for Speech in Neonates." *Developmental Science* 10 (2): 159–64.

Wai, J., D. Lubinski, and C. P. Benbow. 2009. "Spatial Ability for STEM Domains: Aligning over Fifty Years of Cumulative Psychological Knowledge Solidifies Its Importance." *Journal of Educational Psychology* 101: 817–35.

Walker, S. P., T. D. Wachs, S. Grantham-McGregor, M. M. Black, C. A. Nelson, S. L. Huffman, H. Baker-Henningham, et al. 2011. "Inequality in Early Childhood: Risk and Protective Factors for Early Child Development." *Lancet* 378 (9799): 1325–38.

Wang, Y., R. Williams, L. Dilley, and D. M. Houston. 2020. "A Meta-Analysis of the Predictability of LENA™ Automated Measures for Child Language Development." *Developmental Review* 57: 100921.

Watts, T. W., J. Gandhi, D. A. Ibrahim, M. D. Masucci, and C. C. Raver. 2018. "The Chicago School Readiness Project: Examining the Long-Term Impacts of an Early Childhood Intervention." *PLOS ONE 13* (7): e0200144.

Wellman, H. M. 2014. *Making Minds: How Theory of Mind Develops.* Oxford: Oxford University Press.

Werker, J. F. 1989. "Becoming a Native Listener." *American Scientist* 77 (1): 54–59.

Williford, A. P., L. M. Carter, and R. C. Pianta. 2016. "Attachment and School Readiness." In *Handbook of Attachment: Theory, Research, and Clinical Applications,* 3rd ed., edited by J. Cassidy and P. R. Shaver, 639–66. New York: Guilford Press.

Wimmer, H., and J. Perner. 1983. "Beliefs about Beliefs: Representation and Constraining Function of Wrong Beliefs in Young Children's Understanding of Deception." *Cognition 13* (1): 103–28.

Winicki, J., and K. Jemison. 2003. "Food Insecurity and Hunger in the Kindergarten Classroom: Its Effect on Learning and Growth." *Contemporary Economic Policy* 21 (2): 145–57.

Winkler-Rhoades, N., S. C. Carey, and E. S. Spelke. 2013. "Two-Year-Old Children Interpret Abstract, Purely Geometric Maps." *Developmental Science* 16 (3): 365–76.

Wong, C. A., J. S. Eccles, and A. Sameroff. 2003. "The Influence of Ethnic Discrimination and Ethnic Identification on African American Adolescents' School and Socioemotional Adjustment." *Journal of Personality* 71 (6): 1197–232.

Woo, B. M., C. M. Steckler, D. T. Le, and J. K. Hamlin. 2017. "Social Evaluation of Intentional, Truly Accidental, and Negligently Accidental Helpers and Harmers by 10-Month-Old Infants." *Cognition* 168: 154–63.

Wood, J. N. 2013. "Newborn Chickens Generate Invariant Object Representations at the Onset of Visual Object Experience." *Proceedings of the National Academy of Sciences* 110: 14000–5.

Woodward, A. L. 1998. "Infants Selectively Encode the Goal Object of an Actor's Reach." *Cognition* 69 (1): 1–34.

Wynn, K. 1990. "Children's Understanding of Counting." *Cognition* 36 (2): 155–93.

Xu, F., and E. S. Spelke. 2000. "Large Number Discrimination in 6-Month-Old Infants." *Cognition* 74 (1): B1–B11.

Yang, F., Y.-J. Choi, A. Misch, X. Yang, and Y. Dunham. 2018. "In Defense of the Commons: Young Children Negatively Evaluate and Sanction Free Riders." *Psychological Science 29* (10): 1598–611.

Yeager, D. S., P. Hanselman, G. M. Walton, J. S. Murray, R. Crosnoe, C. Muller, E. Tipton, et al. 2019. "A National Experiment Reveals Where a Growth Mindset Improves Achievement." *Nature 573* (7774): 364–69.

Yuan, S., and C. Fisher. 2009. "'Really? She Blicked the Baby?' Two-Year-Olds Learn Combinatorial Facts about Verbs by Listening." *Psychological Science* 20 (5): 619–26.

2

Pedagogy and Curricula Content: Building Foundational Skills and Knowledge

OVERVIEW

This chapter reviews the evidence related to pedagogy and curriculum and offers suggestions for implementation. A child's experience in the classroom is shaped by pedagogy and the curriculum. Pedagogy determines how the educator organizes and facilitates learning. The curriculum determines what aspects of learning are the focus in the classroom. Both play a crucial role in determining the quality of early childhood education (ECE) and complement one another. Pedagogy greatly influences child learning. The role of the ECE educator is most effectively that of facilitator and guide rather than instructor. This has been referred to as a "relational" pedagogy. Beyond ensuring a responsive and supportive relationship between educator and child, there are three key elements of high-quality pedagogy that support children's development: (1) supporting children's spoken and communication skills, (2) supporting children's ability to self-regulate their cognitive and emotional mental processes, and (3) creating opportunities for active learning through play. The chapter also examines the value of a curriculum that supports a child's complete physical, emotional, and cognitive development. A whole-child, evidence-based curriculum should include activities supporting children's development in five areas: physical health

This chapter was written by David Whitebread and Yasmin Sitabkhan.

and development, social and emotional development, preliteracy and pre-numeracy understandings and abilities, ways of understanding the world, and self-expression through the creative arts. The chapter suggests a three-step approach for putting policies into practice, moving from diagnosing the challenges to planning and then to continuous improvement of pedagogy and the curriculum.

INTRODUCTION: THE QUALITY OF CHILDREN'S EXPERIENCE IN ECE

Preschool and the early grades of primary school can promote the development of the skills, knowledge, and attitudes that will enable children to thrive in their schooling and in life.

At the present time, much ECE across the world does not do this well, and many children fail to thrive, do not reach their full academic potential, or drop out of schooling altogether. A major cause of this situation is the transition to overly formal modes of ECE and primary education provision before children are developmentally able to benefit from these approaches (Bingham and Whitebread 2018).

This chapter reviews evidence regarding the most beneficial "process" aspects of ECE provision (that is, the child's direct experience in the setting or classroom) and how they might be most effectively developed within resource-constrained environments in low- and middle-income countries. Process variables most directly affect the quality of children's ECE experience, and fall under two broad headings: (1) pedagogy (how the educator organizes and facilitates the educational experience for the children), and (2) curriculum (what key aspects of the children's development and learning are focused upon).

The main principles set out in this chapter, which underpin the provision of high-quality ECE, are as follows:

- The real strength of high-quality ECE is more commonly not the formal curriculum but the nature and quality of the relationships between the educators and the children in the setting or classroom (Jenkins et al. 2019). This relationship needs to be a key element in initial and continuing educator training.
- Three key elements in ECE pedagogy are associated with children's long-term academic achievement and emotional well-being: practices that support children's communication skills, practices that support children's ability to self-regulate their cognitive and emotional mental processes, and practices that provide opportunities to the children for active learning through play (Whitebread et al. 2019).

- To ensure all children make a secure start to their school trajectories it is important that a whole-child, evidence-based curriculum be provided. This curriculum should include an extensive range of emergent literacy and early mathematics (Anders et al. 2012), alongside elements supporting the children's physical development, social and emotional development, their ways of understanding the world, and their self-expression through the creative arts (Bertram and Pascal 2002).

This chapter reviews research evidence that has identified the key elements of ECE pedagogy and curriculum that predict short- and long-term beneficial outcomes for individual children and for society as a whole. Although this evidence has been largely gathered in high-income countries, much of it has been shown to be relevant across international contexts. However, significant cultural differences exist relating to the qualities that are valued in children and adults and how children and adults relate. If high-quality ECE is to be relevant to children's lives and provide benefit as they grow and become members of their communities, it must also "reflect local values and perspectives on young children's development as well as scientifically established predictors of their cognitive, language, and socio-emotional development" (UNESCO 2015, 55).

In recent years, interventions in low- and middle-income contexts that focus on improving the quality of preprimary teaching and learning have increased. Many of these studies have focused on the learning gains achieved by students, with little mention of the pedagogy involved, making it difficult to know which types of pedagogy have worked in low- and middle-income contexts, under what conditions (for example, scale, cost, government or nongovernment), and how approaches could be replicated. There are, however, some notable exceptions, including studies in Bangladesh and Kenya, and a three-country study in Bangladesh, Tanzania, and Uganda, exploring the role of playful activity in enhancing the quality of children's learning in preschool. The Kenyan study, for example, introduced playful, active learning into math lessons, which normally consisted of listening to the teacher or watching the teacher demonstrate a new concept. By contrast, the intervention involved the children in playing with manipulatives to make meaning of numbers, shapes, and other concepts. Results from a randomized controlled trial involving 2,957 children in treatment and control schools at three time points showed that intervention children's math outcomes were significantly higher as compared with the children in the control schools (Piper, Sitabkhan, and Nderu 2018). The Bangladesh and three-country-study projects are described in the case studies section at the end of this chapter. Although many more such studies in low- and middle-income countries of this type are needed, the evidence so far suggests that the basic principles set out in this chapter hold true with young children everywhere.

KEY ELEMENTS OF HIGH-QUALITY ECE PEDAGOGY

The Nature and Quality of Adult-Child Relationships

The role of the ECE educator is most effectively that of facilitator and guide rather than instructor. This has been referred to as a "relational" rather than an instructional pedagogy (Papatheodorou and Moyles 2008). Numerous studies have shown that direct instruction from an adult has short-term advantages in relation to learning specific facts, but that more indirect adult "scaffolding" of children's exploratory play and learning has longer-term advantages in supporting children's development as learners (Bonawitz et al. 2011).

Extensive research has demonstrated that curiosity is both intrinsic to children's development and can be fostered or inhibited by social interactions between ECE educators and children (Engel 2011).Young children naturally ask a lot of questions of adults about their experiences and are constantly testing out their ideas about the world in which they live (Butler, Ronfard, and Corriveau 2020; Gopnik, Meltzoff, and Kuhl 1999). In high-quality relational pedagogy, educators support young children to develop these natural and powerful ways in which the young human brain is adapted to learn. They do this by paying close attention to children's interests and exploration and helping them pursue these interests to extend their learning, a process called scaffolding. Research on scaffolding has indicated a range of behaviors that the adult educator can use to provide the most effective support for children as developing learners. These behaviors involve close observations of children's exploratory inquiries and problem-solving, showing interest in what the child or children are attempting, sympathetically making suggestions that will extend their ideas and explorations, and providing support that is contingent on their level of understanding, that is, providing more direct support when they are struggling and standing back when they are making good progress (Gillespie and Greenberg 2017; Wood, Bruner, and Ross 1976).

Numerous studies of early "episodes of joint attention" between adults and young children (Tomasello and Farrar 1986), of "sustained shared thinking" (Siraj-Blatchford 2007), and of classrooms supporting children's self-regulation (Perry 1998) have shown the value of adult scaffolding of young children's learning. Evidence from motivational research has also shown that an approach that supports children's sense of autonomy, of competence (or self-efficacy), and of self-worth enhances their belief in themselves as learners and their resilience and perseverance—all aspects that are necessary for their development as powerful and self-motivated learners (Deci and Ryan 2008).

The nature and quality of adult-child relationships and the role of the educator as scaffolder and guide are key; in addition, there is very strong and consistent evidence of the long-term beneficial impact of three further key elements of ECE pedagogy (Whitebread et al. 2019; Whitebread, Kuvalja, and O'Connor 2015). Practices associated with these elements, outlined below, have been consistently shown to predict high levels of long-term academic achievement and emotional well-being:

- *Communicating meaning*. Supporting children in their abilities to represent and communicate their ideas and thoughts through the full range of human symbolic systems
- *Self-regulation*. Providing an appropriate mix of autonomy support, cognitive challenge, and opportunities for reflection known to promote the development of self-regulation
- *Playful learning*. Engaging children's naturally playful ways of exploring the world and developing their abilities

In the remaining parts of this section, evidence is briefly reviewed in relation to the beneficial outcomes of each of these pedagogical elements, and practices that are associated with them are outlined.

Key Takeaways

- The role of the ECE educator is most effectively that of facilitator and guide rather than instructor. This has been referred to as a "relational" rather than an instructional pedagogy.
- There are three key elements of quality ECE pedagogy: (1) supporting children's spoken and communication skills, (2) supporting children's ability to self-regulate their cognitive and emotional mental processes, and (3) creating opportunities for active learning through play.

Element 1: Communicating Meaning

As outlined in chapter 1, from about the age of one year to 18 months, the majority of typically developing children show evidence of starting to make meaning of their world. This is a unique and fundamental aspect of human activity and a crucially important one upon which all human cultural and scientific achievements are founded. Therefore, a key element in any high-quality ECE is that professionals give children the opportunities, materials, and support to represent their perceptions and understandings about the world through a range of linguistic, visual, and physical media. These activities should support children's

- Oral language development, speaking, and listening (Hoff 2013);
- Story-telling and narrative skills (Suggate et al. 2018);
- Exploratory talk (Littleton et al. 2005); and

- Creative arts skills—for example, drawing and other visual media (Papandreou 2014), music (Marsh 2017), and movement and dance (Deans 2016).

This section, which focuses on pedagogy related to children's development of communication skills, concentrates on oral language, exploratory talk, and narrative skills. The other modes of communicating meaning (creative arts, music, and movement and dance) are discussed in Element 3: Playful, Active Learning.

The following practices have been widely researched and shown to significantly affect young children's development of oral language skills.

Book Reading, Story-Telling, and Narrative Skills

There is strong evidence from research with parents and ECE educators that shared and interactive book reading with young children significantly enhances the rate of their vocabulary growth and their overall oral language development.

Although the process of reading a book with children is valuable within ECE contexts, the benefits can be greatly enhanced when an interactive style is adopted. Reviews of research have concluded that a style of shared book reading that is dialogic, in which children are encouraged to be active participants rather than passive listeners, and give extended responses to educators' questions rather than just yes/no answers, is particularly effective in enhancing expressive language development and comprehension skills.

Episodes of Joint Attention

Shared and interactive book reading is a specific example of the broader practice of what has been variously termed "episodes of joint attention" and "sustained shared thinking." Various strands of research have shown that variations in sensitivity to children's interests by parents and educators, and an ability to engage with children in a productive dialogue about what interests them, have considerable significance for children's oral language development.

In line with the general principle of scaffolding rather than instructing, within these episodes, an "attention-following" strategy, building on the child's current interest and attention, supports language development much more effectively than an "attention-shifting" approach in which the adult attempts to switch the child's attention to the adult's own focus of interest (Carpenter, Nagell, and Tomasello 1998).

The value of structuring the ECE environment to enable episodes of joint attention between adult educators and individual children, or small groups, has been definitively demonstrated within a range of studies. For example, a large longitudinal study of about 3,000 children across the

United Kingdom, the Effective Provision of Pre-school Education study, recruited three-year-old children just entering preschool and investigated factors leading to effective ECE provision. This study found that a key element of high-quality ECE provision was the occurrence of episodes of what the researchers termed "sustained shared thinking" between adults and children (Sylva et al. 2004). These episodes were characterized by the development of dialogue between the adult educator and the child, or children, which supported the children to engage in exploratory talk. Children's attendance at a high-quality preschool with this characteristic enjoyed enhanced intellectual and personal gains, even overriding the effects of social disadvantage. These gains persisted throughout the 12 years of the study, culminating in enhanced results on national examinations when the children were 15 years old.

Exploratory Talk and Dialogic Teaching

In addition to practices that have been shown to enhance oral language in young children from the very earliest ages, other experiences need to be provided for children from about four or five years of age to enhance their ability to use language to express their thoughts and ideas, to solve problems, and to work collaboratively with their peers and adults. The three main approaches to support this aspect of oral language development that have been extensively studied are as follows:

- *Dialogic teaching.* The essential notion of dialogic teaching is to teach through dialogue, with educators encouraging children to talk to express and explore their ideas and interests. This approach contrasts with the more traditional instruction model in which the educator uses talk to transmit information to learners.

  There is now extensive research demonstrating that a dialogic approach is more effective in supporting children in their language development and their understanding (Lyle 2008). Strategies commonly used to encourage young children to engage in dialogue include asking open-ended questions; encouraging children to ask questions (which they will do naturally given the chance!); responding positively to their questions; asking children to discuss an idea or problem with a friend, then report back to the whole class on their thinking; asking children how they feel; and modeling the educator's own thinking by saying it out loud. Ultimately, the aim is that children experience the classroom as a "community of learners" rather than a lecture hall, with a range of educational techniques that includes teaching talk (by the educator), learning talk by the children, and organizing interaction.
- *Self-explanations.* One particular teaching strategy that promotes dialogue with young children is to present them with an interesting phenomenon

and ask them to explain it. Studies in this area have investigated children's naive scientific ideas relating to common physical phenomena such as water evaporating, different objects floating or sinking, or water displacement when an object floats with part of it below the water line, like a boat. These studies have shown clear enhancements to young children's critical thinking and improvements in their ability to articulate their ideas. One particular series of studies demonstrates the beneficial effects of children explaining both correct and incorrect ideas and their own reasoning and the reasoning of others (Siegler and Lin 2009).

- *Collaborative problem-solving with peers.* Another particularly effective and popular teaching strategy that promotes children's talk, and that has generated a considerable body of research, involves young children working together in pairs or small groups to collaboratively engage in solving problems. A typical study using this approach investigated the development of five-year-olds' ability to articulate their thinking over a school year. The children were placed in mixed-ability groups of three and asked to agree on a solution to a variety of open-ended problems throughout the year. Compared with a control group, they showed significantly enhanced metacognitive awareness of their own thinking and significantly improved articulation of their ideas. Along with many others, this study also demonstrates that these effects were most pronounced among the children who were the least articulate at the beginning of the year (Perry 1998; Pino-Pasternak, Whitebread, and Neale 2018).

Key Takeaways

- Children need to be given opportunities to communicate meaning by representing their perceptions and understandings about the world through a range of linguistic, visual, and physical media, including activities.
- Children's ability to communicate meaning is influenced by their oral language, exploratory talk, and narrative skills.
- Various specific activities and tools are available that teachers can use to cultivate these skills, including book reading and story-telling. Opportunities to engage in back-and-forth interactions with teachers and peers, as well as opportunities for children to explain themselves, can all build children's ability to communicate meaning.

Element 2: Self-Regulation

As discussed in chapter 1, children's self-regulation and early executive function have been shown to predict both short- and long-term academic achievement and emotional well-being more powerfully than any other aspect of children's early development (Best, Miller, and Naglieri 2011; Bronson 2000; McClelland et al. 2013; McClelland and Wanless 2012; Whitebread 2014a). Studies of practices in the home, in ECE settings, and in primary classrooms aimed at supporting self-regulation have shown that these abilities are highly affected by a range of social influences and so are teachable (Dignath, Buettner, and Langfeldt 2008). In each of these contexts, self-regulation development responds most effectively to facilitative, scaffolding, or relational styles of interaction, as described previously (Perry 1998).

Thus, analyses of ECE settings supporting young children's early development of self-regulatory abilities have identified the following characteristics (Whitebread 2020; Whitebread and Coltman 2011):

- *Emotional warmth* in relationships is developed through responsive and sensitive adult-child interactions that ensure secure attachments. In the United States, a study with more than 800 preschool children found that higher levels of children's cognitive self-regulation developed in classrooms in which the educators more frequently expressed approval of children's behavior and thereby established a positive emotional climate (Fuhs, Farran, and Nesbitt 2013). In Portugal, a study of 200 preschool children found that educator-child closeness predicted improvements in observed self-regulation abilities over the course of a year; similarly to many other studies, the researchers also found that the children who started with low levels of self-regulation benefited the most (Cadima et al. 2016). A positive relationship with the educator is particularly significant if the child is insecurely attached to parents; educators can achieve this relationship by acting as a safe haven, by being present when the child needs help, and by being supportive when the child experiences learning challenges.
- *Children's autonomy* should be supported through the provision of choice and encouragement for children to develop their ideas and interests. A seminal study of classrooms that were supportive of children's self-regulation identified a range of practices supporting children's experience of autonomy, including giving children opportunities for decision-making, setting their own challenges, and assessing their own work; encouraging positive feelings toward challenging tasks; and emphasizing personal progress rather than social comparisons (Perry 1998, 2013). A considerable body of evidence indicates the pivotal role children's experience of autonomy plays in supporting their motivation and feelings of self-efficacy (that is, their belief in their own learning capacity), which underpin their development as self-regulatory learners (Reeve et al. 2008).
- *Cognitive challenge* is provided through engaging tasks and experiences and the support of adults to facilitate and scaffold children's responses. Classroom observations with young children have demonstrated that

classrooms supporting self-regulation are characterized by challenging and open-ended tasks, opportunities for children to control the level of challenge, and the encouragement of positive feelings toward challenge (Perry 1998; Pino-Pasternak, Basilio, and Whitebread 2014). Adult educators in preschool settings enable children to undertake challenging tasks through a range of scaffolding techniques (for example, modeling ways of undertaking the task, providing hints and clues, gradually removing support as children's understanding improves) that have been shown to support self-regulation development (Florez 2011).

- Practices should be in place to provide opportunities for children to *reflect on their learning*, including documentation of children's activities, responses, and ideas; the children's artefacts and the use of photographs and video activities; and collaborative tasks requiring children to talk about their thinking (Carr 2011). A range of studies has shown that the amount of "metacognitive talk" used by adult educators predicts self-regulation gains in young children (Ornstein, Grammer, and Coffman 2010).
- Widely ranging self-regulation interventions have developed types of activities that are likely to *encourage children to talk* about and reflect upon their learning. These include dialogic teaching practices, as discussed previously, cooperative group work (where children work in pairs or small groups to undertake a task or produce something together), and peer tutoring (where one child is asked to teach something he or she knows or can do to another child) (Grau and Whitebread 2018). This approach has been described in an extensive review of educational interventions as "making learning visible," and has been shown to be the most powerful set of interventions in relation to a range of educational gains (Hattie 2009, 2012).

Key Takeaways

- Children's self-regulation abilities are teachable, as they are highly influenced by a range of social factors.
- Classrooms supporting self-regulation are characterized by challenging and open-ended tasks, opportunities for children to control the level of challenge, and the encouragement of positive feelings toward challenge.
- Children's autonomy should be supported through the provision of choice and encouragement for children to develop their ideas and interests, and approaches that encourage children to talk about and reflect upon their learning.

Element 3: Playful, Active Learning

High-quality ECE settings stimulate a considerable amount of metacognitive talk, and a key context for such talk is children's play. Multiple studies have shown impacts of playful, active learning on children's executive functioning, self-regulation, and language development. For example, setting tasks in a playful context has been shown to enhance children's ability to focus their attention and resist distraction (White et al. 2017), to support their working memory (Mistry, Rogoff, and Herman 2001), and to enhance their oral language development (Quinn, Donnelly, and Kidd 2018). Overwhelmingly, the evidence of much recent research (including neuroscience; Pellis and Pellis 2009) suggests that, as the Russian psychologist Lev Vygotsky claimed so many years ago: "In play, the child is always behaving beyond his age, above his usual everyday behaviour; in play he is, as it were, a head above himself" (Vygotsky 1978, 102).

Although there are still many debates concerning the definition of play, the multifaceted nature of play is widely accepted. It is arguably the case that, for each aspect of human development, there is a form of play supporting it. Children can play with other children, with adults, or alone; and play in each of these social contexts can be initiated by the child or by a parent or adult educator (Zosh et al. 2018). In two reviews drawing together a vast array of play research, five broad areas of types of play have been proposed, with each serving different developmental functions (Whitebread et al. 2012; Whitebread et al. 2017). There is also considerable overlap between the types, so a play activity may contain elements of more than one type. In high-quality ECE provision, opportunities for children to engage in all of these types of play, both indoors and, importantly, outdoors, should be supported. The contributions of the different types of play, and activities that support them in ECE settings, are as follows:

- *Physical play* has various subtypes that have a range of cognitive and socioemotional benefits; it is also the type of play for which outdoor provision is important because it opens up a wider range of possible activities (Waite 2017):
  - *Gross motor* (body awareness, coordination, proprioception, balance, strength, stamina activities) and *fine motor* (precision of movement of the hand and fingers, gripping and manipulating tools and objects) play show strong links between physical activity, mental health, personal confidence, and school achievement. They also provide a good grounding for sports activities (Whitebread 2014b) and hand-eye coordination activities (throwing and catching, hitting with a bat or racket), and support concentration and perseverance.
  - *Rhythm and musicality*—dance, gymnastics, and other activities involving rhythm—enhance physical coordination and also have

links to early communication skills, language acquisition, and literacy (Malloch and Trevarthen 2009).

- Studies of *risky physical play*—young children enjoy and need to test out their physical limits—have identified six types of risky play relating to high speed, great heights, dangerous tools, dangerous places, rough and tumble, and getting lost. These types of play are associated with physical confidence and good mental health; children who do not have these opportunities are more prone to anxiety and neuroticism (Jarvis 2010; Sandseter and Kennair 2011).

- *Play with objects* covers a range of ways in which young children interact with objects of all kinds; this type of play supports early understanding of the features of objects and materials and supports a range of mathematical explorations and practical problem-solving. The main subtypes are as follows:
  - *Sensory play* in infancy involves young children, up to about 18 months of age, exploring how objects feel and behave.
  - *Sorting, classifying, and ordering of objects* is a common activity in toddlers and forms a basis for language development (Gopnik and Meltzoff 1992).
  - *Construction play* with recycled materials, wood blocks, construction play materials, and so on enables children to represent people, animals, and objects in their world and to develop their imaginations; it is also an important type of play supporting early mathematical development (Nath and Szücs 2014).

- *Symbolic play* consists of children's play with the means of communication and meaning-making; the main subtypes and associated activities with young children include the following:
  - *Play with words and language.* A playful approach to words and language, through rhyming games, made-up words, word-play in jokes, and so on, predicts language and literacy development in young children, whereas correcting children's language use has a negative effect (Roskos and Christie 2011).
  - *Play with drawing and other visual media.* Preliterate young children first start to represent their ideas and understandings about their world through drawing and should be given opportunities to represent their interests and enthusiasms through these media (Papandreou 2014).
  - *Play with sounds, music and rhythm, and movement and dance.* This type of play supports children's meaning-making in relation to their cultural context, makes an important contribution to young children's well-being, supports their language and literacy development (Marsh 2017), and supports physical development and well-being (Deans 2016).

- *Pretend play,* like all other play types, is universal among young children, but takes many different culturally appropriate forms. It is also a form of play whose development is most clearly enhanced by the involvement of adults as co-players. It develops from simple object substitutions through individual role play and, with adult support, into socially shared narrative play among groups of children. It is the most extensively researched form of children's play (Lillard et al. 2013; Nicolopoulou and Ilgaz 2013) and has been shown to support the following:
  - *Language and literacy development* is enhanced because children must articulate their ideas and effectively communicate with their fellow players (Nicolopoulou et al. 2015).
  - *Social skills, friendships, and emotional well-being* are bolstered because children are obliged to negotiate, share, and support one another to make the play enjoyable and satisfying (Rao and Gibson 2019).
  - *Self-regulation, including cognitive and emotional regulation,* is strengthened because children must regulate themselves to remain in role.
  - *Private speech* is extensively produced during episodes of pretend play and performs the same roles and provides the same developmental benefits as in other contexts discussed directly above (Sawyer 2017).
  - *Creativity* in play requires children to use their imagination, constantly edit and re-edit their narratives, and transform objects, themselves, and others into different roles and scenarios, and predicts a range of creativity measures and indicators later in life (Holmes et al. 2019; Whitebread and O'Sullivan 2020).

  The facilitation of and support for pretend play in ECE requires that opportunities be provided and stimulating stories, play corners, objects, and dressing-up materials be available. To avoid constraining young children's imaginations, it is important that this range of props be simple so as to provide opportunities to create, rather than too narrowly define, particular roles or activities.

- *Games with rules* are the final type of play seen in young children and range from traditional outdoor games (chasing, hiding, skipping, and so on) to card games, board games, and, more recently, modern computer games. Apart from the study of computer games, which is currently extensive and largely inconclusive (Boyle et al. 2016), there is very little rigorous research in this area. Studies have shown the following, however:
  - A facility with outdoor games (ball games, chase, and jumping or singing games), particularly for boys, is related to social competence with their peers (Pellegrini et al. 2002).
  - Playing board games that involve numbers with young children has a significant effect on their number knowledge (Ramani and Siegler 2008; Siegler and Ramani 2008).

Because these games share many of the characteristics of other types of play, and almost always involve social negotiation and the use of precise language, it seems likely that there are social and linguistic benefits arising from games with rules. The negotiation of rules itself also has strong parallels with the social negotiations that occur in social pretend play, and so is most likely to have similar benefits.

The evidence suggests that there is value in the whole spectrum of play (Zosh et al. 2018). Free play, which is child-initiated and controlled by children, and may involve so-called risky play, has been shown to be important for children's mental health (Sandseter and Kennair 2011; Whitebread 2017) and their development of self-regulation (Barker et al. 2014). However, there is also clear evidence that playful learning can be enhanced by the involvement of adults. This is sometimes referred to as "guided play" (or play in which adults are involved as co-players). As discussed previously, to most enhance the quality of the play and learning, adult involvement needs to be of a facilitating or scaffolding nature rather than direct instruction of a body of knowledge structured by the adult educator.

Key Takeaways

- Playful, active learning affects children's executive functioning, self-regulation, and language development.
- Play is multifaceted and can be characterized into five types—physical play, play with objects, symbolic play, pretend play, and games with rules—each of which serves a different purpose.

KEY CURRICULUM ELEMENTS

Much time and effort have been spent by many countries in designing preschool curricula. However, these curricula are often not research based, and the most recent, extensive analysis of curricula widely used in US preschool programs shows that those including a designed, but not evidence-based, curriculum, have no more impact on school readiness (academic and socioemotional outcomes) than those without a curriculum (Jenkins et al. 2019). Given the limited resources that are generally available in low- and middle-income countries, high quality can be most cost efficiently achieved by putting resources into training educators in the relational pedagogy set out in this chapter rather than in devising a highly sophisticated and detailed curriculum.

Chapter 3 addresses how to train teachers on curriculum and pedagogy via initial training and continuing professional development. This section reviews evidence underpinning key principles relating to a high-quality ECE curriculum. To begin with, although curriculum is necessarily organized in subject areas, it is vital that a whole-child approach be adopted. All areas of a young child's development affect all other areas, so nothing should be neglected, including health and nutrition, as well as physical, cognitive, and socioemotional development (Lewallen et al. 2015).

It is vitally important that educators understand play as a key element in preschool pedagogy, the need for them to provide opportunities for children to engage in free play across the curriculum, and the need for them to introduce new skills and areas of knowledge through guided play activities and games (Zosh et al. 2018). Educators also need to be good observers of young children's development so that they can present new activities that are appropriate for their level of development in any curriculum area. This process of formative assessment is a fundamental skill required to be an effective educator, particularly when working with very young children at the preschool level (Arnold 2015; Dunphy 2010).

As set out in chapter 1, the key areas of knowledge and understanding that should be supported within ECE settings relate to physical development, emotional and social development, and early emerging cognitive or knowledge areas—places, number, objects, people's actions and intentions, and people and their social intentions, communication, and language. These areas manifest themselves in complex and interwoven ways across the whole spectrum of knowledge and development, and can most productively be supported through a high-quality ECE curriculum. These areas of the curriculum should include the following:

- Physical health, nutrition, and development
- Emotional and social development
- Emergent literacy and mathematics
- Ways of understanding the world—scientific, historical, and geographical
- Making meaning and self-expression through the creative arts

Physical Health, Nutrition, and Development

The provision of health and nutrition education and services for young children and their families is fundamental to enhancing educational outcomes, particularly in resource-poor low- and middle-income countries, where malnutrition rates are highest. Even in high-income countries, significant proportions of the population are supported by health education programs and the provision of nutritionally balanced school breakfasts and lunches. Children who are ill or hungry show impairments in their playfulness and a range of cognitive abilities, including concentration, perseverance, and self-regulation, all of which directly affect their ability to thrive in

ECE provision, to socialize with their peers, and to learn (Aurino, Wolf, and Tsinigo 2020; Krämer 2017). It is therefore vitally important to include health and nutrition as key elements in the early learning curriculum, shared with both the children and the parents.

Much of the physical development curriculum can be provided through children's physical play. An important principle, however, as with all areas of an early years curriculum, is that simply providing the apparatus and materials and then giving the children the opportunity to play with them is not sufficient. ECE educators need to be trained in young children's early physical development and be aware of activities that can support children's development across the three main areas: movement (running, jumping, climbing, dancing, gymnastics), balance (in static positions on the ground and on apparatus, and during movement, in flight, or on apparatus), and object control (hand-eye and foot-eye coordination when using balls, bats, ropes, hoops, and other equipment).

Emotional and Social Development

Learning is a highly emotional and social experience; humans, and particularly young children, love to learn, and to learn from adults and their peers. Conversely, failure to learn leads to a whole range of negative emotions. ECE programs can foster a social environment that supports children's curiosity, their adventurousness, and their resilience when faced with challenges. Such an ECE environment makes an important contribution to young children's development, including the following:

- *Resilience and coping with stress* can be supported in the ECE setting by the creation of an environment by adult educators in which there are caring relationships, meaningful engagement of the adults with the children, and high expectations (Cefai 2008).
- *Social skills in interacting with others*, including their ability to share, compromise, and negotiate, and, consequently, develop important friendship skills are important. Children begin to develop friendships that can be lasting from a very young age, even before their second birthday (Lewis et al. 1975); friendship is a very powerful aid to the development of social competence (Berger, Cuadros, and Cillesson 2019).

Emergent Literacy and Mathematics

To prepare young children for the two specific areas of literacy and mathematics, which are vitally important symbolic systems supporting the whole range of academic learning and achievement, the ECE curriculum needs to focus on preparatory or "emergent" aspects.

Emergent Literacy and Oral Language

Book reading and the various other oral language and preliteracy practices outlined previously need to be given priority within the ECE setting,
with a particularly strong focus on supporting the young child's oral language development (Dockrell 2019), adopting a playful approach to
emergent literacy (Nicolopoulou et al. 2015), and providing a literacy-rich
environment (books, labels, signs, and so on). General recommendations
regarding ECE practice to provide a literacy-rich environment include the
following:

- Play areas can be equipped with a wide variety of reading and writing
  materials that are relevant to the children's lives and interests and support their engagement in preliteracy activities, including mark making as
  a preliteracy activity to record their ideas and observations. Examples
  include a kitchen area with empty food packets, drink cans, and recipe
  books; a shop or store with price labels, signs, pretend money, and so on;
  or a building site with plans, clipboards, and the like.
- Children need spaces to read, for example, book corners (described in
  chapter 4) where children can "read" picture books either alone or in
  small groups (Reese 2015).
- Children benefit from play activities in which the adult educator plays as
  a co-player and encourages preliteracy activities as part of the play; for
  example, the adult educator can encourage the children to "write" a
  shopping list when they are playing shop, or a menu when they are
  pretending to run a café.

Emergent Mathematics

Early emergent forms of mathematics, including numeracy, shape, and
space, are equally vital in ensuring young children's easy and confident
grasp of formal aspects of the number system, such as counting skills, simple arithmetic, measurement, and basic geometrical and spatial concepts,
together with more advanced aspects of mathematics (Anders et al. 2012).
Playful activities supporting children's emergent mathematics can include
situations in daily living, such as simple card games or board games that
contain numbers and counting; group games like musical chairs, where the
number of chairs goes down one each time; and number songs that often
involve counting up or down (Atkinson 1992). Playful measurement activities should include measurement using body parts, together with other
nonstandard and standard measures of length, volume, area, weight, time,
and so on. In relation to shape and space, playful activities such as working
jigsaw puzzles, building with blocks and construction sets, and identifying
3D shapes and objects in "feely bag" games, are all excellent preparation for
later formal geometric learning (Gifford and Coltman 2015). All of these

activities help children develop a practical understanding of number, measurement, and shape and space before they can go on to deal with the symbolic, standard written forms of formal arithmetic, measurement and geometry, and more advanced mathematical areas (Kamii 2015).

For both literacy and numeracy, it is important not to move on to teaching children the formal, conventional symbolic systems until they have extensive experience of reading, writing, counting, and arithmetic at a practical level, where the communication of meaning is the primary aim. Clear evidence has shown that teaching the formal symbolic systems too early is counterproductive, reduces children's confidence and interest, and undermines their progress as readers, writers, and mathematicians. For example, in relation to reading and writing, a study in New Zealand shows that, by age eleven, children who did not start formal literacy learning until age seven had caught up with children who started when they were five, and that the later starters were better at comprehension and read more for pleasure (Suggate, Schaughency, and Reese 2012).

In similar reviews of the requirements for children to be able to understand and work with symbolic number systems, the necessary executive function development has been indicated, particularly in relation to working memory capacity and control and flexibility of attention (van der Sluis, de Jong, and van der Leij 2007).

Ways of Understanding the World—Scientific, Historical, and Geographical

Young children are endlessly curious about the world in which they live. From as young as two years old, and certainly by three years, they want to know what things are for, or what they do, what they are called, why everything they see is like that, or doing that, or called that. The most helpful and educative response to these questions from an early years educator is not to attempt to provide answers, but to respond with something like, "I'm not sure. I wonder how we could find out?" In this way the educator can introduce the children to the means by which they can explore, investigate, and find out about their world. In other words, the role of the early years educator is not to transmit current scientific, or historical, or geographical knowledge, but to help young children on their first steps to becoming scientists, historians, or geographers. This inquiry learning approach engages the children and makes their learning in these areas meaningful and much more likely to be remembered (McNerney and Hall 2017; Pickford, Garner, and Jackson 2013).

Young children are generally very keen observers of their world, and very keen to try things out and see what works. As a consequence, they have often been called "little scientists." At the preschool level, these natural proclivities can be built upon and extended very effectively as children are introduced to basic scientific methods, including precise measurement (when measuring ingredients in cooking, or measuring plant growth when put in sunny, warm or shady, cold locations), classification (when investigating different types of minibeasts—beetles, spiders, worms, and so on, or which materials feel rough, smooth, slippery, soft, or hard), and experimentation (when finding out what makes objects float, or why a flashlight does not work).

Furthermore, as in everything related to best practice with young children, it is vitally important to place scientific investigations in contexts that are meaningful to the children. This can be achieved by responding to questions the children ask themselves, or it can be orchestrated through a story context (what materials should the three little pigs use to build their houses to stop the big bad wolf blowing them down?), or through presenting the children with a surprising phenomenon that needs to be investigated (such as a spoon looking bent when dipped into a glass of water), or through discussing a scientific question with a puppet who has silly ideas (Coltman 2015).

Making Meaning and Self-Expression through the Creative Arts

It is no surprise that in every culture of the world the activities of adults and the play of young children include representing their experience through story-telling and writing, through model making (including dolls and puppets, junk models, and construction toys), through drawing and other available visual media, through making music, and through dance.

The development of children's drawings has been widely studied, including the artistic, emotional, and cognitive processes driving early scribbling (Coates and Coates 2016) and the development of children's graphic vocabulary and organization (Cox 1992), as a window into children's thinking about their experiences (Jolley 2010). All children in all cultures draw, contributing to their artistic skills, their visual literacy, and their sense of identity. Drawing is also a powerful vehicle for their imaginations and their developing abilities to organize and make meaningful sense of their life experiences.

The development of children's musical abilities has also been an area of considerable study. Research indicating the fundamental developmental links with music, and particularly rhythm, has focused on a number of areas, including the musical structure of early infant-mother dialogue (Malloch and Trevarthen 2009), and the relation between rhythmic sense, language acquisition (Goswami 2019), and early literacy (Huss et al. 2011). What is perhaps unique to music and music making, however, is its power to represent and to evoke emotions and to "uplift, unwind, refocus, relax, reinvent and reflect as children become increasingly comfortable and confident in the world around them" (Bance 2015, 230). Because young children are natural movers, it is no accident that music and songs with this age group are often accompanied by dance, which is a further element of cultural expression and a powerful fusion of musicality, rhythmic sensitivity, and physical abilities.

Creative activities of all kinds are clearly an important element in the early years curriculum. A wide range of materials needs to be available in the early years for children to freely engage in as many forms of creative expression as possible, in addition to an ongoing array of creative activities instigated by the educator to open the children's minds to the many possible forms of creative and personal expression. Providing for young children's activities in the creative arts, however, does not need to be expensive because many of the required materials can be acquired for free. Materials that are natural, recycled, or manufactured can all be used and can be obtained by foraging in the natural environment and from household collections or organized collections from industrial and commercial waste. A report on waste recycling in the Philippines, for example, included reviews of several schemes involving schools collecting waste products for their own use, or as a means of raising funds that could be used to purchase educational materials (Antonio 2010). This type of scheme also incorporates an element of environmental education in an active and meaningful way for young children.

The opportunities for young children to represent their understandings about their world are very much related to the creative arts, and a project approach incorporating elements of all these areas of knowledge and skill is recommended—my family, my village, local animals and their homes, and so on. Such projects give meaning to children's life experiences. Essential to creativity is its open-endedness and the lack of right or wrong answers; indeed, being encouraged to try out new ideas, new techniques, and new ways of observing are all essential to the creative process.

A Note on Documentation and Formative Assessment

Finally, it is worth considering how children's questions, ideas, activities, investigations, and creative processes are documented across the curriculum. This documentation should take two complementary forms. First, openly documenting children's activities, interests, and achievements is important. Displays on the walls, in class books, or in albums, including records of discussions, photos of activities, and children's creative products, provide children with a sense of achievement and opportunities to deepen, record, and further reflect on creative inquiries (Cowan and

Berry 2015). Second, this process of open documentation should go alongside the educator's and child's own records of the child's activities, enthusiasms, and achievements, most helpfully in the form of portfolios. Taken together, these two sets of records enable the educator to assess individual children's development and to make decisions about next steps for individual children and future planning for the class. This reflective style of assessment gives young children ownership and agency in relation to their own learning and has been shown to have positive impacts on children's confidence, motivation, achievements, and self-regulation abilities (MacDonald 2007).

Key Takeaways

- Although curriculum is necessarily organized in subject areas, it is vital that a whole-child approach be considered.
- A whole-child, evidence-based curriculum should include activities supporting children's development in five areas: physical health and development, social and emotional development, emergent literacy and numeracy understandings and abilities, ways of understanding the world, and self-expression through the creative arts.
- Documenting children's activities, interests, and achievements through displays on the walls or in class books or albums, including records of discussions, photos of activities, and children's creative products, can help assess children's development and inform the educator's future planning for the class. Open documentation should be complemented with the educator's and child's own records of individual children's activities, enthusiasms, and achievements.

GUIDANCE ON IMPLEMENTATION

The discussion in the previous section makes a compelling case for the importance of high-quality curricula that reflect research-based pedagogy as a cornerstone of any early childhood program. This section now turns to the "how," focusing on key aspects of implementation. In particular, the "how" is framed in terms of the three elements of pedagogy detailed earlier: (1) communicating meaning, (2) self-regulation skills, and (3) playful learning. To ensure the uptake of these three elements of pedagogy, there are implications for curriculum that support teachers in various ways. This section discusses the necessary conditions for implementation of the three elements of pedagogy and supportive curriculum.

In what ways are these principles enacted in low- and middle-income contexts, and what adaptations can be made to them to fit with cultural models of behavior and interaction? Three areas are discussed below. First, the section considers what needs to be known about the context beforehand to understand how to apply the three key principles of this chapter and then develop supportive curricula and pedagogy. Second, decisions and trade-offs when planning for implementation are discussed. Finally, continuous improvement is considered, along with what is needed to ensure high-quality pedagogy and curriculum.

Diagnose

To develop an effective intervention, the first step is to accurately diagnose what is occurring on the ground. The following areas provide guidance on areas for diagnosis, both for pedagogy and for curriculum revision and development.

- Diagnose *teacher knowledge* using knowledge surveys, interviews, and focus groups to better understand what teachers already know about pedagogy in preschool. This diagnosis can be content-specific (for example, early literacy, early math) as well as general, assessing how educators think children learn best in the early years, and what types of key skills should be emphasized in the early years. For example, one study in the United States carried out a validated survey measuring early childhood teachers' math knowledge and beliefs (Platas 2015).
- Use classroom observations to better understand what *instruction* looks like in ECE classrooms. Specifically, it would be good to understand the role of play in classrooms currently, attitudes toward it as a pedagogy, how self-regulation may manifest itself in the classroom, how teachers support oral language development, and what meaning-making looks like in the specific context.
- Use classroom observations and school visits to learn what types of *materials* are available in schools, both for teachers (such as teacher guides, scoping documents, and so on) and for students (books at appropriate levels, counters, blocks, paper, and others).
- Review the current *curriculum documents* in the country, with special attention to how instruction is divided up (skills-based, content-based, and so on), and whether and how developmental progression is represented. In particular, review curriculum documents, including teacher guides and student books, to understand whether they integrate key principles of pedagogy and how they support teachers in implementing these pedagogies.

- Understand *school and classroom-level support* for teachers' implementation of new ways of teaching, through interviews with key national and district-level personnel. In particular, it is important to understand what support teachers get at the classroom level, who provides that support, how often it is provided, and whether the support is of high quality. For example, in Kenya, district officers are responsible for providing classroom support to preschool teachers. In other contexts, school principals may provide this support.
- *Understand family and community support* for pedagogy. Given that the key principles in this chapter may be unfamiliar ways of teaching for communities and families, it would be good to understand attitudes and knowledge around the key principles. In particular, it would be good to understand what families think about play and its role both in and out of school. For example, one study shows the importance of parental attitudes toward play in Ghanaian preschools (Kabay, Wolf, and Yoshikawa 2017).

Key Takeaway

- When diagnosing conditions on the ground, key aspects to consider include understanding teacher knowledge, observing classroom instruction, knowing what materials are available, reviewing curriculum documents, understanding the level of classroom and school-level support available to teachers and parents, and community views of and support for pedagogy.

Plan for Implementation

To plan for implementation, it is important to identify the necessary conditions for implementation and to devise a sequence for these conditions and what potential constraints to anticipate. In addition, these steps could also be used for continual adaptation of an existing program.

1. Understand how to *contextualize for the elements of pedagogy.* Together with experts and policy makers in the country, there should be discussion about how to design an intervention, including curriculum materials that respect important elements of pedagogy but also respect and reflect cultural ways of teaching and interacting, materials availability, and teacher knowledge. Important considerations include the following:
   - *Playful, active learning and communicating meaning.* In some cultures, playfulness is encouraged, both inside and outside of schooling. In others, play is something that occurs outside of school only. Play may be acceptable between adults and children in some places, but acceptable only among children in other places. These types of

cultural norms should be taken into account when designing and adapting key pedagogical principles. That is not to say that play should not be encouraged, but rather that the implementers will need to understand cultural perceptions and attitudes toward play and work to create pedagogy that fits within classroom norms. For example, in South Africa, implementers developed a "pedagogy of play" that is particular to that context, and describe playful classroom activities that fit within this pedagogy (Solis et al. 2019). These activities may look different than in Western contexts, but they are still based on the same foundations of "playful learning" described in the first part of this chapter.

- *Oral language development and support.* An understanding of how oral language development occurs, and in which language, should be developed. Are the children learning a second language in preschool settings or is it the same language they are learning at home? What is the language policy of the country? These are all important factors that will affect how oral language is supported.

- *Self-regulation.* With an understanding of what types of self-regulatory behaviors may already exist in a certain context, it is important to think about the end goals of this principle, and not simply copy the pathways to the end goals that are used in high-income countries.

- *Availability of materials and resources.* Many contexts with few commercial resources have abundant natural resources (for example, sticks or small pebbles for counting, leaves and sand for artwork) and recycled materials (such as bottle tops to use as counters, jugs, jars, and other household items for dramatic play areas). Procuring, organizing, and building materials is also a good way for the community to be involved in preschool schooling. See photograph 2.1.

Despite the availability of natural and recycled resources, it is important to understand that teachers have a role in curating these environments, and that they need training and experience to do so. Teachers should not be expected to know how to create these environments with available natural resources. In addition, there are some materials, such as books and puzzles, that are not easily created in local environments. The need for these additional resources points to the sustained need for investments in early childhood across the globe.

2. *Prioritize domains of knowledge,* building from developmental progressions and based on country standards documents. In the preschool years, the focus of instruction for key domains such as preliteracy, numeracy, physical health, creative arts, and social-emotional learning should be based on research about how children learn. At this point, it may be important

Photograph 2.1 Examples of Natural and Recycled Resources in Classrooms in Chile

Source: © Used with the permission of Cecrea Program, Ministry of Cultures, Arts and Heritage, Chile. Further permission required for reuse.

to review existing country-level standard documents and recommend and implement changes where possible.

3. *Co-develop scopes and sequences* and curriculum documents, embedding principles for pedagogy. "Scope and sequence" means the breadth of content to teach (scope) and the pacing and order in which to teach them (sequence). Government officials, local curriculum and pedagogy experts, and teachers should convene to develop detailed scopes and sequences of content and pedagogy. These documents should be agreed upon, and a clear plan for what types of documents to produce (for example, teacher guides, textbooks, standards) and how to produce them should be created.

4. *Prioritize support for teachers* that can be embedded in curriculum documents. It is important to ensure that teachers are not overburdened, and that they are not being asked to change everything at the same time. Some recommendations for pedagogy include the following:
   – Prioritize which pedagogies should be focused on first, understanding that not everything can occur at the same time. Develop a plan for how new pedagogies can be introduced to teachers in a structured way without overwhelming them. To prioritize, focus on the high-leverage pedagogies that will foster quality interactions in the classroom.
   – Develop semi-structured teacher guides that provide detailed information on the scope and sequence of what to teach, and that have pedagogical principles built into the instruction. For example, the scope and sequence would support teachers in knowing which

activities to use to teach children how to accurately count 10 objects, as well as when to teach these activities.

– Because some pedagogies may be new and difficult for teachers to implement, it may be good to include extra scaffolding for teachers that illustrates how to implement activities in the classroom, as well as how to support students who may need extra help. Ideally, these materials may provide more support at the beginning of the year and allow for more discretion as teachers become fluent with new pedagogical skills. Materials can also be educative, in that they provide tips and support to teachers in developing key pedagogies, such as observation skills and responsive teaching.

– Curriculum materials should be designed to be simple, practical, and easy to use, with all information easy for the teacher to access and interpret. In particular, materials should provide specific guidance on what types of resources to use and how to use them.

– Training and in-classroom follow-up support should be provided for teachers who are implementing new pedagogy. Simply providing materials for the teacher is not enough. Training and follow-up support is essential. Training should be more intense in the beginning, and emphasize practice over theory. Once in the classroom, teachers need continuous support from coaches, mentors, and peers to improve their practice and take-up of the new pedagogies. Chapter 3 contains a more detailed description of teacher training and support.

5. *Conduct pilot testing and elicit teacher input* on pedagogical approaches and curriculum throughout the process. It is vital that teacher voices are heard and included in the process of introducing new pedagogical approaches and curriculum documents. They should be part of the creation process, not only brought in at the end to pilot test.

6. *Develop a plan for supporting transition to primary school.* Children often struggle in the transition to overly formal and structured primary school programs. In many countries, preschool and grade 1 curricula can be vastly different and not reflective of learning progressions. It is essential that preschools and primary schools work together to ensure a smooth transition for students, including academic learning, socioemotional expectations, and parental expectations.

Exemplar Questions to Guide the Decision-Making Process

Is the pedagogy easy for teachers to implement? Which pedagogies can be embedded in curriculum materials in the most straightforward manner? Focusing on these easier-to-implement pedagogies may allow for quicker uptake, and new, more complicated pedagogies can slowly be introduced throughout the project. For example, in the beginning, an intervention may focus its efforts on providing support to teachers to encourage the development of children's self-regulation. This could be just one daily question or activity that the teacher performs. As teachers become more confident and gain experience with supporting self-regulation, additional small steps can be introduced, in culturally relevant ways.

Where will resources have the greatest impact? It is important to think through which types of resources will be most used in the classroom, and for what purposes, and how many are needed to make a meaningful impact. For example, if teachers are given one set of geometric figures for math, but not provided with any support on how students in small groups can use them, they may end up only in the hands of the teachers and not used as intended.

How can stakeholders be brought in on decision-making and contextualization? In particular, how can community members and parents be used to support the key pedagogical principles and provide extra support to schools?

Despite the most well-thought-out plans and sequence of events, it is rare that any implementation goes exactly as envisaged. For example, a project may be being designed in a country where the curriculum documents need major revision to allow for integration of new pedagogies, but such revision is not possible at the time. In this case, teachers can receive support to use new pedagogies with existing materials. Though not ideal, teacher training and in-classroom support can still allow for integration of new pedagogies as long as explicit links are made between what teachers are being asked to do by the government and the new pedagogies.

Potential Constraints

As with any implementation, there are always constraints to consider and trade-offs to make.

- *Time.* Time is always a constraint—there is never enough time to do everything the way it should ideally be done. Given this, each effort will need to ask hard questions and make decisions about what to prioritize and when.
- *Managing stakeholder expectations and desires.* When working with different stakeholders (for example, government, donor community, parents, community organizations), there are always trade-offs to make in what to emphasize. Key to this negotiation is ensuring that teachers and students do not become overburdened and that the intervention meets their needs.
- *Cost.* Cost is always a limiting factor, and key decisions need to be made about where and when to dedicate the most resources.

Given the challenges and decisions detailed above, it is prudent to take a long-term approach to implementation of the key principles listed in this chapter. Asking teachers and communities to change their behavior and adopt new and unfamiliar practices is difficult, and if not done well tends to fail. There is a large body of literature about the failure of "student-centered," "active," and "play-based" learning in low- and middle-income countries, and relatively few successes, especially at scale. Closer examination of many of these efforts points to various factors, such as lack of alignment with cultural norms and lack of resources. To address these issues, this chapter proposes small steps and changes that are adapted to and respectful of cultural norms, and openness to change and adaptation of long-term goals as the small steps and changes are made.

Key Takeaway

- When planning for implementation, key recommendations include understanding how to contextualize principles for pedagogy; prioritizing domains of knowledge, building from developmental progressions and based on country standards documents; prioritizing support for teachers that can be embedded in curriculum documents; co-developing scopes and sequences and curriculum documents, embedding principles for pedagogy; pilot testing and eliciting teacher input on pedagogical approaches and curriculum throughout the process; and developing a plan for supporting the transition to primary school.

Continuous Feedback and Improvement

Once curriculum materials have been developed, it is tempting to say that they are "final." But curriculum documents are continually evolving. It is important to have a system in place that allows for continual improvement of materials. Once materials have been distributed to teachers, there should be routine observations, interviews, and teacher reports that provide information on how teachers are using the materials and identify key challenges and successes. Revisions should be made to the materials at regular intervals to address these challenges.

When gathering information on how materials are being used, several types of data sources can be useful. First, gather data on how teachers use the materials in the classroom. Through observations by school administrators, district personnel, and other relevant actors, data can be gathered on how teachers interpret the materials and the struggles and successes they have. Analysis of these struggles and successes can provide useful and detailed information for revision. Second, talk with teachers to understand their perceptions and suggestions for improvement of the materials. Separate issues that can be resolved by revising materials from issues that may be better targeted to training and other teacher support. Finally, talk with others in the education system, including students, parents, administrators, and other support personnel, to understand how their suggestions for improvement can be taken into account (see chapter 5).

Key Takeaways

- Curriculum documents are continually evolving. It is important to have a system in place that allows for continual improvement of materials.
- This system of improvement should include gathering data through routine observations and interviews with teachers and others in the education system.

CASE STUDIES

Bangladesh, Tanzania, and Uganda

In Bangladesh, a small study investigated how play was understood, incorporated, and practiced in semi-rural public preprimary classes (Chowdhury and Rivalland 2016). Among the teachers and parents interviewed, a range of activities, including physical exercises, singing, acting, rhyming, games, outdoor play, and drawing, was described as play and seen as a means of developing academic skills by encouraging the children to follow the teacher's instructions in correct ways.

Subsequently, a three-country study in Bangladesh, Tanzania, and Uganda built upon the initial study by introducing 40 play-based preschool Play Labs into rural villages in each country. This larger study investigated the impact of these Play Labs over two years on 720 of the three-to-five-year-old children's physical, cognitive, and social development, and their playfulness, oral language, and self-regulation. These children's progress was compared with that of children living in similar villages, but with either a government- or community-run preschool or no preschool. In addition, the study investigated the features of the children's family situation and the quality of the Play Lab leaders' practices that influenced the children's development. Results indicated a significant change over the course of the study. At the start, for both Play Lab and control children, home factors were related to all aspects of children's development, but by the end these relations remained for the control children only. This result suggests that the Play Labs exerted a greater influence in young children's outcomes compared with the home environment. By the end of just the first year, the Play Lab children had made significantly greater progress in a range of the developmental measures, and the strongest relations were between the quality of Play

Lab leaders' interactions with the children and the children's progress, most noticeably in playfulness and self-regulation (Whitebread and Yesmin 2021).

Two aspects of this intervention that significantly influenced these successful outcomes related to the strong relationships built with the parents and community, and the initial and continuing training of the Play Lab leaders. Parents and community members were crucially involved in the Play Lab from the very start, through a representative committee, and parents (mainly but not exclusively mothers) organized a rota whereby they worked as classroom assistants, made toys and other materials for the children, and carried out routine cleaning and maintenance tasks. This involvement gave them ownership of the Play Lab project and facilitated their education about the pedagogy of the Play Labs, which clearly influenced their own relationships and ways of interacting with their children in the home.

The Play Lab leaders were generally young women who had been successful in their own schooling. Their training consisted of an initial period of a few weeks, during which they were taught the basic skills they would need to lead the Play Lab, which was initially clearly organized with a standard room design, including special corners relating to curriculum areas and a timetable of set activities. Once they were under way, monthly in-service training days were provided at the training center, during which particular aspects of pedagogy or curriculum were addressed in more depth and the teachers had the opportunity to raise and discuss issues of concern.

The governments of the three countries were also involved in the project from the outset and committed, to varying degrees, to work with the project team to roll out Play Labs more widely across their education provision in different areas of the country. The project has demonstrated that this model, involving a paid Play Lab leader and considerable participation by the local parents and community, provides an affordable and high-quality preschool experience for young children that prepares them to make a very successful start to their schooling.

The Philippines

The Philippines government has put special emphasis on early years education as a driver for individual and social development. Through implementation of the Basic Education Act in 2013, the country introduced kindergarten (for five-year-olds) as the first compulsory level of education. This policy shift has required efforts to articulate and align early years and primary education in curriculum development and teacher workforce preparation.

Reviews of the curriculum and other pedagogical documents show that curriculum is sequenced in a way that ensures a continuation in learning trajectories. There is a commitment to promoting active learning and discovery, with the teacher as a facilitator. This aligns with goals around playful learning and is also conducive to enhancing self-regulation skills.

A detailed case study (CEPI 2020, 9) states,

> This requires teachers to promote contextualized activities that would help students make meaning of what is being taught, a clear link to the principle of meaning making. For instance, kindergarten teachers are required to use thematic units or themes that integrate the different domains, following the principle that "children's growth and development is interrelated and interdependent" (DepEd Order No. 47, s. 2016, pp. 4). For instance, in kindergarten there are 7 domains, i.e. Socioemotional Development, Values Development, Physical Health and Motor Development, Aesthetic Development, Mathematics, Physical and Natural Environment and Language, Literacy and Communication. In this grade, it is expected that classrooms would be organized by areas, or activity corners, that would "encourage learners to spend more time engaging in different learning activities within these areas" (DepEd Order No. 47, s. 2016, pp. 17).

Support materials have been created for teachers to implement the National Curriculum, such as the Kindergarten Teacher's Guide created by the Department of Education with technical assistance from Save the Children (Philippines, Department of Education 2017) This document provides weekly guidance on how to address all the skills described in the National Curriculum. This type of guidance, and others like it, illustrates how one country has prioritized quality early education by setting guidelines for curricula and pedagogy that are aligned with research, and then development of resources for teachers to deliver high-quality instruction.

CONCLUSION

The real strength of high-quality ECE is more generally not the formal curriculum, but the nature and quality of the relationships between the educators and the children in the setting or classroom. The role of the ECE educator is most effectively that of facilitator and guide rather than instructor. Beyond ensuring a responsive and supportive relationship between educator and child, three key elements of high-quality pedagogy support children's development: (1) supporting children's spoken and communication skills, (2) supporting children's ability to self-regulate their cognitive and emotional mental processes, and (3) creating opportunities for active learning through play. To ensure all children make a secure start to their school careers, it is important that a whole-child, evidence-based curriculum be provided, which should include activities supporting children's development in five areas: physical health and development, social and emotional development, preliteracy and prenumeracy understandings and abilities, ways of understanding the world, and self- expression through the creative arts. It is vital that ECE educators work with parents to enhance the quality of the home experience and the smooth transition from home to preschool. When planning for implementation, a three-step process is advised, including a diagnosis to understand the current cultural and political context, planning for implementation, and ensuring a plan and process for continuous feedback and improvement.

See table 2.1 for a summary of the key takeaways in this chapter.

Table 2.1 Chapter 2: Summary of Key Takeaways

The nature and quality of adult-child relationships

- The role of the ECE educator is most effectively that of facilitator and guide rather than instructor. This has been referred to as a "relational" rather than an instructional pedagogy.
- There are three key elements of quality ECE pedagogy: (1) supporting children's spoken and communication skills, (2) supporting children's ability to self-regulate their cognitive and emotional mental processes, and (3) creating opportunities for active learning through play.

Element 1: Communicating meaning

- Children need to be given opportunities to communicate meaning by representing their perceptions and understandings about the world through a range of linguistic, visual, and physical media, including activities.
- Children's ability to communicate meaning is influenced by their oral language, exploratory talk, and narrative skills.
- Various specific activities and tools are available that teachers can use to cultivate these skills, including book reading and story-telling. Opportunities to engage in back-and-forth interactions with teachers and peers, as well as opportunities for children to explain themselves, can all build children's ability to communicate meaning.

Element 2: Self-regulation

- Children's self-regulation abilities are highly influenced by a range of social factors and so are teachable.
- Classrooms supporting self-regulation are characterized by challenging and open-ended tasks, opportunities for children to control the level of challenge, and the encouragement of positive feelings toward challenge.
- Children's autonomy should be supported through the provision of choice and encouragement for children to develop their ideas and interests, and approaches that encourage children to talk about and reflect upon their learning.

continued next page

Table 2.1 (*continued*)

Element 3: Playful, active learning

- Playful, active learning affects children's executive functioning, self-regulation, and language development.
- Play is multifaceted and can be characterized into five types—physical play, play with objects, symbolic play, pretend play, and games with rules—each of which serves a different purpose.

Key curriculum elements

- Although curriculum is necessarily organized in subject areas, it is vital that a whole-child approach be considered.
- A whole-child, evidence-based curriculum should include activities supporting children's development in five areas: physical health and development, social and emotional development, emergent literacy and numeracy understandings and abilities, ways of understanding the world, and self-expression through the creative arts.
- Documenting children's activities, interests, and achievements through displays on the walls or in class books or albums, including records of discussions, photos of activities, and children's creative products, can help assess children's development and inform the educator's future planning for the class. Open documentation should be complemented with the educator's and child's own records of individual children's activities, enthusiasms, and achievements.

Diagnose

- When diagnosing conditions on the ground, key aspects to consider include understanding teacher knowledge, observing classroom instruction, knowing what materials are available, reviewing curriculum documents, understanding the level of classroom and school-level support available to teachers and parents, and community views of and support for pedagogy.

Plan for implementation

- When planning for implementation, key recommendations include understanding how to contextualize principles for pedagogy; prioritizing domains of knowledge, building from developmental progressions and based on country standards documents; prioritizing support for teachers that can be embedded in curriculum documents; co-developing scopes and sequences and curriculum documents, embedding principles for pedagogy; pilot testing and eliciting teacher input on pedagogical approaches and curriculum throughout process; and developing a plan for supporting the transition to primary school.

Continuous feedback and improvement

- Curriculum documents are continually evolving. It is important to have a system in place that allows for continual improvement of materials.
- This system of improvement should include gathering data through routine observations and interviews with teachers and others in the education system.

Source: Original table for this publication.
Note: ECE = early childhood education.

REFERENCES

Anders, Y., H. G. Rossbach, S. Weinert, S. Ebert, S. Kuger, S. Lehrl, and J. von Maurice. 2012. "Home and Preschool Learning Environments and Their Relations to the Development of Early Numeracy Skills." *Early Childhood Research Quarterly* 27 (2): 231–44.

Antonio, L. C. 2010. "Study on Recyclables Collection Trends and Best Practices in the Philippines." In *3R Policies for Southeast and East Asia*, edited by M. Kojima, 40–70. Jakarta: Economic Research Institute for ASEAN and East Asia. https://www.eria.org/RPR-2009-10.pdf#page=48.

Arnold, A. 2015. "'When the Chicks Hatch, a Man Will Come and Bring Them Yolk to Eat': Assessment in the Early Years." In *Teaching and Learning in the Early Years*, 4th ed., edited by D. Whitebread and P. Coltman, 77–92. London: Routledge.

Atkinson, S., ed. 1992. *Mathematics with Reason: The Emergent Approach to Primary Maths*. London: Hodder Education.

Aurino, E., S. Wolf, and E. Tsinigo. 2020. "Household Food Insecurity and Early Childhood Development: Longitudinal Evidence from Ghana." *PLOS ONE* 15 (4): e0230965.

Bance, L. 2015. "'I've Got a Song to Sing': Creating a Musical Environment for Children in Their Early Years." In *Teaching and Learning in the Early Years*, 4th ed., edited by D. Whitebread and P. Coltman, 229–45. London: Routledge.

Barker, J. E., A. D. Semenov, L. Michaelson, L. S. Provan, H. R. Snyder, and Y. Munakata. 2014. "Less-Structured Time in Children's Daily Lives Predicts Self-Directed Executive Functioning." *Frontiers in Psychology* 5: 593.

Berger, C., O. Cuadros, and A. H. N. Cillesson. 2019. "Children's Friendships and Social Development." In *SAGE Handbook of Developmental Psychology and Early Childhood Education*, edited by D. Whitebread, V. Grau, K. Kumpulainen, M. McClelland, N. Perry, and D. Pino-Pasternak. London: SAGE.

Bertram, T., and C. Pascal. 2002. *Early Years Education: An International Perspective*. London: Qualifications and Curriculum Authority.

Best, J. R., P. H. Miller, and J. A. Naglieri. 2011. "Relations between Executive Function and Academic Achievement from Ages 5 to 17 in a Large, Representative National Sample." *Learning and Individual Differences* 21 (4): 327–36.

Bingham, S., and D. Whitebread. 2018. "School Readiness in Europe: Issues and Evidence." In *International Handbook of Early Childhood Education*, Vol. I, edited by M. Fleer and B. van Oers. Dordrecht: Springer.

Bonawitz, E., P. Shafto, H. Gweon, N. D. Goodman, E. Spelke, and L. Schulz. 2011. "The Double-Edged Sword of Pedagogy: Instruction Limits Spontaneous Exploration and Discovery." *Cognition* 120 (3): 322–30.

Boyle, E. A., T. Hainey, T. M. Connolly, G. Gray, J. Earp, M. Ott, T. Lim, et al. 2016. "An Update to the Systematic Literature Review of Empirical Evidence of the Impacts and Outcomes of Computer Games and Serious Games." *Computers and Education* 94: 178–92.

Bronson, M. 2000. *Self-Regulation in Early Childhood: Nature and Nurture*. New York: Guilford Press.

Butler, L. P., S. Ronfard, and K. H. Corriveau. 2020. *The Questioning Child: Insights from Psychology and Education*. Cambridge, UK: Cambridge University Press.

Cadima, J., K. Verschueren, T. Leal, and C. Guedes. 2016. "Classroom Interactions, Dyadic Teacher-Child Relationships, and Self-Regulation in Socially Disadvantaged Young Children." *Journal of Abnormal Child Psychology* 44 (1): 7–17.

Carpenter, M., K. Nagell, and M. Tomasello. 1998. "Social Cognition, Joint Attention, and Communicative Competence from 9–15 Months of Age." *Monographs of the Society for Research in Child Development* 63 (4): i–iv, 1–143.

Carr, M. 2011. "Young Children Reflecting on Their Learning: Teachers' Conversation Strategies." *Early Years* 31 (3): 257–70.

Cefai, C. 2008. *Promoting Resilience in the Classroom*. London: Jessica Kingsley Publishers.

CEPI (Centro de Estudios Primera Infancia). 2020. "Case Study: Curricular Review of The Philippines." Background information prepared for this report.

Chowdhury, N. N., and C. Rivalland. 2016. "Conceptualising Play as Pedagogy in the ECE Context of a Developing Country: The Case Study of Bangladesh." *MIER Journal of Educational Studies, Trends and Practices* 1 (2).

Coates, E., and A. Coates. 2016. "The Essential Role of Scribbling in the Imaginative and Cognitive Development of Young Children." *Journal of Early Childhood Literacy* 16 (1): 60–83.

Coltman, P. 2015. "'How Many Toes Has a Newt?' Science in the Early Years." In *Teaching and Learning in the Early Years*, 4th ed., edited by D. Whitebread and P. Coltman, 268–81. London: Routledge.

Cowan, K., and M. Berry. 2015. "'Once There Was Someone Who Walked on the Sky': Creativity in the Early Years." In *Teaching and Learning in the Early Years*, 4th ed., edited by D. Whitebread and P. Coltman, 246–67. London: Routledge.

Cox, M. 1992. *Children's Drawings*. London: Penguin Books.

Deans, J. 2016. "Thinking, Feeling and Relating: Young Children Learning through Dance." *Australasian Journal of Early Childhood* 41 (3): 46–57.

Deci, E. L., and R. M. Ryan. 2008. "Self-Determination Theory: A Macrotheory of Human Motivation, Development, and Health." *Canadian Psychology* 49 (3): 182–85.

Dignath, C., G. Buettner, and H. P. Langfeldt. 2008. "How Can Primary School Students Learn Self-Regulated Learning Strategies Most Effectively?: A Meta-Analysis on Self-Regulation Training Programmes." *Educational Research Review* 3 (2): 101–29.

Dockrell, J. E. 2019. "Language Learning Challenges in the Early Years." In *SAGE Handbook of Developmental Psychology and Early Childhood Education*, edited by D. Whitebread, V. Grau, K. Kumpulainen, M. McClelland, N. Perry, and D. Pino-Pasternak. London: SAGE.

Dunphy, E. 2010. "Assessing Early Learning through Formative Assessment: Key Issues and Considerations." *Irish Educational Studies* 29 (1): 41–56.

Engel, S. 2011. "Children's Need To Know: Curiosity in Schools." *Harvard Educational Review* 81 (4): 625–45.

Florez, I. R. 2011. "Developing Young Children's Self-Regulation through Everyday Experiences." *Young Children* 66 (4): 46–51.

Fuhs, M. W., D. C. Farran, and K. T. Nesbitt. 2013. "Preschool Classroom Processes as Predictors of Children's Cognitive Self-Regulation Skills Development." *School Psychology Quarterly* 28 (4): 347–59.

Gifford, S., and P. Coltman. 2015. "'How Many Shapey Ones Have You Got?' Number and Shape in the Early Years." In *Teaching and Learning in the Early Years*, 4th ed., edited by D. Whitebread and P. Coltman, 281–93. London: Routledge.

Gillespie, L. G., and J. D. Greenberg. 2017. "Empowering Infants' and Toddlers' Learning through Scaffolding." *Young Children* 72 (2): 90–93.

Gopnik, A., and A. N. Meltzoff. 1992. "Categorization and Naming: Basic-Level Sorting in Eighteen-Month-Olds and Its Relation to Language." *Child Development* 63 (5): 1091–103.

Gopnik, A., A. N. Meltzoff, and P. K. Kuhl. 1999. *The Scientist in the Crib: Minds, Brains, and How Children Learn.* New York: William Morrow and Co.

Goswami, U. 2019. "Speech Rhythm and Language Acquisition: An Amplitude Modulation Phase Hierarchy Perspective." *Annals of the New York Academy of Sciences* 1453 (1): 67–78.

Grau, V., and D. Whitebread, eds. 2018. "Relationships between Classroom Dialogue and Support for Metacognitive, Self-Regulatory Development in Educational Contexts." *New Directions for Child and Adolescent Development* 162.

Hattie, J. 2009. *Visible Learning: A Synthesis of 800 Meta-Analyses Relating to Achievement.* London: Routledge.

Hattie, J. 2012. *Visible Learning for Teachers: Maximizing Impact on Learning.* London: Routledge.

Hoff, E. 2013. "Interpreting the Early Language Trajectories of Children from Low SES and Language Minority Homes: Implications for Closing Achievement Gaps." *Developmental Psychology* 49 (1): 4–14.

Holmes, R. M., B. Gardner, K. Kohm, C. Bant, A. Ciminello, K. Moedt, and L. Romeo. 2019. "The Relationship between Young Children's Language Abilities, Creativity, Play, and Storytelling." *Early Child Development and Care* 189 (2): 244–54.

Huss, M., J. P. Verney, T. Fosker, N. Mead, and U. Goswami. 2011. "Music, Rhythm, Rise Time Perception and Developmental Dyslexia: Perception of Musical Meter Predicts Reading and Phonology." *Cortex* 47 (6): 674–89.

Jarvis, P. 2010. "'Born to Play': The Biocultural Roots of Rough and Tumble Play, and Its Impact upon Young Children's Learning and Development." In *Play and Learning in the Early Years*, edited by P. Broadhead, J. Howard, and E. Wood, 61–77. London: SAGE.

Jenkins, J. M., A. A. Whitaker, T. Nguyen, and W. Yu. 2019. "Distinctions without a Difference? Preschool Curricula and Children's Development." *Journal of Research on Educational Effectiveness* 12 (3): 514–49.

Jolley, R. P. 2010. *Children's Pictures.* Chichester, UK: Wiley-Blackwell.

Kabay, S., S. Wolf, and H. Yoshikawa. 2017. "'So That His Mind Will Open': Parental Perceptions of Early Childhood Education in Urbanizing Ghana." *International Journal of Educational Development* 57 (November): 44–53.

Kamii, C. 2015. "Play and Mathematics in Kindergarten." In *Play from Birth to Twelve: Contexts, Perspectives, and Meanings*, edited by D. P. Fromberg and D. Bergen, 197–205. New York: Routledge.

Krämer, M. 2017. "Nutrition and Child Development in Low-and Middle-Income Countries—Evaluation of Three Micronutrient Interventions." Doctoral dissertation, Georg-August-Universität Göttingen.

Lewallen, T. C., H. Hunt, W. Potts-Datema, S. Zaza, and W. Giles. 2015. "The Whole School, Whole Community, Whole Child Model: A New Approach for Improving Educational Attainment and Healthy Development for Students." *Journal of School Health* 85 (11): 729–39.

Lewis, M., G. Young, J. Brooks, and L. Michalson. 1975. "The Beginning of Friendship." In *Friendships and Peer Relationships*, edited by M. Lewis and L. Rosenblum. New York: Wiley.

Lillard, A. S., M. D. Lerner, E. J. Hopkins, R. A. Dore, E. D. Smith, and C. M. Palmquist. 2013. "The Impact of Pretend Play on Children's Development: A Review of the Evidence." *Psychological Bulletin* 139 (1): 1–34.

Littleton, K., N. Mercer, L. Dawes, R. Wegerif, D. Rowe, and C. Sams. 2005. "Talking and Thinking Together at Key Stage 1." *Early Years* 25 (2): 167–82.

Lyle, S. 2008. "Dialogic Teaching: Discussing Theoretical Contexts and Reviewing Evidence from Classroom Practice." *Language and Education* 22 (3): 222–40.

MacDonald, M. 2007. "Toward Formative Assessment: The Use of Pedagogical Documentation in Early Elementary Classrooms." *Early Childhood Research Quarterly* 22 (2): 232–42.

Malloch, S., and C. Trevarthen. 2009. "Musicality: Communicating the Vitality and Interest of Life." In *Communicative Musicality: Exploring the Basis of Human Companionship*, edited by S. Malloch and C. Trevarthen. Oxford: Oxford University Press.

Marsh, K. 2017. "Creating Bridges: Music, Play and Well-Being in the Lives of Refugee and Immigrant Children and Young People." *Music Education Research* 19 (1): 60–73.

McClelland, M. M., A. C. Acock, A. Piccinin, S. A. Rhea, and M. C. Stallings. 2013. "Relations between Preschool Attention Span-Persistence and Age 25 Educational Outcomes." *Early Childhood Research Quarterly* 28 (2): 314–24.

McClelland, M. M., and S. B. Wanless. 2012. "Growing Up with Assets and Risks: The Importance of Self-Regulation for Academic Achievement." *Research in Human Development* 9 (4): 278–97.

McNerney, K., and N. Hall. 2017. "Developing a Framework of Scientific Enquiry in Early Childhood: An Action Research Project to Support Staff Development and Improve Science Teaching." *Early Child Development and Care* 187 (2): 206–20.

Mistry, J., B. Rogoff, and H. Herman. 2001. "What Is the Meaning of Meaningful Purpose in Children's Remembering? Istomina Revisited." *Mind, Culture, and Activity* 8 (1): 28–41.

Nath, S., and D. Szücs. 2014. "Construction Play and Cognitive Skills Associated with the Development of Mathematical Abilities in 7-Year-Old Children." *Learning and Instruction* 32: 73–80.

Nicolopoulou, A., and H. Ilgaz. 2013. "What Do We Know about Pretend Play and Narrative Development? A Response to Lillard, Lerner, Hopkins, Dore, Smith, and Palmquist on 'The Impact of Pretend Play on Children's Development: A Review of the Evidence.'" *American Journal of Play* 6 (1): 55–81.

Nicolopoulou, A., K. S. Cortina, H. Ilgaz, C. B. Cates, and A. B. de Sá. 2015. "Using a Narrative- and Play-Based Activity to Promote Low-Income Preschoolers' Oral Language, Emergent Literacy, and Social Competence." *Early Childhood Research Quarterly* 31: 147–62.

Ornstein, P. A., J. K. Grammer, and J. L. Coffman. 2010. "Teachers' 'Mnemonic Style' and the Development of Skilled Memory." In *Metacognition, Strategy Use, and Instruction*, edited by H. S. Waters and W. Schneider. New York: Guilford Press.

Papandreou, M. 2014. "Communicating and Thinking through Drawing Activity in Early Childhood." *Journal of Research in Childhood Education* 28 (1): 85–100.

Papatheodorou, T., and J. R. Moyles, eds. 2008. *Learning Together in the Early Years: Exploring Relational Pedagogy*. New York: Routledge.

Pellegrini, A. D., K. Kato, P. Blatchford, and E. Baines. 2002. "A Short-Term Longitudinal Study of Children's Playground Games across the First Year of School: Implications for Social Competence and Adjustment to School." *American Educational Research Journal* 39 (4): 991–1015.

Pellis, S., and V. Pellis. 2009. *The Playful Brain: Venturing to the Limits of Neuroscience*. Oxford, UK: One World Publications.

Perry, N. E. 1998. "Young Children's Self-Regulated Learning and Contexts That Support It." *Journal of Educational Psychology* 90 (4): 715–29.

Perry, N. E. 2013. "Understanding Classroom Processes That Support Children's Self-Regulation of Learning." In *Self-Regulation and Dialogue in Primary Classrooms. British Journal of Educational Psychology Monograph Series II: Psychological Aspects of Education – Current Trends, No. 10*, edited by D. Whitebread, N. Mercer, C. Howe, and A. Tolmie, 45–67. Leicester: British Psychological Society.

Philippines, Department of Education. 2017. "Kindergarten Teacher's Guide." Manila.

Pickford, T., W. Garner, and E. Jackson. 2013. *Primary Humanities: Learning through Enquiry*. London: SAGE Publications Limited.

Pino-Pasternak, D., M. Basilio, and D. Whitebread. 2014. "Interventions and Classroom Contexts That Promote Self-Regulated Learning: Two Intervention Studies in United Kingdom Primary Classrooms." *Psykhe* 23 (2): 1–13.

Pino-Pasternak, D., D. Whitebread, and D. Neale. 2018. "The Role of Regulatory, Social, and Dialogic Dynamics on Young Children's Productive Collaboration in Group Problem Solving." *New Directions for Child and Adolescent Development* 162: 41–66.

Piper, B., Y. Sitabkhan, and E. Nderu. 2018. "Mathematics from the Beginning: Evaluating the Tayari Pre-Primary Program's Impact on Early Mathematic Skills." *Global Education Review* 5 (3): 57–81.

Platas, L. M. 2015. "The Mathematical Development Beliefs Survey: Validity and Reliability of a Measure of Preschool Teachers' Beliefs about the Learning and Teaching of Early Mathematics." *Journal of Early Childhood Research* 13 (3): 295–310.

Quinn, S., S. Donnelly, and E. Kidd. 2018. "The Relationship between Symbolic Play and Language Acquisition: A Meta-Analytic Review." *Developmental Review* 49: 121–35.

Ramani, G. B., and R. S. Siegler. 2008. "Promoting Broad and Stable Improvements in Low-Income Children's Numerical Knowledge through Playing Number Board Games." *Child Development* 79 (2): 375–94.

Rao, Z., and J. Gibson. 2019. "The Role of Pretend Play in Supporting Young Children's Emotional Development." In *SAGE Handbook of Developmental Psychology and Early Childhood Education*, edited by D. Whitebread, V. Grau, K. Kumpulainen, M. McClelland, N. Perry, and D. Pino-Pasternak, 63–79. London: SAGE.

Reese, E. 2015. "What Good Is a Picturebook? Developing Children's Oral Language and Literacy through Shared Picturebook Reading." In *Learning from Picturebooks*, 208–22. New York: Routledge.

Reeve, J., R. M. Ryan, E. L. Deci, and H. Jang. 2008. "Understanding and Promoting Autonomous Self-Regulation: A Self-Determination Theory Perspective." *Motivation and Self-Regulated Learning: Theory, Research, and Applications*, edited by D. Schunk and B. Zimmerman, 223–44. New York: Routledge.

Roskos, K., and J. Christie. 2011. "The Play-Literacy Nexus and the Importance of Evidence-Based Techniques in the Classroom." *American Journal of Play* 4 (2): 204–24.

Sandseter, E. B. H., and L. E. O. Kennair. 2011. "Children's Risky Play from an Evolutionary Perspective: The Anti-Phobic Effects of Thrilling Experiences." *Evolutionary Psychology* 9 (2): 257–84.

Sawyer, J. 2017. "I Think I Can: Preschoolers' Private Speech and Motivation in Playful versus Non-Playful Contexts." *Early Childhood Research Quarterly* 38: 84–96.

Siegler, R. S., and X. Lin. 2009. "Self-Explanations Promote Children's Learning." In *Metacognition, Strategy Use, and Instruction*, edited by H. S. Waters and W. Schneider, 85–113. New York: Guilford Press.

Siegler, R. S., and G. B. Ramani. 2008. "Playing Linear Numerical Board Games Promotes Low-Income Children's Numerical Development." *Developmental Science* 11 (5): 655–61.

Siraj-Blatchford, I. 2007. "Creativity, Communication and Collaboration: The Identification of Pedagogic Progression in Sustained Shared Thinking." *Asia-Pacific Journal of Research in Early Childhood Education* 15 (3): 3–23.

Solis, L., K. Khumalo, S. Nowack, E. Bythe-Davidson, and B. Mardell. 2019. "Towards a South African Pedagogy of Play: A Pedagogy of Play." Working Paper.

Suggate, S., E. Schaughency, H. McAnally, and E. Reese. 2018. "From Infancy to Adolescence: The Longitudinal Links between Vocabulary, Early Literacy Skills, Oral Narrative, and Reading Comprehension." *Cognitive Development* 47: 82–95.

Suggate, S. P., E. A. Schaughency, and E. Reese. 2012. "Children Learning to Read Later Catch Up to Children Reading Earlier." *Early Childhood Research Quarterly* 28 (1): 33–48.

Sylva, K., E. C. Melhuish, P. Sammons, I. Siraj-Blatchford, and B. Taggart. 2004. *The Effective Provision of Pre-School Education (EPPE) Project: Technical Paper 12—The Final Report: Effective Pre-School Education*. London: DfES / Institute of Education, University of London.

Tomasello, M., and M. J. Farrar. 1986. "Joint Attention and Early Language." *Child Development* 57 (6): 1454–63.

UNESCO (United Nations Educational, Scientific and Cultural Organization). 2015. *EFA Global Monitoring Report. Education for All 2000–2015: Achievements and Challenges.* Paris: UNESCO.

van der Sluis, S., P. F. de Jong, and A. van der Leij. 2007. "Executive Functioning in Children, and Its Relations with Reasoning, Reading, and Arithmetic." *Intelligence* 35 (5): 427–49.

Vygotsky, L. S. 1978. "The Role of Play in Development." In *Mind in Society: Development of Higher Psychological Processes*, edited by M. Cole, V. John-Steiner, S. Scribner, and E. Souberman, 99–104. Cambridge, MA: Harvard University Press.

Waite, S., ed. 2017. *Children Learning Outside the Classroom: From Birth to Eleven.* London: SAGE.

White, R. E., E. O. Prager, C. Schaefer, E. Kross, A. L. Duckworth, and S. M. Carlson. 2017. The 'Batman Effect': Improving Perseverance in Young Children." *Child Development* 88 (5): 1563–71.

Whitebread, D. 2014a. "The Importance of Self-Regulation for Learning from Birth." In *Characteristics of Effective Learning: Helping Young Children Become Learners for Life*, edited by H. Moylett, 15–35. Maidenhead: Open University Press.

Whitebread, D. 2014b. *The Power of Physical Play* (DVD and Notes). Siren Films, Newcastle-on-Tyne.

Whitebread, D. 2017. "Free Play and Children's Mental Health." *Lancet Child and Adolescent Health* 1 (November): 167–69.

Whitebread, D. 2020. "Influences on the Emergence and Development of Cognitive and Emotional Regulation in Early Childhood." In *Trends and Prospects in Metacognition Research across the Life Span–A Tribute to Anastasia Efklides*, edited by P. Metallidou and D. Moraitou. Dordrecht: Springer.

Whitebread, D., M. Basilio, M. Kuvalja, and M. Verma. 2012. *The Importance of Play: A Report on the Value of Children's Play with a Series of Policy Recommendations.* Brussels: Toy Industries of Europe.

Whitebread., D., M. Basilio, L. O'Sullivan, and A. Zachariou. 2019. "The Importance of Play, Oral Language and Self-Regulation in Children's Development and Learning: Implications for Quality in Early Childhood Education." In *SAGE Handbook of Developmental Psychology and Early Childhood Education*, edited by D. Whitebread, V. Grau, K. Kumpulainen, M. McClelland, N. Perry, and D. Pino-Pasternak. London: SAGE.

Whitebread, D., and P. Coltman. 2011. "Developing Young Children as Self-Regulated Learners. In *Beginning Teaching: Beginning Learning: In Early Years and Primary Education*, edited by J. Moyles, J. Georgeson, and J. Payler. Maidenhead: Open University Press.

Whitebread, D., M. Kuvalja, and A. O'Connor. 2015. *Quality in Early Childhood Education—An International Review and Guide for Policy Makers.* Report for the World Innovation Summit for Education. Doha: WISE.

Whitebread, D., D. Neale, H. Jensen, C. Liu, S. L. Solis, E. J. Hopkins, K. Hirsh-Pasek, and J. M. Zosh. 2017. "The Role of Play in Children's Development: A Review of the Evidence." The LEGO Foundation, Billund, Denmark.

Whitebread, D., and L. O'Sullivan. 2020. "Pretend Play in Young Children and the Emergence of Creativity." In *Mind Wandering and Creativity: Cognitive Processes and Creative Output,* edited by D. Preiss. D. Cosmelli, and J. C. Kaufman. San Diego, CA: Academic Press.

Whitebread, D., and S. Yesmin. 2021. "Factors Contributing to the Effectiveness of Preschool PlayLabs in Bangladesh, Tanzania and Uganda." Paper prepared for the European Early Childhood Educational Research (EECERA) Conference, Zagreb, August 29–September 21.

Wood, D., J. S. Bruner, and G. Ross. 1976. "The Role of Tutoring in Problem Solving." *Journal of Child Psychology and Psychiatry* 17 (2): 89–100.

Zosh, J. M., K. Hirsh-Pasek, E. J. Hopkins, H. Jensen. C. Liu, D. Neale, S. L. Solis, and D. Whitebread. 2018. "Accessing the Inaccessible: Redefining Play as a Spectrum." *Frontiers in Psychology* 9: 1124.

3

Building an Effective Early Childhood Education Workforce

OVERVIEW

A quality workforce that is motivated, engaged, equipped, and rewarded is critical for countries to provide quality early childhood education (ECE) to young children. The relationship between children and early childhood educators is central to how and what children learn. The quality of the ECE educator is one of the most important predictors of educationally rich classrooms and of overall ECE quality. Early childhood educators have a vital role to play in creating positive physical and psychological environments for learning; they can help shape children's educational outcomes and attitudes toward education through their skills and by motivating children. This chapter proposes four key strategies—attracting, preparing, supporting, and retaining—to build an effective and high-quality ECE workforce.

This chapter was written by Nirmala Rao, Emma Pearson, Benjamin Piper, and Carrie Lau.

A VALUED, TRAINED, AND SUPPORTED WORKFORCE IS KEY FOR ECE QUALITY

The unprecedented expansion of center-based ECE programs in low- and middle-income countries (LMICs) provides opportunities to prevent learning gaps that adversely influence children's school achievement. However, one concern associated with this rapid expansion is that there may be a corresponding decrease in the quality of services due in part to a shortage of qualified early childhood educators. (See box 3.1 for a definition of early childhood educators.) LMICs are starting to sharpen their focus on the quality of educators, carers, and instructors in ECE. But all too often educators are young, have no opportunities for training, and are poorly paid. Attracting, preparing, and supporting staff while enhancing the wider ECE system are critical to ensuring that increasing availability of places is matched with rising quality of education

Evidence across the globe suggests that educators who feel valued and supported—through pay, prestige, qualifications, and opportunities for professional development (PD)—tend to perform better and stay longer in the profession than those who do not feel valued. Figure 3.1 illustrates four principles and the broad strategies to attract, prepare, support, and retain ECE educators to enhance preprimary education settings. These four principles frame the rest of this chapter. The chapter also provides an example of how one country, China, has effectively enacted these principles in recent years (see annex 3A).

BOX 3.1

Definition of Early Childhood Educators

This book focuses on early childhood education (ECE), which can be delivered in a variety of different settings, is called different things in different countries, and can be implemented with varying degrees of formality. Accordingly, the workforce that delivers ECE varies highly across countries in many ways, including background, qualifications, function, title, and training. This chapter refers to early childhood educators, or ECE educators, acknowledging that in some countries they may be known as teachers, caregivers, assistants, or even volunteers. This chapter focuses on the workforce that delivers ECE in formalized settings across countries with the primary objective of supporting young children's development and preparation for primary school.

Figure 3.1 Four Strategies to Strengthen the ECE Workforce

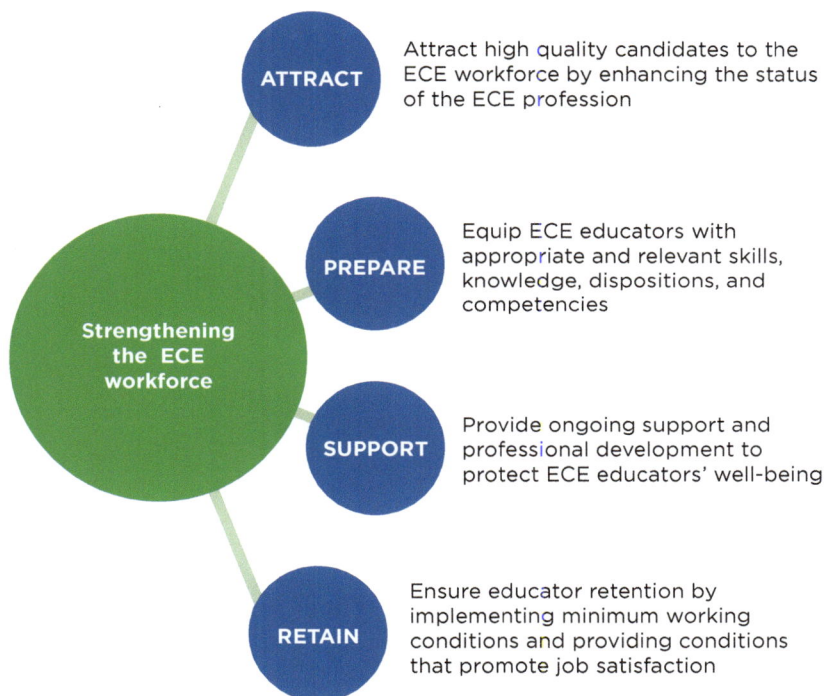

Attract high quality candidates to the ECE workforce by enhancing the status of the ECE profession

Equip ECE educators with appropriate and relevant skills, knowledge, dispositions, and competencies

Provide ongoing support and professional development to protect ECE educators' well-being

Ensure educator retention by implementing minimum working conditions and providing conditions that promote job satisfaction

Source: Original figure for this publication.
Note: ECE = early childhood education.

Successful attainment of these principles is dependent on broader implementation of systemic supports to underpin work across the four areas. These systemic supports should include a transparent system of award and remuneration opportunities; high-quality, relevant, and supportive incremental training and PD; and effective monitoring and evaluation of structural components of ECE that are fed back to, and support, the workforce for effective delivery of ECE. Although the principles outlined here may be equally applicable across ECE and other education sectors, there are important distinctions in the considerations listed within each principle. These distinctions reflect global consensus, embodied in the concept of "nurturing care" (Black et al. 2017), around the importance in ECE of holistic approaches that require close relationships with families and communities. They also reflect international agreement on the unique nature of curriculum focus, pedagogical approaches, physical environments for learning, and interactions between educators and children (Kaga, Bennett, and Moss 2010). Given these distinctions and the younger age of children served in early childhood classrooms, early childhood educators require dispositional attributes that enable them to deliver high-quality educational experiences to young children.

Why Is the Quality of the ECE Educator Important?

Teachers have a critical role to play in creating positive physical and psychological environments for learning. They can shape children's educational outcomes and attitudes toward education through their pedagogical skills and demeanor. The quality of the ECE educator is one of the most important predictors of educationally rich classroom interactions and thereby the quality of the program (Perlman et al. 2016; Slot, Lerkkanen, and Leseman 2015). Like members of any workforce, ECE educators can be vulnerable to stress, and relevant supports are required to ensure that they can respond appropriately to a range of challenges in providing a safe, nurturing environment for young children (Kinkead-Clark 2019). To be effective, ECE educators need to have a unique set of professional and pedagogical knowledge, skills, and dispositions that equip them with the motivation and drive to deliver high-quality educational experiences to young children. These attributes can be acquired through preservice training, in-service programs (for upgrading professional qualifications), or PD activities. A combination of all of these is widely acknowledged as preferable for establishing and maintaining high-quality teaching across both LMICs and high-income countries (HICs).

Key Takeaways

- Early childhood educators have a critical role to play in creating positive physical and psychological environments for learning. They can help shape children's educational outcomes and attitudes toward education through their skills and by motivating children.
- The quality and capacity of the ECE educator are among the most important predictors of educationally rich classrooms and of overall ECE quality.
- To be effective, ECE educators need to have a unique set of professional and pedagogical knowledge, skills, and dispositions that equip them with the motivation and drive to deliver high-quality educational experiences to young children.

ECE EDUCATORS IN LOW- AND MIDDLE-INCOME COUNTRIES FACE UNIQUE CHALLENGES

The principles outlined in this chapter apply equally to LMICs and HICs. However, there are some challenges that are unique to LMICs that should be considered in efforts to develop and sustain a thriving ECE workforce.

Diverse Roles and Qualifications, and Limited Professional Representation

In many countries, ECE educators are employed on an informal basis and tend to be younger than those in other, more formalized education sectors (OECD 2019a). They are less likely than primary or secondary school teachers to be members of trade unions or of professional groups.

Variations in regulatory structures mean that a wide range of professional entry requirements are in place. ECE educators may have no academic background or professional training in ECE, some noncredentialed informal training in ECE, a teaching certificate for ECE or a degree in a nonrelated field, a degree in ECE, or a non-ECE degree with a postgraduate diploma in ECE. Even where professional entry requirements do exist, training opportunities that match these requirements may not yet be available. In 2018, only 60 percent of ECE educators in low-income countries met the minimum academic qualification required to be employed as ECE educators, whereas 80 percent of primary school educators met the minimum required qualifications for employment (UNESCO UIS 2019). This situation is particularly evident in remote and rural areas, where large proportions of ECE educators are unlikely to have attained basic professional entry requirements (Neuman, Josephson, and Chua 2015).

Diverse and Challenging Working Conditions

Many ECE educators work with children in informal, unregulated settings. For example, ECE might refer to community-supported preschools that occupy temporary spaces or mobile programs that serve children in marginalized and geographically remote communities. Although such situations provide important spaces and opportunities for innovation, they also carry the risk of being poor working conditions for some ECE educators. Understanding the unique diversity of settings in LMICs is crucial for ensuring equitable systems that support a thriving workforce.

Where ECE educators have limited access to preparation or training, it is particularly important that they be provided with basic tools to support their practice, including clear, user-friendly curriculum guidelines and supporting materials. To provide high-quality ECE, early childhood educators need to have suitable physical environments for teaching, manageable class sizes, appropriate educational materials, and supportive families and communities, and need to operate within a child-friendly policy environment. However, analyses based on the World Bank's Systems Approach for Better Educational Results: Early Childhood Development (SABER-ECD; World Bank 2019) indicate that 8 out of 13 low-income countries do not have infrastructure standards for non-state preprimary institutions, and 6 out of 13 low-income countries do not have them for state-run facilities. Where regulations do exist, compliance with standards tends to be limited. Out of 37 LMICs that completed the SABER-ECD, only 11 reported compliance with the recommended 1:15 staff-to-child ratios (World Bank 2019). Suggested staff-to-child ratios do not seem to take into account differences in children's needs, such as differences in socioeconomic background (OECD 2019b). In most cases, staff-to-child ratios tend to be lower in urban than in rural areas. Relatedly, where the ratios are higher, there is a tendency for educators to be less qualified, indicating that the least qualified or prepared staff are dealing with more challenging working conditions.

Severe Shortage of ECE Educators in Rural Areas

Early childhood educators in rural areas, where children may be in particular need of high-quality ECE because of resource constraints at home, are in severely short supply. Although not the sole determinant, the shortage of early childhood educators in rural areas has exacerbated disparities between urban and rural areas in the quality of ECE programs (Sun, Rao, and Pearson 2015). In rural and remote areas, ECE educators' roles have traditionally been seen as caregivers or "substitute mothers" with no need for professional training. In rural areas, there are insufficient opportunities for initial and continuing PD to address this lack of qualifications. Furthermore, there are gaps in availability of suitably qualified personnel to monitor ECE quality or to make the kinds of mentoring and supervisory visits that are deemed important in low-resource settings where formal training opportunities may be limited (Neuman and Devercelli 2013). Teachers' lower qualifications can also contribute to retention issues, especially when combined with the lack of parity in pay and in conditions of service with primary school educators.

Regulations are fundamental to improving working conditions and quality; however, the challenges outlined above call for innovative thinking and a level of flexibility around workforce preparation. For example, focusing on in-service training opportunities may be more practical for educators working in remote or hard-to-reach locations.

Key Takeaways

- Increasing professionalization can boost the quality of ECE educators, overcoming the current challenges in many countries of high informality and low qualifications, status, and pay.
- Many ECE educators today are working in very challenging environments, which affects their own well-being and capacity to foster quality early learning.
- Many countries need to address a severe shortage of ECE educators in rural areas to raise overall standards.

FOUR PRINCIPLES FOR AN EFFECTIVE ECE WORKFORCE

The characteristics and behaviors of ECE educators strongly influence the quality of the program they serve and children's learning outcomes. Hence, much needs to be done to ensure that working conditions are attractive to individuals with the potential to contribute significantly to enhancing children's learning. Also crucial are opportunities for these educators to attend high-quality training so that they are well-prepared to undertake their duties and supported and encouraged to stay in the profession. These goals require a coherent preprimary education system that responds to diversities in context outlined in the previous section and that is underpinned by a strong vision supported by consistent and sustained political commitment. This chapter proposes principles that should be part of such a system in promoting an ECE teaching workforce with the skills, support, and motivation needed to deliver quality ECE for children ranging in age from three to six years.

Before the principles illustrated in figure 3.1 are presented, it should be noted that the quantity of the evidence base on the ECE workforce in LMICs is small. There is a dearth of rigorous, detailed, and contextualized research into the impact of ECE educator training on classroom quality, child outcomes, and educator retention. Bearing these caveats in mind, some of the recommendations that are advanced in this chapter are not buttressed by a robust evidence base specifically from LMICs but rely on studies conducted in HICs. The following principles draw from all available evidence from both HICs and LMICs.

Principle 1: Attracting ECE Educators to the Profession

Recruitment of high-quality, committed candidates with adequate qualifications and desired dispositions is clearly critical for developing a thriving workforce. Outlined below are evidence-based insights into conditions around recognition that both inhibit and support recruitment and retention of high-quality educators. Evidence from education systems that are recognized as among the global "top performers" indicates that well-established state support and consistent commitment (regardless of what political party is in power or of shifts in leadership) to a shared vision for education result in a range of benefits that contribute to a well-recognized, well-supported, high-quality workforce (Darling-Hammond et al. 2009). Consistent, sustained national leadership to achieve education goals that yields strong public support and strong systems of governance has been found in Finland, for example, to attract high-quality candidates and to be more effective than an orientation toward achieving immediate results through fragmented reforms that may disenfranchise educators (Ruiz 2011).

Compensation and Recognition

Globally there is a tendency for ECE to operate under relatively informal conditions in comparison with primary and secondary schooling, particularly where attendance is optional. In comparison with their counterparts in primary and secondary schooling, ECE educators are poorly compensated for their work, with SABER-ECD findings indicating parity between ECE and primary school educators in only 6 out of 37 surveyed LMICs (World Bank 2019). ECE educators are also more likely to be working in the private sector, where salaries tend to be lower and less consistent, than in public sector settings (Sun, Rao, and Pearson 2015).

In some LMICs, compensation for ECE educators is amorphous and relies partially or fully on nonfinancial rewards. It may consist of in-kind contributions provided by community members and can stretch to work on a voluntary basis (Neuman, Josephson, and Chua 2015). Because educators' feelings of being valued by society are linked to their salaries (OECD 2019b), it is not surprising that ECE educators earning less than their counterparts in other levels of education may feel undervalued. Low pay and disparities in compensation have implications for the employment and retention of high-quality ECE personnel, both of which are essential for stable environments for children's learning (Neuman, Josephson, and Chua 2015).

Although the complex and diverse settings and situations in which ECE educators work in LMICs require a level of flexibility to innovate, a foundation of minimum standards for compensation and recognition is required so that ECE educators feel valued. As highlighted above, strong systems of governance support high educational expectations and, in turn, a thriving, well-supported, and sustainable workforce.

Social Prestige and Job Satisfaction

There is typically a positive relationship between the social prestige accorded to a profession and working conditions within that profession. In comparison with educators working in primary and secondary schools, the ECE workforce tends to be viewed as less prestigious, given that the minimum qualifications for joining the ECE workforce are often lower and systems for regulation and compensation less well-established. This disparity is often reinforced by the idea that teaching young children is a lower-status occupation (Beteille and Evans 2019). Such assumptions should be challenged and addressed through policies and investments that emphasize the significance of the early childhood years and the skills required to deliver high-quality learning experiences for young children.

Evidence indicates that educators' feelings of personal reward and satisfaction are connected to compensation and social prestige, both of which in turn reflect strong systems of governance and a shared policy vision for education. Job satisfaction is also achieved through systems of support that enable ECE educators to provide high-quality experiences for young children through access to appropriate learning settings and materials, appropriate training and support, and ongoing PD opportunities (Totenhagen et al. 2016).

Key Takeaways

- Recruitment of high-quality, committed candidates with adequate qualifications and desired dispositions is essential to the development of a thriving workforce.
- Attracting ECE educators willing to learn and innovate should be a priority.
- A set of minimum standards for compensation and recognition is required so that ECE educators feel valued and committed.
- Well-established state support and consistent commitment to a shared vision for education contribute to a well-recognized, well-supported, high-quality ECE workforce.

Principle 2: Professional Preparation

ECE is different from other forms of educational provision in several ways, including its connection to communities and emphasis on relationships, focus on children and families, role in supporting transitions between informal early learning and formalized primary school environments, and diversity in curricula and pedagogical approaches. For this reason, although there are core features of quality teaching in ECE settings, contextualized and flexible approaches to training are important (Pearson et al. 2017). To ensure educators are adequately prepared to teach, the right qualifications and training must be provided, including preservice and in-service career development. Those qualifications and that training must be reinforced by professional standards and competency guidelines.

Flexibility and innovation can support and enhance quality early learning. However, these features must be underpinned by systems that outline accountability for and of ECE educators, including recognized competency guidelines or standards to inform professional accreditation and training. Some countries have established accreditation bodies that license ECE educators (for example, in Southeast Asia, the Early Childhood Development Agency in Singapore, the Professional Regulation Commission in the Philippines, and the Teachers Council in Thailand). Some countries also require ECE educators to pass a licensing examination (for example, Cambodia and the Philippines) and regular recertification (SEAMEO and UNESCO 2016). However, significant gaps in the availability of clear competency guidelines or standards for ECE educators remain in many LMICs (Neuman, Josephson, and Chua 2015).

When developing guidelines and systems, it is important to note that the evidence around educator preparation and quality is complex and equivocal. For example, there is growing awareness in HICs that attainment of an undergraduate degree may not in itself sufficiently equip an ECE educator to deliver high-quality educational experiences (Falenchuk et al. 2017). Evidence indicates that the quality and relevance of training are crucial to developing a high-quality ECE workforce, with opportunities for ongoing, workplace-focused PD delivering the most effective results (Darling-Hammond et al. 2009). This evidence supports innovative thinking around provision of training that is rigorous and high quality, yet responsive to context and supportive of the unique aspects of ECE practice, such as connecting to families and communities.

Content of Training

Certain effective pedagogical approaches, outlined further in chapter 2, are recommended for educators in formalized settings and may have relevance for ECE educator preparation. These approaches include identifying alternative pathways for students to learn content, focusing on stimulating thinking and learning, and professional responsibilities, such as communicating with families (Beteille and Evans 2019). However, ECE is distinct in many ways from more formalized primary and secondary schooling. ECE educator preparation should be oriented toward the following key considerations and outcomes:

- Adequate knowledge about the period of early childhood development, content, and pedagogical knowledge (Beteille and Evans 2019)
- Knowledge about play-based approaches and about how to adapt and develop curricula to suit local contexts (Pearson et al. 2017)
- Provision of significant practice time to more effectively implement higher-quality instructional routines (Pearson et al. 2017)
- The ability to accommodate individual learning trajectories

- Socioemotional skills, such as empathy for children and their families (Beteille and Evans 2019; Pearson et al. 2017)
- Creating a growth mindset in students (Beteille and Evans 2019)
- Effective communication and collaboration, problem solving, and reflective practice (Pearson et al. 2017)

The unique characteristics of ECE in LMICs also have implications for the kinds of skills that training should support and promote. These skills include knowledge and familiarity with relevant, localized ECE resources to support curricula; the ability to adapt curricula to contextual needs (for example, diverse linguistic needs); and the ability to connect with families and communities (Neuman, Josephson, and Chua 2015; Pearson et al. 2017; Sun, Rao, and Pearson 2015).

Provision of ECE Training

A key feature of successful training for ECE educators is the incorporation of hands-on, experiential learning in training programs (Pearson et al. 2017). Opportunities to practice so as to internalize principles and to connect what is being learned to their own experiences are important for effective learning among ECE educators (Piper, Mejia, and Betts 2020). Tailoring training to the ECE curriculum, where it exists, is another key requirement, particularly in contexts in which training may be limited, to ensure that any training that is provided focuses on essential skills to support quality learning (Pearson et al. 2017).

It is as important to address how educators learn as it is to make careful choices about what they learn. Because the global literature provides evidence that both preservice education and in-service PD are important, the following sections discuss both of these aspects, with specific reference to LMICs. Preservice education and preparation refers to the training that educators receive before they enter the workforce. Preservice training tends to constitute the dominant approach to preparation in contexts in which there are strict professional entry requirements. In-service training and development opportunities are provided to educators who are actively engaged in the workforce. Mounting evidence suggests that high-quality, workplace-focused, and ongoing PD opportunities can provide a powerful mechanism for strengthening educational workforces. Given the characteristics of ECE, this contemporary focus on in-service training enables the development of high-quality, flexible, and innovative systems of training and preparation for ECE educators.

Preservice training. Preservice training in many LMICs consists of short-term programs (commonly four to six weeks, but as little as a few days). However, very short preservice training is unlikely to provide sufficient skills to equip ECE educators with the confidence and competence to deliver sustained, quality ECE. Ensuring that ECE educators have access to opportunities for ongoing support to nurture appropriate and relevant skills, competencies, and dispositions is therefore critical. Further, a combination of pathways (for both preservice and in-service training) should be provided to ensure that educators have the knowledge, skills, and dispositions to work sensitively with young children, their families, and their communities.

In-service training and PD. Because of the contexts in which many ECE educators work, it has been suggested that in-service PD may be more important, or more appropriate, than preservice training (Neuman, Josephson, and Chua 2015). However, even though in-service training is available to educators in LMICs, duration and relevance vary greatly (Neuman, Josephson, and Chua 2015), underscoring the need to implement a range of certified and recognized pathways for training in ECE. To address this need, it is useful to look at some characteristics and examples of effective ECE in-service programs.

On the basis of a systematic review of PD programs for school educators in the United States, Darling-Hammond, Hyler, and Gardner (2017) distilled elements of effective PD programs, including a content focus, active learning, use of models and modeling, coaching and expert support, feedback and reflection, and sustained duration. Examples of specific relevance to LMICs include the Ghanaian National Nursery Teacher Training Centre's five-day in-service preprimary training, which was followed by two-day and one-day refresher courses at four- and eight-month intervals, respectively. The program offered experiential training and focused on helping educators provide age-appropriate and play-based approaches. Initial findings from a randomized comparison group evaluation indicated that even short periods of in-service training, followed up by refresher courses, could result in significant positive impacts on teaching and classroom quality, as well as child outcomes (Wolf et al. 2019). An evaluation study of a similar program oriented primarily to preservice training showed enhanced curriculum and child development knowledge, but reported little impact on actual teaching quality (Wolf 2018).

The Tayari preprimary program in Kenya supported teachers in more than 2,000 ECE centers and was eventually implemented in four counties. The in-service training was provided by county-level ECE officers with technical support from the Tayari team. Teachers were provided short-term in-service training in each of three terms, with more training time in the first term and less in the third term. The in-service training was connected to a robust coaching and instructional support program provided by government ECE officers. The Tayari external evaluation randomized controlled trial results showed more than 0.30 standard deviation effects in three treatment groups (Ngware et al. 2019), and another randomized controlled trial of Tayari showed similar impacts on school readiness

(Piper, Merseth, and Ngaruiya 2018). The Tayari intervention was unique in that the program showed that effective in-service training could be provided by government officers at large scale, and that the in-service training could be supplemented by consistent coaching and feedback provided by government ECE officers.

Modular approaches to training are offered in Chile and Jamaica (Neuman, Josephson, and Chua 2015). The Jamaican module consists of seven-day workshops over a seven-month period, with a focus on skills for classroom engagement, effective management, and socioemotional development. Evaluation studies found that children in participating educators' classes were rated as having more interest and enthusiasm than others whose educators did not participate. In Chile, 18 training sessions with bimonthly coaching led to significant improvements in outcomes and educator-child interactions, including emotional and instructional support and classroom organization. However, there were no reported significant impacts on children's language or literacy skills (Yoshikawa et al. 2015).

The consensus among experts on whether PD training should be centralized is that it depends on how well prepared government departments are to deliver quality training. When qualified trainers or training materials are in short supply, partnerships among government, nongovernmental, and other agencies working in the field are more likely to result in quality training (Pearson et al. 2017).

Key Takeaways

- To ensure that educators are adequately prepared to teach, they need appropriate preservice training and opportunities for in-service career development.
- Short preservice training alone is unlikely to provide sufficient skills to equip ECE educators with the confidence and competence to deliver sustained quality. Ensuring educators have access to opportunities for ongoing support to nurture appropriate and relevant skills, competencies, and dispositions through in-service training is critical to quality.

Principle 3: Supporting ECE Educators

ECE educators need training, but they also need ongoing support. Strategies for ongoing support and PD to protect ECE worker well-being are crucial for quality. Approaches to providing support include the following:

- Ensuring a culture of mentoring and support that is focused on enabling educators to enhance delivery (not punitive)
- Mentoring through communities of practice

- Supporting curriculum development with ongoing revision and updates to materials and ensuring that materials are widely circulated and applied
- Establishing regulatory frameworks for remuneration, working conditions, and workers' rights
- Establishing clear communication strategies (vertical and horizontal) across multiple relevant departments and sectors
- Building on and involving ECE networks that exist within the country in ECE workforce development initiatives
- Scheduling regular national and regional ECE network and organization activities

Professional Support

Professional support systems for teachers remain an underresearched and underconceptualized aspect of ECE educator development globally despite evidence that effective support systems are a key aspect of a thriving, high-quality workforce. For example, the Organisation for Co-operation and Development (OECD) Starting Strong Teaching and Learning International Survey (OECD 2019b) provides data from OECD countries regarding a range of factors that support or inhibit teacher well-being, and thus the quality of teaching and learning. Across several OECD countries, common stressors include a lack of resources and too many children in classrooms or playrooms. In some countries, administrative duties caused stress as well, but not in all. Preliminary evidence is emerging that similar sources of stress resulting in burnout may exist in LMICs (Lee and Wolf 2018). Emergent research from LMICs adds further insights that highlight the importance of support that is responsive to teachers' broader personal commitments and lives outside of school, as well as their professional needs (Schwartz et al. 2019). Supports for ECE educators can take various forms, from ongoing PD training to opportunities for informal professional gatherings to create a sense of belonging and peer support. Central to all successful support systems is a focus on valuing and supporting as opposed to creating a sense of surveillance.

Professional Development

Professional development (PD) refers to the availability of ongoing training and development opportunities for individuals that support them in advancing their practice and careers. Such opportunities may or may not be certified, but it is important that they be either (1) connected to recognized frameworks for enhanced professional recognition or remuneration or (2) responsive to specific professional practice needs, so that they are valued by teachers as having relevance to career development or for enhancing practice. Many ECE educators may not have access to high-quality preservice training experiences (Hamre, Partee, and Mulcahy 2017). Equitable provision of PD opportunities that are relevant across a range of contexts is therefore key to supporting a thriving workforce. Although evidence suggests that structured pedagogy programs have positive effects on children's literacy and mathematics (Beteille and Evans 2019), in many rural areas access to PD is sparse and requirements are weak (Neuman, Josephson, and Chua 2015; Yang and Rao 2020).

Several studies, conducted in both HICs and LMICs, indicate that supportive, responsive systems that value educator expertise and provide appropriate, relevant opportunities for expanding such expertise are likely to generate educator responsiveness to PD opportunities. Equipping educators with the mindset and opportunities for engaging in lifelong learning about how to help children develop appropriate knowledge, skills, and attitudes generates a positive response to PD opportunities (Beteille and Evans 2019; Schwartz et al. 2019).

Effective support with regard to content should be linked to identified educator needs and should enable educators to have a say in the type of learning they require (Darling-Hammond, Hyler, and Gardner 2017). The inclusion of model curricula and classroom materials is important, and regular evaluation of PD is also considered to be essential to inform ongoing improvements (Darling-Hammond, Hyler, and Gardner 2017).

Many ECE educators may not have access to the types of PD experiences that are likely to be effective (Hamre, Partee, and Mulcahy 2017). Therefore, it is important to identify and develop appropriate mechanisms for designing and implementing quality PD programs that successfully and positively change educators' teaching practices so that ECE quality can be enhanced. One such mechanism can be regular national and regional ECE network and organization activities that support the kinds of peer feedback and assistance that have been associated with effective mentoring and coaching, as outlined below.

Mentoring and Coaching

Several reports have emphasized the importance of following up short-term PD with onsite mentoring and supervision by trained personnel (Beteille and Evans 2019; Darling-Hammond, Hyler, and Gardner 2017). This onsite support is likely to be of particular importance in LMICs, where initial educator preparation is short term, with the implication that follow-up mentoring to support the sustained impact of such training is crucial (Pearson et al. 2017). Effective mentoring and supervision systems can also provide a crucial "feed forward" mechanism that identifies in-service training needs on the basis of direct engagement with frontline workers during observation visits and feedback sessions.

Yoshikawa et al. (2015) report on a successful coaching program for ECE educators in Chile, with coaching and didactic support through PD resulting in moderate to large impacts on emotional support, instructional support, and classroom organization. A key factor that contributed to the success associated with the program was reportedly collaboration between stakeholders at different levels, including educators, principals, and community leaders (Yoshikawa et al. 2015). Another successful example of positive outcomes associated with ongoing mentorship in an LMIC context is the Aga Khan Development Network's Madrasa Early Childhood Development program, in which ECE educators receive center- and field-based training followed by ongoing support provided by Madrasa Resource Centres. According to Rashid and Bartlett (2009), key features of the Madrasa programs are that educators are supported through ongoing, regular mentorship visits; education and training includes a strong focus on providing educators with skills in materials development, using locally available materials and resources; and the preschools are strongly supported by a local management committee that has well-established links with the community. Evaluation studies of this program indicate that specific aspects of the training that educators received as part of their enrollment in Madrasa Resource Centre programs (for example, training in the use of locally available, low-cost materials within a child-centered program) were related to positive outcomes for children (Malmberg, Mwaura, and Sylva 2011).

The Tayari intervention in Kenya used monthly classroom observation and support from a government ECE officer as a key part of the program. The support was scaffolded by a tablet-based coaching system that suggested areas of instructional feedback based on classroom observation results. The data from the coaching visits were included in a county-level dashboard with information about classroom quality and coaching performance. This coaching intervention was part of three different treatment groups, all of which showed meaningful and statistically significant impacts on school readiness at scale (Ngware et al. 2019; Piper, Merseth, and Ngaruiya 2018).

The importance of follow-up mentorship and support for ECE educators is also highlighted in the following expert consensus around characteristics of effective mentoring and supervision by Pearson et al. (2017):

- Observations of practice should be followed up by dialogue and reflection sessions.
- Training should be followed by on-site, ongoing mentoring and supervision.
- Supervisors should be properly trained, experienced, and able to deliver feedback in a nonthreatening manner.
- Systems of supervision and monitoring should include emphasis on self-monitoring (for example, via self-monitoring checklists and forms), and regular sharing sessions with peers should be scheduled.

Emotional Support and Educator Empowerment

The OECD Starting Strong Teaching and Learning International Survey (OECD 2019b) highlights complexities associated with providing effective, efficient supports for educators. Research on ECE educator attrition and take-up of PD opportunities in Ghana similarly highlights the importance of supports that are sensitive to educators' professional values and broader personal commitments (Schwartz et al. 2019). These findings suggest that genuinely supportive systems that result in enhanced teaching and learning are grounded in concerns around valuing teachers, recognizing their contributions to supporting early learning, and ensuring that educators have access to opportunities for enhancing their practice and careers. This support requires attention to multiple elements of "the system" for ensuring quality teaching that range from clear career pathways, to effective systems of mentoring and supervision, to teachers' access to appropriate teaching materials and resources as well as professional support networks.

Pedagogical and Center Leadership

Effective leadership of both pedagogical and administrative aspects of ECE centers is critically important. Consistent evidence across countries supports the notion that better management leads to better outcomes (Beteille and Evans 2019). Good management is key to the provision of good working conditions and opportunities for ongoing PD, which can result in attracting higher-quality educators and having lower turnover rates (Neuman, Josephson, and Chua 2015). However, leaders generally reported being stressed by having too much administrative work (OECD 2019a), implying that there may be insufficient time for them to lead in other aspects of ECE.

Rashid and Bartlett (2009), as cited in Sun, Rao, and Pearson (2015) describe Aga Khan community-based Madrasa preschools in Kenya, Uganda, and Zanzibar as having key features such as strong ongoing mentorship for teachers and both center and field-based training, fully supported by management committees that have strong links with the community. ECE leaders in OECD countries tend to have better qualifications than their frontline staff. In some OECD countries, center directors may have been trained in educational leadership but typically have not had specific leadership training in ECE. This gap points to the need for greater focus on providing ECE leaders across the world with appropriate training so that they can provide the pedagogical and administrative support ECE educators need to deliver quality early learning.

Key Takeaways

- Effective support systems are key to a thriving, high-quality workforce and should focus on *valuing* and *supporting*, not surveillance.
- ECE educators need ongoing support; low-cost communities of learning backed by coaching of educators can help raise quality.

Principle 4: Retaining Quality ECE Educators

Retention of ECE educators is notoriously difficult across almost all countries. Low status, compensation, and qualifications, combined with few opportunities for PD, jeopardize retention of quality educators, particularly in rural and hard-to-reach areas. This retention issue can be attributed to characteristics of the ECE workforce that are recognized globally, including the diverse range of settings in which they work, which results in a high degree of informality and fluidity around workforce regulation and monitoring.

In China, for example, ECE quality varies markedly across regions, and recruitment and retention of appropriately qualified educators in rural areas are particularly challenging (Sun, Rao, and Pearson 2015). A trend for Chinese preschool educators to move from private preschools to government-funded preschools is apparent because of the job security and benefits associated with government-funded jobs (Feng, Tian, and Jiang 2017). A corollary is that the early childhood workforce in private preschools in rural areas is particularly unstable. Further, more than one-third of preschool educators in rural areas in China do not have recognized professional teaching qualifications for ECE (China, MOE 2018b) and have limited opportunities for PD (Yang and Rao 2020). These examples highlight the fragile circumstances in which many ECE educators work. Establishing and maintaining attractive working conditions are critical for better workforce retention. Career progression and satisfaction coupled with better pay, recognition, and rewards also pay dividends. Establishing support systems and opening up opportunities for PD and mentoring can all contribute to better retention.

The recent global COVID-19 (coronavirus) pandemic has drawn further, stark attention to issues around this sector, which in many countries is heavily oriented toward private sector provision. Recent reports indicate that close to 85 percent of South African private preschool operators have been unable to pay educator salaries in the face of COVID-19 (Matlhape 2020).

Key Takeaways

- Retaining high-quality ECE educators is difficult because of common characteristics of the ECE workforce such as low status and compensation, few opportunities for PD, a high degree of informality, and fluidity around regulation and monitoring.
- Establishing and maintaining attractive working conditions are critical for better workforce retention. Career progression and satisfaction coupled with better pay, recognition, and rewards can help with the issue of retention.

- Establishing support systems and opening up opportunities for PD and mentoring can contribute to better retention.

Additional Opportunities for Enhancing the ECE Workforce

The current recognition of the importance of the early years for human and societal development affords opportunities, unparalleled in history, to build and retain an effective ECE workforce. The prioritization of ECE in national policies and the affordances of digital technology offer unique prospects for enhancing the ECE workforces in LMICs.

Countries Are Developing and Amending ECE Policy

The ILO Policy Guidelines for Decent Work for Early Childhood Education Personnel (International Labour Organization 2013) and the SABER-ECD (World Bank 2019) provide global guidelines and frameworks for the early childhood workforce, while the Southeast Asian Guidelines for Early Childhood Teacher Development and Management (SEAMEO and UNESCO 2016) provide regional guidelines. Increasing numbers of LMICs have developed policy and standards for ECE (Vargas-Barón 2015). For example, China released the National Plan for Medium- and Long-Term Education Reform and Development (2010–2020) that universalized pre-school education (China, State Council 2010a, 2010b). India released the National Early Childhood Care and Education Policy, a National Early Childhood Care and Education Curriculum Framework, and the Quality Standards for Early Childhood Care and Education (India, Ministry of Women and Child Development 2013a, 2013b, 2013c) in 2013 and more recently the National Educational Policy 2020, which includes early childhood care and education (India, Ministry of Human Resource Development 2020).

National ECE policies have often included an element of funding for professional preparation and development. However, systems that support education preparation need to be funded sustainably, ensuring that an ECE workforce is appropriately and effectively built over time (rather than via short-term gap filling). Donor agencies have also provided assistance for educator PD because it is seen as a good way to enhance the quality of ECE. Clearly, training provided by donor agencies needs to be aligned with or contribute to national systems for supporting the ECE workforce.

Digital Technology

Ongoing PD can be provided to ECE educators using the advantages of technology. Studies that have evaluated the effectiveness of technology-supported PD for primary and secondary school educators in LMICs have yielded mixed findings. In the Kenyan Tayari program, coaches were provided tablets for instructional support. Program participants showed improvements (Ngware et al. 2019; Piper, Merseth, and Ngaruiya 2018), but the research design precluded an estimate of the impact of the technology separate from the rest of the preprimary intervention. Understanding how and whether technology-enabled support for ECE educators is possible in other LMIC contexts remains an area for additional research. However, evidence on effective ways to harness the power of technology to support in-service ECE educators is still lacking.

GUIDANCE ON IMPLEMENTATION

This section focuses on providing policy makers with guidance on improving the quality of the ECE teacher workforce. Several action steps for policy makers to undertake are provided, along with suggestions on how, practically, these steps can happen.

Diagnose the ECE Situation in Context

Policy makers should diagnose the particular situation in their individual contexts. This diagnosis will help provide a starting point and a sequence for the interventions that are most likely to be effective. Consider the links to the principles described above. Of course, each country is different and the ECE structures that inform policies related to educator preparation and support vary.

- Countries with high enrollment in ECE should manage their educator preparation systems very differently from those with low enrollment. For example, a country with a gross enrollment ratio of 20 percent for preprimary education should have relatively limited qualification requirements because the short-term demand is for a rapid increase in educator availability. Plans should be in place to enhance those requirements over time and to help educators who enter with lower qualifications to upgrade. Countries with gross enrollment ratios of 80 percent or higher should focus more on increasing the requirements for educators, working alongside the treasury, to gradually but meaningfully increase compensation to make the ECE educator position more attractive.
- Countries with a low proportion of professionally trained ECE educators should operate differently from those with high levels of trained ECE educators. If very few educators are trained, the emphasis should be on integrating preservice ECE training with a robust in-service PD structure that can rapidly and effectively improve the skills of educators, ideally with a pathway to upgrading their formal, professional qualifications. These countries could also examine the balance of public versus private

providers of ECE training and focus on encouraging the expansion of private ECE training venues alongside public ones while ensuring quality at those private training sites. If, however, 80 percent of ECE educators are already trained, then the emphasis should primarily be on increasing the relevance and salience of the training itself such that the instructional value of the PD that educators enjoy is significantly higher.

- Policy makers should diagnose the status of their ECE structures using a variety of metrics. They need information on the duration of competing training programs, integration with in-service support structures, cooperation between the health and education sectors in ECE, and the viability of ECE teaching as a profession vis-à-vis the primary education workforce and other opportunities in the market.

Effective Planning for the Longer Term

Planning for improving the quality of the ECE workforce is essential. A low-income country recently announced that it would increase the required duration of professional training for ECE educators from one year to three years. This announcement was met initially with positive feedback externally, but some consternation internally when authorities realized that they had not planned for what would happen to the ECE workforce in the intervening two years. The resulting confusion negatively affected the country because of poor preparation. Mandating changes in the ECE workforce composition does have substantial fiscal impacts. Therefore, it is essential that a country carefully select among different strategies to enhance the quality of its ECE workforce. The strategy chosen must be logical, affordable, and effective in enhancing the quality of the ECE workforce. Ensure that plans include responses to the following issues:

- How many ECE educators are needed, given the changing enrollment rates and increased qualification expectations for the sector? Make sure to plan for both the curvilinear increase in educators required and the significantly increased funding needed for the salaries of ECE educators when their professional qualifications increase.
- How will planning be undertaken for the changes in ECE enrollment over time? If the country is in the midst of rapid expansion, how will that affect both enrollment rates at the macro level and the available seats and classrooms at the micro level? Is the push to increase ECE enrollment affecting children of different ages equally? For example, is the country focusing on increasing enrollment of all three-to-six-year-olds? Or is there an emphasis on enrolling children for one year before the start of formal primary school? Will the country focus on enhancing enrollment of all socioeconomic groups, or will there be income-based or geographical targeting to increase ECE enrollment?

- Many countries are responding to increased demand for ECE enrollment by building ECE classrooms next to schools. Should this be one classroom or more, and might there be consideration of using feeder ECE centers that are closer to where the children live? How do these enrollment rate increases change over time as they approach higher levels? Other contexts suggest that enrollment increases are not linear and that they plateau at certain percentages. Obviously, enrollment changes have financial implications. When enrollment increases, more ECE teachers are needed and they need to be paid. It is strongly recommended that class sizes not increase. Therefore, it is vital to plan for increased funding for ECE educator salaries when increases in ECE enrollment are expected.
- How should private and public ECE educator provision be managed? Many education management information systems do a better job of measuring the provision of ECE educator preparation in public colleges than in private ones or in the level of educator qualifications in the public sector compared with the private sector. Having accurate data from both groups is important, and the country should be realistic in planning when new public colleges can be built compared with planning for increased private provision. If private provision is an important contributor to the ECE workforce, as in Uganda, ECE planning should include regulation and supervision of these private providers. Indonesia, Singapore, the Philippines, and Thailand have all established accreditation bodies that could be seen as exemplars (SEAMEO and UNESCO 2016). Changes to the relative provision of ECE between private and public providers have implications for country budgets. Although increased private provision reduces the ability of a policy maker to manage all elements of ECE educator quality, it is one strategy for reducing the financial burden on the government when there is increased enrollment in ECE.

Coordinate and Integrate

ECE is, at its core, an integrated function. Policy makers should place a much heavier emphasis on coordination and integration in ECE. Some examples include the following:

- *Coordination with ministries of health and social services.* The design of ECE differs by country, but for many LMICs education and health overlap to some degree. Many ECE programs fail primarily because of weak integration of these sectors' priorities, funding, and support. This is of particular interest in contexts in which COVID-19 infection concerns should inform how coordination occurs between ministries, particularly because water, sanitation, and hygiene and referral pathways for health concerns are paramount. Effective policy makers considering ECE workforce development should include health and social services leadership and ideas in the design for ECE workforce development.

- *Coordination with ministry of education departments.* ECE is a subsector that is affected by the ECE directorate itself, the curriculum department or body, the teacher training department, and the materials management department if it is separate from the curriculum body. It is important that ECE policy makers understand the wide range of stakeholders that are required to be influenced if the ECE program is going to be effective. In many cases, these directorates or departments operate independently, and each of them influences how ECE workforce decisions are made.
- *Integration of primary educator curriculum.* Students who leave ECE and enter primary school often experience substantial shocks given the vast differences pedagogically and affectively between ECE and primary school. Effective ECE leaders will consider the integration of the ECE educator training curriculum and the primary educator training curriculum. And, in many cases, the primary educator curriculum could learn from the ECE educator curriculum.
- *Integration of preservice and in-service support.* ECE educator support structures require increased integration between preservice and in-service support. Many ECE systems are currently treating these two portions of ECE educator support separately, which reduces the effectiveness of both and, more important, makes it difficult for educators to actualize the skills acquired or reinforced in either. In some countries, including South Africa, certificate-level ECE training courses integrate initial educator training, induction processes, and continuing PD.
- *Integration of teacher service modalities.* How teachers are hired, managed, and paid often differs within a single country. For example, some ECE teachers are formally hired at the national or local levels. Other ECE teachers are hired by school boards, and still others with less formal training only receive a small stipend, and sometimes inconsistently. These service modalities differ based on the wealth and urbanicity of these locations, with more rural locations often having the less formal management structures. It is important for ECE systems to have reliable data on these ECE teacher arrangements, along with structures for supporting the less formal teacher relationships, so that reforms focused on improving outcomes include the wide range of teacher service arrangements common in LMICs.

Monitor and Evaluate

The principles described in this chapter are important guidelines for policy makers to use to monitor and evaluate their policy choices. Effective data management can help leaders determine where policy changes are stuck in implementation bottlenecks and how the overall system can improve on the basis of increased fidelity of implementation in particular areas. Overall, effective monitoring will help policy makers implement an effective ECE workforce strategy and allow for rapid adjustments to strategy and sequencing of particular policy options. Policy makers considering how to improve ECE educator provision and support should develop effective monitoring systems to manage this process with the following characteristics:

- *Teacher data.* A severe weakness in many systems is a lack of a robust ECE educator database that will allow the country's leaders to consider at the aggregate level how the ECE educator workforce matches the demand for educators. Even more important, data are required to understand how the workforce could be reorganized to reduce oversupply in some areas and manage gaps in others.
- *Student learning and educator skills.* The metric that matters most is student learning outcomes. The quality of a country's ECE educator workforce is best measured by the proportion of learners who are prepared for school. ECE educator development structures that have impressive data but little learning are ineffective, so knowing both how educators are being developed and what their impact is on learning is essential. An initial indicator of learning outcomes could be the skills that educators have and the pedagogical methods that they use, but both of these metrics are analytically complex.

Key Takeaways

- The country context—levels of enrollment, existing training and qualifications, and institutional capacity—will shape the policy approach to increasing workforce quality.
- Building a quality ECE workforce takes time; planning is critical to ensure sustained gains in workforce quality.
- Coordination and integration are vital to achieving wider gains; and monitoring and evaluation can help underpin success.

Quick Actions to Improve the ECE Workforce

This section focuses on practical steps that countries can take to maximize the quality of the ECE workforce. The suggestions below follow the four principles highlighted throughout the chapter and suggest quick actions that can be taken immediately.

Attract

To attract quality potential ECE educator candidates, countries should take several steps:

- Consider the career pathways for ECE educators. Even if the starting salary is low, educators will be more likely to be attracted to the profession if there is a clearly defined career educator ladder.
- Consider that the key behavior needed from educators is willingness to use engaging methods inherent to successful ECE implementation. Thus, it is crucial to focus on attracting engaged and active educators who will implement new methods and strategies. A full 56 percent of countries do not require postsecondary qualifications for ECE educators, so it is particularly important to attract motivated individuals to the profession (World Bank 2019).
- Communicate to candidates and the broader field of potential educators that the country is interested in a diverse ECE workforce. Given that the vast majority of ECE educators is female, countries can reduce gender inequity by actively using recruitment messages that indicate the country's interest in men, minorities, and other groups who are underrepresented in the ECE workforce.

Prepare

Several methods can be used for designing preservice programs that effectively develop the skills needed for a high-quality ECE workforce.

- Ensure that preservice programs for ECE educators include practicum activities. Even if the length or complexity of the technical components of the intervention must be reduced, it is essential that preservice preparatory programs include one or two rounds of practicum with supervision and feedback from program lecturers. During the practicum, trainees should co-teach with the classroom educator, thereby learning by doing. They also need to have significant opportunities to teach, totaling several weeks during each round. Performance on the practicum should be a substantial portion of the evaluation of preservice trainees, who should be evaluated using clear, behavior-based measurement of classroom pedagogy. The Ghana National Nursery Teacher Training Centre training program provides a set of experiential opportunities that have had an impact on behavior.
- Preservice programs should focus on creating opportunities for trainees to practice activities and skills after observing instructional modeling. When determining the amount of time that should be spent on lecture, discussion, modeling, and practice, programs should focus on increasing

instructional modeling from skilled ECE educators and on time for train-ees to practice those skills. Every idea or item of instructional content that ECE trainees are exposed to should be associated with time practic-ing those skills.

- The content of teacher preparation should be related to instructional realities at the intersection of the existing ECE curriculum, the materials available in the market, and the skills needed for educators to develop educator-made instructional materials. Classroom time should focus on practical opportunities for educator trainees to practice preparing lesson plans and instructional materials given the combination of curriculum, ready-made materials, and educator-made materials available to regular educators.

- The preservice structure should be designed to provide multiple path-ways to the teaching market. Kenya, for example, has several different certification pathways for ECE, including certificates, diplomas, and higher education. Kenya's ECE educators come from both public and pri-vate ECE colleges, providing flexible pathways for Kenya's workforce.

Support

Teachers are adult learners. Support structures targeted to ECE educators as adult learners who require a package of instructional support are essential to improving workforce quality. Countries that are serious about increasing the quality of their educators should undertake the following:

- Policy makers should find a way to staff a coaching instructional support system. ECE educators need regular classroom instructional feedback from others who know what quality teaching looks like. Evidence sug-gests that one coach tasked with supporting educators in 20 ECE centers would be able to provide instructional coaching on a consistent basis (Wilichowski and Popova 2021). That coaching should include classroom observations, instructional feedback, and ongoing support (Piper, Mejia, and Betts 2020). An educator can be upgraded to this position, or an external officer can be hired. Care should be given to select coaches who have the skills to provide instructional feedback to ECE teachers. In par-ticular, coaches should be selected on the basis of their merit and instruc-tional quality rather than seniority or other factors that do not directly relate to improved learning outcomes. These coaches need to be provided with scaffolded tools with which to identify instructional challenges and with support to ensure the feedback between coaches and educators focuses on key instructional behaviors. This system will pay for itself in improved learning outcomes. Chile, for example, uses an instructional support system to maximize educator improvement and improved learn-ing outcomes (Yoshikawa et al. 2015), as did the Aga Khan Foundation's

Madrasa program (Rashid and Bartlett 2009) and the Tayari ECE intervention in Kenya (Piper, Merseth, and Ngaruiya 2018).

- Low-cost communities of learning should be developed to supplement the coaching systems. Depending on the context and the size of ECE school clusters, communities of learning meetings should be held at the school level or the cluster level. Clusters are sets of geographically proximate schools. School-level communities of learning are easier to manage because there are no transport costs, but the training is less likely to be implemented at a high level of fidelity or quality, given the lower skill levels of the facilitator of the meetings at the school level. The cluster level is more likely to have higher-quality facilitators, but the distances that educators must travel will require reimbursement of transport costs or a change to the educators' terms of service to include travel to the meetings. In either case, these communities of learning should focus on reinforcing particular skills of educators. Careful thought should be given to allowing the communities of learning agenda to be educator created, capitalizing on the demand for PD. Structured topics to address specific instructional issues could also be developed, allowing for more detailed focus on what coaches identify as the weaknesses in classroom implementation. Recent evidence suggests that WhatsApp, Telegram, or other social media platforms might be able to buttress the ability of teachers to communicate with each other beyond the scheduled meetings.

Retain

A few key elements are fundamental to the retention of ECE educators.

- Countries should develop modest PD programs that tie successful engagement in short-term courses and attendance at communities of learning meetings to the educator career ladder. What educators need to do to be licensed and to keep that license should be very clear, and these PD activities should primarily be related to these requirements.
- Teacher career ladders should be planned for carefully, ensuring that countries can afford the salaries necessary for the higher levels of the ladder. These ladders should provide not only incentives for retention over time but also the PD engagement and other educator behaviors important to the profession's codes within the particular country to ensure teachers have a true pathway for career progression.
- Soft incentives are important to retention of ECE educators. Soft incentives include recognition in meetings, certificates, small low-cost rewards, and positive reinforcement in public. Countries with sufficient funding should consider increasing pay to ensure that educators are retained, but even these countries should make the profession more attractive by offering structured soft incentives.

Choosing among Quick Actions

This chapter provides a long list of potential actions that countries and leaders can take to improve the quality of the ECE workforce. The sequence of these actions depends on the realities of the context, and policy makers should not necessarily undertake these activities sequentially. Instead, policy makers should consider initially implementing a small set of essential activities to more rapidly capitalize on quick wins that can increase the viability of future actions. Two priorities could be selected initially to show that the system can be responsive to the needs of the ECE educator workforce; these priorities can provide the foundation for a broader ECE educator intervention package. The initial two priorities should be based on the results of the diagnostic analysis described at the beginning of this section.

CONCLUSION

A high-quality ECE workforce is essential to ensuring ECE quality. This chapter highlights the importance of attracting, preparing, supporting, and retaining suitable individuals as ECE educators. Table 3.1 provides more specific information on these four principles along with suggestions for implementing these principles. The chapter also emphasizes the importance of mandated, high-quality preservice training; opportunities for continuing PD; emotional support; and adequate compensation for a quality workforce. Policy makers are encouraged to undertake the evidence-based steps discussed in the "Quick Actions" section as soon as possible. These practical steps, which can be implemented right away, have the potential to generate substantial positive impacts on the quality of the ECE workforce and, in turn, young children's learning outcomes. However, a singular focus on the workforce is simply not sufficient to effectively promote development and learning in early childhood centers. A systems approach is essential in LMICs where standards for operation of early childhood programs are nonexistent, relatively low, or simply not implemented. Early childhood educators need to have suitable physical environments for teaching, manageable class sizes, appropriate educational materials, and supportive families and communities; and they need to operate within a child-friendly policy environment to ensure that they can provide nurturing care for all young children. Table 3.2 provides a review of the key takeaways in this chapter.

Table 3.1 Summary of Strategies for Building an Effective ECE Workforce

Principles	Principles for good practice	Considerations for ECE workforce in low-resource settings
Attract	• Enhance status of ECE and ECE workforce through public engagement and communication. • Emphasize recruitment of high-quality, committed candidates with appropriate entry requirements (including educational, experiential, and dispositional requirements).	• Identify strong leaders in the field to enhance status and attract candidates (also see chapter 5). • Develop entry requirements to suit specific needs and contexts (that is, skills in linguistic diversity or working in emergency situations may be required in some contexts and not others) and then update or revise entry requirements as workforce becomes increasingly skilled.
Prepare	• Implement a range of certified and recognized pathways for training in ECE. • Equip ECE educators with appropriate and relevant contextually responsive skills, knowledge, dispositions, and competencies for working specifically in community-oriented ECE settings.	• Ensure ECE training is adequate for delivery of ECE curriculum. Use hands-on approaches that provide opportunities for experiential learning. • Ensure widespread availability to educators through flexible modes of training and professional development that respond to unique needs (geographical access and transport; diverse training contexts, including ECE in hard-to-reach communities or emergency situations; linguistic diversity). • Ensure training includes content on inclusive practices that address unique diversity in LMIC contexts (that is, children in slum areas; children of migrant workers; children in remote, ethnically and linguistically diverse communities). • Emphasize dispositions and skills that enable ECE educators to cope and respond (creativity in developing materials; advocacy for ECE; building community and multisectoral partnerships). • Ensure that attendance at training is rewarded and recognized.

continued next page

Table 3.1 (*continued*)

Principles	Principles for good practice	Considerations for ECE workforce in low-resource settings
Support	Establish and maintain strategies for ongoing support and professional development to protect ECE worker well-being: • Coaching and instructional support • Mentoring through communities of practice • Regular national and regional ECE network and organization activities • Regulatory frameworks for remuneration, working conditions, and workers' rights	• Support curriculum development with ongoing revision and updates to materials. Ensure that materials are widely circulated and applied. • Build on and involve ECE networks that exist within the country in ECE workforce development initiatives. • Ensure a culture of mentoring and support that is focused on supporting educators to enhance delivery (not punitive). • Establish clear communication strategies (vertical and horizontal) across multiple relevant departments and sectors.
Retain	Establish and maintain attractive working conditions: • Teacher-student ratios • Classroom facilities • Career progression and satisfaction • Remuneration	• Provide ongoing contextualized, intensive training rather than generalized, theoretical training that may be ineffective for focused preparation, through which educators can see the positive impact of their practice on children. • Establish strong working teams at the district and local level to provide coaching and mentoring for ECE educators that signal value attached to their role and impact. • Establish and implement clear, transparent reward mechanisms that recognize ongoing training and career progression.

Source: Original table for this publication.
Note: ECE = early childhood education; LMIC = low- and middle-income country.

Table 3.2 Chapter 3: Summary of Key Takeaways

A valued, trained, and supported workforce is key for ECE quality

- Early childhood educators have a critical role to play in creating positive physical and psychological environments for learning. They can help shape children's educational outcomes and attitudes toward education through their skills and by motivating children.
- The quality and capacity of the ECE educator are among the most important predictors of educationally rich classrooms and of overall ECE quality.
- To be effective, ECE educators need to have a unique set of professional and pedagogical knowledge, skills, and dispositions that equip them with the motivation and drive to deliver high-quality educational experiences to young children.

ECE educators in low- and middle-income countries face unique challenges

- Increasing professionalization can boost the quality of ECE educators, overcoming the current challenges in many countries of high informality and low qualifications, status, and pay.
- Many ECE educators today are working in very challenging environments, which affects their own well-being and capacity to foster quality early learning.
- Many countries need to address a severe shortage of ECE educators in rural areas to raise overall standards.

Principle 1: Attracting ECE educators to the profession

- Recruitment of high-quality, committed candidates with adequate qualifications and desired dispositions is essential to the development of a thriving workforce.
- Attracting ECE educators willing to learn and innovate should be a priority.
- A set of minimum standards for compensation and recognition is required so that ECE educators feel valued and committed.
- Well-established state support and consistent commitment to a shared vision for education contribute to a well-recognized, well-supported, and high-quality ECE workforce.

Principle 2: Professional preparation

- To ensure that educators are adequately prepared to teach, they need appropriate preservice training and opportunities for in-service career development.
- Short preservice training alone is unlikely to provide sufficient skills to equip ECE educators with the confidence and competence to deliver sustained quality. Ensuring educators have access to opportunities for ongoing support to nurture appropriate and relevant skills, competencies, and dispositions through in-service training is critical to quality.

Principle 3: Supporting ECE educators

- Effective support systems are key to a thriving, high-quality workforce and should focus on valuing and supporting, not surveillance.
- ECE educators need ongoing support; low-cost communities of learning backed by coaching of educators can help raise quality.

continued next page

Table 3.2 (*continued*)

Principle 4: Retaining quality ECE educators

- Retaining high-quality ECE educators is difficult because of common characteristics of the ECE workforce such as low status and compensation, few opportunities for PD, a high degree of informality, and fluidity around regulation and monitoring.
- Establishing and maintaining attractive working conditions is critical for better workforce retention. Career progression and satisfaction coupled with better pay, recognition, and rewards can help with the issue of retention.
- Establishing support systems and opening up opportunities for PD and mentoring can contribute to better retention.

Guidance on Implementation

- *Diagnose the ECE situation in context.* The country context—levels of enrollment, existing training and qualifications, and institutional capacity— will shape the policy approach to increasing workforce quality.
- *Effective planning for the longer term.* Building a quality ECE workforce takes time; planning is critical to ensure sustained gains in workforce quality.
- *Coordinate and integrate.* Coordination and integration are vital to achieving wider gains, and monitoring and evaluation can help underpin success.

Source: Original table for this publication.
Note: ECE = early childhood education; PD = professional development.

ANNEX 3A: ATTRACTING, PREPARING, SUPPORTING, AND RETAINING ECE EDUCATORS IN CHINA

Table 3A.1   Attracting, Preparing, Supporting, and Retaining ECE Educators in China

Principles	Examples of good practices in China
Attract	• Under the *Teacher's Law* (National People's Congress, 1993), ECE educators are required to have completed a postsecondary ECE training program at an accredited tertiary institution. • In 2012, the Ministry of Education (MOE) issued the "Professional Standards for Preschool Teachers (Trial Version)" (China, MOE 2012a) to establish professional and competency standards for ECE educators. • To ensure ECE educators' job security and social benefits, more quotas of formally established posts (*bianzhi*) and professional titles (*zhicheng*) have been allocated, especially in remote rural areas (China, MOE 2017b; China, State Council 2010c). For example, in Zhejiang province, it is explicitly stated that at least one ECE educator must hold a *bianzhi* in each preschool classroom in remote rural areas (China, MOE 2019b).

continued next page

Table 3A.1 (*continued*)

Principles	Examples of good practices in China
Attract	• To attract educators (in ECE and in primary and secondary school education) to work in underdeveloped areas, the Free Teacher Education Program (FTEP) provides monetary incentives for undergraduate studies. In turn, teachers graduating from the FTEP are required to work in their hometown for six years, with at least one year in rural areas. The FTEP also supports teachers' pursuit of a part-time master's degree after they have worked for one year upon graduation (China, State Council 2018).

Prepare	• The MOE encourages tertiary institutions to establish five-year associate degree programs to increase the number of places in preservice teacher preparation programs (China, State Council 2010c).
	• Stringent program standards and quality assurance mechanisms are in place to regularly monitor the quality of preservice teacher education programs in tertiary institutions (China, MOE 2016b, 2018a). The standards address (1) program and course objectives, (2) graduation requirements, (3) coursework content and teaching, (4) community engagement and practicum experience, (5) background and qualifications of course instructors, (6) facilities and resources, (7) quality assurance self-monitoring, and (8) student career development. The quality of preservice teacher education programs is rated on the basis of the eight standards and is categorized as Level 1 (minimum requirement), Level 2 (good quality), and Level 3 (extraordinary). The validity period is six years.
	• The training in preservice teacher education programs emphasizes hands-on approaches and practices:
	  – The teaching content includes examples of good practices from preschools (China, MOE 2017b).
	  – Practicum experiences with professional support are provided, including (1) requirement for at least one semester of practicum (18 weeks); (2) dual-mentor approach in professional support (supervision by instructor from the preservice teacher education program and cooperating teacher from the practicum site); (3) different modalities of practicum, for example, micro-teaching, observation, and student teaching in practicum sites; and (4) long-term school-university partnership (China, MOE 2016b, 2017b).

continued next page

Table 3A.1 (*continued*)

Principles	Examples of good practices in China
Support	• Since 2010, the National Teacher Training Program (NTTP) has been providing continuous professional development in underdeveloped and remote rural areas. The NTTP provides different modalities and approaches to training, for example, short-term intensive face-to-face training (workshops, seminars, field practice, observation) and online learning (China, MOE 2011a). NTTP providers are obligated to evaluate and monitor the quality of the delivery of professional development training under the supervision of local governments (China, MOE 2019a). In 2020, the MOE issued 11 guidelines to regulate the quality of the NTTP, with differentiated targets for novice teachers, master teachers, rural teachers, principals, and teacher educators (China, MOE 2020). • The MOE requires preschools to invest 5 percent of their annual expenditure in supporting teacher professional development to ensure that each teacher spends at least 360 hours on professional development activities in a five-year cycle (China, MOE 2012b). • Novice teachers are required to receive 120 hours of induction and mentoring (China, MOE 2011b). For example, in Shanghai, all novice teachers receive one year of standardized community-based induction and mentoring organized by the Education Bureaus at the district level. The Education Bureau specifies clear and established mentoring protocols, and requires the process of induction to be documented in the novice teacher induction manual (Shanghai Municipal Education Commission 2012).
Retain	• Professional development communities are formed at the regional level, wherein high-quality preschools provide professional development and curriculum support to other preschools within the same district. In rural areas, central township preschools take on the responsibility for supporting teacher professional development in village preschools within the same administrative region (China, MOE 2017a). • Preschools are required to meet national standards for working conditions and regulations on class size, teacher-child ratio, classroom facilities, and teaching materials (China, MOE 2016a). • The MOE has increased remuneration and subsidies for ECE educators in remote rural areas (for example, pay for teachers without *bianzhi* is equal to pay for those with *bianzhi*; housing is provided) (China, MOE 2015).

continued next page

Table 3A.1 (*continued*)

Principles	Examples of good practices in China
Retain	The provision of professional titles (*zhicheng*) is prioritized for teachers with *bianzhi*, providing a career progression for teachers. However, in some provinces, such as Shandong and Guangdong (for example, Shenzhen), all eligible teachers, including those who work in the private sector without *bianzhi*, are equally awarded professional titles (Shandong Province Education Department 2019; Shenzhen Education Bureau of Bao'an District 2019).

Sources: China, MOE 2011a, 2011b, 2012a, 2012b, 2015, 2016a, 2016b, 2017a, 2017b, 2018a, 2018b, 2019a, 2019b, 2020; China, State Council 2010c, 2018; Shandong Province Education Department 2019; Shanghai Municipal Education Commission 2012; Shenzhen Education Bureau of Bao'an District 2019.
Note: ECE = early childhood education.

REFERENCES

Beteille, T., and D. K. Evans. 2019. "Successful Teachers, Successful Students: Recruiting and Supporting Society's Most Crucial Profession." World Bank Policy Approach to Teachers. World Bank, Washington, DC. http://documents .worldbank.org/curated/en/235831548858735497/Successful-Teachers -Successful-Students-Recruiting-and-Supporting-Society-s-Most-Crucial -Profession.pdf.

Black, M. M., S. P. Walker, L. C. H. Fernald, C. T. Andersen, A. M. DiGirolamo, C. Lu, D. C. McCoy, et al. 2017. "Early Childhood Development Coming of Age: Science through the Life Course." *Lancet* 389 (10064): 77–90. https://doi .org/10.1016/S0140-6736(16)31389-7.

China, MOE (Ministry of Education of the People's Republic of China). 2011a. "Circular on the Implementation of National Teacher Training Programs for Preschool Teachers" (in Chinese). http://www.moe.gov.cn/srcsite/A10 /s7058/201109/t20110905_146630.html.

China, MOE (Ministry of Education of the People's Republic of China). 2011b. "Suggestions on Strengthening the Teacher Training for Primary and Secondary School Teachers" (in Chinese). http://www.gov.cn/gongbao/content/2011 /content_1907089.htm.

China, MOE (Ministry of Education of the People's Republic of China). 2012a. "The Issuance of Professional Standards of Kindergarten Teachers (Trial Version), Professional Standards of Primary School Teachers (Trial Version), and Professional Standards of Secondary School Teachers (Trial Version)" (in Chinese). http://old.moe.gov.cn//publicfiles/business/htmlfiles/moe/s7232 /201212/xxgk_145603.html.

China, MOE (Ministry of Education of the People's Republic of China). 2012b. "Suggestions on Reinforcing the ECE Workforce" (in Chinese). http://www .gov.cn/zwgk/2012-09/07/content_2218778.htm.

China, MOE (Ministry of Education of the People's Republic of China). 2015. "Circular on the Implementation of Rural Teacher Supporting Program" (in Chinese). http://www.moe.gov.cn/jyb_xxgk/moe_1777/moe_1778/201506 /t20150612_190354.html.

China, MOE (Ministry of Education of the People's Republic of China). 2016a. "Preschool Working Regulation" (in Chinese). http://www.moe.gov.cn/srcsite /A02/s5911/moe_621/201602/t20160229_231184.html.

China, MOE (Ministry of Education of the People's Republic of China). 2016b. "Strengthen Pre-service Teacher Educational Practicum" (in Chinese). http:// www.moe.gov.cn/srcsite/A10/s7011/201604/t20160407_237042.html.

China, MOE (Ministry of Education of the People's Republic of China). 2017a. "Suggestions on the Implementation of the Third Round of Three-Year Action Plans of Early Childhood Education 2017–2020" (in Chinese). http://www .moe.gov.cn/srcsite/A06/s3327/201705/t20170502_303514.html.

China, MOE (Ministry of Education of the People's Republic of China). 2017b. "Circular on the Implementation of Quality Standards of Pre-Service ECE Teacher Preparation Program (Trial)" (in Chinese). http://www.moe.gov.cn /srcsite/A10/s7011/201711/t20171106_318535.html.

China, MOE (Ministry of Education of the People's Republic of China). 2018a. "Revitalization of Teacher Education from 2018 to 2022." http://www.moe .gov.cn/srcsite/A10/s7034/201803/t20180323_331063.html.

China, MOE (Ministry of Education of the People's Republic of China). 2018b. 2017 年全国教育事业发展统计公报 (China Education Statistics Year Book of 2017). http://www.moe.gov.cn/jyb_sjzl/sjzl_fztjgb/201807/t20180719_343508.html.

China, MOE (Ministry of Education of the People's Republic of China). 2019a. "Circular on the Implementation of National Teacher Training Program for Preschool, Primary, and Secondary School Teachers in 2019" (in Chinese). http://www.moe.gov.cn/srcsite/A10/s7034/201903/t20190315_373529.html.

China, MOE (Ministry of Education of the People's Republic of China). 2019b. "The Response to the No.3836 Proposal in The Second Session of the 13th National People's Congress" (in Chinese). http://www.moe.gov.cn/jyb_xxgk/xxgk_jyta /jyta_jijiaosi/201912/t20191204_410821.html.

China, MOE (Ministry of Education of the People's Republic of China). 2020. "Circular on the Issuance of 11 Documents of Teacher Training" (in Chinese). http://www.moe.gov.cn/s78/A10/A10_gggs/A10_sjhj/202003 /t20200330_436306.html.

China, State Council (State Council of the People's Republic of China). 2010a. 国家 中长期教育改革和发展规划纲要 (Outline of the National Plan for Medium- and Long-Term Education Reform and Development (2010–2020)) (in Chinese). http:// www.gov.cn/jrzg/2010-07/29/content_1667143.htm.

China, State Council (State Council of the People's Republic of China.) 2010b. 当前 发展学前教育的若干意见 (State Council's Suggestions on the Current Development of Early Childhood Education) (In Chinese). http://www.gov.cn/zwgk/2010-11/24 /content_1752377.htm.

China, State Council (State Council of the People's Republic of China). 2010c. "Suggestions on Current Development of Preschool Education" (in Chinese). http://www.gov.cn/zwgk/2010-11/24/content_1752377.htm.

China, State Council (State Council of the People's Republic of China). 2018. "Upgrading the Free Teacher Education Program" (in Chinese). http://www.gov.cn/zhengce/content/2018-08/10/content_5313008.htm.

Darling-Hammond, L., M. E. Hyler, and M. Gardner. 2017. *Effective Teacher Professional Development*. Palo Alto, CA: Learning Policy Institute.

Darling-Hammond, L., R. C. Wei, A. Andree, N. Richardson, and S. Orphanos. 2009. *Professional Learning in the Learning Profession: A Status Report on Teacher Development in the United States and Abroad*. Palo Alto, CA: School Redesign Network at Stanford University.

Falenchuk, O., M. Perlman, E. McMullen, B. Fletcher, and P. S. Shah. 2017. "Education of Staff in Preschool Aged Classrooms in Child Care Centers and Child Outcomes: A Meta-Analysis and Systematic Review." *PLOS ONE* 12 (8): e0183673.

Feng, W., P. Tian, and H. Jiang. 2017. 区域幼儿园教师队伍配置进展与优化路径研究- 基于北京市2010-2015年的实证分析 ("Research on the Progress and Optimization Paths of District-Based Allocation of Kindergarten Teachers— Based on the Empirical Analysis of Beijing from 2010 to 2015"). *Teacher Education Research* 29 (3): 39–45.

Hamre, B. K., A. Partee, and C. Mulcahy. 2017. "Enhancing the Impact of Professional Development in the Context of Preschool Expansion." *AERA Open* 3 (4). https://doi.org/10.1177/2332858417733636.

India, Ministry of Human Resource Development. 2020. "National Educational Policy 2020." Ministry of Human Resource Development, New Delhi. https://www.education.gov.in/sites/upload_files/mhrd/files/NEP_Final_English_0.pdf.

India, Ministry of Women and Child Development. 2013a. "National Early Childhood Care and Education (ECCE) Curriculum Framework." Ministry of Women and Child Development, New Delhi. https://wcd.nic.in/sites/default/files/national_ecce_curr_framework_final_03022014%20%282%29.pdf.

India, Ministry of Women and Child Development. 2013b. "National Early Childhood Care and Education (ECCE) Policy." Ministry of Women and Child Development, New Delhi. https://wcd.nic.in/sites/default/files/National%20Early%20Childhood%20Care%20and%20Education-Resolution.pdf.

India, Ministry of Women and Child Development. 2013c. "Quality Standards for Early Childhood Care and Education (ECCE)." Ministry of Women and Child Development, New Delhi. http://www.nipccd-earchive.wcd.nic.in/sites/default/files/PDF/Quality%20Standards%20for%20ECCE.pdf.

International Labour Organization. 2013. "ILO Policy Guidelines on the Promotion of Decent Work for Early Childhood Education Personnel." International Labour Office, Sectoral Activities Department, Geneva.

Kaga, Y., J. Bennett, and P. Moss. 2010. *Caring and Learning Together: A Cross-National Study on the Integration of Early Childhood Care and Education within Education*. Paris: United Nations Educational, Scientific and Cultural Organization.

https://bangkok.unesco.org/content/caring-and-learning-together
-cross-national-study-integration-early-childhood-care-and.

Kinkead-Clark, Z. 2019. "Using Temperament-Based Approaches to Negotiate the Terrains of Crisis in Jamaican Early Childhood Classrooms." *Journal of Early Childhood Teacher Education* 41 (3): 209–22. https://doi.org/10.1080/10901027 .2019.1609142.

Lee, S. S., and S. Wolf. 2018. "Measuring and Predicting Burnout among Early Childhood Educators in Ghana." *Teaching and Teacher Education* 78: 49–61. https://doi.org/10.1016/j.tate.2018.10.021.

Matlhape, G. 2020. "The Early Childhood Workforce in Times of COVID-19— Are They Adequately Supported?" Webinar, Early Childhood Workforce Initiative. https://www.earlychildhoodworkforce.org/content/early-childhood -workforce-times-covid-19-are-they-adequately-supported.

Malmberg, L.-E., P. Mwaura, and K. Sylva. 2011. "Effects of a Pre-School Intervention on Cognitive Development among East-African Pre-School Children: A Flexibly Time-Coded Growth Model." *Early Childhood Research Quarterly* 26 (1): 124–33. https://doi.org/10.1016/j.ecresq.2010.04.003.

Neuman, M. J., and A. E. Devercelli. 2013. "What Matters Most for Early Childhood Development: A Framework Paper." Systems Approach for Better Education Results (SABER) Working Paper 5, World Bank, Washington, DC.

Neuman, M. J., K. Josephson, and P. G. Chua. 2015. "A Review of the Literature: Early Childhood Care and Education (ECCE) Personnel in Low- and Middle-Income Countries." Early Childhood Care and Education Working Paper 4, United Nations Educational, Scientific and Cultural Organization, Paris.

Ngware, M., N. Hungi, P. Wekulo, M. Mutisya, C. Faye, J. Njagi, N. Muhia, E. Wambiya, H. Donfouet, and C. Oduor. 2019. *Impact Evaluation of Tayari School Readiness Program in Kenya*. Nairobi: African Population and Health Research Centre. https://aphrc.org/wp-content/uploads/2019/07/Kenya_ECDE_ImpactEvalution _TayariFINAL_20022019.pdf.

OECD (Organisation for Economic Co-operation and Development). 2019a. *Education at a Glance 2019: OECD Indicators*. Paris: OECD Publishing. https://doi.org/10.1787/f8d7880d-en.

OECD (Organisation for Economic Co-operation and Development). 2019b. *Providing Quality Early Childhood Education and Care: Results from the Starting Strong Survey 2018*. Paris: OECD Publishing. https://doi.org/10.1787/301005d1-en.

Pearson, E., H. Hendry, N. Rao, F. Aboud, C. Horton, I. Siraj, A. Raikes, and J. Miyahara. 2017. "Reaching Expert Consensus on Training Different Cadres in Delivering Early Childhood Development at Scale in Low-Resource Contexts." UK Government Department for International Development, London. https:// www.gov.uk/dfid-research-outputs/reaching-expert-consensus-on-training -different-cadres-in-delivering-early-childhood-development.

Perlman, M., O. Falenchuk, B. Fletcher, E. McMullen, J. Beyene, and P. S. Shah. 2016. "A Systematic Review and Meta-Analysis of a Measure of Staff/Child Interaction Quality (the Classroom Assessment Scoring System) in Early Childhood Education and Care Settings and Child Outcomes." *PLOS ONE* 11 (12): e0167660.

Piper, B., J. Mejia, and K. Betts. 2020. *Teacher Support Guidelines for Coaching and Communities of Practice.* Research Triangle Park, NC: RTI International.

Piper, B., K. Merseth, and S. Ngaruiya. 2018. "Scaling Up Early Childhood Development and Education in a Devolved Setting: Policy Making, Resource Allocations, and Impacts of the Tayari School Readiness Program in Kenya." *Global Education Review* 5 (2): 47–68. http://ger.mercy.edu/index.php/ger /article/view/397.

Rashid, N., and K. Bartlett. 2009. "Training Professionals for Quality ECCD Practice: Lessons from the Madrasa Programme and AKF." Conference presentation at the First Technical Workshop of the Africa Early Childhood Care and Development Initiative, Zanzibar, October 25.

Ruiz, M. J. G. 2011. "OECD, PISA and Finnish and Spanish Comprehensive School." *Procedia—Social and Behavioral Sciences* 15: 2858–63. https://doi.org/10.1016/j .sbspro.2011.04.203.

Schwartz, K., E. Cappella, J. L. Aber, M. A. Scott, S. Wolf, and J. R. Behrman. 2019. "Early Childhood Teachers' Lives in Context: Implications for Professional Development in Under-Resourced Areas." *American Journal of Community Psychology* 63 (3–4): 270–85. https://doi.org/10.1002/ajcp.12325.

SEAMEO (Southeast Asia Ministers of Education Organization) and UNESCO (United Nations Educational, Scientific and Cultural Organization). 2016. *Southeast Asian Guidelines for Early Childhood Teacher Development and Management.* Bangkok: SEAMEO; UNESCO Bangkok.

Shandong Province Education Department. 2019. "Circular on Conferring Teacher Professional Titles for Preschool, Primary School, and Secondary School Teachers of 2019" (in Chinese). http://edu.shandong.gov.cn/art/2019/12/9 /art_11990_8162131.html.

Shanghai Municipal Education Commission. 2012. "Suggestions on the Novice Teacher Standardized Training for Preschool, Primary, and Secondary School Teachers" (in Chinese). http://www.shanghai.gov.cn/nw2/nw2314/nw2319 /nw12344/u26aw31503.html.

Shenzhen Education Bureau of Bao'an District. 2019. "Circular on Promoting the Quality of Minban Preschool, Primary School, and Secondary School" (in Chinese). http://sso.sz.gov.cn/pub/baqzfzx2017/jyj/zwgk/zxwj/201908/t2019 0805_18108611.htm.

Slot, P. L., M. K. Lerkkanen, and P. P. Leseman. 2015. "The Relations between Structural Quality and Process Quality in European Early Childhood Education and Care Provisions: Secondary Analyses of Large Scale Studies in Five Countries." CARE—European Early Childhood Education and Care. http:// ecec-care.org/fileadmin/careproject/Publications/reports/CARE_WP2_D2__2 _Secondary_data_analyses.pdf.

Sun, J., N. Rao, and E. Pearson. 2015. "Achieving Goal 1. Policies and Strategies to Enhance the Quality of Early Childhood Educators." Background paper prepared for the Education for All Global Monitoring Report 2015, *Education for All 2000– 2015: Achievements and Challenges.* Paris: United Nations Educational, Scientific and Cultural Organization. http://unesdoc.unesco.org/images/0023/002324 /232453e.pdf.

Totenhagen, C. J., S. A. Hawkins, D. M. Casper, L. A. Bosch, K. R. Hawkey, and L. M. Borden. 2016. "Retaining Early Childhood Education Workers: A Review of the Empirical Literature." *Journal of Research in Childhood Education* 30 (4): 585–99. https://doi.org/10.1080/02568543.2016.1214652.

UNESCO (United Nations Educational, Scientific and Cultural Organization) Institute of Statistics. 2019. UIS.Stat. http://data.uis.unesco.org/.

Vargas-Barón, E. 2015. "Policies on Early Childhood Care and Education: Their Evolution and Some Impacts." Background paper prepared for the Education for All Global Monitoring Report 2015, *Education for All 2000–2015: Achievements and Challenges.* Paris: United Nations Educational, Scientific and Cultural Organization.

Wilichowski, Tracy, and Anna Popova. 2021. "Structuring Effective One-to-One Support." Guidance Note, World Bank, Washington, DC.

Wolf, S. 2018. "Impacts of Pre-Service Training and Coaching on Kindergarten Quality and Student Learning Outcomes in Ghana." *Studies in Educational Evaluation* 59: 112–23.

Wolf, S., J. L. Aber, J. R. Behrman, and E. Tsinigo. 2019. "Experimental Impacts of the 'Quality Preschool for Ghana' Interventions on Teacher Professional Well-Being, Classroom Quality, and Children's School Readiness." *Journal of Research on Educational Effectiveness* 12 (1): 10–37. https://doi.org/10.1080/19345747.2018.1517199.

World Bank. 2019. *Systems Approach for Better Educational Results (SABER): Early Childhood Development (ECD).* Washington, DC: World Bank. http://saber.worldbank.org/index.cfm?indx=8&pd=6&sub=1.

Yang, Y., and N. Rao. 2020. "Teacher Professional Development among Preschool Teachers in Rural China." *Journal of Early Childhood Teacher Education* 42 (3): 219–44. https://doi.org/10.1080/10901027.2020.1726844.

Yoshikawa, H., L. Diana, C. Snow, E. Treviño, M. C. Barata, C. Weiland, C. Gomez, et al. 2015. "Experimental Impacts of a Teacher Professional Development Program in Chile on Preschool Classroom Quality and Child Outcomes." *Developmental Psychology* 51 (3): 309–22. https://doi.org/10.1037/a0038785.

4

Creating Early Childhood Education Environments That Promote Early Learning

OVERVIEW

Early childhood education (ECE) environments greatly influence children's learning experiences as well as their health and development more generally. The right learning environment is about more than just space, expensive buildings, or equipment. It is, at its best, about creating an environment conducive to learning and that ensures children feel safe, make sense of the world, and feel empowered, understood, and free to learn actively and flexibly. Five principles underpin an environment conducive to quality early learning: (1) overall safety, (2) pedagogical organization, (3) spatial flexibility, (4) empowerment and authorship, and (5) child-centered design. These five principles can help create a supportive and nurturing early learning environment that reflects local cultures, landscapes, and community experiences. The right learning environment helps children learn about themselves, others, and the world's diversity. It is centered around learning relationships between children, adults, and materials, and is based on flexible encounters rather than rigid teaching.

This chapter was written by Cynthia Adlerstein and Alejandra Cortázar.

CREATING SAFE, FLEXIBLE, AND CREATIVE SPACES TO LEARN

Creating the right environment for quality early learning is about more than bricks and mortar, furniture, equipment, books, and blackboards. It is not just an issue of "space," buildings, architecture, and classroom layout (Robson and Mastrangelo 2018). The right learning environment allows children to interact with their teachers and the world in a way that helps them learn and understand the world better (Byers et al. 2018; OECD 2017a).

Learning environments can be built and organized in many different ways. No single environment or approach is best. However, environments that are participatory and that open up opportunities for dynamic learning and interaction will be more conducive to quality ECE.[1] It is the culturally sensitive use of physical space and time to support multiple learning experiences and diverse pedagogical practices that makes quality learning environments possible (Cleveland et al. 2018).

This chapter discusses five principles for achieving supportive and nurturing learning environments for ECE (figure 4.1). The chapter summarizes

Figure 4.1 Five Key Principles for Quality Learning Environments

many pedagogical perspectives, research-based innovations, and mainstream international evidence on creating and maintaining quality learning environments (Cleveland 2018; OECD 2017b; UIS 2012).

Overall safety is the first key principle, highlighting the minimum protective conditions that must be in place before any type of educational provision can begin. Once settings meet an appropriate level of safety, the next attribute is the *pedagogical organization* of ECE learning environments, meaning that every part of the physical learning environment should be thoughtfully planned and intended to motivate specific teaching and learning opportunities. The third principle is *spatial flexibility*: the chapter illustrates how quality ECE environments should move from rigid teacher-centered arrangements to multifunctional and open spaces with various learning centers and adaptable zones for children's exploration and collaborative group learning. *Empowerment and authorship*, the fourth principle, highlights the importance of providing opportunities for children, teachers, and families to be able to personalize early learning spaces throughout the teaching-learning process. Finally, the fifth principle focuses on *child-centered design* in learning environments, including child-adult ratios, child group sizes, child accessibility, and access to learning opportunities. Together, these five principles provide the foundations for quality ECE environments. The chapter explores the ideas behind the five principles and how they are put into practice. It also looks at how political, economic, social, and regional differences shape a quality environment. The discussion then turns to how to translate these principles into policy and practice.

PRINCIPLES OF QUALITY EARLY LEARNING ENVIRONMENTS IN ECE

Overall Safety: Minimal Protective Conditions for Learning

Safety must come first. Ensuring children's overall safety should always be the top priority. A secure and protective space must minimize possible risks and dangers (UIS 2012). Teachers and children must feel safe (Cleveland et al. 2018). Safe physical learning environments not only protect children, teachers, and communities, but also have explicit protocols and codes of conduct that promote a sense of care within the community and an awareness of safety among teachers, families, and learners.

Overall safety depends on engaging the whole community, on parental involvement, and on participatory decision-making with teachers and children. In Rwanda, school safety conditions are managed by parents' committees and teachers. Families help build adobe walls around a school's compound to stop outsiders and goats from wandering around. Parents and children tend vegetable gardens to grow produce for the school and plant shade trees with teachers for outdoor safe play. The Turkish Ministry of Education, through the Child-Friendly Schools Program (a United Nations Children's Fund model), involves families and communities to ensure that students feel safe and respected and to create a healthy life for the whole school community (Miske 2010). Teachers and parents are considered frontline monitors of safety. They take turns watching over children in hallways and playgrounds, and make school maps for children so that they can point out where they may feel unsafe at school.

Learning environments rooted in safety and minimum protective conditions for all young children should include hygienic conditions with culturally sensitive facilities, reasonable air quality and noise levels, security protocols, and universal accessibility for all members of the community.

Water, sanitation, and hygiene are essential components of overall safety. Appropriate hygiene practices, such as handwashing, controlled garbage disposal, and ending open defecation, can be compromised in the absence of adequate water supply and suitable toilets. The lack of clean water, washing systems, and hygiene materials contributes to children missing education and performing poorly because of parasites and illnesses. In several countries, such as India, Malawi, and Vietnam, although sanitation campaigns have improved children's understanding of hygienic habits and handwashing (Masangwi et al. 2012), a high percentage of defecation in school grounds, unfit latrines, and age-inappropriate handwashing facilities for the youngest children continue to impede healthy practices and toxin-free environments (Fauziati 2016; Patil et al. 2015; Xuan et al. 2013).

Safe learning environments provide adequate toilet facilities, garbage disposal, and handwashing in classrooms or in centers' common spaces (Cobanoglu and Sevim 2019). For example, in Mindanao, the Philippines, ECE centers and primary schools purchased cost-effective, sturdy 500-gallon plastic water tanks, rainwater catchment devices, rubber pipes, and washbasins. Community volunteers constructed water supply systems to improve the health and handwashing habits of 200 children and to irrigate medicinal and vegetable school gardens to reduce hunger.

Evidence suggests that, out of all architectural features (light, temperature, size, and so on), low air quality and high noise levels are the ones that have a direct negative impact on learning (EEF 2019). Learning spaces with no ventilation often have higher concentrations of carbon dioxide, which can influence child cognition, affecting word recognition, among other things (EEF 2019). High noise levels (for example, settings under a flight path, near transportation hubs or expressways, or close to construction) can also have a measurable detrimental impact on learning. Having windows to capture natural light and generate cross ventilation and using natural outdoor spaces for classes are cost-effective ways to improve air quality and overcome these problems. In Kerala, India, a school near a busy road planted vegetable and fruit gardens on either side of the school building. The gardens include passion fruit vines and other creeping vines that create a natural "plant-made" roof, under which children spend considerable time daily. They have transformed the school surroundings into healthy spaces that reduce noise and high temperatures during summer classes. The new gardens have motivated the whole community to convert and maintain unused school spaces into places for organic farming. All students have plants allotted to them so that watering and assessing growth are everyday responsibilities. Some school time is dedicated to learning in the gardens. Time is also allocated for cultivation before and after school, including with parents and teachers.

Standard day-to-day safety is important. For example, electrical cables should be concealed, and outlets placed out of the reach of children; ramps should be designed for students with disabilities; and stairs should be well-lit and wide enough to accommodate students safely. The handrails should be durable. Shelves, wardrobes, and drawers should not have sharp or dangerous spikes or corners; and structures should be free of hazardous materials. All settings should have warning signs at eye level for children and emergency exit evacuation plans known by members of the community.

Safe learning environments are culturally sensitive and reflect local conditions. For example, in the early days of ECE expansion in Ethiopia, some schools transformed their dirt floors into smooth and clean surfaces for learning with layers of plaster and floor paint because desks and chairs were not affordable. Children received clean, brightly colored floor mats that they could sit on after removing their shoes, not only providing a pleasant and neat classroom but also offering the children, teachers, and parents an understanding of the importance of hygiene and cleanliness, even in an environment with little or no resources for furniture (UNICEF 2006).

Security protocols to manage emergencies (earthquakes, floods, fire, and the like) and universal access to safe spaces are necessary for overall safety (Britto 2017; Duarte, Jaureguiberry, and Racimo 2017). ECE centers and schools should provide educators and children with the necessary places and instructions to minimize hazardous environments (Cobanoglu and Sevim 2019) and to manage the community's safety during emergencies. An interesting low-cost example of evacuation equipment combining safety and child well-being is the Chilean evacuation slide. Public ECE centers with nursery provision (children aged two years and under) have evacuation slides on the outside of buildings for children and adults to use from second-floor rooms in an emergency.

Key Takeaways

- Children's and teachers' safety must come first; without it, there can be no learning.
- Safe physical learning environments protect children, teachers, and communities; and they have explicit protocols and codes of conduct that promote a sense of care within the community and safety awareness among teachers, families, and learners.
- Making overall safety possible involves the active participation of children, families, and teachers.

Pedagogical Organization: Spaces That Promote Exploration, Interaction, and Collaboration

Quality learning environments for ECE offer educational content and practices that build knowledge and engage children in meaning-making (Devine-Wright 2009). Every part of the ECE setting (hallways, classrooms, common rooms, and bathrooms) seeks to motivate specific learning opportunities and outcomes (Adlerstein, Manns, and González 2016). The pedagogical organization of the environment reflects educational purposes and beliefs of how children learn and should always be coherent with and support curricular aims, learning standards, or the educational objectives to which communities agree. Pedagogical organization is not a single correct layout, but the way educators, families, and children organize their resources to learn and spend time in an educational environment.

Pedagogical organization is always a result of educational choices. Spatial thinking can be developed by ECE teachers to build quality learning environments (Cortés Loyola, Adlerstein Grimberg, and Bravo Colomer 2020; Luka 2014). Pedagogically organized environments are recognized as the second priority for teachers and educators (out of 81) in the Organisation for Economic Co-operation and Development's TALIS Starting Strong Survey 2018. Research suggests pointless decoration and overcrowded spaces should be avoided (Sim et al. 2019). Learning centers, play areas, and exploration zones should be encouraged to promote adult-child and child-child interaction and hands-on learning. Pedagogical organization can turn low-cost, basic infrastructure and spaces into exploration centers and art zones.

For example, some urban kindergartens in Vietnam equipped several high hall windows with stools and observation resources (binoculars, soil, books, and the like) to enable children to connect with the natural and urban landscape. Likewise, in Chilean public nursery schools, inaccessible windows and skylights in hallways were covered with colored cellophane paper to enable new aesthetic experiences for two- and three-year-old children.

Pedagogical organization through zoning and learning areas, such as a home corner, a building zone, a classroom library, or science and sensory exploration sections, is not new. The idea of organizing different play zones and areas to encourage children's self-activity emerged from Froebelian pedagogy (Cortés Loyola, Adlerstein Grimberg, and Bravo Colomer 2020). Though evidence is not conclusive on which learning centers and what materials are the most effective, the collaborative experiences that emerge within these learning centers are consistently associated with positive learning (EEF 2019). Pedagogically organized centers in ECE require much more than just seating children together with certain materials. Learning spaces support pedagogical organization so that all children can access learning materials and experiences that promote interaction, sustained shared thinking, and collaboration. Learning spaces should consider distributing resources and display technologies (digital screens, tablets, and the like) that enable teachers and children to develop precise tasks and learning experiences in small groups and through independent exploration (Cleveland et al. 2018).

The CENDIs (Centros de Desarrollo Infantil del Frente Popular Tierra y Libertad, or Early Childhood Centers of the Popular Front "Land and Freedom") in Monterrey, Mexico, turned classrooms into "learning laboratories" for children's exploration, free play, and problem-solving. Walls display objects of knowledge as visual aids for teaching and learning. These include word flashcards, local object photographs, and snapshots of social practices. Some surfaces and furniture (chair backs, shelves, tables) are used to organize the material creatively. They are also used to showcase projects, challenges, and discoveries. Reading corners, small spaces to rest, and low windows with baskets holding magnifying glasses, plant pots, and notebooks to observe and record plants' growth help children and teachers explore, discover, and learn together. A clock on the wall of each classroom, an extensive calendar, and a graphic timeline with daily tasks give structure to the school day. The CENDIs' learning environments organize pedagogical sites and resources so that children engage in learning at all times and in diverse ways; the environment encourages them to take on individual challenges, collective responsibilities, and collaborative problem-solving.

In Ethiopia, India, and Kenya, teacher-centered classrooms have blossomed into stimulating learning spaces through the use of pocket boards with word cards, picture cards, and numerical cards; wall boards painted with indigenous ink; alphabets, numbers, and mat signs; cut-outs and story outlines on walls; and low-cost or no-cost teaching aids in learning corners. According to UNICEF (2019), the average cost of converting a standard Kenyan classroom into a stimulating learning environment is US$25.

Key Takeaways

- ECE centers' physical environment should be planned to motivate teaching and learning opportunities.
- With low-cost and locally available materials, walls, windows, and organized play zones or corners can become playful and stimulating learning spaces.
- ECE learning environments should be organized so that all children can access learning materials and experiences that promote exploration, interaction, and collaboration.

Spatial Flexibility: Adaptable Places for Flexible Learning

Adaptable spaces, or areas that can be rearranged according to different teaching and curricular needs, are crucial to quality early learning. Spatial flexibility complements stable and fixed learning centers by fostering multifunctional places that are readily responsive to emergent teaching-learning needs (OECD 2017b). It promotes a sense of openness and spaciousness (Kennedy 2010) necessary to engage in learning and supports the growth of ideas (Gandini 2005), collaboration, and creativity (Adlerstein, Manns, and González 2016). Flexible spaces can encourage more effective teaching (Anderson-Butcher et al. 2010; Oblinger 2007), educators' teamwork, better planning, and a greater focus on personalized learning. They also improve children's self-reliance to undertake initiatives and work collectively in groups (Dekker, Elshout-Mohr, and Wood 2006; Fielding 2006). This idea strongly contrasts with early "schoolification" in ECE centers, which mimics traditional classrooms in primary school.

Flexibility replaces the idea of a single teacher-centered and individual-learner classroom arrangement (typically a board and front-facing seating of students) with various multipurpose artifacts, materials, and places that reflect the nuances of different knowledge areas and diverse learning experiences working simultaneously and connectedly.

Flexible environments often have fewer but better resources. They should provide permanent rotation and renovation, involving purposeful circulation pathways and areas for the whole group to encounter different learning interactions (exploration, observation, creation, communication, and exhibition). The idea is to facilitate learning anywhere, allowing all indoor and outdoor spaces to be learning tools themselves (OECD 2013). Spatial flexibility is possible with simple and locally available resources. It encourages creativity inside and outside the classroom. Raised platforms and large carpets can support performances, group meetings, or floor-based activities. Potted plants, magnifying glasses, rocks, shells, nature books, pencils, and paper on a windowsill can create opportunities for exploration.

Spatial flexibility is always a challenge for teachers and educators. It is not just about opening or enlarging spaces. It requires more planning around activities, behavior, transitions, and sound control. Flexibility encourages early childhood educators to shift from closed, rigid classrooms to learning spaces where learning ebbs and flows depending on learning needs and teaching circumstances (Oblinger 2007). Educators are more likely to adapt and rearrange rooms differently if they have been encouraged by training and policies to plan spatial flexibility, take risks, and experiment with versatile use of spaces to develop new pedagogical strategies.

Flexible learning environments demand a transition from classrooms based on the three S's (static, safe, and sanitary) to environments grounded in the three A's (adaptable, agile, and attuned to the local context). Safe and clean settings are an essential condition for educational environments, but without transformable spaces deep learning is less likely to occur (Richardson and Mishra 2018). The availability of open-ended materials and areas directly affects the variety of activities that children engage in and the learning opportunities available to them (Beghetto and Kaufman 2014; Cleveland 2018; Dudek 2012).

Flexible learning environments allow agile conversion of spaces and easy adaptation, facilitate connectedness and movement between classrooms or learning centers, and support robust social encounters for learning in different types of groupings. Flexible learning environments offer more open design and good sightlines with break-out areas and shared spaces for learning near classrooms that make circulation easy. For example, instead of expensive and rigid walls (such as concrete, brick, or wood) for adjoining classrooms and learning centers, flexible dividers can be made of varied materials, such as midrise shelves, curtain-like fabric partitions, versatile furniture like light-weight tables, climbing walls, platforms, and movable whiteboards. This approach allows the entire learning environment to become one large space, while also retaining the possibility of partitioning it into traditional classrooms or learning sections. The "less is more" trademark of flexibility fosters spacious, uncluttered, and action-inviting classrooms (Cleveland et al. 2018) with places for hands-on experiences and links to the outdoors (visually and physically), following children's movement, play, and exploration interests.

In Chilean public kindergartens, classrooms are continually rearranged for children and teachers to undertake different reading and literary projects. Though all kindergartens have classroom libraries (by national regulation) and reading areas, flexibility (as a practice and of furniture) enables educators to temporarily transform the whole space into different places for the children to enjoy literature simultaneously in different ways. Curtain dividers, multipurpose shelves, and assembled furniture allow children to circulate within the classroom, recreating characters with puppets and building scenery and dialogue for performances. Mats, blankets, fabric, cushions, and rugs easily enable spatial flexibility in classrooms, replacing traditional rigid chairs and demarcating flows to support focused behavior and overall competency with tasks (Moore 1996; Maxwell 2007). They are low-cost compared with school furniture and more comfortable for younger children. These materials are easy to use to delimit places for individual work, rest and calm activities, free play, or gathering to celebrate. They can help provide a flexible and dynamic hands-on environment for learning. They provide cues that guide children's activities, and possible uses are easy to understand or imagine. The use of transportable elements such as dividers and signposts makes environments familiar and appealing, supporting children's autonomy, guiding their use without direct teacher intervention (Arndt 2012). Flexibility means using space in many ways for diverse and stimulating activities.

The AEIOtú kindergarten network in Colombia offers active, flexible, child-driven spaces that connect children and teachers in diverse ways to promote learning. AEIOtú centers provide opportunities for progressive improvements in learning in low-socioeconomic neighborhoods. Children can move from listening to one speaker (traditionally the teacher explaining or demonstrating) speaking to the whole group, to working in small groups on project-based activities, working independently (reading, searching, or experimenting), or coworking with an adult. Although specific places for each kind of learning experience (a lecture hall, an art room, a light center, a drama zone) could accommodate each type of work, the transitions between activities can often be immediate and conducive to the learning experience. AEIOtú spaces can be easily reconfigured without the need for expensive infrastructure or technological equipment. Shelves and fabric curtains work as dividers that children can open, and tables and chairs are moveable according to children's interests. Light switches are installed at child-hand height, and materials are kept in transparent containers to allow easy access when needed.

Key Takeaways

- Flexible spaces can encourage more effective teaching, teamwork, and planning among educators, as well as self-reliance among children to undertake initiatives and work collectively in groups.
- Multifunctional and open environments that are grounded in the three A's (adaptable, agile, and attuned) are more effective at promoting children's exploration and collaborative learning than rigid teacher-centered arrangements based on the three S's (static, safe, and sanitary).

Empowerment and Authorship: Creating Opportunities for Cocreation

Learning environments can offer educational opportunities and communicate pedagogical values and beliefs. They can enable or hinder a shared sense of ownership between children and educators (Miller 2019; OECD 2017b; Wall 2015). In ECE, quality learning environments empower children as learners and as full participants in experiences that build knowledge and share identity and cultural belonging (Dahlberg, Moss, and Pence 2005; Mills and Comber 2013). Empowerment is grounded in a learning culture in which teachers and students are invited to make active choices about where to work and have the freedom to change spaces to suit their teaching and learning interests and priorities (Cleveland et al. 2018). Empowering learning environments provide a sense of belonging and ownership. They encourage community members to fill the given spaces with new meanings of coexistence and continuous learning through their shared design. Quality learning environments allow children to decide how to organize space, furniture, and materials to support their learning projects, allowing them, along with teachers, to find their voice and to find meaning by sharing their ideas around a learning center (Adlerstein, Manns, and González 2016).

The empowering principle does not require expensive and sophisticated resources (McGregor 2003); quite the opposite, it delegates spatial decision-making to engage children and adults in spatial thinking and building (Ferrare and Apple 2010) and allows mastery of the learning environment (Cleveland 2018; Cleveland et al. 2018). In other words, it allows children to be a part of self-selected learning places and provides them with opportunities to choose materials and experiences that change the learning space throughout the day. Examples include using two- and three-dimensional display spaces such as shelves, boards, and stools of different heights for children to showcase their projects and celebrate their achievements.

Numerous studies highlight the importance of empowering learning environments for staff job satisfaction and worker retention (OECD 2019). Promoting better working conditions for ECE teachers by, for example, protecting areas to test pedagogical ideas and experiment with different spatial arrangements or to try out new structures and places for play can help increase staff performance and fulfillment. Empowering learning environments improve ECE teachers' collaboration to monitor children's learning processes (Cleveland et al. 2018; OECD 2009, 2019).

The MAFA program (Modelamiento de Ambientes Físicos de Aprendizaje, or Physical Learning Environments Modeling System) developed in Chilean public kindergartens is an example of empowering physical learning environments. The MAFA program uses a system of three building blocks: First, wooden pieces can be arranged into multipurpose supports to replace traditional school furniture. Second, a play resource for teachers and children is provided to share their thinking on how to set up the physical spaces for learning. Third, through the system's app—MAFApp—teachers can document the innovative and collaborative ways they use space. ECE teachers receive training that encourages a new mindset and inspires them to join a virtual community of practice. The MAFA program empowers adults and children to engage in new spatial thinking. It provides a sense of ownership that progressively improves learning environments' quality through democratic interactions and children's place-awareness (how and where they learn).

Setting up a MAFA classroom costs 30 percent less than setting up a regular classroom in a school or kindergarten. ECE teachers also feel more competent in improving the quality of their learning environments (Adlerstein-Grimberg and Bralic-Echeverría 2021). A MAFA classroom also encourages parental engagement and new behaviors of responsibility for maintaining these outcomes (Adlerstein and Pardo 2017).

Key Takeaways

- Giving children, teachers, and families opportunities to personalize and change learning environments promotes a sense of belonging and ownership, and offers opportunities for cocreation.
- Empowering environments are not finished spaces. Instead, they offer children and teachers ongoing learning opportunities to rethink and complete them.

Child-Centered Design: The Right Space, Class Size, and Child-Adult Ratios

Both built and natural learning environments for young children should be child-centered in design. They should reflect children's developmental characteristics, social and cultural practices, and everyday interests. Making meaningful ECE learning environments requires appropriate scaling and accessibility, reasonable child-adult ratios, and class sizes that allow personalized and playful interactions.

Appropriate child scaling means that physical and cultural surroundings are within reach of children. Spaces should reflect the developmental perspective and sociocultural possibilities to produce secure spatial attachment (Pilowsky 2016). A child-centered (or child-meaningful) scale refers to spaces and resources that are catchable, climbable, and conquerable for children's learning without physical and cultural barriers (Cleveland 2018).

In other words, scaling ensures children can navigate their environment easily and comfortably.

As a rule, objects should be at eye level for four-to-six-year-olds, or 95 centimeters from the floor (Bernard van Leer Foundation 2019). Objects and places with social uses should be in easy reach, in children's field of vision, the right size, and have a homey feel (see, for example, photograph 4.1). There is a need for domestic-style interiors that do not look institutional (Cleveland et al. 2018) and that boost the availability of authentic materials and encourage practices that bring everyday lives into the settings. When ECE staff can scale resources and sociocultural diversity into the physical environment, they provide more favorable opportunities for healthy development among minority children and improve children's cognitive development. For example, instead of using oversized chairs and tables that leave children with their feet dangling, appropriate scaling ensures other socially relevant ways of sitting or resting.

Photograph 4.1 Scaling Environments within Children's Reach

Source: Image courtesy of Cynthia Adlerstein. Further permission required for reuse.

The Peruvian kindergarten network, Casa Amarilla, developed a local version of the Reggio Emilia approach for disadvantaged communities. Children were interested in exploring urban architecture and how construction worked, especially tunnels and bridges. Responding to these interests, educators scaled building spaces and climbing artifacts with recycled structures and materials (for example, plastic pipes, cardboard boxes, pieces of wood, as seen in photograph 4.2) for the children to build and experiment with. This helped the children understand how workers build tunnels.

Class or group size is also essential to quality early learning. As the size of a class or teaching group gets smaller, teachers can interact more frequently with each child and develop a range of pedagogical approaches to teach responsively, improving learning opportunities and outcomes (EEF 2019). When groups are smaller, and child-adult ratios are low, high-quality pedagogical practices may significantly affect children by providing more frequent interactions (Pianta et al. 2009) and sustained shared thinking (Purdon 2016; Siraj-Blatchford 2009). Research shows that a low child-adult ratio correlates with more verbal interaction and more responsive and extended dialogue (Siraj-Blatchford et al. 2002). Also, group work is achievable with lower child-adult ratios, creating more active and sustained engagement, higher-order reasoning, and responsive interactions (Blatchford et al. 2006).

Conversely, classrooms with more children are more likely to feature teacher-centered pedagogies. Crowded learning environments disrupt interactions with increased levels of interpersonal conflict, intensifying children's solitary play and teachers' time in addressing classroom conflicts due to crowding (Evans and Hygge 2007; Mathews and Lippman 2020). Larger group sizes increase stress for children and staff (Legendre 2003; Valente et al. 2012), which leads to an increase in absenteeism and teachers' burnout and retirement (OECD 2019).

Photograph 4.2 Recycled Structures and Climbing Artifacts

Source: Images courtesy of Cynthia Adlerstein. Further permission required for reuse.

Reducing child-adult ratios does cost more. Policy makers with limited budgets and overcrowded classrooms must set realistic standards and support teachers in managing group sizes meaningfully. The correct classroom size and the appropriate child-adult ratio are not unique or exact numbers. Instead, the calculation should ensure that all learners have access to environments that foster their development as human beings (UIS 2012). While working to address high child-adult ratios, countries can explore tactics to promote better classroom environments and increased interactions even in overcrowded learning spaces, including hiring assistants, using shift models, rotating children between outdoor and indoor spaces, and implementing group-based activities, among others. According to the most decisive evidence that currently exists (from primary schools in the United States), the critical issue in group size appears to be whether the reduction of ratios is sufficient to allow educators to develop new teaching skills and approaches that reduce their stress, burnout, and absenteeism.

Density reduction can be achieved by using classroom space more flexibly and creatively, reducing the need for multiple pieces of furniture (Lippman 2013), and zoning spaces with learning centers that enable an agile flow during play and learning-group experience. In CEIP Andalucía, Seville (Spain), students are brought together in mixed groups (ethnicity, gender, motivation, performance), encouraging them to help each other and better understand the learning process. The whole class is regularly divided into small interactive groups of four or five students. The lessons comprise activities that last 15 or 20 minutes and are accompanied by a teacher or another adult. Once the time devoted to one activity has finished, the adults rotate to another group to spend some time with all the groups every lesson. Each group carries out a different activity, but the general subject matter of all activities is the same.

Key Takeaways

- ECE learning environments should be child-centered in design, reflecting children's developmental characteristics, social and cultural practices, and everyday interests.
- Spaces and resources that are scaled for and accessible to children, and child-adult ratios and class sizes that allow personalized and playful interactions, promote early learning.

PUTTING POLICY INTO PRACTICE: CREATING THE RIGHT LEARNING ENVIRONMENTS

Governments (central, regional, and local) in low- and middle-income countries can take several steps to provide children with quality early learning environments.

Situation Analysis: What to Look Out For

The first step in taking action is to understand the starting point. This volume proposes that policy makers explore the following issues in a local situation analysis, based on the five principles of quality early learning environments. By addressing these issues, policy makers can better understand whether learning environments in the country respond to young children's needs. The following section presents a list of potential questions to ask as part of a situational analysis of ECE learning environments.

Overall Safety

Do centers meet minimal hygiene and safety conditions so that children can learn? Is a clean water supply ensured for handwashing? Is garbage disposal controlled? Can light, noise, and temperature in ECE centers be controlled so children can engage in learning and playful experiences? Are the materials and physical environments accessible to all children and adults? Are safety protocols and places of evacuation known by all community members? Do families and community members participate in ensuring safety and maintaining healthy practices?

Pedagogical Organization

Is the pedagogical value of everyday objects and spaces being recognized? Have different areas and zones been organized for children to engage in various learning experiences? Does the environment reflect what children are exploring, learning, and solving in their everyday lives? Does the physical environment include learning aids that support different teaching strategies (clocks, books, new word panels, responsibility charts, and so on)? Do children have access to places that foster different interactions and actions, such as sharing, exploring, moving, resting, collaborating, expressing, and so on? Do children have spaces where they can rest, be calm, play, create, and run?

Spatial Flexibility

Is the learning environment easily adaptable for different types of experiences and groupings? Is furniture multipurpose and easy to adjust for diverse uses? Can furnishings be used as dividers and breakers of whole space? Are children able to circulate and flow through the different learning centers? Can children easily connect indoor and outdoor areas during learning experiences? Are materials open-ended, inviting children to create, build, imagine, and solve? Do natural and meaningful materials predominate in the learning environment?

Empowerment and Authorship

Do children have opportunities to personalize their learning environments? Do learning environments document and show children's thoughts, actions, and decisions? Do teachers invite children to arrange spaces and exhibit their projects and learning processes? Are displays child- and adult-made? Do teachers have support to test new spatial arrangements and teaching places? Do families, children, and teachers feel their environment expresses a shared identity?

Child-Centered Design

Does the learning environment feel cozy and homey? Does the learning environment include objects that children and the community treasure in their everyday lives? Is the physical environment scaled to be within reach of all children? Are there enough adults in the learning environment to interact responsively with children? Does the ratio of children to educators allow children's exploration, free play, and collaborative learning? Does the number of children in the learning environment ensure a comfortable noise level? Does the size of the learning space allow children to move without disruption? Can children see through the windows, or are they too high for them? Does the learning environment include authentic and natural resources for learning, such as rocks, seashells, seeds, and branches? Are walls painted and not overcrowded with visual aids?

How to Do It

The implementation of some of the principles in this chapter requires standards and regulations. Implementation of others does not. This section presents both.

Standards and Regulations

The principles of overall safety and child-centered environments are part of what are known as structural quality indicators and relate to space, safety and sanitary conditions; the number of children per group; and the child-adult ratio and class size, among others (Slot 2018). These two principles can be implemented through the development of standards, norms, or regulations. Regulations allow countries to ensure that ECE programs meet minimum conditions. Many countries establish quality standards for ECE center licenses, accreditation, or certification. Although setting standards may seem easy or straightforward, the challenge is to ensure that meeting them is affordable, which means that standard setting must go hand in hand with support.

Chile is a case in point. Standards were set, but when they became mandatory fewer than 10 percent of programs were able to meet them because they had not received support to improve conditions. South Africa is another example. It defined standards in 2009 for ECE programs (DBE and UNICEF 2009), but they have not been fully implemented (Atmore, van Niekerk, and Ashley-Cooper 2012). Similiarly, Jamaica developed a governance structure, the Early Childhood Commission, to assess and monitor standards for all ECE programs. However, it did not provide support to programs to meet the standards or assess the feasibility of the standards it set (UNICEF 2020).

Learning from these examples, the following seven steps are proposed for countries to develop ECE structural quality standards:

1. *Conduct a country study to assess the quality of ECE learning environments.* Though it might be difficult to get information on all ECE programs in a country, a representative sample is crucial. This study should provide information about the situation on the ground and will serve as a baseline for estimating the costs of any improvement.
2. *Assess the feasibility of raising standards.* Each country needs to assess whether it is feasible to improve ECE conditions. For example, if a high percentage of programs have no running water, it is important to know whether it is feasible to solve that problem or whether there are other suitable alternatives. The same issue applies to teacher shortages or classroom size. When assessing feasibility, being creative to try to find many different solutions is important. For example, using outdoor spaces for teaching is one option in a country with mild temperatures if classrooms are too small.
3. *Set standards.* Standards should be set that are challenging but at the same time achievable.
4. *Calculate the quality gap.* It is important to calculate the quality gap, that is, the distance between program reality and standards. This measurement can be used to determine the level of support needed.
5. *Support programs to achieve standards and bridge the gap* by providing resources and technical assistance. This support can include resources for improving facilities, hiring staff, or providing technical assistance.
6. *Make standards official.* For standards to work they need to be legally binding. Meeting standards could be a prerequisite for new programs. Old programs should be given time to make changes to meet new standards.
7. *Develop a certification or monitoring system.* An independent institution is helpful for assessing and monitoring standards. It is important to define how often programs need to be certified, to determine whether programs will be visited, and to outline the potential consequences of failing to meet standards.

Other Implementation Strategies

The principles of pedagogical organization, spatial flexibility, and empowerment and authorship can be implemented through one or more of the following strategies:

- *Technical orientations or guidelines.* Orientations provide stakeholders with guidance on how to practically implement certain ideas or concepts, usually via publications given to professionals, families, or both. Many countries provide technical orientations for ECE providers so that they can meet requirements and be aligned with the proposed principles. Guidelines can be accompanied by professional development to ensure a higher level of implementation (Guskey 2002). For example, most infrastructure guidelines are developed by architects or designers, in consultation with ECE experts (Guskey 2002). This type of document can advise providers on how to build ECE centers that respond to children's needs and requirements. One example is the Rwanda Child Friendly Schools Infrastructure Standards and Guidelines (Rwanda, Ministry of Education 2009). It sets standards for infrastructure and describes good practices for schools to follow. Another example is the New South Wales Childcare Planning Guideline (NSW Department of Planning and Environment 2017) in Australia, which provides orientation for planning based on seven principles: context, adaptive learning spaces, built forms, safety, sustainability, landscape, and amenity.

- *Specific programs.* Another alternative for introducing a new idea is to develop a specific program to be implemented in ECE centers. Programs can be developed and rolled out by private providers or governments. There are several examples of interesting programs (public and private) that promote some of the principles presented in this chapter. Programs are generally focused on one or two principles and aim to promote children's learning and development by improving the learning environment. Patio Vivo Foundation in Chile is a program that uses outdoor spaces for pedagogical purposes. The organization works in collaboration with the center or school community to design and provide outdoor spaces that are aligned with the curriculum. Patio Vivo is an example of the implementation of the principles of flexibility, empowerment, and pedagogical intent.[2]

  Forest schools (in Scandinavian countries, Australia, New Zealand, and the United Kingdom) are models of how outdoor space and nature can be used for pedagogical purposes. They illustrate the principles of flexibility and pedagogical intent. Forest schools are ECE programs in which children, led by trained educators, spend most of their day outside engaged in learning activities in the woods or other natural environments. These programs usually have a small facility with bathrooms and a space for children to keep their belongings and stay inside in case of extreme weather (Williams-Siegfredsen 2012).

- *Professional development opportunities.* Professional development allows educators to practice new strategies, reflect on their pedagogical practices, and make changes to and adapt learning environments. When a country wants to make changes at the practice level, professional development is a good strategy. A good example of how to promote the principles outlined above through professional development is the Faros Program from the Transforma Foundation in Peru. Through professional development, technical assistance, and assessment of the learning environment, the foundation supports programs to provide children with learning environments that respond to children's needs. This support includes weekly visits to schools; on-site and off-site training opportunities for teachers, coaches, and directors; and continual dialogue and support. The foundation works with families and communities to transform learning environments, starting with the materials families and communities can provide, such as recycled materials from factories where parents work. The program ensures facilities meet basic conditions, such as adequate bathrooms, and provide children with flexible spaces full of natural materials where they can engage in multiple learning experiences.[3]

- *Communication strategies* (seminars, campaigns). When the goal is to introduce a new idea in society, it is important for it to gain acceptance. For example, if a country wants to increase outdoor play, it might generate a communication campaign presenting evidence of the benefits of outdoor play for learning. This activity will ensure that all stakeholders—center directors, early childhood educators, parents, teachers, and the community—understand the changes early childhood centers need to make to accomplish this goal. One example of these types of campaigns is Canada's "Make Room for Play," created by the nongovernmental organization ParticipACTION. The campaign highlighted how screen use reduces play time. Another example is the British "Love Outdoor Play" campaign by the charity Play England, which promoted children's outdoor experiences, experimentation with nature, and use of public spaces.

There are many strategies and steps to take to achieve quality. Attaining that goal also requires political will, resources, technical capacity, and a well-trained workforce, which may vary depending on each country's stage in attaining quality.

In countries in the early stages of attaining quality, the private sector, international agencies, and nongovernmental organizations provide enriched early learning environments through programs, professional development, and communication strategies. Governments have the opportunity to learn from these experiences to inform their public programs. Countries in the early stages have no ECE standards or regulations. It is possible that they have attempted regulation but that it was not finalized or approved. In some cases, the regulations have not been successful. The focus in these countries tends to be on access rather than quality.

Countries in the mid stages have developed standards and guidelines for ECE environments or share common principles in their curricular guidelines. However, there are no mechanisms for assessment, monitoring, or certification of standards. It is also possible that the government, in addition to privately run programs, has specific programs and professional development or communication strategies that foster one or more of the principles outlined in this chapter. In these countries, a focus on quality is developing. Nonetheless, governance structures, financing, or technical capacity to fully implement quality policies may be absent.

Countries in more advanced stages have public ECE systems that share a common view of a desired early learning environment. They have a coherent curriculum, professional development, and quality standards. These countries have standards for ECE programs with clear technical guidelines on how to achieve them, as well as a governance structure with mechanisms for assessing, monitoring, and certifying them. These countries still use professional development and communication strategies to promote and foster some of the principles. The focus of ECE policies in these countries is on quality.

Monitoring Progress

Programs and countries can assess the quality of ECE learning environments. This assessment can be undertaken at different levels, depending on the goal and the resources.

Inside ECE programs, both educators and principals can assess learning environments to develop improvement plans or to evaluate the need for renovating, maintaining, or accommodating spaces or practices. Those performing an assessment need an assessment instrument and time to conduct the observation and provide feedback to educators. It is critical to consider resources to finance improvements in weak areas.

Local or central government can assess the quality of learning environments to monitor compliance with standards. Professionals trained in using assessment instruments need to go on site visits to perform classroom observations.

Countries and programs may develop their own instruments depending on their standards or choose to use instruments that are available on the market, such as the following:

- *The environment rating scales* (Infant/Toddler Environment Rating Scale, Early Childhood Environment Rating Scale, Family Child Care Environment Rating Scale). These scales allow an assessment of different services to be made, including infant care, family childcare, and center-based care. The environment rating scales assess both indoor and outdoor spaces as well as the availability and use of materials and interactions. Educators and supervisors can identify the specific areas that are strong and weak and understand which actions need to be taken to improve the quality of the environment (Harms, Clifford, and Cryer 1998).

- *The MAFA system* (described earlier in this chapter) has also designed an evaluation model designated ME.MAFA. It has six dimensions for assessing the quality of the learning environment: flexible, symbolically meaningful, pedagogically intended, inclusive, empowering, and promoting well-being. This evaluation tool was designed to be used easily by educators, principals, and supervisors. It does not require specific training. It can also be used for professional development and to provide feedback (Adlerstein, Manns, and González 2018).
- *Children's Physical Environment Rating Scale* (CPERS). The focus of this scale is planning, overall architectural quality, indoor activity spaces, and outdoor play areas. Its aim is to assess whether areas need to be developed, expanded, or renovated; it does not assess more subjective components of the learning environment (Moore and Sugiyama 2007).

Country Constraints to Achieving Quality

Countries may face several constraints when trying to implement these principles. A common obstacle is a lack of technical capacity. Many low- and middle-income countries have few or no ECE or early child development specialists in their central governments. The ECE workforce is also often not well trained, which makes it difficult to turn principles into practice.

As in any other sector, ECE needs specialists. In the short term, governments could ask for international advice. However, in the long run it is important to strengthen the ECE workforce and support universities or other institutions in building national capacity. Some countries offer grants to study abroad in exchange for returning home to work. Other countries provide incentives so that the best students study education at university.

Another potential obstacle is unrealistic expectations within the standards developed by policy makers and other stakeholders. Improving quality is a slow and costly process. Countries tend to set higher standards than they can achieve and afford. Or they do not assess the feasibility of accomplishing the standards. Setting feasible intermediate goals—to provide drinking water in preschools, for example—creates the opportunity to set more ambitious goals later. Although many countries realize the importance of quality learning environments for ECE, they do not necessarily have sufficient resources to invest or the willingness or ability to prioritize

ECE in the face of competing demands. Worldwide, many countries invest fewer resources in ECE than in other levels of education (UNICEF 2019).

Finally, another potential obstacle is what has been called "schoolification", which refers to a tendency to mimic primary school environments in ECE programs. In many countries, ECE programs look like primary school programs, with children as young as age three sitting in rows of chairs listening to an educator deliver content. Most principles described in this chapter cannot be accomplished under these conditions (Williams-Siegfredsen 2017).

Key Takeaways

- **Situation analysis.** Whether learning environments in a country respond to young children's needs can be better understood by conducting a situation analysis using the five principles as a benchmark. Understanding where a country is with regard to quality is helpful to the design of strategies to improve quality over time.
- **Strategies to create ECE environments that promote early learning.** Implementation of the principles in this chapter calls for different strategies:
  - *Safety* and *child-centered design*. These principles are best implemented through the development of standards, norms, or regulations.
  - *Pedagogical organization, spatial flexibility,* and *empowerment and authorship*. These principles can be implemented through guidelines, programs, professional development, and communication strategies.
- **Setting realistic goals.** Improving quality is a slow and costly process that requires setting realistic goals that are achievable and affordable. Conducting regular monitoring and providing support for the achievement of goals can help create spaces that promote early learning.

CONCLUSION

This chapter focuses on ECE learning environments as the educational habitats where children should find a plethora of nurturing opportunities, experiences, and resources to help them develop as individual human beings and thrive as a part of society. The understanding of quality learning environments goes far beyond the built facilities or the physical arrangement of classrooms. The chapter advocates for places that interconnect social, cultural, temporal, and physical aspects for teachers and children to engage in shared experiences of learning.

Quality ECE learning environments have a place-based pedagogical core that relies on viable participatory transformation processes. Involving children, families, and educators in the ongoing process of making learning environments is critical to boosting a sense of belonging and adopting shared responsibility to sustain learning improvements. There is no single correct layout or architectural material that proves to be the best in all circumstances. The pedagogical use of authentic local resources and support for innovative teaching methodologies make quality learning environments possible. Therefore, learning environments that positively affect children's development are a result of innovative space design sustained with innovative teaching and learning practices (Mahat et al. 2018; Young et al. 2019).

Drawing on this perspective, establishing effective ECE learning environments requires consideration of five key principles at the practitioner, management, and policy levels to develop different mechanisms and strategies. Implementation of these five principles requires regulations, technical orientation or guidelines, specific programs, professional development opportunities, and communication strategies. Furthermore, it is a dynamic process as children, educators, and families change through time and as theoretical and empirical knowledge grows.

Table 4.1 reviews the takeaways presented in this chapter.

Table 4.1   Chapter 4: Summary of Key Takeaways

Overall safety: Minimal protective conditions for learning

- Children's and teachers' safety must come first; without it, there can be no learning.
- Safe physical learning environments protect children, teachers, and communities; and they have explicit protocols and codes of conduct that promote a sense of care within the community and safety awareness among teachers, families, and learners.
- Making overall safety possible involves the active participation of children, families, and teachers.

Pedagogical organization: Spaces that promote exploration, interaction, and collaboration

- ECE centers' physical environment should be planned to motivate teaching and learning opportunities.
- With low-cost and locally available materials, walls, windows, and organized play zones or corners can become playful and stimulating learning spaces.
- ECE learning environments should be organized so that all children can access learning materials and experiences that promote exploration, interaction, and collaboration.

continued next page

Table 4.1 (*continued*)

Spatial flexibility: Adaptable places for flexible learning

- Flexible spaces can encourage more effective teaching, teamwork, and planning among educators, as well as self-reliance among children to undertake initiatives and work collectively in groups.
- Multifunctional and open environments that are grounded in the three A's (adaptable, agile, and attuned) are more effective at promoting children's exploration and collaborative learning than rigid teacher-centered arrangements based on the three S's (static, safe, and sanitary).

Empowerment and authorship: Creating opportunities for cocreation

- Giving children, teachers, and families opportunities to personalize and change learning environments promotes a sense of belonging and ownership and offers opportunities for cocreation.
- Empowering environments are not finished spaces. Instead, they offer children and teachers ongoing learning opportunities to rethink and complete them.

Child-centered design: The right space, class size, and child-adult ratios

- ECE learning environments should be child-centered in design, reflecting children's developmental characteristics, social and cultural practices, and everyday interests.
- Spaces and resources that are scaled for and accessible to children, and child-adult ratios and class sizes that allow personalized and playful interactions, promote early learning.

Putting policy into practice: Creating the right learning environment

- *Situation analysis.* Whether learning environments in a country respond to young children's needs can be better understood by conducting a situation analysis using the five principles as a benchmark. Understanding where a country is with regard to quality is helpful to the design of strategies to improve quality over time.
- *Strategies to create ECE environments that promote early learning.* Implementation of the principles in this chapter calls for different strategies:
  - *Safety* and *child-centered design.* These principles are best implemented through the development of standards, norms, or regulations.
  - *Pedagogical organization, spatial flexibility,* and *empowerment and authorship.* These principles can be implemented through guidelines, programs, professional development, and communication strategies.
- *Setting realistic goals.* Improving quality is a slow and costly process that requires setting realistic goals that are achievable and affordable. Conducting regular monitoring and providing support for the achievement of goals can help create spaces that promote early learning.

Source: Original table for this report.
Note: ECE = early childhood education.

Table 4.2 summarizes good and risky practices and provides some implementation verification questions for monitoring the process.

Table 4.2 Summary of Good and Risky Practices

Principle	Good practices and decisions that strengthen	Risky practices and decisions that weaken	Guiding questions
Overall Safety Nontoxic habitats and healthy practices make all feel safe.	• Have access to clean water. • Have handwashing systems. • Implement hygienic practices. • Use natural light, air flow, gardening, and organic farming to overcome noise, temperature, and poor air quality. • Raise safety awareness by having, sharing, and practicing safety protocols for emergencies. • Involve community in safety maintenance through observation turns, mapping violence, and building security in settings.	• ECE settings without clean water services and sanitation facilities. • ECE spaces without airflow, natural light, and noise dampers. • ECE setting next to industries that manage hazardous or toxic elements.	• Are there minimum safety and hygiene requirements for ECE programs? • Are there mechanisms to ensure compliance with safety and minimum hygienic requirements? • Is there public funding for maintenance?
Pedagogical Organization Various learning centers and interest spots build knowledge and engage children in meaning-making.	• Use all spaces and objects as learning drivers to foster a specific learning experience or outcome. • Organize learning centers and zones that all children can understand and access. • Ensure learning centers and areas have clear tasks and experiences for small-group or individual work.	• Decorate walls and spaces with stereotyped images and/or branded products. • Place materials on the perimeter of the room walls, leaving the center empty. • Overcrowd spaces with different resources and materials. • Store materials out of children's reach, just for adults' access and use.	• Is the ECE workforce trained to prepare and organize the environment pedagogically? • Does the government offer guidelines, programs, or professional development to help ECE staff implement pedagogically intentional spaces?

continued next page

Table 4.2 (*continued*)

Principle	Good practices and decisions that strengthen	Risky practices and decisions that weaken	Guiding questions
Spatial Flexibility Multipurpose spaces respond to emergent teaching-learning interests and needs.	• Continually rotate and change all materials and resources to maintain children's wonder and raise new interests and projects. • Have open-ended materials and spaces that teachers and children can easily adapt for different purposes. • Use simple objects and spaces as dividers to break the whole space into different learning places, pathways, and flows. • Use signposts and points of interest to design pathways and sightlines that connect the indoor and outdoor learning experiences. • Encourage teachers and children to explore and try out flexible uses of space and time, for example by moving meal and self-care routines to outdoor spaces. • Have teachers plan and synchronize the flexible use of space, based on children's interests. • Enjoy spatial flexibility with children and families.	• Overcrowd classrooms with pedagogical resources and materials. • Punish or disparage children's and teachers' efforts to try out spatial flexibility • Impose a single layout for classrooms and common areas.	• Do infrastructure regulations or guidelines promote the flexible use of spaces? • Do ECE programs have both indoor and outdoor spaces? • Is there public and social understanding of the importance of the use of outdoor spaces? • Is the ECE workforce trained to be flexible in the use of spaces and adaptation to children's needs?

continued next page

Table 4.2 (*continued*)

Principle	Good practices and decisions that strengthen	Risky practices and decisions that weaken	Guiding questions
Empowerment and Authorship Children and educators actively cocreate learning places that express their knowledge and meaning-making.	• Give children the opportunity to personalize classroom spaces, rearranging furniture and materials according to new ideas and projects. • Include photographs and children's creations that reflect their personal interests and experiences in learning centers and common areas to make them a collective matter. • Talk about inhabiting environments with children, and deliberate with them better ways of doing so. • Share responsibility for organizing indoor and outdoor spaces with children and families by cocreating new places for learning and living together. • Communicate on walls, furniture, and surfaces the ideas, projects, and experiences that teachers and children are developing. • Listen to children's ideas, interests, and practices to extend them in the design of new spaces.	• Define the classroom layout permanently. • Compel the use of the same materials, resources, and spaces for all children within determined learning experiences. • Make educators and managers alone decide how to design learning spaces. • Make children organize, clean up, or rearrange the environment by using competition or awards.	• Do the curriculum and other policy instruments allow adaptation for children's ideas and interests? • Is the ECE workforce trained to identify and respond to children's interests and needs? • Is there a shared understanding of the central role of children in cocreating their learning process?

continued next page

Table 4.2 (*continued*)

Principle	Good practices and decisions that strengthen	Risky practices and decisions that weaken	Guiding questions
Child-Centered Design Space size, child-adult ratios, and scaled materials make the environment cozy, culturally significant, and reachable for all children.	• Provide a cozy, homey environment with meaningful objects that capture children's everyday lives. • Use natural resources and authentic cultural objects to create multisensory landscapes (sounds, fragrances, textures, lights, and flavors). • Make material handy for children, and ensure they can reach and have access to the different materials and learning resources. • Permanently renovate the resources that are available in learning centers with children's and the community's treasured items.	• Overcrowd spaces and surfaces with learning aids and pedagogical resources. • Use artificial and stereotyped materials that underestimate relevant cultural objects and practices. • Forbid children from bringing personal meaningful objects to school (toys, favorite blanket, or loved pillow). • Let resources deteriorate and lose the power to motivate and amaze children. • Prefer perfectly adult-organized spaces over imperfectly child-organized places. • Store learning resources in high, unreachable shelves or in hermetically sealed containers.	• Are there minimum requirements (standards) for child-adult ratio and group size for ECE programs? • Are there minimum requirements (standards) for indoor and outdoor spaces for ECE programs? • Are there mechanisms to ensure compliance with structural quality requirements? • Is there financial support for ECE programs to comply with requirements or standards? • Is the ECE workforce trained to make child-centered design decisions?

Source: Original table for this publication.
Note: ECE = early childhood education.

NOTES

1. This chapter uses the acronym ECE for "early childhood education" instead of ECEC (for "early childhood education and care") or ECCE (for "early childhood care and education") because, in coherence with a pedagogical standpoint of learning environments, "care" is at the ethical nature of any education level and should not be exclusively confined to services for young children. Likewise, the chapter assumes that learning environments have a pedagogical core that makes the right to education possible, whereas early childhood care services are solely oriented to children's and families' social protection and welfare.
2. For more information, see "Projects" (http://patiovivo.cl/proyectos/).
3. For more information, see "Transforma" (http://transforma.org.pe/transforma ---que-hacemos.html).

REFERENCES

Adlerstein, C., P. Manns, and A.González 2016. *Pedagogías para habitar el jardín infantil. Construcciones desde el modelamiento del ambiente físico de aprendizaje (MAFA).* Santiago, Chile: Ediciones UC.

Adlerstein, C., P. Manns, and A. González. 2018. *Valorar El Modelamiento Del Ambiente Físico De Aprendizaje En La Educación Parvularia. Manual para la aplicación de ME.MAFA.* Santiago, Chile: Ediciones UC.

Adlerstein, C., and M. Pardo. 2017. "Highlights and Shadows in ECEC Policy in Latin America and the Caribbean." In T*he SAGE Handbook of Early Childhood Policy,* edited by L. Miller, C. Cameron, C. Dalli, and N. Barbour. New Delhi: SAGE Publications.

Adlerstein-Grimberg, C. Y., and A. Bralic-Echeverría. 2021. "Heterotopic Place-Making in Learning Environments: Children Living as Creative Citizens." *Magis* 14. https://doi.org/10.11144/Javeriana.m14.hpml.

Anderson-Butcher, D., H. Lawson, A. Iachini, P. Flaspohler, and J. Bean. 2010. "Emergent Evidence in Support of a Community Collaboration Model for School Improvement." *Children and Schools* 32: 160–71.

Arndt, P. A. 2012. "Design of Learning Spaces: Emotional and Cognitive Effects of Learning Environments in Relation to Child Development." *Mind, Brain, and Education* 6 (1): 41–48.

Atmore, E., L. J. van Niekerk, and M. Ashley-Cooper. 2012. "Challenges Facing the Early Childhood Development Sector in South Africa." *South African Journal of Childhood Education* 2 (1): 120–39.

Beghetto, R., and J. Kaufman. 2014. "Classroom Contexts for Creativity." *High Ability Studies* 25 (1): 53–69.

Bernard van Leer Foundation. 2019. "An Urban95 Starter Kit: Ideas for Action." Bernard van Leer Foundation, The Hague.

Blatchford, P., E. Baines, C. Rubie-Davies, P. Bassett, and A. Chowne. 2006. "The Effect of a New Approach to Group Work on Pupil-Pupil and Teacher-Pupil

Interactions." *Journal of Educational Psychology* 98 (4): 750–65. https://doi .org/10.1037/0022-0663.98.4.750.

Britto, P. R. 2017. *Early Moments Matter for Every Child*. New York: United Nations Children's Fund.

Byers, T., M. Mahat, K. Liu, A. Knock, and W. Imms. 2018. *A Systematic Review of the Effects of Learning Environments on Student Learning Outcomes*. Melbourne: University of Melbourne, LEaRN. http://www.iletc.com.au/publications/reports.

Cleveland, B. 2018. "Why Innovative Learning Environments? Stories from Three Schools That Helped Establish an Ongoing Space and Pedagogy." In *School Space and Its Occupation: Conceptualising and Evaluating Innovative Learning Environments*, edited by S. Alterator and C. Deed, 39–65. Boston: Brill Sense. https://doi .org/10.1163/9789004379664_004.

Cleveland, B., P. Soccio, R. Mountain, and W. Imms. 2018. "Learning Environment Design and Use: Towards Effective Learning Environments in Catholic Schools (TELE): An Evidence-Based Approach (2015–2017)". Catholic Education Melbourne.

Cobanoglu, F., and S. Sevim. 2019. "Child-Friendly Schools: An Assessment of Kindergartens." *International Journal of Educational Methodology* 5 (4): 637–50. https://doi.org/10.12973/ijem.5.4.637.

Cortés Loyola, C., C. Adlerstein Grimberg, and Ú. Bravo Colomer. 2020. "Early Childhood Teachers Making Multiliterate Learning Environments: The Emergence of a Spatial Design Thinking Process." *Thinking Skills and Creativity* 36. https://doi.org/10.1016/j.tsc.2020.100655.

Dahlberg, G., P. Moss, and A.Pence. 2005. *Más allá de la calidad en educación infantil*. Barcelona: Grao.

DBE (Department of Basic Education) and UNICEF (United Nations Children's Fund). 2009. *National Early Learning and Development Standards for Children Birth to Four Years (NELDS)*. Pretoria: Department of Basic Education. https://www .unicef.org/southafrica/media/1746/file/ZAF-national-early-learning-and -developmentstandards-for-children-birth-to-4-years-2011.pdf.

Dekker, R., M. Elshout-Mohr, and T. Wood. 2006. "How Children Regulate Their Own Collaborative Learning." *Educational Studies in Mathematics* 62: 57–79.

Devine-Wright, P. 2009. "Rethinking NIMBYism: The Role of Place Attachment and Place Identity in Explaining Place-Protective Action." *Journal of Community and Applied Social Psychology* 19 (6): 426–41.

Duarte, J., F. Jaureguiberry, and M.Racimo. 2017. *Suficiencia, equidad y efectividad de la infraestructura escolar en América Latina según el TERCE*. https://publications.iadb .org/bitstream/handle/11319/8158/Suficiencia-equidad-y-efectividad-de-la -infraestructura-escolar-en-America-Latina-segun-el-TERCE.PDF?sequence=3.

Dudek, M. 2012. *Children's Spaces*. Abingdon, Oxon: Routledge.

EEF (Education Endowment Foundation). 2019. "Built Environment." EEF, London. https://educationendowmentfoundation.org.uk/education-evidence /early-years-toolkit/built-environment.

Evans, G., and S. Hygge. 2007. "Noise and Performance in Adults and Children." In *Noise and Its Effects*, edited by L. Luxon and D. Prasher. London: Whurr Publishers.

Fauziati, E. 2016. "Child Friendly School: Principles and Practices." *The First International Conference on Child-Friendly Education* 95–101.

Ferrare, J., and M. Apple. 2010. "Spatializing Critical Education: Progress and Cautions." *Critical Studies in Education* 51 (2): 209–21.

Fielding, M. 2006. "Leadership, Radical Student Engagement and the Necessity of Person-Centred Education." *International Journal of Leadership in Education* 9: 299–313.

Gandini, L. 2005. *In the Spirit of the Studio: Learning from the Atelier of Reggio Emilia.* New York: Teachers College Press.

Guskey, T. 2002. "Professional Development and Teacher Change." *Teachers and Teaching* 8 (3): 381–91. doi:10.1080/135406002100000512.

Harms, T., R. M. Clifford, and D. Cryer. 1998. *Early Childhood Environment Rating Scale—Revised Edition (ECERS-R).* New York: Teachers College Press.

Kennedy, M. 2010. "In Position to Learn." *American School & University* 82 (6): 20–22.

Legendre, A. 2003. "Environmental Features Influencing Toddlers' Bioemotional Reactions in Daycare Centers." *Environment and Behavior* 35 (4): 523–49.

Lippman, P. C. 2013. "Designing Collaborative Spaces." *Campus Technology* 26 (9): 21–26.

Luka, I. 2014. "Design Thinking in Pedagogy." *Journal of Education, Culture, and Society* 5 (2): 63–74. https://doi.org/10.15503/jecs20142.63.74.

Mahat, M., C. Bradbeer, T. Byers, and W. Imms. 2018. "Innovative Learning Environments and Teacher Change: Defining Key Concepts." Technical Report 3/2018, University of Melbourne. https://doi.org/10.13140/RG.2.2.12508.28802.

Masangwi, S., A. Grimason, T. Morse, N. Ferguson, and L. Kazembe. 2012. "Community Knowledge Variation, Bed-Net Coverage and the Role of a District Healthcare System, and Their Implications for Malaria Control in Southern Malawi." *Southern African Journal of Epidemiology and Infection* 27 (3): 116–25.

Mathews, E., and P. C. Lippman. 2020. "The Design and Evaluation of the Physical Environment of Young Children's Learning Settings." *Early Childhood Education Journal* 48: 171–80. https://doi.org/10.1007/s10643-019-00993-x.

Maxwell, L. 2007. "Competency in Child Care Settings." *Environment and Behavior* 39 (2): 229–45.

McGregor, J. 2003. "Making Spaces: Teacher Workplace Topologies." *Pedagogy, Culture and Society* 11 (3): 353–77. https://doi.org/10.1080/14681360300200179.

Miller, V. 2019. "Creating the Third Teacher through Participatory Learning Environment Design: Reggio Emilia Principles Support Student Wellbeing." In *School Spaces for Student Wellbeing and Learning,* edited by H. Hughes, J. Franz, and J. Willis. Singapore: Springer. https://doi.org/10.1007/978-981-13-6092-3_13.

Mills, K. A., and B. Comber. 2013. "Space, Place, and Power: The Spatial Turn in Literacy Research." *International Handbook of Research on Children's Literacy, Learning, and Culture,* edited by K. Hall, T. Cremin, B. Comber, and L. C. Moll, 412–23. New York: John Wiley and Sons. https://doi.org/10.1002/9781118323342.ch30.

Miske, S. 2010. "Child Friendly Schools—Safe Schools." Keynote Speech at the Second International Symposium on "Children at Risk and in Need of Protection." Ankara, Turkey, April 24, 2010.

Moore, G. 1996. "How Big Is Too Big? How Small Is Too Small? Child Care Facility Design." *Child Care Information Exchange* 110: 21–24.

Moore, G., and T. Sugiyama. 2007. "The Children's Physical Environment Rating Scale (CPERS): Reliability and Validity for Assessing the Physical Environment of Early Childhood Educational Facilities." *Children, Youth and Environments* 17 (4): 24–53. http://www.colorado.edu/journals/cye.

NSW Department of Planning and Environment. 2017. *Childcare Planning Guideline: Delivering Quality Childcare for NSW.* Sydney: NSW Department of Planning and Environment. https://www.planning.nsw.gov.au/-/media/Files/DPE/Guidelines/child-care-planning-guideline-2017-08.pdf.

Oblinger, D. G. 2007. "Space as a Change Agent." Educause. https://www.educause.edu/research-and-publications/books/learning-spaces/chapter-1-space-change-agent.

OECD (Organisation for Economic Co-operation and Development). 2009. *Creating Effective Teaching and Learning Environments. First Results from TALIS.* Paris: OECD Publishing. https://doi.org/10.1787/9789264068780-en.

OECD (Organisation for Economic Co-operation and Development). 2013. *Innovative Learning Environments.* Educational Research and Innovation. Paris: OECD Publishing. https://doi.org/10.1787/9789264203488-en.

OECD (Organisation for Economic Co-operation and Development). 2017a. "An OECD Framework for a Module on the Physical Learning Environment." Revised edition. OECD Publishing, Paris.

OECD (Organisation for Economic Co-operation and Development). 2017b. *The OECD Handbook for Innovative Learning Environments.* Paris: OECD Publishing. https://doi.org/10.1787/9789264277274-en.

OECD (Organisation for Economic Co-operation and Development). 2019. *Good Practice for Good Jobs in Early Childhood Education and Care.* Paris: OECD Publishing. https://doi.org/10.1787/64562be6-en.

Patil, S. R., B. F. Arnold, A. L. Salvatore, B. Briceno, S. Ganguly, J. M. Colford, and P. J. Gertler. 2015. "The Effect of India's Total Sanitation Campaign on Defecation Behaviors and Child Health in Rural Madhya Pradesh: A Cluster Randomized Controlled Trial." *PLOS Medicine* 11 (8). https://doi.org/10.1371/journal.pmed.1001709.

Pianta, R., W. Barnett, M. Burchinal, and K. Thornburg. 2009. "The Effects of Preschool Education: What We Know, How Public Policy Is or Is Not Aligned with the Evidence Base, and What We Need to Know." *Psychological Science in the Public Interest* 10 (2): 49–88. doi:10.1177/1529100610381908.

Pilowsky, M. 2016. *Apego espacial: La lugaridad en el aprendizaje.* Santiago, Chile: Ediciones JUNJI. https://www.junji.gob.cl/cuaderno-1-la-lugaridad-en-el-aprendizaje/.

Purdon, A. 2016. "Sustained Shared Thinking in an Early Childhood Setting: An Exploration of Practitioners' Perspectives." *Education 3-13* 44 (3): 269–82. https://doi.org/10.1080/03004279.2014.907819.

Richardson, C., and P. Mishra. 2018. "Learning Environments That Support Student Creativity: Developing the SCALE." *Thinking Skills and Creativity* 27 (March): 45–54. https://doi.org/10.1016/j.tsc.2017.11.004.

Robson, K., and S. Mastrangelo. 2018. "Children's Views of the Learning Environment: A Study Exploring the Reggio Emilia Principle of the Environment as the Third Teacher." *Journal of Childhood Studies* 42 (4): 1–16. https://doi.org/10.18357/jcs.v42i4.18100.

Rwanda, Ministry of Education. 2009. "Child Friendly Schools Infrastructure Standards and Guidelines 2009." Ministry of Education, Kigali. https://www.preventionweb.net/files/15377_rwandachildfriendlyschoolsinfrastru.pdf.

Sim, M., J. Bélanger, A. Stancel-Piątak, and L. Karoly. 2019. "Starting Strong Teaching and Learning International Survey 2018 Conceptual Framework." OECD Education Working Paper 197, OECD Publishing, Paris. https://doi.org/10.1787/106b1c42-en.

Siraj-Blatchford, I. 2009. "Conceptualising Progression in the Pedagogy of Play and Sustained Shared Thinking in Early Childhood Education: A Vygotskian Perspective." Faculty of Social Sciences–Papers. University of Wollongong.

Siraj-Blatchford, I., K. Sylva, S. Muttock, R. Gilden, and D. Bell. 2002. *Researching Effective Pedagogy in the Early Years.* Research Report 356. London: Department for Education and Skills. http://www.dcsf.gov.uk/research/data/uploadfiles/RR356.pdf.

Slot, P. 2018. "Structural Characteristics and Process Quality in Early Childhood Education and care: A Literature Review." OECD Education Working Paper 176, OECD Publishing, Paris. https://doi.org/10.1787/edaf3793-en.

UIS (United Nations Educational, Scientific and Cultural Organization Institute for Statistics). 2012. *A Place to Learn: Lessons from Research on Learning Environments.* Montreal: UIS.

UNICEF (United Nations Children's Fund). 2006. *The Child Friendly School Manual.* New York: UNICEF. http://www.unicef.org/publications/files/Child_Friendly_Schools_Manual_EN_040809.pdf.

UNICEF (United Nations Children's Fund). 2019. *A World Ready to Learn: Prioritizing Quality Early Childhood Education.* New York: UNICEF.

UNICEF (United Nations Children's Fund). 2020. *Access and Equity in Early Childhood Education: Evaluation of Five Countries in Latin America and the Caribbean.* Panama City: UNICEF. https://www.unicef.org/lac/media/11041/file/Access-Equity-in-Early-Childhood-Education.pdf.

Valente, D. L., H. M. Plevinsky, J. M. Franco, E. C. Heinrichs-Graham, and D. E. Lewis. 2012. "Experimental Investigation of the Effects of the Acoustical Conditions in a Simulated Classroom on Speech Recognition and Learning in Children." *Journal of the Acoustical Society of America* 131 (1): 232–46.

Wall, G. 2015. "Modern Learning Environments: Impact on Student Engagement and Achievement Outcomes." New Zealand Ministry of Education Research Report.

Williams-Siegfredsen, J. 2017. *Understanding the Danish Forest School Approach: Early Years Education in Practice,* Second Edition. London: Routledge. https://doi.org/10.4324/9781315542027.

Xuan, L. T. T., T. Rheinländer, L. N. Hoat, A. Dalsgaard, and F. Konradsen. 2013. "Teaching Handwashing with Soap for Schoolchildren in a Multi-Ethnic Population in Northern Rural Vietnam." *Global Health Action* 6 (1). https://doi.org/10.3402/gha.v6i0.20288.

Young, G., D. Philpott, E. Butler, K. Maich, and S. Penney. 2019. "Exploring the Impact of Quality Early Child Education on Special Education: Can We Prevent Placement in Special Education?" *Exceptionality Education International* 29 (3): 6–21.

5

The Role of Management, Leadership, and Monitoring in Producing Quality Learning Outcomes in Early Childhood Education

OVERVIEW

Effective leadership and management are crucial for the delivery of quality early childhood education (ECE). Good leaders and managers have a positive impact on children's learning, health, and well-being through their ability to promote several key aspects of quality ECE, including supporting and motivating ECE teachers, fostering positive learning environments, and promoting strong partnerships with families. This chapter identifies ways to raise the quality of ECE in low- and middle-income countries (LMICs) through

- *Better leadership and management*—Ensuring leaders are educated, trained, and supported in administration, pedagogy, and building partnerships;
- *Good policies*—Improving recruitment, evaluation, and monitoring while providing standards, regulations, and guidelines; and
- *Investing in data and accountability*—Raising standards and performance through quality assurance.

This chapter was written by Iram Siraj, Violeta Arancibia, and Juan D. Baron, with outstanding research assistance from Catalina Lillo.

INTRODUCTION

Effective leadership and management[1] are critical for the delivery of quality in ECE centers and have a positive effect on children's learning, health, and social outcomes as well as their well-being. Growing empirical evidence demonstrates that a leader's role and actions affect student outcomes and that, after teachers, ECE center management is likely to be the second most important in-school determinant of learning (Bloom et al. 2015; Fryer, Levitt, and List 2015; Leithwood et al. 2004; Robinson 2007). Moreover, sound management systems are critical to achieving quality. This chapter reviews the evidence on the contribution of school leaders to ECE quality. It also looks at management and policies that lead to quality learning for children in ECE.

In high-income countries, management systems, policies and proce-dures, and general management expertise are widely available. This may not be the case in LMICs. Leadership responsibilities may not be clearly defined, and many countries have no consistent cadre of trained and quali-fied teachers or school leaders and may rely heavily on informal arrange-ments, with teachers filling the role of leaders but without specific qualification criteria.

Most LMICs lack the "top down" infrastructure, management training, operational resources, and practical administration and finance skills to run efficient and effective services. Anecdotal evidence suggests that most LMICs also lack evidence-based, high-quality pedagogy and opportunities for professional development at a system scale. Consequently, most princi-pals in LMICs have neither a strong pedagogical background nor manage-ment skills, leading to inefficient management practices and hampering the quality of ECE.

This lack of professionalization is not unique to ECE (for a review, see Adelman and Baron 2019). Establishing effective leadership and manage-ment in ECE centers is, however, both more challenging and more urgent than in the rest of the education system. The challenge is compounded by the fact that ECE services tend to be delivered by a mixture of differently motivated profit-seeking and not-for-profit chains and a plethora of micro-businesses.

These factors have led to a fragmented ECE system within LMICs, with a splintered workforce that currently requires ECE leaders who are more capa-ble, better trained, more highly qualified, and much better resourced and supported than they are currently. "New and improved" leaders could shape a fairer culture and a higher quality of ECE services. These principals would enable better management practices and hence better student outcomes.

Evidence on the impact of more effective leadership on students' learn-ing outcomes in ECE centers in LMICs is limited. Most such studies have focused on either primary or secondary education (for example, Blimpo, Evans, and Lahire 2015; Bloom et al. 2015; Leithwood et al. 2004; Mbiti 2016) or on high-income countries (Muijs et al. 2004; Siraj-Blatchford and Manni 2007). However, several aspects of the literature on school leadership in LMICs are relevant for ECE.

This chapter looks at the emerging evidence and suggests key determinants and enablers of effective ECE leadership in LMICs, including three key elements: (1) good management and leadership, which includes leading in administrative, pedagogical, and partnership areas; (2) policies to support effective ECE management that include school leader recruitment, evaluation, and training; and (3) quality assurance for service delivery and effective use of data to foster improvement. This chapter then draws policy implications and provides implementation guidance to improve ECE management in LMICs.

KEY ELEMENTS OF HIGH-QUALITY ECE MANAGEMENT AND LEADERSHIP

This section outlines three areas for effective ECE service delivery: Good management and leadership at the school level, policies at the system level, and explicit quality assurance systems based on data. All three do not apply to all ECE educational systems. However, these areas show the complexity of the leader's role and the need for environments that support quality services.

Good Management and Leadership at the School Level

The actual functions an ECE leader performs to lead and manage ECE centers may vary depending on contextual factors, including the type of provision or whether the preschool is attached to a primary school, among others. In all contexts, however, school leaders perform many different activities. The role of a school leader is complex. It requires multiple competencies, both pedagogical and administrative, as well as the socioemotional skills to develop and build partnerships with teachers, parents, students, nongovernmental organizations (NGOs), administration officials, and others in the education system. To support effective management, it is necessary to clearly define the specifics of the school leader's expected role and the functions the position entails (as well as the functions of others in leadership roles in the school). These expectations must be developed with the participation of management specialists, ECE leaders in practice, and teachers, and must be contextually appropriate. These expectations should also be clear to the ECE leaders and other members of the system and should be adapted to different contexts of the school (such as ECE as part of a larger school, community-run ECE, privately provided ECE, and so on).

Administrative Activities

Managers and leaders spend most of their time on administrative tasks, even more so when activities are not standardized, well defined, or planned. To save time on administration, education systems need to define roles, responsibilities, and processes, as well as create the capacity to carry out those activities. Technology, school procedure manuals, training videos, and coaching can help. The following are key administrative tasks that school leaders, management teams, or even some teachers in small schools do day to day.

Planning for responsible and efficient management and allocation of resources. Resource allocation establishes the climate of a setting, which, in turn, influences and affects learning (Sim et al. 2019). This is not only about pens, paper, toys, pedagogical material, and textbooks: The management of staff roles and responsibilities also requires careful allocation and planning—as does the distribution of responsibilities and salaries. The equitable allocation of responsibilities and salaries encourages both staff engagement and staff buy-in to a shared culture with common priorities. The National College for Education Leadership program, which has helped Jamaica succeed in increasing students' access to schools and improving educational quality, identified efficient allocation of fiscal resources as crucial for school management (Nannyonjo 2017).

Recording all expenditures in a transparent manner is vital. The senior manager should prioritize what the center needs to spend, after its basic fixed costs, to meet effective standards. Leaders need to plan and manage resources to meet short-, medium-, and long-term goals. They must project income and costs through budgets to ensure safety, quality, equity, and sustainability. In Senegal, for instance, school leaders were required to provide budget plans for teaching and learning materials as well as for teacher training (Barrera-Osorio et al. 2009). Stakeholders should be able to see the center's structural organization, for example, its senior management team, support staff, hours worked, specific roles from leading to cleaning, and a well-organized allocation of educational resources (for example, books, toys, materials, information technology equipment, and administrative systems). Every center's biggest expenditure item is staff salary costs, which are usually funded in LMICs by a mix of government grants, foreign and local donations, and fees paid by learners' parents or carers.

Preparing and managing budgets systematically. Managers must be financially literate to be effective. If ECE leaders lack financial literacy, it is crucial that they acquire such knowledge and skills through training. For example, they need to grasp the difference between recurring expenditures (that is, salaries, resources, maintenance and repairs, fixed overhead) and capital expenditures (buildings, machinery, new facilities), and between a cash flow statement, an income and expenditure account, and a balance sheet—and to be comfortable and competent with all three.

Increasing fiscal allocation without systematic planning and organizational reform does not lead to school improvement (Barrera-Osorio et al. 2009). Lack of financial planning and literacy inevitably leads to compromising the delivery of a quality service to children, staff, and parents. Effective financial management is always flexible and able to respond rapidly, given that leaders must handle changes in pupil numbers, the percentage of children with special needs, changes in local taxation, the rise in bad debt when a local economy struggles through drought and inflation, seasonal fluctuations as parents relocate after harvest, and the impact of armed conflicts, to name a few. To respond, effective managers must develop a solutions-focused financial approach based on children's needs. For example, a decentralized budget allocation to make the budget fit school needs improved the quality of education in Mozambique (World Bank 2007).

Using appropriate systems to record, manage, and plan finances. The particular form or system of financial management depends on the size and complexity of the ECE facility or school and the context in which it operates, for example, state, private, or local community enterprise. Attempts at one-size-fits-all systems are doomed to fail; however, there is plenty of guidance at the country level and online. For example, Scotland has established Heads Together, a national online community for school leaders to share their experiences, which includes a platform for exchanging management practices, including around financial matters (Pont, Nusche, and Moorman 2008). Recording, managing, and planning finances often requires a minimum of record-keeping guidance that responds not only to the capacity of schools but also to record-keeping regulations. In some cases, a software package may be preferred, but the sophistication of its functionality depends on the user's computer skills and the ECE center's budget, which can be a high barrier to entry for many centers in LMICs.

In 2019, after more than a decade of struggling with poor financial management, which had led to debt and low salaries, a small rural community school in Chilanga, Zambia, created three bespoke Excel systems to help manage its fee income, staff payroll, and income and expenditures. The available commercial packages were too expensive, so the school built its own, with help from its trustees, to meet its precise needs. Within six months, through far better fiscal management, the school managed to become debt free and to increase staff salaries by 33 percent. It is possible for an NGO or others working with school systems to create similar simple, relevant, financial management systems and to provide them free of charge to micro-businesses in LMICs—in the same way that some NGOs provide free child assessment measures, medicines, water, and so on.

Ongoing financial micromanagement is essential, but so are an annual formal review and a three-year forecast, which could involve benchmarking against similar schools. Forecasting includes considering (and projecting) learner numbers, class or group sizes, staff costs and salary increases, planned maintenance, longer-term capital development, local economic context, and government plans. In Honduras, PROHECO schools with school councils engaged school leaders and teachers in overseeing the budget, recruiting and paying teachers, updating school facilities, and recording teachers' and students' attendance. This effort significantly reduced student dropout (Barrera-Osorio et al. 2009). Some of these multiyear plans and systems in LMICs are top down, that is, required of the local school or ECE center by government or commercial chains, but the individual leader of a center needs to fulfill these requirements themselves.

Leading staff recruitment and staff development (when applicable). People are every organization's biggest resource. Recruiting, investing in staff, and retaining the best should be every ECE center's top priority. Recruiting, inducting, appraising, supporting, developing, rewarding, and promoting staff require clear, equitable, simple, and transparent systems. The Organisation for Economic Co-operation and Development (OECD), for example, highlights the benefits of teacher and leadership development for schools (OECD 2019, 153–88). Schools are now seen as venues where teachers have continuous professional development opportunities. Many countries have recruitment and retention strategies, including the reform in India to recruit teachers on contracts, the extra teacher program in Kenya to allow school communities to recruit teachers, and the pay-for-performance mechanism in Brazil (Bruns, Filmer, and Patrinos 2011). However, strategies to recruit contract teachers have brought medium-term challenges in many countries because contract teachers have sought formalization and regularization within the civil service. In many countries the issue of pay for performance has been contentious and politically unviable.

Effective management involves using appropriate policies for each phase of the employment process. These policies can come from a regional government, an NGO, or the private sector. But most ECE centers in LMICs are micro-businesses, which means local school leaders need to establish these employment systems themselves. Effective management systems contain simple descriptions of systems for staff recruitment, development, and management that are relevant and deliverable for any low- or middle-income country. An effective system includes policies and procedures that promote equality, staff responsibilities, recruitment, health and well-being, remuneration, probation, annual leave, sick leave, maternity and paternity leave, performance management, staff conduct, grievance, discipline, and dismissal. All policies should align with government, legal, and local needs. In the Carrera Magisterial program in Mexico, for example, teachers' salaries are linked to the results of their annual appraisal, which consists of peer review, the leader's evaluation, and student performance (McEwan and Santibáñez 2005).

Communicating openly and consistently with appropriate authorities. Effective management also involves clear lines of accountability. Of course, the proximal accountability is to the learning and well-being of the children, staff, and families. But ECE leaders are also the interface between this local context and the wider structures that support the school or ECE center. In many OECD countries, the main responsibility of school leadership has shifted from managing inputs to improving teachers' and children's outcomes, hence, the need to adapt national requirements to local needs to construct school-level criteria (Pont, Nusche, and Moorman 2008).

Pedagogical Leadership

A new paradigm in developing countries has been gathering steam—the importance of the pedagogical role of the school leader or management team in supporting teachers (Bambrick-Santoyo 2012). Most developing countries rely on school leaders exclusively for administration, leaving pedagogical support for teachers to outside stakeholders. Even when schools are well-resourced, the pedagogical leadership of a school leader is crucial to give coherence to school activities, to provide continuous support to teachers, and to prioritize ECE. Pedagogical leadership means putting support to teachers at the center of the management of the school, not only supplying inputs and material but also providing feedback, organizing management teams and teachers to better identify students with deficiencies, and providing resources to students who need them most.

Putting learning at the center of leadership. Learning should be the main outcome of all activities in the school, in particular for ECE students who are developing foundational skills that will determine their future educational trajectories. Prioritizing children's best interests would kick-start the transformation of ECE services in LMICs. Thus, it is important to develop child-centered practices that management should encourage, support, and sustain (see chapters 2 and 4). Understanding the multifaceted nature of quality is crucial, and young children's learning and well-being should be at the heart of the ECE center's agenda (Sim et al. 2019). Important aspects include the following, for example (Sim et al. 2019, 11):

- Staff-child interaction, including the process quality of staff-child interaction and the monitoring and assessment of children's development, well-being, and learning
- Center characteristics, including structural quality characteristics, pedagogical and administrative leadership, climate, and stakeholder relations

- Leader and staff characteristics, including background and initial preparation, professional development, well-being, and professional beliefs about children's development, well-being and learning, and self-efficacy

Adapting the curriculum appropriately. An effective ECE manager also understands both pedagogy and how it affects management and adaptation of the curriculum to be fit for purpose. According to Everard, Morris, and Wilson (2004), school leaders should be well versed in national curriculum reform and should know how to match the national curriculum, or a chosen curriculum, to the needs of the children. LMICs face additional challenges, such as multi-age classrooms, given that some children enter school as older nonreaders without school experience, are retained because of particular needs, or reenter at an older age when a family's finances or priorities change.

An effective manager involves all staff in curriculum development and delivery, and provides all staff with tools for appropriate planning, assessment, and recording of learning progression in systems (for reporting within the school and to parents). Creating a sense of ownership and providing support to those delivering the curriculum are important. In a survey of 1,850 school leaders, Barber, Whelan, and Clark (2010) find that coaching teachers and improving curriculum were regarded as the most important skills of high-performing school leaders.

Good ECE leaders are contextually literate, and they link the curriculum to children's everyday lives in their local community and context. Without this relevance, every school and ECE center risks a high level of dropout early in a child's learning journey, particularly in LMICs if parents and children fail to see the point of investing their limited resources and time in early education.

Using appropriate child assessment systems accurately and methodically. An effective ECE manager uses appropriate child assessment systems accurately and methodically. Leaders are aware of any local standards for reporting child learning and progress. Leaders should also assist teachers in using their own assessments of how a child is progressing in all key domains of development and in recording their development consistently and methodically. In India, teachers were trained to use report cards to record children's reading performance to guide their teaching practice (Banerjee et al. 2010). Apart from accurate measurement, recording and reporting also allow for more formative assessment, which, in turn, aids planning and progression for children as individuals or in small groups. This also helps teachers create the optimal environments for learning and spaces for play, small group teacher-led activities, and larger group sessions.

Setting the direction, pace, culture, and strategy. High-performing schools demonstrate the strength and value of developing a long-term strategy that aligns closely with their mission and vision (Bloom et al. 2015). Regardless of whether the school leader or head teacher is self-aware and holds a clear, systematic educational philosophy and vision, the leader must have strategies and practices to influence others to deliver the vision (York-Barr and Duke 2004). For LMICs with existing stocks of leaders and teachers, this means establishing a strategy to professionalize those school leaders and teachers (OECD 2019). This objective is best addressed by providing a continuous and specialized professional development strategy for ECE and primary school leaders serving children age three to six years.

Establishing and facilitating smooth transitions for children. The National Center on Parent, Family, and Community Engagement in the United States suggests three transitions for ECE attention: from home to a care or preschool facility, within ECE programs, and from kindergarten classes to elementary school. These transitions present both opportunities and challenges for the child, the family, and the education provider.

Effective leadership at school and in government includes developing the skills necessary to assess current transition practices, to understand what has been effective and what needs to be changed, to partner with families through transitions, and to ask families and older children to share their experiences of transitions. Successful transition entails (1) providing guidance and reassurance to children and families on the environment, activities, learning expectations, and routines in the ECE center; (2) planning transitions so they are timely and predictable and occur according to each child's needs and pace; and (3) preparing families to help meet their children's needs as they move to the new setting and inviting parents to stay in the new setting. Transitions are most successful when families are engaged in planning and decision-making, and when there are systems for sharing information about their child's strengths and challenges with the ECE center or school. Reciprocal, two-way communication systems are vital in every aspect of ECE.

Developing and integrating both a "big-picture" and a local contextual understanding. The most effective school leaders are those who understand and address their challenges with a systemwide perspective (Talan, Bloom, and Kelton 2014) and who also communicate effectively both outward and inward. This involves communicating well with local government, with community members and other stakeholders, and with staff, families, and the children themselves (Siraj-Blatchford and Manni 2007).

Good local ECE leadership involves developing an appreciation of the setting's whole picture and full context, through grasping the relations and interactions of each part in the "whole service" provision. This big-picture understanding is an essential and distinct characteristic of leadership, and it is the particular leadership skill that enables local leaders to accurately identify the changes they need to make for improvement (Siraj-Blatchford and Sum 2013).

Effective leadership integrates big-picture understanding and multidirectional communication to create the necessary solid thought base for a knowledge management structure that facilitates the flow of information and the capture of appropriate data. These, in turn, create the evidence base for improved decision-making and accountability.

Providing reflective supervision and continuous staff development. ECE leaders who provide their staff with consistent guidance, monitoring, and reflective supervision are a distinctive feature of high-performing ECE services (Siraj-Blatchford and Manni 2007). Howes, James, and Ritchie (2003) also find that reflective supervision predicted the impact of African American and Latino preschool teachers' training programs on children's learning outcomes. Barber, Whelan, and Clark (2010) show that school managers achieve most success through supporting staff development, and Robinson (2007) finds that a school leader's advocacy of, and participation in, teacher learning and development had a significant impact on students' learning outcomes.

Partnerships

Partnerships are crucial for ECE centers. They provide support, both financial and in kind; advocate for the importance of ECE; help mobilize other parts of the education system to deliver at school; guarantee that families work with schools to help support child learning and development; and provide an external source of accountability.

Building a strong ECE-families partnership. Research shows that family expectations and parental involvement have a great impact on children's learning (Leithwood, Sun, and Schumacker 2019). Other studies indicate that parenting intervention programs can promote both parent-child interaction and parents' engagement in children's book-reading and play activities (Engle et al. 2011).

In India, Banerjee et al. (2010) find that students' learning outcomes improved when school leaders used report cards to keep parents updated on school information and when they implemented a training program to promote parental engagement in children's learning. Similarly, in Jamaica, parents became engaged in their children's learning process through reading the information contained in their Child Health and Development Passport (Word Bank 2015).

ECE managers can learn to promote family engagement through ongoing contact, sharing children's developmental information, home visits, and helping parents strengthen the early home learning environment (Melhuish et al. 2008). The earlier section on transitions is also relevant to family partnership, as is a later section on school committees.

Key Takeaways

ECE leaders have complex and varying responsibilities, requiring wide-ranging skills in the following areas:

- *Administration.* The ability to efficiently plan and manage the allocation of resources is crucial to quality ECE leadership and management because the majority of a school leader's time is spent on these tasks.
- *Pedagogical leadership.* Good leaders put learning at the center of leadership and help teachers adapt curriculum, use assessment appropriately, and support children's transitions. Good leaders also understand system-wide challenges and local context and balance the two; they also support staff development.
- *Partnerships.* Developing and fostering positive school and family partnerships is a key role for school leaders.

ECE Management at the System Level

Many education systems in developing countries lack clear definitions of how schools, and in particular ECE centers or schools with ECE classrooms, should be managed. There is no guidance on who does what, how, and under what conditions. This situation creates challenges for monitoring, supporting, and ultimately guaranteeing quality service delivery and improvements in children's foundational skills. There are usually no policies on standards for ECE centers that include learning outcomes, no outcomes for management, no quality assurance mechanisms, and no managerial organization that helps teachers to better use resources and engage students and parents. These policies are necessary to guarantee the coherent expansion of the system, to facilitate accountability, to implement quality measurement and control, to target resources more efficiently, and to guarantee that children are safe and learning in ECE classrooms. Moreover, when these elements exist, the context is not necessarily considered. For example, the requirements for urban schools are the same as for rural schools, which usually have fewer available resources. When policies are enacted, there is insufficient capacity building and strategic communication to make sure that stakeholders understand their roles and responsibilities.

Policies to Support ECE Management at the System Level

Improving the selection and evaluation of ECE leaders. Educational authorities in LMICs usually select teachers with the longest working experience and best teaching performance in schools to serve as school leaders (Adelman and Baron 2019). Without specialized training, however, great teachers may not make good leaders or efficient managers. Instead, when selecting ECE leaders, formal training, skills, and qualifications should be combined with formative assessment.

Studies indicate that ECE leaders' educational qualifications can predict the effectiveness of their leadership. For example, Perlman et al. (2019) explore the association between directors' characteristics and supervision practice in 80 ECE centers and find that the directors' years of working experience and level of education predicted their engagement in supervision meetings with teachers. In England, the National Professional Qualification for Headship increased leaders' performance when it made formal qualifications mandatory for school leaders (Barber, Whelan, and Clark 2010).

Moreover, common competencies shared by effective leaders in existing studies act as indicators when selecting school leaders. These competencies include knowledge and experience of pedagogy and management, interpersonal skills to work with community members, personal identity (that is, self-reflection and self-awareness), and the capability to collaborate with and motivate staff (New Venture Fund 2018). In LMICs with a tradition of hierarchy or management by direction, training programs need to be established to support leaders in taking risks and trusting staff.

Because high rates of school leader turnover have a negative effect on school achievement (Barber, Whelan, and Clark 2010; Bartanen, Grissom, and Rogers 2019), potential leaders could join a pre-appointment program to assess their leadership ability and commitment before taking a formal position. Bloom et al. (2016) developed the World Management Survey and the Management and Organization Practice Survey (MOPS) to measure leaders' abilities through interviews. The World Management Survey includes open-ended questions to measure leaders' ways of monitoring and assessing. By contrast, MOPS includes closed questions about, for example, the frequency of monitoring. Lemos and Scur (2016) have tailored and verified MOPS in Colombia, India, and Mexico.

Often, LMICs do not have rigorous systems for selecting leaders for their schools. At times, this means that a teacher with classroom experience is selected without ensuring that they have the necessary administrative and pedagogical leadership competencies.

International experience shows that two sets of criteria tend to be applied when selecting ECE leaders: academic credentials and the professional background that allows for the proper selection of staff. Academic credentials refer to the candidate's professional diploma, which gives preference to the title of teacher. Professional background refers to teaching experience. Yet, in some LMICs, ECE leaders may not even have a teaching degree and, in some cases, lack teaching experience as well. In those cases, leaders are often hand-picked by the political authority in office.

Internationally, many leaders are selected from senior positions in other sectors with no direct teaching experience and little knowledge of how to supervise teachers (New Venture Fund 2018), particularly in the large for-profit ECE chains. It may be difficult for these leaders to handle teaching, curriculum, and managerial responsibilities wisely and effectively. Instead, a more distributed form of leadership can empower existing skilled teachers to share responsibilities and foster ECE improvement.

Snell and Swanson (2000) identify a framework to help school leaders develop distributed leadership. It contains five dimensions: (1) empowering skilled teachers to promote their agency and willingness to take on challenges; (2) developing teachers' professionalism and deepening their understanding of pedagogy and children's abilities; (3) fostering reflection to promote teachers' agency and personal responsibility; (4) advocating collaboration instead of competition; and (5) requiring creating and planning to promote teachers' flexibility in teaching. These dimensions are especially important for those sole leaders and managers who want to develop their teachers and engage in successful planning for their center, and also for the wider ECE system in LMICs.

Informal teacher-leaders can also influence school-based professional development and influence their peers to improve teaching practice and children's learning outcomes (Poekert, Alexandrou, and Shannon 2016). According to the OECD Teaching and Learning International Survey (a global, large-scale survey to investigate teachers and the learning environment in schools), stronger distributed leadership can foster a culture of shared responsibilities and positive teacher-student relationships (OECD 2016).

Developing school-based management in fragmented ECE systems. Effective leaders are influential not only administratively but also pedagogically (Adelman and Baron 2019). Instead of controlling through bureaucracy, they empower through providing clarity: they maintain the organization's direction and pace, cultivate staff and parent engagement, encourage (and expect) high-quality service, and develop a positive working environment through a sense of common purpose, shared mission, and collective desire for development and change.

In a review of 134 studies, Robinson (2007) identifies five types of school-based management (SBM) practices that have a significant impact on children's learning outcomes: setting goals, teachers' training, a supportive environment, evaluating teaching, and curriculum and strategic resourcing.

Of course, at the ECE center level in LMICs, ECE leaders within the government sector, and within the large private and NGO chains, often have limited decision-making powers. However, they can still have some autonomy over the implementation and adaptation of the curriculum to fit their local needs (OECD 2009). For example, Yang (2019) finds that even the most highly regulated Chinese preschool leaders were able to initiate curriculum innovation through careful planning and experimentation.

SBM reforms have been initiated in some LMICs to improve the effectiveness of financing and the whole education service (Blimpo, Evans, and Lahire 2015). In Zambia, for example, after many small community schools fell into debt in the difficult national economic conditions, the Department of Education began providing all head teachers with in-service business and finance management training. Some LMICs have established local school committees to engage the school leaders and parents in controlling the school administration through increased professionalism and school-community collaboration (Barrera-Osorio et al. 2009). And in other LMICs different local stakeholders have started to work together to monitor school performance, to raise funds and examine the finances, and to recruit and train teachers (Barrera-Osorio et al. 2009).

Maeshall and Bunly (2017) evaluate the treatment effects of the Education Sector Support Scale-Up Project (a form of SBM reform in Cambodia) in 238 rural primary schools. They find that awarding small grants for SBM to schools was linked to better school performance and higher levels of student achievement.

In Kenya, SBM intervention empowered school committees to monitor and assess teachers' attendance and performance (Duflo, Dupas, and Kremer 2011). In other LMICs, school management has been empowered to hire and fire teachers and to link teachers' salaries to their performance, and teachers' instructional quality and students' learning outcomes improved (Bruns, Filmer, and Patrinos 2011).

In those LMICs where small ECE sole leaders have very limited decision-making power, SBM could be implemented where needed and local information can empower the local community and decentralize decision-making (Blimpo, Evans, and Lahire 2015).

Training and Support for Management

Effective management and effective leadership entail different skill sets. The widespread "bi-functioning" of these two roles in LMICs calls for pre-service and continuous in-service leadership training that supports the development of both sets of skills as well as for improved recruitment and evaluation of ECE leaders.

Designing and delivering effective preservice and in-service training for ECE leaders. Continuous pragmatic training is essential to developing the core skills of ECE leaders. Relevant and well-designed training is especially important in LMICs, given ECE leaders' dual role of leader and manager in small ECE centers. To be effective, training should occur both before appointment and throughout service.

In most LMICs there is no initial training for school leaders. The possibilities for development and specialization in leadership and management are very scarce or do not exist. Leadership has gained relevance only in recent years; in LMICs some leaders have one or two years of teacher training, and in some countries have only secondary education. For example, in Chile, there was no training on leadership focused on ECE until recently, where teachers who opted for training in this area now take leadership courses or postgraduate courses for teachers and school system leaders.

To improve children's learning, all ECE leaders need to take responsibility for staff development, including supervising and assessing teacher performance, mentoring and planning teacher professional development, and cultivating a reflective and collaborative working culture (OECD 2015)—in addition to attending to their own ongoing development and learning.

ECE leaders can play a key role in ensuring that teachers feel supported and have effective pedagogical training (see chapter 3). In a systematic review of research from LMICs, Evans and Popova (2016) find that teachers' pedagogical training made their teaching more relevant to children's developmental needs and improved the children's learning. When staff start to see that their professional learning leads directly to better child outcomes, they begin to grasp that professional learning makes their work more satisfying and purposeful. This can lead, in turn, to staff who feel more supported, to increased staff attendance and retention, and, consequently, to reduced recruitment costs.

Siraj-Blatchford and Manni (2007) analyze leadership data from the Effective Provision of Preschool Education longitudinal study (Sylva et al. 2004), reviewing 12 ECE centers identified as having added value to children's cognitive and social outcomes. They identified a range of "effective leadership practice categories," which are valuable when training effective ECE leaders in LMICs. These include identifying and articulating a collective vision, building common purposes, effective communication, encouraging reflection, supporting professional development, monitoring and assessing practice, building a learning culture, encouraging and facilitating parent and community partnerships, strong contextual literacy (a good grasp of the needs of the local community, families, and the children), and focusing on education (that is, a mixture of a sound curriculum and experiential and guided learning alongside play).

The research evidence suggests that effective preservice and in-service training must involve helping ECE leaders understand how to motivate staff; create the time and space for professional conversations that contribute to excellence in indoor and outdoor teaching practice; ensure all decisions are informed by evidence and empirical data, including their own data that encompass staff, parents, and children's voices; maintain a rigorous and equal focus on equity and excellence; and build a community and culture of learning and collective efficacy that always prioritizes the child's best interests.

Some basic school leader and manager training has already been adopted in a few LMICs, for example, Colombia, Mexico, and Zambia (Adelman and Baron 2019). Mutale et al. (2017) report that, in Zambia, participants' confidence and management skills improve after participating in a leadership and management training program. The spotlight at the end of this chapter provides some lessons learned from 12 countries on the state of policies that support ECE management.

Key Takeaways

- When selecting ECE leaders, formal training, skills, and qualifications should be combined with formative assessment. Continuous pragmatic training is essential to develop the core skills of ECE leaders.
- To improve children's learning, all ECE leaders need to take responsibility for staff development, such as supervising and assessing teacher performance, mentoring and planning teacher professional development, and cultivating a reflective and collaborative working culture (OECD 2015), in addition to attending to their own ongoing development and learning.
- School-based management can be an effective approach to empowering school leaders and school communities.

Quality Assurance Sytems to Improve ECE Service Delivery

Monitoring and accountability are essential for effective leadership. Monitoring provides important information about school functioning, teacher performance, and child learning. Monitoring and accountability also shed light on leaders' own performance.

According to Miller and Smith (2011), an effective accountability system includes standards, evaluation systems, and compliance mechanisms. UNESCO (2017) has constructed a framework of school accountability to engage governments, schools, teachers, parents, students, and international organizations in providing higher-quality education. Quality assurance systems are also being developed for pretertiary education in countries such as Haiti and Pakistan.

Establishing an effective and efficient system of quality that includes monitoring and accountability requires every part of the education system to work together in improving ECE at all levels, given that support and accountability never rest with a single stakeholder (Siraj-Blatchford and Sum 2013).

This section suggests four measures for monitoring and accountability for better school management: (1) set comprehensive and localizable standards; (2) establish an evaluation and accountability system; (3) use data efficiently to promote compliance mechanisms and target support; and (4) empower and evaluate school committees. Together, these measures constitute a quality assurance system that can be implemented by agencies seeking to improve ECE services.

Develop Comprehensive and Localizable Standards
Formal standards can promote internal and external inspection of school operations, but it is important to carefully consider how incentives may shift behavior and the range of potential unintended consequences that could result—and to be ready to improve and adjust reforms to correct for early missteps. For example, in Hong Kong SAR, China, the Quality Assurance Framework (QAF) was established in 2007 to monitor the quality of ECE programs and promote preschool improvement. As part of this effort, only non-profit-making kindergartens that met the QAF's requirements could access government subsidies (Yang, Wang, and Li 2017). To meet the requirements, the local ECE leader-manager must guide the center's staff through both an internal self-evaluation and an external quality review conducted by the Education Bureau (Yang, Wang, and Li 2017).

Miller and Smith (2011) identify three types of accountability standards that have been established in some LMICs: (1) input-based standards about class size, teachers' qualifications, and school equipment; (2) process-based standards about teaching and learning processes; and (3) outcome-based standards for testing and assessing children's learning outcomes (Miller and Smith 2011).

A United Nations Educational, Scientific and Cultural Organization report (UNESCO 2017) reviews standards in 71 school systems and finds that, overall, they focus on infrastructure (for example, the playground, the provision of teaching materials and water), teaching and learning (for example, teacher-child ratio, teacher qualification, maximum number of children), and children's physical health, protection, and safety (first-aid facilities, clean water, toilet provision).

The motivations, stages, and stakeholders involved in the process of developing standards will vary by country. It is, however, possible to distinguish two approaches to develop standards: the top-down model, which is more hierarchical and mainly involves experts and government entities, and the bottom-up model, in which various communities, education stakeholders, and other social organizations participate equally in the development of policy documents.

Many countries have established profiles for their school leaders' or head teachers' functions, often referring only to their administrative or management roles and neglecting the fundamental requirement for the school leader to be the pedagogical leader. It is, therefore, important to have transparent agreement about the necessary knowledge and responsibilities of school leaders.

Standards of practice and the school leaders' knowledge and school management responsibilities should include community engagement, resource management, and the educational environment. With these standards, the country has a common reference point regarding the expectations for a quality ECE school. The standards and their respective indicators should be clear, significant, and few, with the goal of preventing an excessive bureaucratic burden in supervision and evaluation. Most cases propose between four and six standards or dimensions that are then subdivided into two to three substandards or indicators.

Any new framework for ECE standards in LMICs would, ideally, be developed with the collaborative participation of all stakeholders: management experts, pedagogy specialists, center leaders, teachers, and parents. To be useful and productive, these emerging standards must fit local circumstances, be achievable by local center leaders, and have the widest possible approval. They must be clear, specific, attainable, and relevant to the educational context, and take into consideration the local context, families, children's well-being, resources, and the wider educational community.

Using the template set out earlier as a base, organizations can produce comprehensive ECE standards that incorporate input, process, and outcome elements of school accountability. Moreover, considering the contextual differences of local preschools in LMICs, the standards-setting organization could instruct local school committees to adapt the general standards to their local conditions and needs (Pritchett 2015). This approach could help policy makers and implementers support management infrastructure and develop a more contextually literate and individualized model.

Establish an Evaluation, Support, and Accountability System Based on Data

After setting relevant standards for ECE, an evaluation system is needed to ensure the standards are implemented and promote ECE improvement. In England, for example, well-established standards have been used increasingly in evaluation and managerial processes, and the results of the evaluation can guide further improvement (UNESCO 2017). Inspection reports are available publicly through the internet, which can motivate public engagement in school operations (Miller and Smith 2011). In Colombia, however, the results of inspections using set standards were used to decrease government investment in low-performing schools, which may lead to school closures (OECD 2015). Therefore, the tools for and the objectives of monitoring are important considerations when designing strategies for supervision, monitoring, and data collection.

The Chilean model for preschool center management offers a good example of clear standards. The model has five dimensions, each able to serve as a rubric for evaluation: (1) leadership, including strategic vision, center management, results-focused management, and planning; (2) standards focused on family and community; (3) pedagogical management, including curricular management standards, pedagogical interactions, and environments conducive to learning; (4) integral well-being, which includes a good environment, healthy living, and safe educational spaces; and (5) resource management, which includes human resources and operational management. What is interesting about this model is that it does not strongly divide the ECE leader's responsibilities between pedagogical leadership and administrative management—both are the ECE leader's responsibility.

ECE leaders can use existing measures to monitor the quality of their pedagogical interaction, curriculum, and children's learning environment in classrooms, such as the Teacher Instructional Practices and Processes System (Seidman et al. 2013), the Measure of Early Learning Environments (as revised for LMICs), the Early Childhood Environment Rating Scale-Extension (Sylva, Siraj-Blatchford, and Taggart 2010), and the Sustained Shared Thinking and Well-being Scale (Siraj, Kingston, and Melhuish 2015). These measures all require training before use (which can be provided in-house), and they all provide clear practice indicators and items that teachers can use for their own development through professional conversations and for self or external assessment.

It is important to note that assessments in ECE face challenges distinct from those in other levels of education systems. Emphasis should be on conducting assessments in settings that are comfortable, familiar, non-threatening, and of interest to the child, and that incorporate the child's developmental considerations, cultural considerations, and the potential to measure disabilities (for example, Bowman, Donovan, and Burns 2001).

Some measures of child development specifically for LMICs are being built and can be used for school and external assessment. The most common method of collecting information is through ECE leader, teacher, parent, and child interviews; classroom activity observation; recess and other spaces; and meeting attendance. Surveys are also a helpful data-collection tool. Some systems focus on student assessments, whereas others use school evaluations. As a result, there are divergent approaches that, on the one hand, promote quality improvement through student knowledge assessments and, on the other hand, consider the need to use external evaluations that verify the quality of ECE according to the latest standards and indicators. Examples of student assessment tools include the East

Asia-Pacific Early Child Development Scales by Rao, Sun, and Becher (2015), which were developed for children ages 36–71 months in East Asia and have demonstrated satisfactory internal consistency for assessing children's developmental outcomes. Another is the International Development and Early Learning Assessment (Save the Children 2011), which is an open access tool that has been used in more than 60 LMICs to evaluate child learning outcomes. In addition, examples of tools designed for large-scale monitoring of child outcomes include the Anchor Items for the Measurement of Early Childhood Development (AIM-ECD) (Pushparatnam et al. 2021) and the Early Childhood Development Index (ECDI2030) (UNICEF 2021).

Other cases adhere to a model of professional accountability, focusing mainly on the sustainable development of the capabilities of professionals within the establishment. In Latin America, Brazil follows this model, seeking to improve the quality of services through the development of the internal capacity of each center. Special emphasis is placed on avoiding any kind of competition or comparison between preschools, seeking to improve the working conditions of professionals as part of their quality standards (CIDE 2017).

Improving the monitoring and evaluation (or inspection) of school management has both a medium- and a long-term impact, and follow-up must be undertaken to sustain the positive impacts (World Bank 2015). According to the Starting Strong Survey 2018 (OECD 2019), ECE leaders need to monitor and assess children to improve learning, identify children with particular needs, evaluate the program, and monitor trends over time and for high stakes accountability (OECD 2019, 43–44).

Use Data Efficiently to Promote Compliance Mechanisms and Target Support

Compliance mechanisms need to be established to check that school standards and evaluation systems are being implemented consistently and correctly. The development of global digital networks and advanced technology has helped school monitoring systems considerably, and they are valuable for reducing costs of data collection and monitoring.

Data-based compliance mechanisms have been adopted by several LMICs (for example, Brazil, Ghana, Haiti) to monitor educational quality and student attendance. In Balochistan, Pakistan, for example, mobile phones are now used for data collection to improve schools' decision-making processes. The data collected include teacher attendance, student enrollment, school budgets, and provision of basic facilities. The real-time nature of these data allows timely and continuous monitoring of the school system, which can promote evidence-based decision-making (Baron and Salazar 2018a).

In Peru, technology-based data collection is also undertaken in schools and the data are sent to the Ministry of Education for feedback and evaluation. Local government can also take targeted actions to improve service delivery (Baron and Salazar 2018b). The effective use of data can also provide parents and other stakeholders with information on resource allocation, school operations, and students' learning outcomes (Bruns, Filmer, and Patrinos 2011); it can also guide parents' selection of better-functioning schools, thus forcing ECE services to work according to existing standards and guidelines (Miller and Smith 2011). To generate the necessary buy-in, programs must provide parents with easy access to straightforward information regarding a given school's performance results. Quality data and data platforms are therefore essential to informing parents and school administrators alike regarding a school's performance. In time, data-based evaluation will greatly assist ECE leaders' decision-making for managing and changing the ECE services for young children and their families.

Data in the quality assurance system or accountability system can be used to target scarce resources to the parts of the system where resources are needed. Data then become important not only for tracking progress but also for identifying how to allocate human and financial resources more efficiently.

Empower and Evaluate School Committees

Decentralization initiatives, including improving empowerment of and investment in school committees, can also improve schools' accountability—school committees can assist in localizing official standards and can act as school-based inspectors who collect and report data.

In LMICs, governments commonly appoint more teachers in an attempt to control class size and to produce better learning outcomes (Mbiti 2016). Unfortunately, increasing quantity without improving quality and accountability makes next to no difference to children's learning outcomes. Improving the accountability of teachers, and promoting their professional quality, is what matters.

Empowering school committees to, for example, recruit teachers and renew their contracts has been found to decrease teacher absenteeism and improve teaching (Muralidharan et al. 2016). Duflo, Dupas, and Kremer (2011) conducted a randomized experiment in Kenya and found that teachers who had been recruited with contracts issued directly by schools spent more time on instruction than those appointed centrally.

Hanushek, Link, and Woessmann (2013) find, however, that school autonomy made little difference in low-performing school systems. Therefore, the evaluation of SBM plays an important role. Demas and Arcia (2015) developed the School Autonomy and Accountability (SAA) tool to monitor SBM by evaluating the participation of the school committee, schools' financial management, personnel management, students' learning, and the use of information.

Key Takeaways

- Quality assurance systems can help improve school management and ECE service delivery.
- Quality assurance systems entail monitoring and accountability measures, including
  - Developing comprehensive and localizable standards;
  - Establishing an evaluation, support, and accountability system based on data;
  - Using data efficiently to promote compliance mechanisms and target support; and
  - Empowering and evaluating school committees.

PUTTING POLICIES INTO PRACTICE

This section puts forward the policy implications for diagnosis, implementation, and monitoring of effective ECE management and leadership. It draws policy implications from the evidence discussed in the previous section, but the main insights come from high-income countries and more developed school systems. Therefore, it is important to gather evidence as reforms progress in LMICs. This section presents a road map for decision-makers to implement the principles outlined above to boost the effectiveness of management and leaders' work in ECE centers to promote and support quality learning. The implementation plan is anchored in the development and support of the school leader as the fundamental element of effective management.

Diagnostics

To implement managerial, policy, and quality assurance reforms in ECE, the current situation and policies must be understood. Only then will it be possible to identify concrete opportunities to make changes that increase quality. To gain a complete picture of the ECE system from the managerial, policy, and quality assurance standpoints, the following types of studies would be helpful:

- *ECE national context diagnostic of policies.* The first task is to thoroughly map existing national institutions to gain a clear idea of how they operate. A key activity at this juncture would be to review evaluations (if they exist) to understand viable models for eventual scale-up. Mapping must also include a review of existing policies, regulations, and institutional supports in different countries. When beginning the design stage, the cultural characteristics of the country and the society's beliefs in relation to ECE must be considered.

- *National context quantitative mapping.* Given the diversity of ECE modalities, it is possible to find a wide array of school leaders in educational centers. For example, in ECE centers that are attached to primary schools, the position of an ECE leader is most likely filled by the general school head. Given that school leaders have so many responsibilities, they usually do not have the time or knowledge to manage ECE. In a few cases, schools with preschool, kindergarten, first grade, or second grade as the initial grade have a head who leads the educational cycle, focusing on ECE classes. In rural areas in LMICs, multi-age classrooms are common, and a teacher who is also the school leader attends to children between four and six years old, and sometimes as old as seven. In urban areas, public and formal ECE centers are most common; most of the time they have a school head. Therefore, it is necessary to collect reliable data about the national ECE situation, including number of centers and their diverse management and provision modalities; rural versus urban; private versus public; age and enrollment of students; number of teachers; and leaders' attributes (data on age, education, recent in-service training themes, years of experience, and so on). Given the multidisciplinary focus of ECE, which ministry is responsible for it? The ministry of health, ministry of education, ministry of women, multiple ministries, or the community?

- *Public policy review in relation to teachers and ECE leaders.* An important question for policy makers is whether there is a teacher career trajectory that includes school leaders, a management career ladder for school leaders, or both. This is important, given that incentives, not necessarily all monetary, will be needed to recruit and train school leaders. It is also important to review whether the teacher and school management policies are coordinated and coherent with the higher objectives of the system. This is not always the case; generally the higher education initiatives regarding teacher training, in-service training, and professional development policies established by the ministries are disjointed and often out of touch with the reality of the centers. Nevertheless, programs can be developed and, at the same time, visualization of a policy for a school management career can begin. It is important that the leader realize that, if he or she is required to undergo a change process, the work conditions will need to adjust to a certain extent. It is necessary to have political buy-in that translates into having the necessary funds to implement the policies.

- *Management teams' and school leaders' time-use study.* It would be important to form a clear picture of the time demands for the management of ECE schools or centers, making clear distinctions for different arrangements.
- *Assessment of training opportunities for ECE leaders.* Key questions here might include the following: What training programs exist? Do they include intense practice, or are they only theoretical? What is the academic component? What incentives exist to attend? Are continuous support, guidance, and materials available to school administrators and managers? Do they know who should carry out activities, when, and how? It is important to identify standards or expectations for school managers and leaders, paying particular attention to the leader's pedagogical role. These are important questions to be answered before moving into implementing stand-alone programs.
- *Tools, data study, and monitoring and evaluation.* It is important to understand what data the country is already producing on management, enrollment, quality assurance, and any other aspects related to ECE. It is also important to identify what tools, if any, have been used and adapted to measure inputs, their use, and learning outcomes at the school level. Moreover, it is important to identify what other tools (apps, paper questionnaires, informal networks) are used by supervisors to gather data, support management of schools, and disseminate policy and implementation information from higher levels of the ministry.

Implementation Plan: Enabling Conditions and Road Map

Implementation should be driven by two factors: (1) data from the diagnostics and (2) the goals of the ECE system that the country wants to put in place. Implementation must also consider funding envelopes and a time horizon. There are a few required conditions to improve the quality of ECE centers through management and leadership.

Political buy-in. Political buy-in is necessary to ensure investments are made in aspects of quality that may be harder to quantify but are as or more important than visible outcomes such as infrastructure or attendance. Political buy-in is also necessary to establish ECE as a long-term state policy, ensuring the necessary resources for implementation and evaluation.

Performance standards for ECE center leaders. The first section of this chapter highlights the importance of reference framework standards to lead the improvement of center leaders' performance and effectiveness. To establish performance standards, it is first important for stakeholders to develop a common reference framework according to the specific context. This needs to be agreed on and communicated carefully. The more consultation that occurs, the easier implementation will be. Many countries have profiles for leaders' functions, but these profiles refer only to their administrative functions. The need for leaders to also be pedagogical leaders is not specified in those profiles. Therefore, what is important is to have a clear, specific, and transparent agreement on the knowledge and responsibilities of school leaders (Anderson et al. 2008; Ingvarson and Kleinhenz 2006).[2]

Performance standards must be developed with the participation of several groups: management specialists, school leaders in practice, and teachers. The standards are an agreement about what each entity expects from its leaders, so they must have the widest possible approval. They must be clear, specific, attainable in their achievement, and relevant to the educational context, taking into consideration the local territory and the educational community. Once developed, investing enough time in the elaboration, discussion, and diffusion of standards is key. Upon completion, the leader is empowered, and the leader's role becomes more valuable in the educational center. Leaders value having a common and clear framework and performance guide. They also value having pedagogical purpose in their administrative actions.

One of the challenges of setting standards for the management of ECE centers is that preschool education for children ages four to six years is increasingly incorporated into primary education establishments in many countries. Standards of leadership between preprimary and primary schools are not very different. However, one of the main differences hinges on the central role of ECE leaders in well-being and communication with families. Some countries aim to integrate the preschool leader and the management team. Others look to an in-service training program for school leaders that focuses on children's educational development from the earliest stages to facilitate the transition from preschool to the first grades of primary education. Such a program provides an opportunity to train center leaders and families about the advantages of promoting transition mechanisms, yet it is not often addressed in LMICs.

Another challenge is reconciling different types of modalities and levels of education (from nursery school to kindergarten) in a single quality framework or among a set of standards. It is a pending issue, but the idea is to move forward with a general framework that is flexible enough to accommodate the different modalities of the centers.

It is recommended that standards be developed first, and then the diagnosis of in-service leaders' competencies and knowledge can be carried out to give the study a stronger theoretical framework and develop the necessary data-collection tools.

Evaluation of competencies of current ECE center leaders. The next step to improve the quality of ECE centers is to evaluate the competencies of leaders, including those who lead stand-alone centers or who lead primary schools that incorporate ECE, in both urban and rural contexts. This evaluation must be based on standards, and its objective is to visualize, both for policy decisions and for the leaders themselves, the gap between current performance and performance standards. This is essential for training and to establish the competencies of leaders. The diagnosis requires knowledge of demographics, leaders' work experience, types of education and training, salaries, working hours, and so on. Many LMICs do not have such up-to-date statistics.

This evaluation informs decision-makers about the needs for in-service training. On the basis of the findings of these diagnostics, decisions can be made to prioritize the allocation of available resources to the neediest geographic areas or demographic groups: Do children in the most vulnerable sectors have fewer effective school leaders? Are there rural or urban areas where leaders are weaker? An additional benefit of evaluating the competencies of current leaders is that doing so can lead to the identification of effective directors throughout the country who could be engaged to support training efforts.

In-service training programs for ECE center leaders. When standards have been validated and a diagnostic has been carried out, the next step is to make a strategic decision: train leaders within the system, select new ones, or both. In LMICs, the most strategic decision is to bet on training, given that it is most likely that the diagnostic will show many shortcomings in the performance of current school leaders. It should also be acknowledged that few LMICs offer initial training processes for leaders, resulting in a limited supply of candidates. Therefore, it would be more appropriate to simultaneously train leaders in practice and recruit new candidates for training before selection and hiring.

Organizing an effective leadership training program for ECE centers presents challenges and entails a gradual process that includes an evaluation of results. In LMICs, developing a simultaneous national program for all school leaders would be complex. Experience in different countries in Latin America (Chile, the Dominican Republic, Peru) shows that initially conducting a pilot program in one region of the country benefits operations and quality of service.

Provide quality training programs for school leadership. Training for ECE leaders must be well planned. It is the responsibility of the ministry of education, along with professional and higher education institutions, to design coherent, cumulative, and integral training experiences, as well as to deal with the results.

The design should first include an assessment of the leaders' competencies and knowledge based on established standards. The assessment's results identify the gap between leaders' current work and expected standards.

This exercise allows adjustments in the training plan to be made that correspond to needs. For example, gaps faced by leaders in rural areas will be different from those in urban areas. Therefore, the programs must be tailored to each context, and training plans adjusted to the different ECE modalities.

The training program must develop pedagogical management and leadership abilities in center leaders. On the one hand, the objective of training is to develop abilities in leaders, including strategic vision, team building, the capacity to negotiate and effectively communicate, empathy, and a sense of self-sufficiency, among others. On the other hand, training should equip participants with certain professional knowledge, such as managerial leadership, decision-making based on real school data, early childhood inclusion and equality, and sensitivity to ethnic, cultural, and linguistic diversity. Leaders need to know and develop the necessary skills to incorporate the heterogeneity of the children, to use pedagogical practices in preschools, to conduct evaluations, and to lead with a strong understanding of the curriculum. This will allow leaders to support their teachers' professional development, carry out project management, and so on. Nevertheless, studies show that some school leaders feel less prepared for administrative roles, such as financial management, and that they feel more prepared for roles as educators of ECE and in establishing relationships with staff (Hayden 1997; Muijs et al. 2004). Therefore, a good leadership training program should strengthen their administrative skills alongside their pedagogical management and leadership abilities.

The instructors in training programs need to be well-educated in management and educational leadership. This is perhaps the greatest difficulty in carrying out effective training programs. Most instructors in LMICs are academics from education departments that in general are removed from the real and concrete problems leaders face. They tend to focus more on theory than practice. Often, they are not up to date on the study of management or educational leadership. In turn, these countries look to district-level or regional leaders who lack the knowledge and experience in this kind of training program, given that their main focus has always been supervision.

Training needs to be focused and specific to the context of school leaders. One of the frustrations among adult students in training is the inevitable gap between theoretical ideas in their studies and their capacity to apply these ideas in their work. Successful training models are based on the premise that the immediate application of new knowledge to real-life situations strengthens lessons learned. For training to be effective, the examples used should relate to real problems and concerns that participants face in their work. The training should intertwine theory with the idiosyncratic problems that leaders face. Case studies, effective leader modeling, and program improvement plans are just a few examples of teaching strategies to make these connections practical. Active learning methods promote skills acquisition. Training programs that include modeling followed by role playing and performance feedback offered in an emotionally supportive atmosphere have been successful in several studies (for example, Dufrene et al. 2005; Sterling-Turner, Watson, and Moore 2002). Evidence also supports the importance of mentors who are instructors with leadership experience and who can accompany leaders in their daily work to monitor improvements and provide performance feedback. The inclusion of mentors increases the overall cost of training programs but ensures their quality.

Training should be focused on the leader as the agent of change. Effective leaders create a vision that serves to catalyze change. The leader needs to be prepared to overcome obstacles and encourage progress. Exposure to different models of change and the opportunity to develop abilities to ensure necessary reforms are successful are essential to training programs. Good professional development programs for early childhood administrators include both aspects: they take people to higher levels of knowledge and ability (what they know) while altering thought processes to deepen their understanding of their professional practice (how they do it).

Inclusion of an evaluation component is important. Training evaluations should include the leader's learning results: new knowledge acquisition, skills and abilities learned, changes in behavior seen in new work practices, changes in the school's organizational climate, quality of teaching practices, and parent satisfaction. In general, training programs include evaluations based on satisfaction with the service rendered but rarely provide an evaluation that measures the level of learning achievement in new practices. The second type of evaluation is essential to promoting real change in quality and a better understanding of the training's effectiveness.

Participants' career growth should be encouraged and supported. Wherever possible, training should translate into merit-based incentive systems and promotions in the leader's career path. The idea is to make sure that what is taught in training is used in the classroom.

Leader networks can be created in ECE centers. The professional role of an early education leader is often lonely. As such, training experiences should include opportunities for peer support and to generate territorial networks.

The resources and pedagogical support required will depend on the type of training program, that is, whether it is only in-person or both in-person and online, and whether it includes shadowing and mentoring. Also, the length of the program is an important budget consideration. In general, a program that focuses on developing abilities and good practices needs to take into account the significant time required to absorb, develop, and consolidate new abilities. Leadership training is more intense and requires more time than management training because it implies fundamental changes in the way people envision their roles and solve problems. Therefore, although shadowing increases the cost of training programs, it makes them more effective. Well-written manuals for leaders are also an important tool for their day-to-day operations. The trainees should focus on developing good practices and how to face multiple challenges that come with effective school management.

Identify and select new ECE school leaders. Once the standards are established and an in-service training program for leaders has been created, the education system needs to improve its leadership selection system. There is little information about selecting leaders specific to the ECE context, but the experience of selecting school leaders can provide important insights. Ontario's education system uses early and effective identification of future leaders within the organization, which ensures the development of their talents over time through leadership experiences from inside the existing establishment along with other similar strategies (Barber, Whelan, and Clark 2010). The Ontario school leader selection system is a valuable model because it includes an effective leadership identification, selection, and development system that is integrated into a harmonious and effective network that strengthens school systems (Barber, Whelan and Clark 2010).

Implement quality assurance and data-collection systems. On the basis of the previous discussion of standards, procedures, and definitions of roles and responsibilities, a quality assurance system can be developed to track implementation, measure improvement, and identify challenges. This system will serve as a quantitative measurement of ECE centers' standards that leaders need to improve on every year. It should include measurable indicators, aligned with the standards, that serve as an easy way to develop improvement plans that school leaders can use to better manage the school and to compare themselves with other schools. Such a quality assurance system will also help policy makers identify where to deploy more resources to tackle dire conditions or the lack of improvement.

Monitoring of Implementation

Just as school leaders need to have clear roles, responsibilities, accountability, and tools that facilitate their work, the implementation of programs and reforms for ECE management and leadership must follow similar principles. Successful implementation will depend on the quality of available resources, planning, monitoring, and path correction to overcome challenges. Therefore, the existence of capable ECE departments in ministries or service delivery cells that can monitor and evaluate progress is fundamental for improvement in ECE services. The process in each country, especially in LMICs, is not easy. Nevertheless, the lessons learned in other countries and contexts provide valuable inputs for leadership implementation. The foremost challenge is to carry out a rigorous implementation process that includes mobilizing human resources, funding, and political will.

Key Takeaways

Countries can improve the quality of their ECE leadership through the following steps:

- Diagnose the current challenges and circumstances.
- Plan for implementation to ensure political support for reforms, standard setting, evaluation, monitoring, quality assurance, and training in both management and educational leadership.
- Monitor implementation to evaluate progress and improve services.

CONCLUSION

ECE leaders fulfill the crucial roles of managing ECE centers, supporting educators, and engaging with families. ECE leaders recruit educators and staff, monitor whether curricula and pedagogical approaches are implemented with fidelity in the classroom, and provide instructional support. They also make key decisions about the school's physical environment and resources and are an important link to families and broader communities. The uniquely wide-ranging dual set of responsibilities for ECE leaders, both managerial and pedagogical, means that effective ECE leaders need to be proficient in both skill sets, especially given the low capacity and challenging working conditions that undermine motivation and retention in the ECE sector. It is critical that strong ECE leader training programs be developed, with a focus on leadership, pedagogical and administrative management, and coordination with the rest of the educational system. Effective leadership and management are crucial in enabling several key aspects of quality ECE, including supporting and motivating ECE teachers, fostering positive learning environments, and promoting strong partnerships with families.

See table 5.1 for a review of key takeaways from this chapter.

Table 5.1 Chapter 5: Summary of Key Takeaways

Good management and leadership at the school level

- *Administration.* The ability to efficiently plan and manage the allocation of resources is crucial to quality ECE leadership and management because the majority of a school leader's time is spent on these tasks.
- *Pedagogical leadership.* Good leaders put learning at the center of leadership and help teachers adapt curriculum, use assessment appropriately, and support children's transitions. Good leaders also understand systemwide challenges and local context and balance the two; they also support staff development.
- *Partnerships.* Developing and fostering positive school and family partnerships is a key role for school leaders.

ECE management at the system level

- When selecting ECE leaders, formal training, skills, and qualifications should be combined with formative assessment. Continuous pragmatic training is essential to developing the core skills of ECE leaders.
- To improve children's learning, all ECE leaders, including leader-managers, need to take responsibility for staff development, such as supervising and assessing teacher performance, mentoring and planning teacher professional development, and cultivating a reflective and collaborative working culture (OECD 2015), in addition to attending to their own ongoing development and learning.
- School-based management can be an effective approach to empowering school leaders and school communities.

Quality assurance for service delivery and data

- Quality assurance systems can help improve school management and ECE Service Delivery.
- Quality assurance systems entail monitoring and accountability measures, including
  - Developing comprehensive and localizable standards;
  - Establishing an evaluation, support, and accountability system based on data;
  - Using data efficiently to promote compliance mechanisms and target support; and
  - Empowering and evaluating school committees.

Putting policies into practice

The crucial steps a country can take to improve the quality of its ECE leadership include the following:

- Diagnose the current challenges and circumstances.
- Plan for implementation to ensure political support for reforms, standards setting, evaluation, monitoring, quality assurance, and training in both management and educational leadership.
- Monitor implementation to evaluate progress and improve services.

Source: Original table for this publication.
Note: ECE = early childhood education.

ECE Management: Some Lessons from the Field

With the support of the World Bank's Early Years Fellows,[a] information was collected in 12 countries using a brief questionnaire to gain an understanding of policies around and support to early childhood education (ECE) management (see annex 5A). The countries were Angola, Brazil, Burundi, Cameroon, the Arab Republic of Egypt, El Salvador, Jordan, Mali, Morocco, North Macedonia, Pakistan, and Tunisia. From responses to the short questionnaire, along with desk reviews, the following conclusions about the state of policies and support for ECE can be drawn:

- *Private ECE centers tend to have higher autonomy.* One of the most important differences is the degree of management autonomy in private centers. Most private kindergartens are not attached to a private primary school and have a principal that is exclusively focused on ECE in comparison with the public systems.
- *Clear policies for ECE management are lacking.* There is no clear policy regarding leadership in ECE centers. There are countries where ECE centers typically have a leader who is the managerial or administrative representative; this situation applies to both public and private providers (Angola, Brazil, El Salvador, North Macedonia, Mali, Tunisia). In other cases, public ECE centers (called kindergarten classrooms) are attached to primary schools. The primary school head is responsible for the school as a whole unit,

including kindergarten classrooms. In these countries, school headmasters usually designate another teacher to support them with specific functions (Angola, Cameroon, Egypt, Jordan, Pakistan), and in others, such as Morocco, the concept of ECE school leadership does not currently exist. There are no school heads at all in many countries' community schools.

- *Government still plays a major role in hiring.* In most countries, hiring processes are carried out by the ministry of education at both the national and regional levels. In other cases, they are carried out by municipalities. The difference between public and private sector ECE centers is that private centers can directly select and hire teachers.
- *Qualifications needed for leadership vary greatly across low- and middle-income countries.* Most countries require ECE leader candidates to have a high school diploma and between five and ten years of professional experience working in a school. However, the qualification requirements are diverse among countries in the sample. For example, Jordan requires a master's degree, whereas other countries require only a high school diploma (North Macedonia, Pakistan), nine years of education (Burundi), or just previous experience (Angola). Some countries do not even have an established framework for school leaders, and the role is carried out in a more informal way (Morocco). In Cameroon, most ECE center leaders do not have to achieve a special qualification before being appointed head of an ECE center. In Angola, although Presidential Decree 129/17 of June 16 (Status of ECE Subsystem) states that heads of schools should be ECE teachers with at least five years of experience, there are many cases in which other arrangements constitute the main criteria for nominations in public institutions.
- *Terms for appointments of school leaders do not tend to be fixed.* The term duration is not specified, nor is the number of times a leader can be reappointed.
- *In general, school leaders cannot hire or evaluate teachers because other ministerial or municipal authorities have the authority to do so.* In Morocco, for example, school principals are evaluated for functions related to the primary school only and there is no regulatory framework for the preschool level. The exception is Cameroon, where the headmaster or headmistress can select, hire, and evaluate teachers. These evaluations have consequences for the professional advancement of teachers. Parent-teacher associations, using the guidance of the headmasters or headmistresses, can also hire teachers to meet needs in specific academic institutions. In private schools, school leaders do hire and evaluate their teaching staff and their results may have consequences.
- *Regarding specific training for ECE leaders or coordinators,* there are in-service training programs in Angola, Brazil, Cameroon, Egypt, Mali, and Pakistan. In the other countries surveyed, no national in-service training

program is in place for ECE leaders. The themes of these training programs are not specified, except in Brazil, where the emphasis is on operational management, food programs, and the like. The need for ECE leader and coordinator training is urgent. In Brazil, for example, the School Census for manager position professionals has a field on specialization courses for ECE. Of the 91,399 professionals who are registered under the Census, only 11 percent have taken a preschool-related specialization course.

- *There are no incentives for those who attend director training programs,* except in Cameroon, Egypt, and Pakistan, where these are more related to salary increases for assuming director functions. By contrast, community ECE leaders in rural areas, where the most vulnerable children learn and sometimes have only one teacher, do not receive any training (Cameroon, Mali).

It is evident that the reality of the role of the ECE center leader does not match with what the theory and international good practices propose. While recognizing the efforts that these countries are making, continual and sustained change will be needed to accelerate quality ECE. Behind each ECE leader are teachers and countless students whose physical, intellectual, emotional, and social development are at risk at this critical stage of their development.

In this complex context, there are some countries that have made efforts to increase access to education, usually focusing on access to primary grades. However, ECE is crucial for building good cognitive and social foundations that would make primary school more productive for children. The focus should be on integrating and mainstreaming ECE management into the management and regulatory framework of primary education. This integration will require specialized management and leadership who understand the need for investments and quality service delivery. This means training leaders—who not only take on the administrative tasks of the center but also provide pedagogical leadership—on how to accompany and support their teachers, effectively observe classrooms, give timely feedback, monitor each child's progress related to the curriculum, and build a strong and nurturing relationship with parents. Unfortunately, little of this in practice is seen in the low- and middle-income countries surveyed.

[a] The authors would like to thank the World Bank Early Years Fellows who answered the survey: Saed Alzawahreh, Amna Ansari, Bárbara Barbosa, Martin Galevski, Etienne A. Guirou, António Felix B. Jerónimo, Soukaina Tazi, Sara Velásquez, Rana Yacoub, and Zeineb Ben Yahmed.

ANNEX 5A: QUESTIONNAIRE SURVEY

Background: The World Bank team is working to illustrate the diversity and complexity of early childhood education (ECE) school leadership in low- and middle-income countries. We appreciate your support in filling out the following survey that will help us capture the heterogeneous nature of ECE learning centers for our forthcoming publication.

Instructions: Please completely answer the following questions by providing detailed responses and documenting sources of information. Please provide sources and links to reference all of your answers.

Questions:

1. Is there a principal or school coordinator position in ECE centers? Make any distinction to whether your answer refers to public or private.
2. Who is the acting principal or coordinator figure? (Teacher, administrator, other) Make any distinction to whether your answer refers to public or private.
3. What is the professional background of the principal in ECE centers? What higher education degree(s) do they have (if any)? Do they have any certifications? What percentage of principals only have a secondary education diploma?
4. How many principal/coordinator figures are in schools? Is there only one school principal for all grades (including ECE) or is there also a principal for the ECE grades?
5. Who chooses the principal/coordinator position at the ECE center/grades?
6. What entity (if any) designates the person in charge of selecting the principal/coordinator position at the learning center? If possible, please share the corresponding law or norm that determines this.
7. How long does the principal/coordinator position term last? Are there term contracts or term limits?
8. Is there an entity or assigned individual that evaluates the principal/coordinator's performance?
9. Can the principal/coordinator select, hire, and evaluate teachers? Do these evaluations have consequences?
10. Is there any national public or private in-service training for ECE principals?
11. Do principals or ECE coordinators have any academic incentives?
12. Is there anything else you would like to share about ECE school leadership?

NOTES

1. A few caveats are in order: First, we use "management" and "leadership" interchangeably; for clear distinctions, see Davies (2003). Second, when referring to the principal's role, we have in mind a broader definition of principal, in the sense that it is not the individual but the management team that performs the "role of the principal." Third, most of the (limited) strong evidence on management practices on outcomes come from higher-income countries or is for a different level of education, not necessarily ECE, for which the research and the evidence are more limited.

2. A good example of these standards is the case study of Chile for management of preschool centers. The Chilean model includes five dimensions and each of them serves as a rubric for evaluation: (1) leadership along the lines of strategic vision standards, center management, results-focused management, and planning; (2) standards focused on family and community; (3) pedagogical management, including curricular management standards, pedagogical interactions, and environments conducive to learning; (4) integral well-being, referring to a good environment, healthy living, and safe educational spaces; and (5) resource management, referring to human resources and operational management. What is interesting about this model is that it does not strongly divide the principal's responsibilities in terms of pedagogical leadership and administrative management. Both are the principal's responsibilities.

REFERENCES

Adelman, M., and J. Baron. 2019. "School Principals as Effective Leaders and Managers: A Critical Piece of the Learning Puzzle." Unpublished.

Anderson, M., P. Gronn, L. Ingvarson, A. Jackson, E. Kleinhenz, P. McKenzie, B. Mulford, and N. Thornton. 2008. "OECD Improving School Leadership Activity. Australia: Country Background Report." Australian Council for Educational Research, Melbourne.

Bambrick-Santoyo, P. 2012. *Leverage Leadership: A Practical Guide to Building Exceptional Schools*. San Francisco, CA: John Wiley & Sons, Inc.

Banerjee, A. V., R. Banerji, E. Duflo, R. Glennerster, and S. Khemani. 2010. "Pitfalls of Participatory Programs: Evidence from a Randomized Evaluation in Education in India." *American Economic Journal: Economic Policy* 2 (1): 1–30.

Barber, M., F. Whelan, and M. Clark. 2010. "Capturing the Leadership Premium: How the World's Top School Systems Are Building Leadership Capacity for the Future." McKinsey and Company. http://mckinseyonsociety.com/downloads/reports/Education/schoolleadership_final.pdf.

Baron, J., and I. P. Salazar. 2018a. "Review of Monitoring Experiences: Cases." Unpublished.

Baron, J., and I. P. Salazar. 2018b. "Semáforo escuela Peru's School Monitoring System." Unpublished.

Barrera-Osorio, F., T. Fasih, H. Patrinos, and L. Santibañez. 2009. *Decentralized Decision-Making in Schools. The Theory and Evidence of School-Based Management.* Washington, DC: World Bank.

Bartanen, B., J. A. Grissom, and L. K. Rogers. 2019. "The Impacts of Principal Turnover." *Educational Evaluation and Policy Analysis 41* (3): 350–74.

Blimpo, M. P., D. K. Evans, and N. Lahire. 2015. "Parental Human Capital and Effective School Management: Evidence from The Gambia." Working Paper 7238, World Bank, Washington, DC.

Bloom, N., R. Lemos, R. Sadun, and J. Van Reenen. 2015. "Does Management Matter in Schools?" *Economic Journal* 125 (584): 647–74.

Bloom, N., R. Lemos, R. Sadun, D. Scur, and J. Van Reenen. 2016. "International Data on Measuring Management Practices." *American Economic Review* 106 (5): 152–56.

Bowman, B., S. Donovan, and S. Burns, eds. 2001. *Eager to Learn: Educating Our Pre-schoolers.* Washington, DC: National Academy Press.

Bruns, B., D. Filmer, and H. Patrinos. 2011. *Making Schools Work: New Evidence on Accountability Reforms.* Human Development Perspectives. Washington, DC: World Bank.

CIDE. 2017. "Estándares de oportunidades de aprendizaje en Educación Parvulario: evidencia comparada." Universidad Alberto Hurtado, Santiago.

Davies, Brent. 2003. "Leadership and Management Processes." In *Handbook of Educational Leadership and Management,* edited by Brent Davies and John West-Burnham. London: Pearson Longman.

Demas, A., and G. Arcia. 2015. "What Matters Most for School Autonomy and Accountability: A Framework Paper." Systems Approach for Better Education Results (SABER) Working Paper 9, World Bank. Washington, DC.

Duflo, E., P. Dupas, and M. Kremer. 2011. "Peer Effects, Teacher Incentives, and the Impact of Tracking: Evidence from a Randomized Evaluation in Kenya." *American Economic Review* 101 (5): 1739–74.

Dufrene, B. A., G. H. Noell, D. N. Gilbertson, and G. J. Duhon. 2005. "Monitoring Implementation of Reciprocal Peer Tutoring: Identifying and Intervening with Students Who Do Not Maintain Accurate Implementation." *School Psychology Review* 34 (1): 74–86.

Engle, P. L., L. Fernald, H. Alderman, J. Behrman, C. O'Gara, A. Yousafzai, M. Cabral de Mello, et al. 2011. "Strategies for Reducing Inequalities and Improving Developmental Outcomes for Young Children in Low-Income and Middle-Income Countries." *Lancet* 378 (9799): 1339–53.

Evans, D. K., and A. Popova. 2016. "What Works to Improve Learning in Developing Countries? An Analysis of Divergent Findings in Systematic Reviews." *World Bank Research Observer* 31 (2): 242–70.

Everard, K. B., G. Morris, and I. Wilson. 2004. *Effective School Management.* London: SAGE.

Fryer, R. G., S. Levitt, and J. A. List. 2015. "Parental Incentives and Early Childhood Achievement: A Field Experiment in Chicago Heights." Harvard University, Cambridge, MA. https://scholar.harvard.edu/files/fryer/files/gecc_final.pdf.

Hanushek, E. A., S. Link, and L. Woessmann. 2013. "Does School Autonomy Make Sense Everywhere? Panel Estimates from PISA." *Journal of Development Economics* 104: 212–32.

Hayden, J. 1997. "Directors of Early Childhood Services: Experience, Preparedness and Selection." *Journal of Australian Research in Early Childhood Education* 1: 49–61.

Howes, C., J. James, and S. Ritchie. 2003. "Pathways to Effective Teaching." *Early Childhood Research Quarterly* 18: 104–20.

Ingvarson, L., and E. Kleinhenz. 2006. "Estándares profesional de práctica y su importancia para la enseñanza." *Revista de Educación* 340: 265–95.

Leithwood, K., K. Seashore Louis, S. Anderson, and K. Wahlstrom. 2004. *How Leadership Influences Student Learning: A Review of Research*. Minneapolis, MN: University of Minnesota; Ontario: University of Ontario; New York: Wallace Foundation. http://conservancy.umn.edu/bitstream/11299/2035/1/CAREI ReviewofResearch How Leadership Influences.pdf.

Leithwood, K., J. Sun, and R. Schumacker. 2019. "How School Leadership Influences Student Learning: A Test of The Four Paths Model." Unpublished.

Lemos, R., and D. Scur. 2016. "Developing Management: An Expanded Evaluation Tool for Developing Countries." London School of Economics, Center for Economic Performance, London.

Maeshall, J. H., and A. Bunly. 2017. "School Grants and School Performance in Rural Cambodia." *Journal of Development Effectiveness* 9 (3): 305–28.

Mbiti, I. M. 2016. "The Need for Accountability in Education in Developing Countries." *Journal of Economic Perspectives* 30 (3): 109–32.

McEwan, P., and L. Santibáñez. 2005. "Teacher and Principal Incentives in Mexico." In *Incentives to Improve Teaching, Lessons from Latin America*, edited by Emiliana Vegas. Washington, DC: World Bank.

Melhuish, E., K. Sylva, P. Sammons, I. Siraj-Blatchford, B. Taggart, and M. Phan. 2008. "Effects of the Home Learning Environment and Preschool Center Experience upon Literacy and Numeracy Development in Early Primary School." *Journal of Social Issues* 64 (1): 95–114. doi:10.1111/j.1540-4560.2008.00550.x.

Miller, L. J., and S. C. Smith. 2011. "Did the No Child Left Behind Act Miss the Mark? Assessing the Potential Benefits from an Accountability System for Early Childhood Education." *Educational Policy* 25 (1): 193–214.

Muijs, D., C. Aubrey, A. Harris, and M. Briggs. 2004. "How Do They Manage? A Review of the Research on Leadership in Early Childhood." *Journal of Early Childhood Research* 2 (2): 157–69.

Muralidharan, K., J. Das, A. Holla, and A. Mohpal. 2016. "The Fiscal Cost of Weak Governance: Evidence from Teacher Absence in India." Policy Research Working Paper 7579, World Bank, Washington, DC.

Mutale, W., A. T. Vardoy-Mutale, A. Kachemba, R. Mukendi, K. Clarke, and D. Mulenga. 2017. "Leadership and Management Training as a Catalyst to Health System Strengthening in Low-Income Settings: Evidence from the Implementation of the Zambia Management and Leadership Course for District Health Managers in Zambia." *PLOS ONE* 12 (7): 1–24.

Nannyonjo, H. 2017. *Building Capacity of School Leaders: Strategies That Work—Jamaica's Experience*. Washington, DC: World Bank.

New Venture Fund. 2018. "Developing Early Childhood Leaders to Support Strong, Equitable Systems: A Review of the Early Childhood Leadership Development Landscape." New Venture Fund, Washington, DC. https://www.arabellaadvisors.com/wp-content/uploads/2018/04/New-Venture-Fund_Packard_report_v7.pdf.

OECD (Organisation for Economic Co-operation and Development). 2009. *Improving School Leadership: The Toolkit*. Paris: OECD Publishing. https://www.oecd.org/education/school/44339174.pdf.

OECD (Organisation for Economic Co-operation and Development). 2015. *Students, Computers and Learning: Making the Connection*. Paris: OECD Publishing.

OECD (Organisation for Economic Co-operation and Development). 2016. *School Leadership for Learning: Insights from TALIS 2013*. Paris: OECD Publishing. https://read.oecd-ilibrary.org/education/school-leadership-for-learning_9789264258341-en#page3.

OECD (Organisation for Economic Co-operation and Development). 2019. *TALIS 2018 Results (Volume I): Teachers and School Leaders as Lifelong Learners*. Paris: OECD Publishing. https://doi.org/10.1787/1d0bc92a-en.

Perlman, M., N. Howe, C. Gulyas, and O. Falenchuk. 2019. "Associations between Directors' Characteristics, Supervision Practices and Quality of Early Childhood Education and Care Classrooms." *Early Education and Development* 31 (4): 507–23.

Poekert, P., A. Alexandrou, and D. Shannon. 2016. "How Teachers Become Leaders: An Internationally Validated Theoretical Model of Teacher Leadership Development." *Research in Post-Compulsory Education* 21 (4): 307–29.

Pont, B., D. Nusche, and H. Moorman. 2008. *Improving School Leadership, Volume 1: Policy and Practice*. Paris: OECD Publishing.

Pritchett, L. 2015. "Creating Education Systems Coherent for Learning Outcomes: Making the Transition from Schooling to Learning." Working Paper 15/005, Research on Improving Systems of Education (RISE).

Pushparatnam, A., D. A. Luna Bazaldua, A. Holla, J. P. Azevedo, M. Clarke, and A. Devercelli. 2021. "Measuring Early Childhood Development among 4–6 Year Olds: The Identification of Psychometrically Robust Items across Diverse Contexts." *Frontiers in Public Health* 9: 569448. https://doi.org/10.3389/fpubh.2021.569448.

Rao, N., J. Sun, and Y. Becher. 2015. "Assessing Early Development and Learning across Cultures: The East Asia Pacific—Early Child Development Scales." *Assessment and Development Matters* 7: 21–25.

Robinson, V. M. J. 2007. "School Leadership and Student Outcomes: Identifying What Works and Why." ACEL Monograph Series, Australian Council for Educational Leaders, Winmalee, Australia. http://www.saspa.com.au/wp-content/uploads/2016/02/Robinson.pdf.

Save the Children. 2011. *The International Development and Early Learning Assessment*. London: Save the Children. https://idela-network.org/mou-form/.

Seidman, E., M. Raza, S. Kim, and J. M. McCoy. 2013. *Teacher Instructional Practices and Processes System (V.5) – TIPPS*. New York: New York University.

Sim, M. P. Y., J. Belanger, A. Stancel-Piątak, and L. A. Karoly. 2019. "Starting Strong Teaching and Learning International Survey 2018 Conceptual Framework." Education Working Paper 197, OECD Publishing, Paris. https://doi.org/10.1787/106b1c42-en.

Siraj, I., D. Kingston, and E. Melhuish. 2015. *Assessing Quality in Early Childhood Education and Care. Sustained Shared Thinking and Emotional Wellbeing (SSTEW) Scale for 2–5-Year-Olds Provision.* London: UCL and IOE Press.

Siraj-Blatchford, I., and L. Manni. 2007. *Effective Leadership in the Early Years Sector.* London: Institute of Education, University of London.

Siraj-Blatchford, I., and C. Sum. 2013. "Understanding and Advancing System Leadership in the Early Years." National College for Teaching and Leadership, Nottingham.

Snell, J., and J. Swanson. 2000. "The Essential Knowledge and Skills of Teacher Leaders: A Search for a Conceptual Framework." Paper presented at the annual meeting of the American Educational Research Association, New Orleans, LA, April 24–28.

Sterling-Turner, H. E., T. S. Watson, and J. W. Moore. 2002. "The Effects of Direct Training and Treatment Integrity on Treatment Outcomes in School Consultation." *School Psychology Quarterly* 17: 47–77.

Sylva, K., E. C. Melhuish, P. Sammons, I. Siraj-Blatchford, and B. Taggart. 2004. *The Effective Provision of Pre-School Education (EPPE) Project: Final Report.* London: DfES/Institute of Education, University of London.

Sylva, K., I. Siraj-Blatchford, and B. Taggart. 2010. "Early Childhood Environment Rating Scale-Extension." Teachers College Press, New York.

Talan, T. N., P. J. Bloom, and R. E. Kelton. 2014. "Building the Leadership Capacity of Early Childhood Directors: An Evaluation of a Leadership Development Model." *Early Childhood Research and Practice* 16 (1): 1–10.

UNESCO (United Nations Educational, Scientific and Cultural Organization). 2017. *Accountability in Education: Meeting Our Commitments.* Paris: UNESCO Publishing.

UNICEF (United Nations Children's Fund). 2021. "Early Childhood Development Index 2030: A New Tool to Measure SDG Indicator 4.2.1." https://data.unicef.org/resources/early-childhood-development-index-2030-ecdi2030/.

World Bank. 2007. *What Is School-Based Management?* Washington, DC: World Bank.

World Bank. 2015. *World Bank Support to Early Childhood Development: An Independent Evaluation.* Washington, DC: Independent Evaluation Group, World Bank.

Yang, W. 2019. "Moving from Imitation to Innovation: Exploring a Chinese Model of Early Childhood Curriculum Leadership." *Contemporary Issues in Early Childhood* 20 (1): 35–52.

Yang, W., J. Wang, and H. Li. 2017. "Achieving a Balance between Affordability, Accessibility, Accountability, Sustainability and Social Justice: The Early Childhood Education Policies in Hong Kong." In *Early Childhood Education Policies in Asia Pacific,* edited by H. Li, E. Park, and J. J. Chen, 51–71. Singapore: Springer.

York-Barr, J., and K. Duke. 2004. "What Do We Know about Teacher Leadership? Findings from Two Decades of Scholarship." *Review of Educational Research* 74 (3): 255–316.

6

Toward Quality Early Learning: Systems for Success

OVERVIEW

Implementing high-quality, effective, and equitably distributed early learning services is necessary empirically and conceptually, but is challenging practically. No matter how effective specific curricula and pedagogy, particular learning environments, or even individual educators and leaders are, they are insufficient to fully advance early learning. Early learning sits at the vortex of a diverse array of existing programs, institutions, and systems, each laden with unique and highly influential histories, regulations, workforces, financing mechanisms, governance approaches, and data and accountability requirements. To successfully implement and scale early learning services, the requisite understanding of how these institutions and systems function and interact renders an examination of systems thinking, composition, and infrastructure essential. Such an analysis indicates that (1) early learning can be an effective bridge for linking the often disparate early childhood and education systems, and (2) attention to these systems and the infrastructure that supports them is crucial for sustaining effective early learning efforts and for realizing returns on fiscal and human investments in young children.

This chapter was written by Sharon Lynn Kagan and Caitlin M. Dermody.

INTRODUCTION

Why end a volume on early learning with a chapter on systems? What are systems and how are they relevant to early learning? In tackling these two questions, this chapter contextualizes the challenges inherent in bringing the ideas presented throughout this book to fruition and, hopefully, to scale. Earlier chapters address individual elements that support early learning. This chapter explains why all elements are important to consider as part of a system and why systems thinking is essential to delivering quality early learning at scale. The chapter begins by acknowledging the contemporary vulnerability of early learning efforts, underscoring how their recent and rapid global expansion risks, however inadvertently, exacerbating deeply rooted practices and policies that inhibit successful implementation. Drawing on systems theory, research, and practice, the chapter presents a fresh perspective on how early learning services might be considered, designed, implemented, and scaled within the context of the existing systems that frame them.

BACKGROUND AND CHALLENGES: A SYSTEMS IMPERATIVE

Background and Challenges

Anchored by well-researched and well-publicized scholarship from diverse fields that extolls the benefits of high-quality early learning[1] as an elixir of children's individual competence and the overall social and economic advancement of countries, early learning programs are increasingly in the spotlight, although they are underfunded compared with primary and secondary schools. Throughout the world, these early childhood services have received augmented public support and resource allocations, enabling the enrollment of increased numbers of young children (Lancet Early Childhood Development Series Steering Committee 2016; UNICEF 2019; Vargas-Barón et al. 2019).

However, as promising as this may seem, in reality, all is not so rosy. Regardless of these increased investments in early learning programs, children's gains are not strong (Barnett 2008; Fukkink, Jilink, and Oostdam 2017; Love et al. 2013; US Department of Health and Human Services 2010; van Huizen and Plantenga 2018) and are often not sustained (Lipsey, Farran, and Durkin 2018; Shuey and Kankaras 2018; Whitehurst 2018). Moreover, accelerators of effectiveness are lacking; programs are not all of high quality, are not equitably distributed, are sometimes inefficient, and are often difficult to sustain and scale, resulting in limited maximization of the considerable investments being made in them (OECD 2017a; Reid et al. 2019; UNESCO 2019; UNICEF 2019; Watson 2012).

Complicating the fragility of contemporary early learning programs, their origins make them precarious. All services for young children and their families are not the purview of any single discipline, profession, or ministry. Owing their existence to multiple disciplines (for example, education, psychology, economics, and political science), such services typically (and sometimes simultaneously) exist in ministries as varied as education, social services, welfare, or community and economic development. As a specific subset of these services, early learning services straddle diverse and often ill-cemented social and governmental structures. Laden with these inconsistencies, and further burdened by inchoate and dispersed governmental fiscal commitments, early learning programs in many countries are fragmented in intention and delivery, and burdensomely confusing to families, providers, and policy makers.

Early learning services are awash with weighty challenges, many of them raised in this volume: How can early learning services that are responsive to the contemporary needs of children and their diverse learning conditions and environments be produced? How can the gains children make in early learning programs be sustained as they transition to primary school? How can continuity between preschool and primary services be promoted to maximize their impact? How can services be designed that adequately address the increasingly diverse populations that are being and will be served? In short, how do we ensure that the programs and services that are created foster the outcomes desired for all programs and services, and for all children? Typical policy responses to these and other trenchant questions include the development of new pedagogical strategies, the layering on of more programs or services, or reaching out to new and previously un- or underserved populations.

This chapter suggests that such efforts, however well intentioned and necessary, are insufficient to address the broad and challenging issues that now confront those attempting to advance early learning services. It suggests that solutions to complex issues demand more than a simple adding on of more services, no matter their quality or individual merit. Acknowledging the magnitude and depth of contemporary challenges, coupled with the perilous base on which early learning services sit, means that policy makers need to think differently—and far more boldly—if the hope is to enhance and durably scale early learning services and, most important, advance the well-being of the children such services purport to serve.

Understanding Systems: The Chapter's Focus

Addressing these realities conceptually and practically demands fresh thinking. Fresh thinking involves the intentional broadening of perspectives and questing for inventive ways of understanding the problems that are typically constrained by conventional responses. Germane to the focus of this chapter, it means considering early learning services broadly and systemically. To do so, policy makers must distinguish between early learning and early learning services, define systems and understand systemic thinking, plan for change by conceptualizing early learning services holistically and interactively, and implement contextually responsive and respectful systems.

Distinguishing between Early Learning and Early Learning Services

Early childhood education and care (ECEC) is characterized by its commitment to fostering child-centered pedagogy. Its definition is fairly—though not thoroughly—agreed upon, and typically considered to span the years from birth to eight. *Early learning* is a developmental and pedagogical construct that refers to what and how children learn. Inherently, then, early learning is spontaneous and ubiquitous: it takes place everywhere young children exist—in their homes, communities, fields, playgrounds, parks, and community environments. But early learning as the term is used in this volume is quite different; it refers to the learning that occurs at more formalized center-based experiences that have been intentionally established to support early learning in programs for children ages three to six years.

As such, *early learning services* (as distinguished from early learning) are characterized by the planned and organized efforts that take hold in myriad institutional entities—childcare programs, prekindergarten and kindergarten services, and schools that work to promote early learning. In this sense, early learning services are amoebae-like: although bound by a pedagogical nucleus (early learning), the services sprawl, taking on diverse shapes and often adopting the patina of their host setting. Thus, as used herein, *early learning* is a pedagogical construct, whereas *early learning services* is an institutional construct. As an institutional construct, early learning services are committed to advancing children's learning within and across the programs and settings in which they are being provided.

Defining Systems and Thinking Systemically

To date, most programmatic and policy efforts concerned with improving early learning services have focused on the child, the classroom, the pedagogical approach, and sometimes the program as the primary units of analysis. Although essential to the advancement of pedagogy and programming, such perspectives represent only one important dimension of early learning services. This chapter suggests that, beyond their focus on children, classrooms, and individual programs, early learning services must be conceptualized and understood as part of a larger and more complex system.

Because systems are complex, an analogy may help clarify what they are and illuminate their importance to early learning services. Consider that early learning services or programs are like automobiles; they have consistent properties. For automobiles, the properties are wheels, doors, and turn signals; for early learning services, the properties are curriculum, pedagogy, and centers. These properties may vary in detail (for example, automobiles are different colors and early learning services use different curricula and take place in different centers), but both are tangible and identifiable. Both automobiles and early learning services have clear functions; they are designed to get us places (for example, automobiles transport people to specific locations and early learning services prepare students for school and lifelong learning experiences). Both automobiles and early learning services are direct, identifiable, concrete entities that users experience.

But neither automobiles nor early learning services can function in isolation. Carrying the analogy further, they both need infrastructure to support them. The infrastructure for each takes different forms. Automobiles need a physical infrastructure (for example, highways, bridges, tunnels), a regulatory infrastructure (for example, driver's licenses, stop signs, speed surveillance mechanisms), and a fiscal infrastructure (for example, car financing and insurance supports). These infrastructural supports make automobiles useful, safe, and operational at scale. Simply building more and more automobiles without attending to corresponding efforts to improve the infrastructure diminishes their utility. Without attention to the physical infrastructure, roads get clogged up and are weakened by overuse; without attention to the fiscal infrastructure, rampant automotive production can leave unpurchased automobiles consigned to showroom lots. It is the combination of the automobiles and the infrastructure that makes the automotive transportation system both workable and effective.

Similarly, early learning services need and rest on essential infrastructure that also brings them to fruition and renders them effective. The infrastructure that supports early learning services, although historically overlooked in the literature, has become a key theme in recent scholarship. Although no perfect consensus exists regarding these infrastructural elements, they often include financing, governance, regulation and accountability, workforce capacity, data collection and use, family and community engagement, and links with other services (Kagan and Cohen 1997). Collectively, these infrastructural elements combine with early learning services (that is, the direct services) to form a system. Kagan and Cohen (1997) note that a simple equation represents this relationship: a system is composed of, or equals, the direct early learning services plus the infrastructure.

Moreover, Kagan and Cohen (1997) suggest that the direct services and all seven elements of the infrastructure are needed for a system to function, expressed formulaically as eight (the direct service and the seven infrastructure elements) minus one (either the direct service or any single element of the infrastructure) equals zero, making the system null, because all eight elements are essential to forming a coherent and functioning system. And, more consequentially, only when the total system is addressed can the desired and often-absent systemic outcomes be produced that enable the creation and scaling up of early learning services of merit. Systemic outcomes, as opposed to individual or programmatic outcomes, include early learning services that are high quality, equitably distributed, efficiently designed and executed, efficiently financed and governed, and durably scaled (Kagan and Roth 2017). Systems thinking and implementation address these outcomes; programmatic thinking can not and does not.

Planning for Change: Conceptualizing Holistically and Interactively

Beyond defining and acknowledging the importance of systems thinking, and the essentiality of addressing all elements of the system, the processes associated with how systems are conceptualized and change need to receive some attention. Planning systems demands broad-based conceptualization of the $8 - 1 = 0$ formula, but it also requires acknowledging that systems are not static. On the contrary, they are highly dynamic and constantly in flux in sometimes predictable, but often unpredictable, ways. Systems are contoured by the ways in which their elements interact. Changes in any single element of the infrastructure often affect the full system. Because of systems' interactive nature, systems planners and thinkers must not only think holistically (for example, $8 - 1 = 0$) but also plan for such interactions.

With an eye toward improving the overall system, scholars are working to discern how different systemic elements are linked and how they influence one another (Britto et al. 2014; Kagan et al. 2016; Marope and Kaga 2015; Naudeau et al. 2010; Vargas-Barón 2015). Although the consensus on these interactions is still developing, the literature consistently underscores the liabilities of thinking about elements of a system independently, a practice still widely operative. Recently, for example, enhancing workforce capacity has been touted as a near panacea for addressing the lion's share of the problems associated with early learning services. In reality, enhancing the quality of workers, however popular and necessary, is not the sole solution to related and recurring workforce challenges (for example, supply, retention, turnover) that early learning programs face.

Myriad factors, represented by elements of the system, contribute heavily to workforce capacity (for example, garnering the durable funding to support increased compensation, overcoming the ravages of hybridized governance and differential salaries that encourage staff to shift from one program to another, or dealing with accountability and regulatory approaches that set different staffing requirements, even within a single jurisdiction). Workforce capacity cannot be meaningfully enhanced without attending to infrastructural elements, including, at a minimum, finance, governance, regulation, and accountability. In short, understanding how diverse system elements interact with one another to support quality early learning is a correlate of effective systems thinking and planning and a prerequisite for its advancement and scalability.

Implementing Contextually Respectful Systems

Understanding systems that influence early learning services means acknowledging that although systems thinking may be comparatively recent in this field, the systems that encase early learning services are not. To best consider how to implement improved early learning services, the magnitude of contextual variation on early learning services and the contexts in which such services generally sit must be acknowledged (Kamerman and Kahn 1989). In some countries, early learning services, and ECEC services in general, are an acknowledged part of the social infrastructure, benefiting from large public support and full funding. In other countries, early learning services are not always defined as a durable part of the social fabric, leaving the services limited in scope, reach, and sometimes even duration. Because early learning services are products of their country's social history and historical context, they not only vary but also may demand different areas and levels of focus.

For example, in a country with very few resources devoted to early learning services, considerable attention will need to be focused on the funding element of the infrastructure, whereas countries that support early learning services well may need to address funding less. Or, in a country that routinely eschews accountability, attention to complex regulatory enforcement might be much less intense than in a country that heavily attends to frequent assessment measures and processes. In this sense, systems implementation is shaped by context. Determining how to design and implement quality and aligned early learning services demands that we both take a systems perspective and inform it with clear understandings of the context. Fortunately, and buttressed by examples of emerging systems that frame early learning services work globally (Kagan 2018; OECD 2017a; Reid et al. 2019; UNESCO 2019; UNICEF 2019; Urban et al. 2012), this chapter provides examples of how such efforts can be implemented using contextually grounded, systemic perspectives.

Key Takeaways

- Early learning services need and rest on an essential *infrastructure* that entails seven elements: financing, governance, regulation and accountability, workforce capacity, data collection and use, family and community engagement, and links with other services.

- All seven elements of infrastructure combine with early learning services to form a system. All elements need to work in harmony with the service to deliver quality early learning.
- Understanding how diverse system elements interact with one another to support quality early learning is a prerequisite for its advancement and scalability.

SYSTEMS THAT FRAME EARLY LEARNING SERVICES

Systems Thinking in General

Challenges that face the vast array of services that support young children are neither new nor unique to this field. Transcending disciplines, institutions, and populations, systemic challenges have existed for decades, evoking a rich and varied theoretical base.[2] In general, systems theory is framed by five themes: there is a functional link between the elements or parts of a system and the whole; system elements and the whole exist in relationship to one another; system elements change over time and are influenced by one another, new knowledge, and altered contexts; such change is often unpredictable and nonlinear; and change exists within a web of causality so that a change in one element affects other elements and the entire system.

Germane to all systems work, and especially to ECEC programs and early learning services, Ackoff (2010) suggests that systems and the "messes" they evoke can be dealt with through absolution (ignoring the mess and hoping the current situation self-corrects), resolution (creating a good-enough response), solution (creating a response that generates the best possible outcome for the current system), or dissolution (redesigning the system to eliminate the mess). This chapter contends that early childhood programs and early learning services may be characterized by the first two courses of action: absolution and resolution. With regard to absolution, many early learning advocates either consciously (because it is so challenging) or unconsciously (because of a lack of understanding) ignore the systems mess. Others who want to see immediate gains are resolved to move forward with programmatic advances because a "good-enough" solution may be timely and achievable. Ackoff (2010) and other systems thinkers, including this chapter's authors, regard absolution and resolution as insufficient generally.

Where young children are concerned, given the proven benefits of quality early learning programs, neglecting systems thinking is morally wrong, strategically unwise, and inimical to our collective social well-being.

Many—but Two Focal—Systems

To begin to address systemic challenges associated with early learning services, it must be acknowledged that the "mess" was not created by any single program or discipline. Consequently, its solution must be grounded in multiple disciplines and the institutional systems that bring them to reality. Many systems influence young children, including the family system, the (embryonic in most countries) ECEC system, the education system, the health system, the welfare system, the neighborhood or housing system, and the economic and political systems. Despite their distinct functions, structures, and cultures, they all are supported by public policies that often reinforce their insularity and render them somewhat impervious to change. Embedded in the social and operational fabric of countries, they all influence young children, albeit to different degrees.

But do all these systems affect early learning services, the focus of this volume, to the same degree? Throughout this volume, and as noted, early learning services refer to the array of activities that children ages three to six experience when they are in center-based education services outside the home; such services primarily focus on developing and delivering pedagogical opportunities to advance young children's learning. Using this definition, early learning services around the world are delivered through two main systems: ECEC and education (figure 6.1). Some countries deliver

Figure 6.1 Early Learning as a Bridge Linking Two Systems

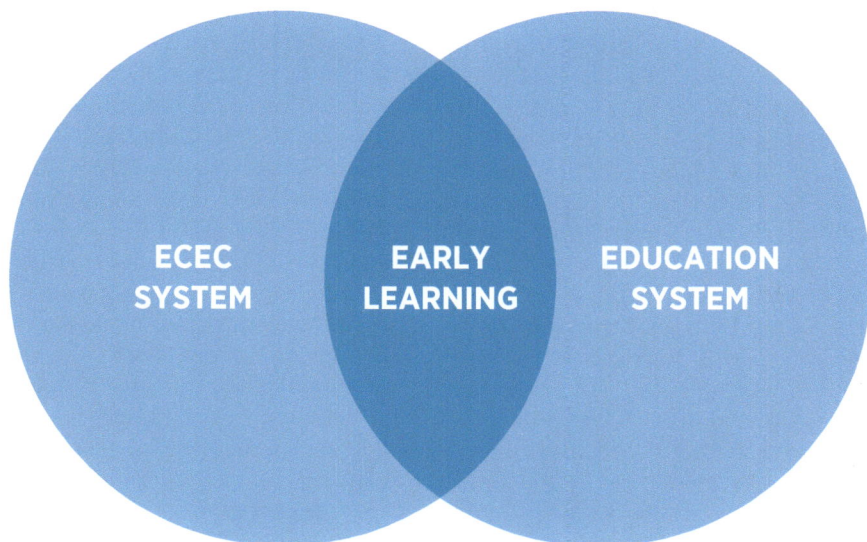

Source: Original figure for this publication.
Note: ECEC = early childhood education and care.

most early learning services through an ECEC system, other countries deliver them through the national or local education system, and others use a combination of the two.[3]

Irrespective of which system has the legal authority for early learning, alignment between the ECEC and education systems is critical. But each of these systems has its own perspectives, values, methodologies, and pedagogies; as a result, the systems are often hesitant to change. Moreover, and as noted herein, alignment efforts have typically primarily addressed pedagogical and program alignment, with scant attention accorded to alignment of systemic elements that compose the infrastructure. In contrast, and presenting a fresh perspective, this chapter contends that, to achieve alignment and to scale early learning services, all elements of the infrastructure must also be aligned. To accomplish this alignment, and as a prelude to discussing how early learning can be implemented and scaled, the chapter discusses and provides examples of ECEC systems, describes their elements, and then discusses the education system. By presenting each system individually, the chapter aims to sketch their contextual and operational distinctions, identify the position of early learning within them, and, critical to the thesis of this chapter, more clearly determine the systemic challenges that need to be addressed and aligned to advance and scale early learning services.

The ECEC system

ECEC system efforts in action. In comparison with the education system, the emergence of ECEC systems is quite recent and, in some countries, still nascent. However embryonic, ECEC systems are gaining popularity and emerging across the globe in response to the expansion of services for young children and their families. As new research promoted increased funding for ECEC programs in the late twentieth and early twenty-first centuries, many countries—particularly present-day high-income countries, but low- and middle-income countries as well—expanded their services for young children. Often such expansion took place somewhat hurriedly, typically with limited long-term planning and under the aegis of different ministries. Rapid expansion, although welcome, had diverse side effects, including questionable quality, inequitable distribution among populations, and uncertainty regarding programmatic distinctions, availability, and accessibility for parents, the public, and policy makers. These sometimes chaotic and often confusing conditions propelled the need for a more systematic and efficient approach to service delivery. ECEC systems were born of necessity to coordinate often disparate and burgeoning services.

Long advocated in the United States (Kagan and Cohen 1997; Sugarman 1991), ECEC systems work is now being implemented globally. For example, Chile Crece Contigo, a major systems initiative in Chile, coordinates efforts among the Ministry of Social Development and other line ministries, with the goal of promoting consistent management and regulation of services. In Colombia, De Cero a Siempre coordinates ECEC among different agencies, with both national and subnational coordinating mechanisms. Singapore consolidated ECEC from the Ministries of Education, Health, and Community, Youth, and Sports to create a single Early Childhood Development Agency in 2013 (Bull and Bautista 2018). In the Republic of Korea, although there is no single governance entity, the Office of Government Policy Coordination (part of the Prime Minister's Secretariat) has been tasked with coordinating efforts between the Ministry of Education and the Ministry of Health and Welfare (Moon and Landsberg 2018). And in Hong Kong SAR, China, despite its strong private sector orientation, the government recognizes systemic differences and fosters alignment of programs through economic incentives (Rao and Lau 2018).

Understanding ECEC systems. Beyond these implementation efforts, ECEC systems work is receiving scholarly attention. Often launched with the goal of better understanding systems, discerning their impact, and producing data that will improve their quality, such studies in countries around the world complement efforts in the field (Adams et al. 2019; Araujo et al. 2016; Bertram and Pascal 2016; Kagan et al. 2016; Kagan and Landsberg 2019; Meloy, Gardner, and Darling-Hammond 2019; Neuman, Roth, and Kagan, forthcoming; OECD 2001, 2017a, 2017b; Vargas-Barón 2013; Weiland and Yoshikawa 2013; World Bank 2018). To garner a contemporary perspective on this issue, a recent comparative analysis examines ECEC systems and their infrastructure in six jurisdictions—Australia; England; Finland; Hong Kong SAR, China; Korea; and Singapore (Kagan and Landsberg 2019).

In all these high-performing countries, the study finds that, although the direct services and the ministries under whose auspices they operate varied considerably, the countries demonstrated strong infrastructure commitments in five pillar areas: strong policy foundations (pillar I); durable funding and governance structures (pillar II); knowledgeable and supported workforce and families (pillar III); informed, individualized, and continuous pedagogy (pillar IV); and data that are used to drive improvement (pillar V). Moreover, the study finds that, under ideal circumstances, these five pillars would be supported by 15 well-defined and well-implemented building blocks, as depicted in figure 6.2.

Noting that not all countries implemented each of the 15 building blocks in the same way or to the same degree, the study acknowledges the importance of conceptualizing systems that include all 15 blocks, with the understanding that specific implementation patterns and processes will vary. First, under ideal conditions, building a functional ECEC system requires a strong policy foundation, defined as one that recognizes both the social and economic importance of investing in young children. Countries with strong policy foundations also respect the distinct needs of families, communities,

Figure 6.2 The Elements of the ECEC System

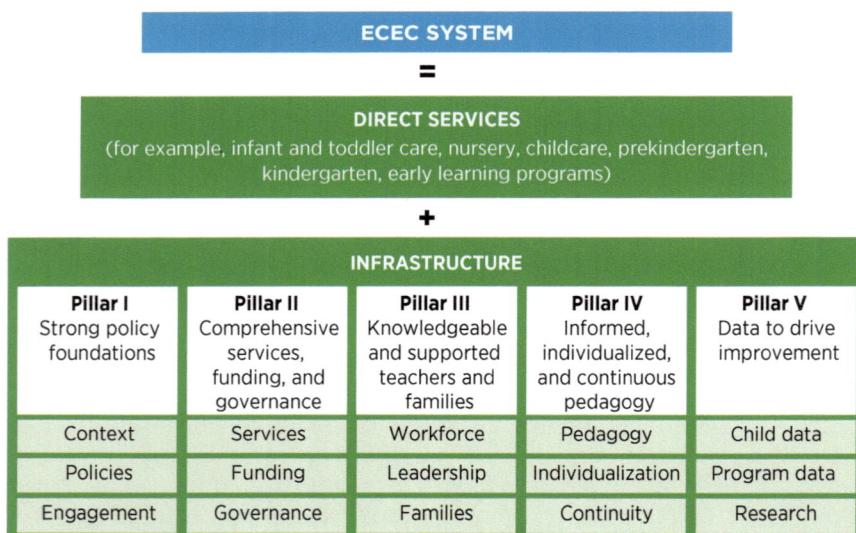

ECEC SYSTEM				

=

DIRECT SERVICES				
(for example, infant and toddler care, nursery, childcare, prekindergarten, kindergarten, early learning programs)				

+

INFRASTRUCTURE				
Pillar I Strong policy foundations	**Pillar II** Comprehensive services, funding, and governance	**Pillar III** Knowledgeable and supported teachers and families	**Pillar IV** Informed, individualized, and continuous pedagogy	**Pillar V** Data to drive improvement
Context	Services	Workforce	Pedagogy	Child data
Policies	Funding	Leadership	Individualization	Program data
Engagement	Governance	Families	Continuity	Research

Source: Original figure for this publication adapted from Kagan 2019.
Note: ECEC = early childhood education and care.

and states, and have found effective ways to engage populations and smoothly link levels of government.

Second, ECEC systems are built on physical and fiscal structures that ensure the stability and quality of the services; they have specific early childhood governance structures that seek to encourage transparency and coordination among programs and services, thus fostering their collective efficiency and equity. Third, strong ECEC systems provide for their people. The workforce is well trained and justly compensated, thus reducing turnover; leadership is cultivated and prepared; and families are meaningfully engaged in programs and services. Fourth, ECEC systems provide child-centered, individualized pedagogy that promotes continuity of experiences and learning for young children. Finally, strong ECEC systems plan for the collection and use of data to improve direct pedagogical services for children, the quality of programs, and the overall design of services. ECEC systems also boast research capacity that addresses the challenges inherent in delivering diverse services to young children and their families.

The Education System

Unlike ECEC systems, which are still emerging, long-established education systems that plan and deliver educational services to their populations exist in all countries. In addition to being well established, education systems are an acknowledged part of the social fabric of nations and regarded as essential to societal advancement and well-being. Education systems enjoy attitudinal supports such that their existence is not questioned. In part, this support may occur because there is a general understanding of the purposes of education, what schools do, how they function, and why they need to be supported. In short, these givens mean that in all countries education systems are accepted realities, underpinned by values and mechanisms that institutionalize them across time and place.

Globally, education systems share similar goals; they exist to expedite and provide educational services that are high in quality, equitably distributed, efficient, and sustained over time. Beyond stated goals that are both transparent and reasonably consistent, education systems are characterized by specified hierarchies, clearly delineated boundaries, and sophisticated infrastructure. Most education systems function with defined governance and administrative hierarchies in which lines of authority are crisp and decision-making powers are clearly distributed. For example, education systems boast defined boards of education that are distinct from their administrative personnel. Individual schools within the education system function primarily under the aegis of the public sector with considerable public fiscal support, although private sector educational services are becoming more widespread.

In addition, most education systems adhere to federal, state, and local regulations that pertain to all schools and consider public input in their governance, with such input carrying considerable sway in many countries. In other words, hierarchies, with their established governance and accountability mechanisms, are clear. Additionally, most education systems delineate different kinds of boundaries. They have specified "catchment" areas where their schools and services are located and for which they have responsibility. They set boundaries regarding the ages of children who are required to attend school. And they clearly delineate boundaries regarding who can be employed in the schools, typically establishing requirements for personnel, salary levels, and common salary schedules. Finally, education systems have sophisticated infrastructure: they have professional pipelines to prepare teachers through institutions of higher education, organized accountability and data procedures, and consistent funding and governance mechanisms.

Important to note, although countries conceptually regard education in general as an essential part of the social infrastructure and share clarity of hierarchies, boundaries, and broad infrastructural elements, the educational services they provide and how they provide them vary considerably. Indeed, they vary on most operational characteristics (for example, ages of compulsory attendance, per student expenditures, number of days that constitute a year, intensity and duration of monitoring, and number and range of services for diverse populations). They also vary on the amount of their fiscal commitments to education (OECD 2019) and the ways in which they engage with the private sector and other systems (health, welfare, social services). Indeed, systems and how they change differ in no small measure because they are contextually contoured by their sociocultural (for example, values, beliefs, heritage, religion) and economic-political (for example, demographics, social thinking and movements, government leadership, funding) contexts (see annex 6A).

Comparing ECEC and Education Systems

As noted, ECEC and education systems are quite different, in part because they are centered on different developmental stages, and are regarded somewhat differently by the public. Mature, stable, and deeply embedded in the social fabric of nations, education systems are the bedrock of societies and—in many communities—the center of community life. Their very patterns of being, replete with unique histories, cultures, and belief systems, are well instantiated and sometimes reluctant or impervious to change, as countless scholars have long noted (Lightfoot 1978; Sarason 1971; Wagner 1994) and innumerable practitioners can attest. Moreover, they have well-honed infrastructure that helps foster coherence among schools. By contrast, ECEC systems are still in formation, emerging often without public understanding or public support. Fragile, shifting, and still malleable, ECEC systems are quite porous given that their functions and structures are still being defined. Given these differences, it is both challenging and inaccurate to equate ECEC and education systems.

Despite these differences, ECEC and education systems are both rooted in their contexts. Both are concerned with advancing learning and seek to provide rich educational opportunities that are culturally, developmentally, and contextually appropriate. Moreover, they both rest on infrastructure that needs support. Although operationally manifesting quite differently, the pillars and building blocks applicable to ECEC systems globally and described in figure 6.2 apply to education systems. For example, most education systems include the capacity to monitor and regulate their services and routinely have dedicated entities to collect, process, and use data for instructional or management improvement. How they do this (with what frequency, for which children, using which measures) varies, but education systems develop data to drive improvement (pillar V). Similarly, all education systems seek to engage knowledgeable and supported teachers and families. Although they have diverse requirements for teachers and different approaches to fostering their pedagogical quality, education systems address this pillar (pillar III) as well as the others proffered for

ECEC systems. Moreover, both ECEC and education systems need public understanding and support to foster their quality and durability in an ideal scenario (pillar I).

In addition to these structural similarities, the two systems share a critical link, notably their efforts to advance children's quality early learning experiences. Increasingly, they both serve young children, sharing the intention of supporting early learning. They understand that the early years lay the important foundation for later learning, and they retain commitments to advancing children's "readiness" for and success in school.

The Alignment Challenge

Because ECEC and education systems exist independently from one another, all too frequently they have only modest interactions and limited alignment. Even though they sometimes serve children of the same ages and have a similar focus on learning, ECEC and education systems often have quite distinct philosophies and pedagogies with regard to early learning (Kagan and Tarrant 2010; Pianta, Cox, and Snow 2007; Sameroff and Haith 1996). As noted, they often have personnel who are prepared and compensated differently, and they have different programmatic regulatory requirements and different approaches to and measurements of quality. They are often financed and governed quite differently, with ECEC services sometimes functioning primarily in the market sector and educational services in the public sector. Consequently, these contextual differences pose a major challenge for those concerned with advancing early learning services. The task at hand, then, is not only to build functional ECEC systems that honor developmental theories and methodologies but also to align them with the values and orientations that prevail in the more established education system. Determining how to create continuous early learning opportunities that both transcend and link ECEC and education systems is the issue to which the chapter now turns.

Key Takeaways

- Although many systems affect young children, both the ECEC system and the education system are crucial for the delivery of early learning services.
- Alignment between the ECEC and education systems is limited, but critical for delivering quality early learning services.
- To achieve alignment and to scale early learning services, elements of the infrastructure in both systems, such as compensation, training, pedagogy, regulatory requirements, and measures of quality, must be aligned.

A SYSTEMIC APPROACH TO ALIGNING AND DELIVERING EARLY LEARNING

Aligning Early Learning Services: A Brief Retrospective

Transition and Alignment Efforts

Efforts to create links and continuity between the institutions that serve young children are not new. Understanding why they evolved and how they fared, however briefly, is an important prelude to understanding the need for and nature of the contemporary reconceptualization of early learning services, as presented in this volume. Dating back to criticisms of the inability of the Head Start Program in the United States to enable its participants to sustain the gains made into the earliest years of schooling (Rivlin and Timpane 1975), continuity and transition efforts burgeoned in the United States.[4] Learning from these endeavors, attempts to create activities that ease children's transition into formal school have taken hold, typically not part of national policies, but as programmatic efforts. Such efforts take the form of preparatory visits, parent and teacher training, and shared student reports (Ahtola et al. 2011; Mow, Jones, and People 2015; OECD 2017b).

These "transition" activities—affecting only some children, only some of the time—have been superseded by work that promotes more comprehensive and durable approaches to alignment. Rather than focus on one-time, often intermittent activities, more sustained approaches are taking hold. Pedagogical alignment calls for the alignment of curriculum, standards, assessments, teacher competencies, certification requirements, and compensation (Kagan 2010; Kagan and Kauerz 2012; Shuey et al. 2019), irrespective of where young children receive services. For example, a common pedagogical orientation in the form of a national framework characterizes children's early learning experiences in economies as diverse as Australia; England; Finland; Hong Kong SAR, China; and Singapore (Kagan and Landsberg 2019).

Looping—in which teachers teach in a preschool setting one year and follow some or all of their children into formal school—is growing in popularity. ECEC certification requirements are being aligned with schools, and funding models for early learning are adopting the school funding formula (NIEER 2019). The development of individual learning plans that are designed in ECEC programs and move with the children into the schools are operative in England and Finland. Indeed, an entire movement aligning preschool through third grade is striving to foster more penetrating and durable alignment (Atchison and Diffey 2018b; Kauerz 2010). Moreover, multisectoral efforts that link ECEC programs to health, mental health, and behavioral support services are under way (Kagan and Landsberg 2019).

Alignment Realities

Despite these worthwhile efforts, systemic fragmentation between the ECEC and education systems remains both an indisputable and a challenging reality, in part because of the interventions themselves. Most efforts to redress systemic schisms are highly idiosyncratic, isolated, and sporadic; they are largely unevaluated, trial efforts, working to establish proof of concept. Lacking broad-scale fiscal support, these efforts may be locally designed and engineered to honor local traditions, histories, and cultures, but therefore remain difficult to generalize both regionally and nationally. Moreover, and transcending the direct services themselves, the interventions are often constrained by the limited attention accorded to the systems' distinct and terribly misaligned infrastructural supports. For example, few alignment efforts transcend a programmatic focus to address the systems' inconsistencies in teacher preparation and certification, program monitoring, funding, and governance, to mention a few.

The alignment challenge is manifested in several ways. Limited coordination across sectors is a common challenge across countries; in many countries where infrastructure efforts are under way, staffing remains insufficient to overcome alignment challenges. Romania, for example, has coordinated offices of early education but has employed only limited staff (Adams et al. 2019) to enable comprehensive systemic alignment. In short, a major problem, and one more fully addressed below, is that most current alignment efforts do not reflect systemic thinking and consequently do not address the infrastructural elements that could promote durable alignment.

Positioning Early Learning Services

Caught in the vortex of the embryonic ECEC system and the established education system, where do early learning services fit? And, more important, how should their alignment with both systems be conceptualized and planned for? Three principles, each with distinct intentions, guide this chapter's responses to this seminal question. First is a framing principle that situates early learning: early learning services are not the sole purview of either the ECEC or the education system; rather, they transcend and are highly pertinent to both systems. Second is a conceptual principle: because early learning services typically sit at the confluence of two major systems, systems thinking must be understood as a prelude to their alignment. Third is an operational principle: because early learning services not only shape but are shaped by how they are implemented, consideration must be given to the existing properties of each system, with the goal of honoring each system's thinking and context.

Regarding the first principle—framing or situating early learning—early learning services fit squarely in the province of both the ECEC and education systems. Portrayed graphically in figure 6.3, it is not conceptualized as a separate system; rather, as early learning services advance, they must be a part of both the ECEC and the education systems. The position in each of these two host systems may vary across locales and time. For example, in country X, early learning services may be more closely aligned with the ECEC system whereas, in country Y, they may be more associated with the education system. Moreover, given the emerging nature of ECEC systems, such associations within any given country may shift as more consolidated approaches to ECEC evolve. Although not a single system, early learning services must seek to be represented in both and to align both. It is the bridge that spans and helps link the ECEC and education systems.

The second principle, one that is more conceptual, acknowledges the essentiality of systems thinking to the advancement of early learning services. It is predicated on the reality that programmatic efforts to support transitions, as noted above, have been neither widespread nor remarkably successful. To prevent such intermittent approaches, early learning services will need to address both components of a system—its programs and its infrastructure—with a heavy emphasis on the infrastructure elements or building blocks enumerated in figure 6.3. For example, early learning services will need unique standards, measures of implementation and accomplishment, professional capacity, and family and community engagement at pivotal times. These programs will need fiscal and governance support, as well. The point is that, in designing effective early learning, its advocates must look well beyond the direct services and consider ways that the infrastructure for early learning can be either developed or infused into the existing ECEC and education systems. Although early learning services do not need to develop a separate systemic *structure,* they must be conceptualized systemically with consideration for how systemic functions will be advanced through attention to infrastructure elements.

Third, operationalizing early learning services cannot be understood as the simple insertion of programs or activities into one or both systems, or even picking elements from each system that best suit early learning's intentions. It is not about the "schoolification" of the early learning curriculum or only about shaping primary pedagogy to better resemble that practiced in quality ECEC programs. Rather, systemic alignment demands that the context help shape the intervention. Doing this well means that early learning advocates must understand and assess the philosophies, internationalities, and capacity associated with both the ECEC and education systems, noting how they do, or can be contoured to, support early

Figure 6.3   Early Learning and the ECEC and Education Systems

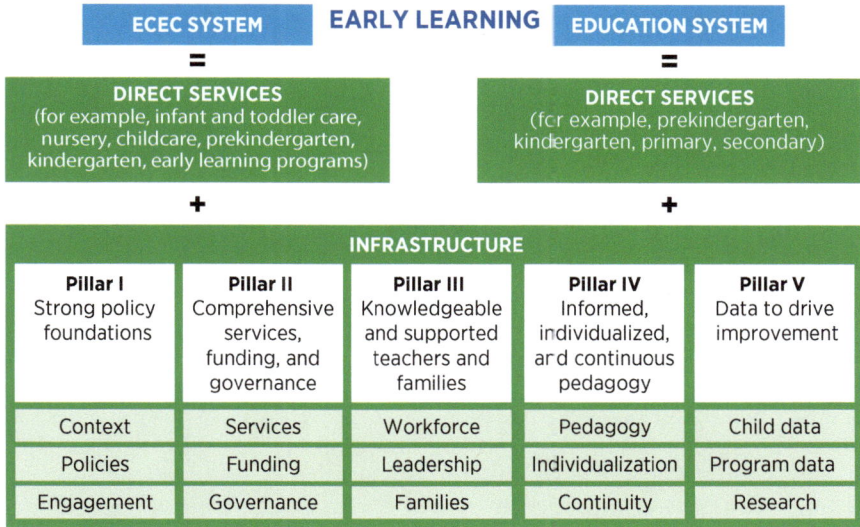

ECEC SYSTEM	EARLY LEARNING	EDUCATION SYSTEM
=		=

DIRECT SERVICES (for example, infant and toddler care, nursery, childcare, prekindergarten, kindergarten, early learning programs)		DIRECT SERVICES (for example, prekindergarten, kindergarten, primary, secondary)
+		+

INFRASTRUCTURE				
Pillar I Strong policy foundations	**Pillar II** Comprehensive services, funding, and governance	**Pillar III** Knowledgeable and supported teachers and families	**Pillar IV** Informed, individualized, and continuous pedagogy	**Pillar V** Data to drive improvement
Context	Services	Workforce	Pedagogy	Child data
Policies	Funding	Leadership	Individualization	Program data
Engagement	Governance	Families	Continuity	Research

Source: Original figure for this publication.
Note: ECEC = early childhood education and care.

learning services. Systemic alignment, then, becomes not simply a programmatic intervention, but a steady, sequenced, and highly focused effort to align the key elements, practices, and supportive infrastructure across these two focal systems. It evokes strategies that align relationships, activities, and learning tools that are continuous, despite facility and system boundaries; it aligns pedagogy, practices, and programs across and between the two systems (Kagan 2010). Indeed, it calls for a systemic approach to alignment, one that understands and honors context.

A Systems Approach To Alignment

To accomplish such alignment, it is helpful to return to the five pillars that characterize ECEC and education systems to detect where promising alignment potential exists (figure 6.3).

- Referring to pillar I, alignment will be enhanced if strong policy foundations exist within and between the two host systems to create a social context that values early learning, as it does primary and secondary education. In addition, it means that, when policies are developed in one system, potential consequences are discerned in the other.

- Regarding pillar II, early learning services must support diverse and comprehensive strategies that advance alignment while understanding that common funding and governance strategies are needed. For example, specific strategies are required to ensure that, irrespective of whether children's programs are in the ECEC or the education system, they are comparably funded to adequate levels and that systems-driven funding disparities are eliminated.
- As expressed in pillar III, early learning services must address the nature and quality of the workforce and its leadership. That is, teachers across systems should be comparably trained, have equal opportunities for professional development and advancement, and be compensated equitably according to their experience and preparation levels. Provisions for engaging families should be analogous for programs in either the ECEC or the education system.
- Acknowledging pillar IV, pedagogy and curriculum must be aligned so that comprehensive early learning standards, which specify what children should know and be able to do, exist across all programs and systems. Similarly, comprehensive curriculum and curriculum frameworks (what is taught) and child-centered pedagogy (how it is taught) must be honored in both systems.
- Finally, addressing pillar V, child-appropriate assessments of children and assessments of programs must be similar, irrespective of the program in which the child is enrolled, and must be sequential over time. Early learning services espouse links with families and foster the development and use of data as children traverse systems. This means that uniform data should be collected within each system and that those data should be shared when children make the transition from the ECEC system to the education system.

In short, systemic alignment between ECEC and education systems is characterized by a commitment to continuity within direct services and an infrastructure that advances pedagogical, programmatic, and policy continuity for children age three to age six, irrespective of the institutional setting or encasing system.

However challenging, if done well, such systemic alignment offers many benefits. First, focusing on alignment acknowledges the reality of the two systems and can be a catalyst for institutional reform across them. Second, by aligning the understanding of child-centered quality pedagogy across the systems, a more synchronized and scientifically grounded approach, one long advanced by learning theorists, can be initiated in the early years and sustained through children's primary schooling years. Third, aligning services and learning opportunities for children could reduce the negative effects of navigating challenging transitions, thereby fostering the potential for enhanced and sustained outcomes. Finally, this approach bolsters the quality and efficiency of services for both ECEC and education systems by creating intellectual synergy for children and operational synergies for the delivered services.

Key Takeaways

- Early learning is the bridge that links the ECEC and education systems; it must be considered a part of both, even if its position in each of these two host systems varies across time and context.
- Systemic fragmentation between the ECEC and education systems remains a reality.
- Systems thinking is essential to advancing early learning: it can lead to institutional reforms, reduce challenges of transitions for children, and boost efficiency and quality of learning.

IMPLEMENTING QUALITY EARLY LEARNING BY ADDRESSING COMPLEX SYSTEMS

Having considered systemic alignment conceptually, the next step is to foster its implementation. Challenging though this may be, there are workable strategies, drawn from diverse parts of the world that are illustrative and useful.

Based on global learning, four sequential strategies are presented: understanding the context, designing early learning services, implementing quality early learning services, and assessing and improving early learning services. Buttressing the many suggestions proffered in this volume, each of these strategies is discussed below, along with recommendations.

Strategy 1: Understanding the Context

Early learning services are shaped by three foundational contexts that heavily influence implementation: country contexts, systems contexts generally, and ECEC and education systems contexts. Understanding these contexts and how they influence early learning services is essential to successful implementation.

Country Contexts

All policies and services for children are framed by their country contexts, which are composed of seminal beliefs, values, and social, historical, political, and economic circumstances. Understanding the context means discerning how inherent country norms and cultural practices influence the development of young children as well as the services they receive. For example, Nordic countries, steeped in a welfare state tradition, offer robust services for young children through the public sector. By contrast, many Asian countries rely on more entrepreneurial and private sector services. Sometimes geographically large countries devolve policies and programs to subnational units (states or provinces). By contrast, small countries (in the sense of either population or geography) can retain a centralized approach to early learning, often facilitating early learning's implementation and consistency throughout the country. Moreover, the overall economic status of a country influences how able it is to commit to early learning services in general, and then where and how it elects to use its resources, with most low- and middle-income countries providing direct services to children before developing the necessary infrastructure to deliver quality services.

Because contexts vary, findings from many studies underscore that there can be no single model or approach to systems that will work in all countries (Kagan 2018; Montie, Claxton, and Lockhart 2007; Neuman and Devercelli 2013). Acknowledging such diversity, however, does not mean that systemic alignment lessons cannot be beneficially shared. Indeed, countries can and must learn from other countries, while being vigilant about the need to adapt policies to the home context. Implementation begins with determining the degree to which the social givens, or the elements of the context, are fixed or malleable, and the degree to which those that are malleable can be changed. Thus, understanding both the importance of country context and the status of country context is a first step in implementing quality early learning services.

Systems Contexts Generally

As this chapter suggests, systems thinking is essential to the process of significantly advancing early learning services; however, its defiance of linearity, individual autonomy, tidiness, and completion makes it difficult to grasp. Unlike a simple programmatic intervention that can be parachuted into a context, systems work requires understanding that, first, systems have unique structures and processes and, second, systems are viewed and understood from multiple perspectives (Checkland 1985). As such, systems work means dealing with more than one structure or one discipline, each of which is contextually embedded. This more expansive orientation also means that systems work demands that attention be paid to the fiscal and operational context of programs. It means understanding the political orientation of the country (for example, social welfare versus mixed market economic orientations; democratic versus autocratic political orientations). And it means conceptualizing the structural design and relationships of diverse governmental and nongovernmental entities (for example, centralized versus decentralized governmental structure; stringent versus modest accountability requirements) as systems are evoked. In short, systems work demands an understanding of the contexts within which they are designed and implemented.

For early learning services, leaders must understand the nature of children's learning and development, the number and nature of existing early learning programs, the degrees to and ways in which they are funded, the governance mechanisms that have been tried or now exist, the capacity of institutions to prepare and train professionals, the caliber of the accountability system, and the extent to which early learning services are aligned with both the ECEC and education systems. It also means being prepared to deal with the process of systemic implementation (for example, living with ambiguity, loosely configured outcomes, interacting systemic elements, and collaborative and often daunting processes) that is inimical to systems work of any kind.

ECEC and Education Systems Contexts

Because early learning services sit at the vortex of and transcend two systems, their implementation is heavily influenced by these host contexts. As discussed earlier in this chapter, despite their differences, ECEC and education systems share fundamental functions (for example, the advancement of learning, the delivery of quality services, and the development of institutional efficiency and sustainability). As such, work within them can be grounded in similar goals and understandings about how to bring about change. As discussed elsewhere with regard to early learning efforts (Kagan 2018; Kagan and Gomez 2015), the development of a theory of change can ground individuals from diverse backgrounds and perspectives in a set of common expectations about what is to happen and how changes may unfold. Specifically, and as demonstrated in annex 6A, a theory of change specifies the inputs necessary to achieve change, variables to consider in the process of implementing change, and the desired outcomes (Coffman 2012; Connell and Kubisch 1998; Greenfield 2009; Yoshikawa et al. 2018). In its early stages, the development of a theory of change should include diverse stakeholders who represent different constituencies and who recognize the importance of systemic alignment. Although a theory of change can guide early learning efforts, context contours and those involved are bound to honor diverse institutional and personal cultures and histories.

Recommendations Related to Understanding the Context

- Consider how contexts influence early learning service provision and systemic alignment.
- Build and popularize shared understandings of systems and systemic elements; strategically use the systems framework to design and advance the implementation of early learning services.
- Build in contextual assessments as an early step in the process, and design early learning services predicated on these understandings.
- Develop or adopt a theory of change to guide the process of change and to delineate the intended outcomes; ensure that stakeholders are part of the entire design process.

Strategy 2: Designing Early Learning Services

As discussed, the motivation for mounting ECEC programs has been driven by forces external to the child, notably by major social needs or goals. By contrast, the impetus for developing early learning services emanates internally—from those in the field who understand the complex challenges inherent in overcoming years of uncoordinated service delivery; it is their felt need for greater coherence and continuity across systems that not only frames early learning services work but also imbues it with urgency and energy.

Establishing Boundaries

As a part of understanding early learning services through a systemic lens, the boundaries or universe of the early learning services as well as the infrastructure that supports them must be determined. Boundaries are the "cut-off points of analysis" (Midgley 2008) and address questions such as: Do early learning services embrace childcare, residential care, or foster care for children of this age, or do they include only those services labeled as educational? Do they include services that carry through the primary years of school? Do they refer to services funded only by government or by a combination of public and private sector resources? Moreover, boundary definition addresses the degree to which comprehensive early childhood development efforts originating outside of schools (that is, services emanating from the health, mental health, and social sectors) are included.

Beyond determining the universe of services encompassed in efforts to foster systemic alignment, consideration must be given to the populations to be covered by the intended alignments. To what degree should learning service provision be universalized for all children or focus on specific groups? Often, for example, given comparative underrepresentation of some populations, such as children from lower-income, migrant, rural, and special needs backgrounds, work to prioritize these populations is being considered in alignment efforts (Bertram and Pascal 2016; Neuman and Devercelli 2013; OECD 2001, 2016).

Once boundaries delineate the included programs and people, each element of the infrastructure can be accordingly defined (Checkland 2000). Governance would address how these programs or services are delivered, with the goal of considering ways to link the governance of ECEC and education systems. At the pedagogical level, such boundaries might include the alignment of curriculum and pedagogical frameworks, teacher qualifications, and assessments that are the same in both systems. Programmatically, boundary setting might design regulations and monitoring mechanisms according to the same standards; it might include ways of engaging families that transcend the formal systems. In other words, setting the boundaries establishes the frame for the systems, that is, the area to which systemic efforts are directed.

Needs Assessment

Once boundaries are established, needs assessments determine the current status of the direct early learning services and the infrastructure that supports them. Such stocktaking provides critical information that shapes the scope of the efforts and guides the development of an initial plan. Two conditions characterize the needs assessment: First, however well elaborated, needs are considered emergent and subject to refinement or modification, requiring that reassessment take place. Second, the overarching design, rationale, and protocol must be understood by, and include, multiple participants (for example, families, community leaders, elected officials, representatives of nongovernmental organizations), with the goal of incorporating diverse perspectives into the plan. The aim of broad participation in the early stages of systems work is to create common, realistic appraisals of what does or does not exist and to bring diverse perspectives into dialogue. To carry out such assessments, a number of different strategies can be used, including, for example, systemic action research (Burns 2007), systemic interventions (Midgley 2006), and participatory system dynamics modeling (Hovmand 2014). Regardless of the strategy used, the data produced must be carefully analyzed and considered, usually by participants involved in the planning, with the goal of creating a theory of change that guides action. Such plans of action typically are composed of both short- and long-term goals and often use multiple strategies concurrently (Midgley 2006).

Recommendations Related to Designing Early Learning Services

- Foster broad-based participation in all facets of the design process.
- Delineate the boundaries of early learning services.
- Plan for and fund an inclusive, contextually driven needs assessment.
- Use data from the needs assessment to establish short- and long-term action priorities.
- Recognize that there is no single design strategy that works in all contexts, and that often systemic alignment strategies are contoured and recontoured over time.

Strategy 3: Implementing Quality Early Learning Services

To bring aligned early learning services to fruition, four major conditions must be considered: the influence of relationships, the importance of structures, the critical role of people and leaders, and the presence of essential resources—public commitment, time, and money. Each is discussed below.

The Influence of Relationships

All early learning services are based on relationships: relationships among the individuals involved in bringing the services to reality and relationships among institutions comprising the systems that encase the services. Regarding individuals, successful implementation requires paying attention to diverse relationships that predate the system planning and evolve because of it, managing these relationships, and recognizing that diverse (and sometimes unconventional) constituencies are a centerpiece of systems implementation. Although institutions are composed of individuals, institutions have their own cultures, and sometimes quite historic relationships that influence the implementation of early learning services. Whether smooth or laden with competition, inconsistencies of values, or differing pedagogical orientations, these legacy institutional relationships must be understood and addressed. Statements of common intentions, memoranda of understanding, or contracts are strategies that can help clarify relationships, roles, and responsibilities and help vertically align early learning services with primary schools and other education services.

The Importance of Structures

Trans-institutional relationships that support early learning need to be cemented through formal structures or mechanisms: task forces, in- and cross-program committees, boards, commissions, and even the establishment of new ministries have been used as mechanisms to do this. Usually somewhat formal, structured, and regularized, these mechanisms bring diverse voices to the table and provide the impetus or backbone for the implementation of early learning services across ECEC and education systems. Often termed boundary spanning mechanisms (BSMs) (Aldrich and Herker 1977; Tushman and Katz 1980), these efforts carry out multiple functions—systems goal setting, planning, and accountability—and vary in design, support, and degree of authority. Some are staffed with designated personnel and large budgets; others are administered collaboratively with less formal roles prescribed. Whatever their organizational structure, these hubs often engage in planning, systems design, ongoing evaluation, and increasingly interdisciplinary professional development. BSMs, deemed "institutional anchors" by SABER-ECD (Systems Approach for Better Education Results–Early Childhood Development), are a recurring policy recommendation for low- and middle-income countries striving to create early learning services (Adams et al. 2019; World Bank 2018). They are also used to create links among levels of government and diverse services, particularly in decentralized contexts, where community, regional, state, and federal services overlap (Britto, Engle, and Super 2013; Naumann et al. 2013). Regardless of their design or intent, BSMs conceptually provide structures for coordinating a range of services throughout sectors, ministries, and levels of government.

Countries that are advancing early learning services have a good deal of experience with different kinds of BSMs. With England and Finland as key examples, single ministries are often responsible for the development of curriculum, information coordination, standards setting for children and teachers, and, in some cases, monitoring and accountability for aligning ECEC and education systems. According responsibility for early learning to two ministries is also quite common, but leading countries that have embraced this split structure, such as the Republic of Korea, must work to instantiate continuity among them (Kagan and Landsberg 2019). Through the development of common frameworks, common professional development, common career requirements, and common career ladders, they achieve functional alignment (Kagan and Landsberg 2019), sometimes resulting in the formation of a structure. Finally, the creation of an entirely new entity to guide the development of early learning programs is taking hold in some countries (for example, Singapore) and in a number of states within the United States (for example, Alabama, Georgia, and Massachusetts) (Atchison and Diffey 2018a). The creation of a new entity enables the realization of structural and functional alignment, although contextual differences influence the facility with which these new agencies are created.

However important, BSMs have caveats related to their implementation. First, creating structures is complicated and is highly contextually driven, making their establishment easier in some contexts than others. Second, systems thinking and planning are often spearheaded by an impassioned and understanding leader, country or county elected officials, or an elected official's spouse, resulting in structures that are politically laden and often vulnerable to shifts in political power. Third, BSMs often begin with great euphoria, only to be later burdened by realities associated with cross-system work. Despite their limitations, these BSMs can foster the kinds of cross-system links that are needed to advance all-too-hybridized early learning services.

The Critical Role of People and Leaders

At the heart of any organization, and often predictive of its success, is the capacity of the individuals who lead and populate it. Early learning services are not an exception, despite the reality that in most countries early learning personnel are not universally well trained or well compensated. Throughout this volume, the need to provide outstanding and ongoing professional learning opportunities for teachers has been noted. However, leaders, who are sometimes overlooked, also need to be cultivated and prepared to guide the evolution of early learning. As the field grows and as challenges mount, specified leadership for early learning will be needed more than ever before. Leadership development must be regarded as essential to the advancement of early learning. To attain this level of leadership, professional development opportunities that attract individuals from diverse backgrounds or with diverse ideas must be consciously created. Such efforts need to be anchored in systems literature generally (Ackoff 1999; Checkland 1985; Forrester 1994; Overton 2013; Senge 2006) and acknowledge the different, multiple, and changing forms that leadership takes (Ackoff 2010; Senge, Hamilton, and Kania 2015). Such efforts must prepare individuals to lead within and across agencies and organizations and to recognize distinctions between titular, shared, and operational leadership.

The Presence of Essential Resources: Public Commitment, Time, and Funding

Fortified by research, data now clearly indicate the benefits of early learning to individuals and societies. Less well documented, the benefits of linking early learning services have not been widely popularized, so their importance is often not well understood by families or the public. Ensuring that such information is widely understood and shared is fundamental to procuring public support for advancing early learning. But such recognition does not happen without careful attention and strategic planning, in part because of the still-idiosyncratic nature of such efforts. In addition, the timing of early learning efforts is highly varied because of the complexity of creating synergy among institutions and systems. Smith and Thelen (2003) explain that, just as elements of development, such as neural reactions or bodily growth, happen on different time scales for different individuals, each unique early learning services effort will vary in the timing of its development. In one context, the establishment of an assessment approach may take months; in another, years. Fortunately, when adopting systemic thinking, something that begins as a planning effort may quickly evolve into action. In addition, something that begins in one element of the infrastructure may generate spillover effects in another. For example, the development of a national framework to enhance pedagogical quality may result in the need for greater monitoring to ensure its implementation, or greater compensation to foster the continuity of the workforce. Time, although hard to predict but essential to consider, is a critical implementation variable.

No less significant than timing, the availability of resources and their uses, over time, are part of systemic thinking. Often buoyed by public and media calls for increased investment, early learning funding is increasing. However, funding is often of short duration, restricted in its use, and challenging to access, making the intended benefits somewhat limited. Funding is essential to bridge the ECEC and education systems, and it is also the fulcrum on which the quality, equitable distribution, and sustainability of early learning services balance. Systemic thinking means that long-term plans for fiscal sustainability are essential to the implementation process.

Recommendations Related to Implementing Quality Early Learning Services

- Publicize the importance and benefits of institutional links for young children.
- Prioritize the development of relationships that foster vertical and horizontal continuity among institutions and systems.
- Design an early learning services structure that suits the context, taking the value and pitfalls associated with diverse structures and BSMs into consideration.
- Focus on developing and sustaining capacity at provider and leader levels.
- Consider the role of public commitment, time, and resources as the implementation takes hold.

Strategy 4: Assessing and Improving Early Learning Services

There is widespread agreement on the need to assess both the implementation and outcomes associated with early learning services. From an implementation perspective, learning about successes, preferred implementation sequences, or pitfalls could ease the challenge by revealing the systemic elements that are essential implementation priorities. Further, having solid data on outcomes, if positive results accrue, could boost support for early learning services, just as positive program results from early childhood programs have fueled the political will for ECEC efforts (Belfield et al. 2006; Campbell et al. 2002; Reynolds et al. 2002).

However, there is little consensus on the precise outcomes that should characterize these services. Traditionally, effectiveness in early learning programs has been measured by two variables: the quality of the program (as assessed by process and structural variables) and the outcomes achieved for children. More complex, hybridized, and contextually grounded, the assessment of early learning services needs a different set of metrics and a different set of outcomes, including outcomes that accrue not only to the child but also to the family, to pedagogy, and to the alignment of the host systems. Although this chapter offers one set of outcomes (quality, equity, sustainability, and efficiency of early learning systems that pertain to children, programs, families, and institutions), these are not necessarily agreed upon generally.

Even if outcomes were both agreed upon and clearly specified, there are limited metrics and tools with which to assess them. Creating metrics is complicated and often involves a skill set that is not traditionally part of the expertise of early learning thinkers. For example, to measure systemic efficiency, economists who are able to create efficiency tools must be engaged. To create a measure of sustainability, one must determine what should be sustained, which poses a challenge given that systems work is designed to be evolutionary and adaptive. By design, systems are successful to the degree that their results are cumulative and adaptive to changing contexts. Therefore, early learning services metrics need to be contextually as well as universally relevant—the former to ensure fidelity to systems' individuality and the latter to ensure accurate data aggregations across systems.

Comprehensive data-collection and -analysis capacity needs to be operational. In many countries, baseline data systems, although improving, are still quite fragile, even within a single ministry. Because early learning services tend to transcend agencies and ministries, the complexities are compounded and require cross-agency collaboration and alignment in data collection and analysis. Such cross-agency efforts must grapple with issues of shared responsibility, confidentiality, quality control, and systemic efficiency. To date, efforts to establish such comprehensive data systems are taking hold in Brazil and other countries; sometimes the efforts come about in response to national crises (for example, environmental issues, food security), with the lead agencies taking responsibility for inspiring comprehensive systems data development.

Beyond coming to a consensus on desired outcomes, creating metrics, and developing data-collection capacity within and among institutions, effective ways of using the data to improve early learning services and aligned systems must be considered. Such data utilization and data sharing are particularly crucial, given that early learning transcends systems and given that it is an emerging field. There are lessons to be learned across countries about notable processes for advancing systems work in community engagement, consolidated financing systems, integrated data systems, consolidated governance, and other areas in early learning that are begging for more information. As such, mechanisms for data sharing and utilization within and across countries are needed.

Recommendations Related to Assessing Early Learning Services

- Create a process or mechanism to define outcomes and their indicators for early learning services.
- Develop, pilot, and validate systemic metrics and tools that address the above outcomes and indicators.
- Update data systems to effectively collect and use early learning services data that transcend ECEC and education systems.
- Support data efforts that create and disseminate empirically driven, useful, and innovative information directly related to early learning services and the systems that encase them.

Key Takeaways

- To implement quality early learning services, it is important to structure those services to suit the context, prioritize continuity among institutions and systems, and sustain capacity at the provider and leader levels.
- The benefits of institutional linkages for young children should be stressed to underlie implementation efforts.

CONCLUSION

This chapter presents a systems approach to implementing early learning services that fosters their quality, equitable distribution, scalability, and efficiency. Predicated on data and capturing the lived experiences from countries around the globe, this chapter affirms that, although much has already been accomplished to this end, much remains to be done.

Creating early learning services that are guided by systems thinking and systems alignment is not for the faint of heart. Nor is this work for those who want instant success. Rather, this work needs patient, recurrent long-term vision, support, and scholarship. In the long run, understanding the potency of systems thinking to advance early learning services is among the most pressing needs and the greatest opportunities.

Table 6.1 reviews the takeaways presented in this chapter.

Table 6.1   Chapter 6: Summary of Key Takeaways

Background and challenges: A systems imperative

- Early learning services need and rest on an essential *infrastructure* that entails seven elements: financing, governance, regulation and accountability, workforce capacity, data collection and use, family and community engagement, and links with other services.
- All seven elements of infrastructure combine with early learning services to form a system. All elements need to work in harmony with the service to deliver quality early learning.
- Understanding how diverse system elements interact with one another to support quality early learning is a prerequisite for its advancement and scalability.

Systems that frame early learning services

- Although many systems affect young children, both the ECEC system and the education system are crucial for the delivery of early learning services.
- Alignment between the ECEC and education systems is limited, but critical for delivering quality early learning services.
- To achieve alignment and to scale early learning services, elements of the infrastructure in both systems, such as compensation, training, pedagogy, regulatory requirements, and measures of quality, must be aligned.

A systemic approach to aligning and delivering early learning

- Early learning is the bridge that links the ECEC and education systems; it must be considered a part of both, even if its position in each of these two host systems varies across time and context.
- Systemic fragmentation between the ECEC and education systems remains a reality.
- Systems thinking is essential to advancing early learning: it can lead to institutional reforms, reduce challenges of transitions for children, and boost efficiency and quality of learning.

Implementing quality early learning by addressing complex systems

- To implement quality early learning services, it is important to structure those services to suit the context, prioritize continuity among institutions and systems, and sustain capacity at the provider and leader levels.
- The benefits of institutional linkages for young children should be stressed to underlie implementation efforts.

Source: Original table for this publication.
Note: ECEC = early childhood education and care.

ANNEX 6A: ECEC SYSTEMS THEORY OF CHANGE

Originally posited by Kagan and Gomez (2015) for ECEC systems, expanded by Kagan et al. (2016), and further refined for the Early Advantage study (Kagan 2018), the following theory of change takes a systems perspective. Although designed for ECEC systems rather than education systems, the theory's central tenets can be applied to both host systems of early learning services; it provides a functional pathway, defined boundaries, observable inputs, and achievable outputs and outcomes. Presented in figure 6A.1, the theory suggests that, when essential programs and services (A) are supported by a clearly delineated infrastructure (B), they will yield an effective ECEC system (C). The system will then produce desired *outputs* (high-quality, equitably distributed, sustainable, and efficient services) (D); and, when these outputs are combined with family supports (E), positive outcomes in the form of positive child and family well-being will ensue (F). Econo-political (for example, demographics, social thinking and movements, governmental leadership, funding) (G) and sociocultural (for example, values, beliefs, heritages, religions) (H) contexts surround and heavily influence implementation of the theory of change.

Figure 6A.1 ECEC Systems Theory of Change

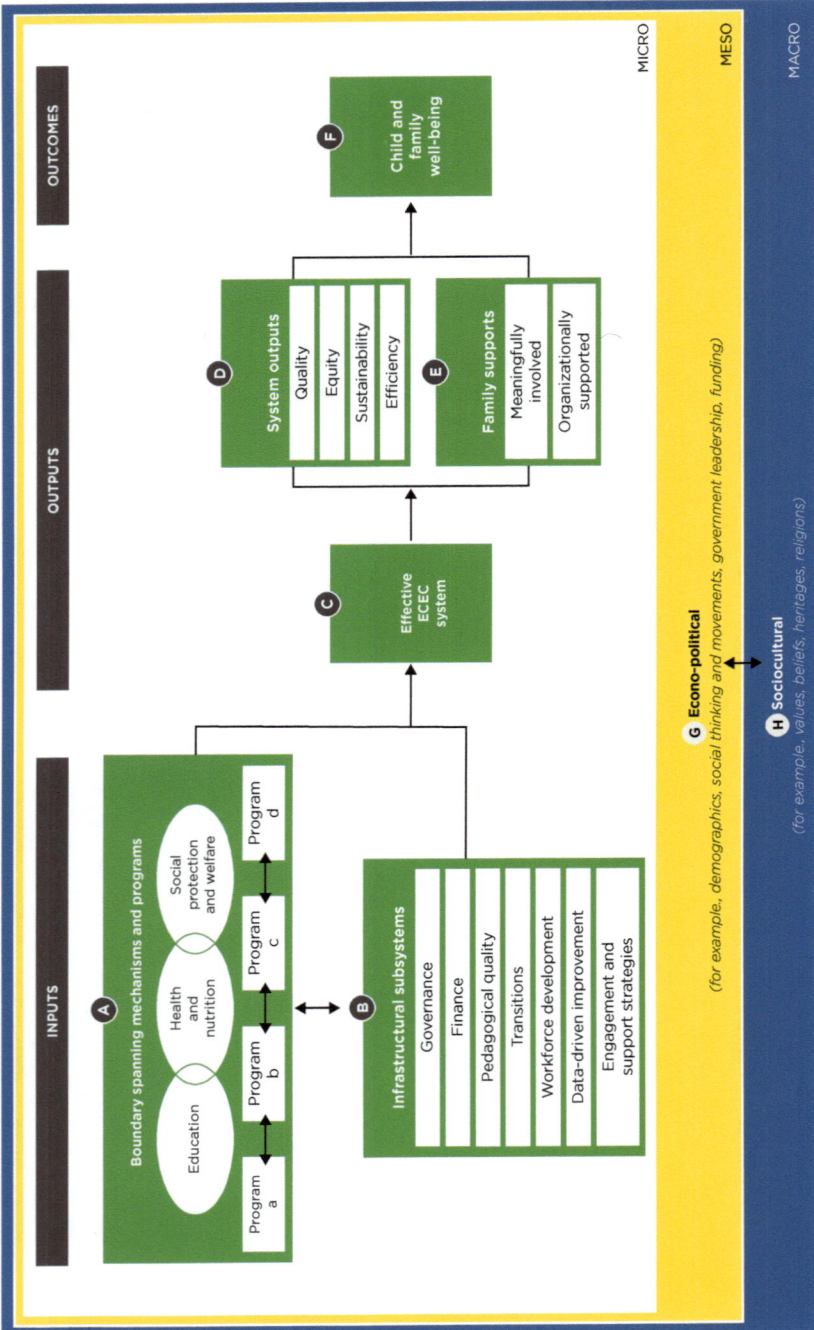

Source: Original figure for this publication adapted from Kagan 2018.
Note: ECEC = early childhood education and care.

NOTES

1. Reflecting rapidly changing ideas within an equally dynamic field, the following distinctions regarding the services children receive are made for clarity. *Early childhood development* refers to the wide array of offerings available to young children (birth to age eight) and their families, including family childcare, center-based services (taking place in childcare, nurseries, day nurseries, prekindergarten, kindergarten, and schools), home visiting programs, parenting education and support, and health and nutrition services. *Early childhood education and care* (ECEC), a subset of early childhood development, refers to the array of programs that are expressly established to support the early learning and development of young children, typically serving children from birth to entry into formal school, including services such as nursery, childcare, prekindergarten, and kindergarten. *Early learning services* or *programs*, as used herein, are a subset of ECEC, and refer to center-based programs that have been intentionally established to support early learning for children ages three to six.

2. Systems work dates back to the nineteenth century, an era of rapid social progress, but gained currency later, emanating from domains as diverse as biology (von Bertalanffy 1950), linguistics (Banathy 1968), sociology (Parsons 1951), ecological development (Odum 1983), organizational theory and management (Senge 2006), systems dynamics (Forrester 1970), and even developmental psychology (Bronfenbrenner 1979). For the purposes of this chapter, the works of many systems theoreticians (Forrester 1970, 1971, 1994; Overton 2013; Senge 2006; Smith and Thelen 2003) were synthesized.

3. Provision of early learning services varies greatly around the world. In countries where early learning services are the purview of more than one system, sometimes services are split by children's age, with the ECEC system providing services for younger children (for example, three-to-four-year-olds), while the year immediately before primary school (five-to-six-year-olds) is provided by the local education system. In other cases, both systems deliver services for children age three to age six in parallel.

4. Accelerated by federal investments in demonstration efforts, Project Follow Through, Head Start Planned Variation, and Project Developmental Continuity aimed to promote continuity between early childhood programs and services offered by the public schools. Mostly pedagogical or curricular in nature, these efforts noted and tried to ameliorate institutional differences, sadly only with modest success as found by the National Transition Study and the National Head Start/Public School Early Childhood Transition Study (Love et al. 1992; Ramey et al. 2000).

REFERENCES

Ackoff, R. L. 1999. *Re-Creating the Corporation: A Design of Organizations for the 21st Century.* New York: Oxford University Press.

Ackoff, R. L. 2010. *Systems Thinking for Curious Managers.* Devon, UK: Triarchy Press.

Adams, L., A. Sava, M. Moarcas, and C. Ulrich Hygum. 2019. "Romania Early Childhood Development: SABER Country Report 2019." Systems Approach for Better Education Results, World Bank, Washington, DC.

Ahtola, A., G. Silinskas, P. L. Poikonen, M. Kontoniemi, P. Niemi, and J. E. Nurmi. 2011. "Transition to Formal Schooling: Do Transition Practices Matter for Academic Performance?" *Early Childhood Research Quarterly* 2 (3): 295–302.

Aldrich, H., and D. Herker. 1977. "Boundary Spanning Roles and Organization Structure." *Academy of Management Review* 2 (2): 217–30.

Araujo, M. C., Y. Cruz-Agayo, A. Jaimovich, and S. L. Kagan. 2016. "Drawing Up an Institutional Architecture." In *The Early Years: Child Well-Being and the Role of Public Policy,* edited by S. Berlinski and N. Schady, 179–201. Washington, DC: Inter-American Development Bank.

Atchison, B., and L. Diffey. 2018a. "Governance in Early Childhood Education." Education Commission of the States, Washington, DC.

Atchison, B., and L. Diffey. 2018b. "Initiatives from Preschool to Third Grade: A Policymaker's Guide." Education Commission of the States, Washington, DC.

Banathy, B. H. 1968. *Instructional Systems.* Belmont, CA: Fearon Publishers.

Barnett, W. S. 2008. "Preschool Education and Its Lasting Effects: Research and Policy Implications." Education and the Public Interest Center, Boulder, CO; and Education Policy Research Unit, Tempe, AZ. http://epicpolicy.org/publication /preschooleducation.

Belfield, C., M. Nores, W. S. Barnett, and L. Schweinhart. 2006. "The High-Scope Perry Preschool Program: Cost-Benefit Analysis Using Data from the Age-40 Follow-up." *Journal of Human Resources* 41 (1): 162–90.

Bertram, T., and C. Pascal. 2016. *Early Childhood Policies and Systems in Eight Countries.* Hamburg: International Association for the Evaluation of Educational Achievement.

Britto, P. R., P. L. Engle, and C. M. Super, eds. 2013. *Handbook of Early Childhood Development Research and Its Impact on Global Policy.* Oxford: Oxford University Press.

Britto, P. R., H. Yoshikawa, J. van Ravens, L. A. Ponguta, M. Reyes, S. Oh, and R. Seder. 2014. "Strengthening Systems for Integrated Early Childhood Development Services: A Cross-National Analysis of Governance." *Annals of the New York Academy of Sciences* 1308 (1): 245–55.

Bronfenbrenner, U. 1979. *The Ecology of Human Development.* Cambridge, MA: Harvard University Press.

Bull, R., and A. Bautista. 2018. "A Careful Balancing Act: Evolving and Harmonizing a Hybrid System of ECEC in Singapore." In *The Early Advantage 2: Building Systems That Work for Young Children,* edited by S. L. Kagan and E. Landsberg, 155–81. New York: Teachers College Press.

Burns, D. 2007. *Systemic Action Research: A Strategy for Whole System Change.* Bristol, UK: Policy Press.

Campbell, F. A., C. T. Ramey, E. Pungello, J. Sparling, and S. Miller-Johnson. 2002. "Early Childhood Education: Young Adult Outcomes from the Abecedarian Project." *Applied Developmental Science* 6 (1): 42–57.

Checkland, P. 1985. "Achieving 'Desirable and Feasible' Change: An Application of Soft Systems Methodology." *Journal of the Operational Research Society* 36 (9): 821–31.

Checkland, P. 2000. "Soft Systems Methodology: A Thirty Year Retrospective." *Systems Research and Behavioral Science* 17 (S1): S11–S58.

Coffman, J. 2012. "Evaluating Systems Building Efforts." In *Early Childhood Systems: Transforming Early Learning*, edited by S. L. Kagan and K. Kauerz, 199–215. New York: Teachers College Press.

Connell, J., and A. Kubisch. 1998. "Applying a Theory of Change Evaluation Approach to the Evaluation of Comprehensive Community Initiatives: Program, Prospects, and Problems." In *New Approaches to Evaluating Community Initiatives: Theory, Measurement, and Analysis*, edited by K. Fulbright-Anderson, A. Kubisch, and J. Connell, 15–44. Aspen, CO: The Aspen Institute.

Forrester, J. W. 1970. "Systems Analysis as a Tool for Urban Planning." *IEEE Transactions on Systems Science and Cybernetics* 6 (4): 258–65.

Forrester, J. W. 1971. "Counterintuitive Behavior of Social Systems." *Technological Forecasting and Social Change* 3: 1–22.

Forrester, J. W. 1994. "System Dynamics, Systems Thinking, and Soft OR." *System Dynamics Review* 10 (2–3): 245–56.

Fukkink, R., L. Jilink, and R. Oostdam. 2017. "A Meta-Analysis of the Impact of Early Childhood Interventions on the Development of Children in the Netherlands: An Inconvenient Truth?" *European Early Childhood Education Research Journal* 25 (5): 656–66.

Greenfield, P. M. 2009. "Linking Social Change and Developmental Change: Shifting Pathways of Human Development." *Developmental Psychology* 45 (2): 401–18.

Hovmand, P. S. 2014. *Community Based System Dynamics*. New York: Springer.

Kagan, S. L. 2010. "Seeing Transition through a New Prism: Pedagogical, Programmatic, and Policy Alignment." In *Transitions for Young Children: Creating Connections across Early Childhood Systems*, edited by S. L. Kagan and K. Tarrant, 3–17. Baltimore, MD: Paul Brookes.

Kagan, S. L., ed. 2018. *The Early Advantage 1: Early Childhood Systems That Lead by Example*. New York: Teachers College Press.

Kagan, S.L. 2019. "The Quest for Social Strategy". In *The Early Advantage 2: Building Systems That Work for Young Children*, edited by S.L. Kagan and E. Landsberg, 1–19. New York: Teachers College Press.

Kagan, S. L., M. C. Araujo, A. Jaimovich, and Y. C. Aguayo. 2016. "Understanding Systems Theory and Thinking: Early Childhood Education in Latin America and the Caribbean." In *The SAGE Handbook of Early Childhood Research*, edited by A. Farrell, S. L. Kagan, and E. K. M. Tisdall, 163–84. London: SAGE Press.

Kagan, S. L., and N. E. Cohen. 1997. "Not by Chance: Creating an Early Care and Education System for America's Children." Abridged Report, The Quality 2000 Initiative, Bush Center in Child Development and Social Policy at Yale University, New Haven, CT.

Kagan, S. L., and R. E. Gomez, eds. 2015. *Early Childhood Governance: Choices and Consequences.* New York: Teachers College Press.

Kagan, S. L., and K. Kauerz, eds. 2012. *Early Childhood Systems: Transforming Early Learning.* New York: Teachers College Press.

Kagan, S. L., and E. Landsberg, eds. 2019. *The Early Advantage 2: Building Systems That Work for Young Children.* New York: Teachers College Press.

Kagan, S. L., and J. L. Roth. 2017. "Transforming Early Childhood Systems for Future Generations: Obligations and Opportunities." *International Journal of Early Childhood* 49 (2): 138–54.

Kagan, S. L., and K. Tarrant, eds. 2010. *Transitions for Young Children: Creating Connections across Early Childhood Systems.* Baltimore, MD: Paul H. Brookes Publishing Co.

Kamerman, S. B., and A. J. Kahn. 1989. "The Normative/Ideological Context of Policy Formation Family Policy: Has the United States Learned from Europe?" *Review of Policy Research* 8 (3): 581–98.

Kauerz, K. 2010. *PreK-3rd: Putting Full-Day Kindergarten in the Middle.* New York: Foundation for Child Development.

Lancet Early Childhood Development Series Steering Committee. 2016. "Advancing Early Childhood Development: From Science to Scale, an Executive Summary for *The Lancet's* Series." *Lancet.* http://iin.oea.org/pdf-iin/RH/2018/2Lancet%20ECD%20Executive%20Summary.pdf.

Lightfoot, S. L. 1978. *Worlds Apart: Relationships between Families and Schools.* New York: Basic Books.

Lipsey, M. W., D. C. Farran, and K. Durkin. 2018. "Effects of the Tennessee Prekindergarten Program on Children's Achievement and Behavior through Third Grade." *Early Childhood Research Quarterly* 45: 155–76.

Love, J. M., R. Chazan-Cohen, H. Raikes, and J. Brooks-Gunn. 2013. "What Makes a Difference? Early Head Start Evaluation Findings in a Longitudinal Context." *Monograph from the Society for Research in Child Development* 78.

Love, J. M., M. E. Logue, J. V. Trudeau, and K. Thayer. 1992. *Transitions to Kindergarten in American Schools, Final Report of the National Transition Study.* Washington, DC: Office of Planning and Policy.

Marope, P. T. M., and Y. Kaga. 2015. *Investing against Evidence: The Global State of Early Childhood Care and Education.* Paris: UNESCO Publishing.

Meloy, B., M. Gardner, and L. Darling-Hammond. 2019. *Untangling the Evidence on Preschool Effectiveness: Insights for Policymakers.* Palo Alto, CA: Learning Policy Institute.

Midgley, G. 2006. "Systemic Intervention for Public Health." *American Journal of Public Health* 96 (3): 466–72.

Midgley, G. 2008. "Systems Thinking, Complexity and the Philosophy of Science." *Emergence: Complexity and Organization* 10 (4).

Montie, J. E., J. Claxton, and S. D. Lockhart. 2007. "A Multinational Study Supports Child-Initiated Learning: Using the Findings in Your Classroom." *YC Young Children* 62 (6): 22–26.

Moon, M., and E. Landsberg. 2018. "Progress via Innovation and Investment: Setting the Stage for Greater Harmonization in the Republic of Korea."

In *The Early Advantage 2: Building Systems That Work for Young Children*, edited by S. L. Kagan and E. Landsberg, 128–54. New York: Teachers College Press.

Mow, V. L., C. Jones, and J. People. 2015. *Evaluation of the Transition to School Statement*. Sydney: Center for Education Statistics and Evaluation.

Naudeau, S., N. Kataoka, A. Valerio, M. J. Neuman, and L. K. Elder. 2010. *Investing in Young Children: An Early Childhood Development Guide for Policy Dialogue and Project Preparation*. Washington, DC: World Bank

Naumann, I., C. M. McLean, A. Koslowski, E. K. M. Tisdall, and E. Lloyd. 2013. "Early Childhood Education and Care Provision: International Review of Policy, Delivery and Funding." Scottish Executive. https://www.research.ed.ac.uk /portal/files/12434956/Early_Childhood_Education_And_Care_Provision.pdf.

Neuman, M. J., and A. E. Devercelli. 2013. "What Matters Most for Early Childhood Development: A Framework Paper." SABER Working Paper Series 5, World Bank, Washington, DC.

Neuman, M. J., J. Roth, and S. L. Kagan. Forthcoming. *A Compendium of International Early Childhood Systems Research*. Washington, DC: National Center on Education and the Economy.

NIEER (National Institute for Early Education Research). 2019. *The State of Preschool 2018: State Preschool Yearbook*. New Brunswick, NJ: Rutgers Graduate School of Education.

Odum, H. T. 1983. *Systems Ecology: An Introduction*. Hoboken, NJ: Wiley.

OECD (Organisation for Economic Co-operation and Development). 2001. *Starting Strong I: Early Childhood Education and Care*. Paris: OECD Publishing.

OECD (Organisation for Economic Co-operation and Development). 2016. *Education at a Glance 2016*. Paris: OECD Publishing.

OECD (Organisation for Economic Co-operation and Development). 2017a. *Starting Strong 2017: Key OECD Indicators on Early Childhood Education and Care*. Paris: OECD Publishing.

OECD (Organisation for Economic Co-operation and Development). 2017b. *Starting Strong V—Transitions from Early Childhood Education and Care to Primary Education*. Paris: OECD Publishing.

OECD (Organisation for Economic Co-operation and Development). 2019. *Education at a Glance 2019*. Paris: OECD Publishing.

Overton, W. F. 2013. "A New Paradigm for Developmental Science: Relationism and Relational-Developmental Systems." *Applied Developmental Science* 17 (2): 94–107.

Parsons, T. 1951. *The Social System*. London: Routledge and Kegan Paul Ltd.

Pianta, R. C., M. J. Cox, and C. Snow, eds. 2007. *School Readiness and the Transition to Kindergarten in the Era of Accountability*. Baltimore, MD: Paul H. Brookes Publishing Co.

Ramey, S. L., C. T. Ramey, M. M. Phillips, R. G. Lanzi, C. Brezausek, C. R. Katholi, S. Snyder, and F. Lawrence. 2000. *Head Start Children's Entry into Public School: A Report on the National Head Start/Public School Early Childhood Transition Demonstration Study*. Washington, DC: Administration on Children, Youth and Families, US Department of Health and Human Services.

Rao, N., and C. Lau. 2018. "Responsive Policymaking and Implementation: Enhancing ECEC System Quality and Equity in Hong Kong." In *The Early*

Advantage 2: Building Systems That Work for Young Children, edited by S. L. Kagan, and E. Landsberg, 99–127. New York: Teachers College Press.

Reid, J. L., S. A. Melvin, S. L. Kagan, and J. Brooks-Gunn. 2019. "Building a Unified System for Universal Pre-K: The Case of New York City." *Children and Youth Services Review* 100: 191–205.

Reynolds, A. J., J. A. Temple, D. L. Robertson, and E. A. Mann. 2002. "Age 21 Cost-Benefit Analysis of the Title I Chicago Child-Parent Centers." *Educational Evaluation and Policy Analysis* 24 (4): 267–303.

Rivlin, A. M., and P. M. Timpane, eds. 1975. *Ethical and Legal Issues of Social Experimentation*. Washington, DC: Brookings Institution.

Sameroff, A., and M. Haith, eds. 1996. *The Five to Seven Year Shift: The Age of Reason and Responsibility*. Chicago: University of Chicago Press.

Sarason, S. B. 1971. *The Culture of School and the Problem of Change*. Boston: Allyn and Bacon.

Senge, P. M. 2006. *The Fifth Discipline: The Art and Practice of the Learning Organization*. New York: Currency Doubleday.

Senge, P., H. Hamilton, and J. Kania. 2015. "The Dawn of System Leadership." *Stanford Social Innovation Review* 13 (1): 27–33.

Shuey, E. A., and M. Kankaras. 2018. "The Power and Promise of Early Learning." OECD Education Working Paper 186, OECD Publishing, Paris.

Shuey, E., K. Najung, A. Cortazar, X. Poblete, L. Rivera, M. J. Lagos, F. Faverio, and A. Engel. 2019. "Curriculum Alignment and Progression between Early Childhood Education and Care and Primary School: A Brief Review and Case Studies." OECD Education Working Paper 193, OECD Publishing, Paris.

Smith, L. B., and E. Thelen. 2003. "Development as a Dynamic System." *Trends in Cognitive Sciences* 7 (8): 343–48.

Sugarman, J. 1991. *Building Early Childhood Systems*. Washington, DC: Child Welfare League of America.

Tushman, M. L., and R. Katz. 1980. "External Communication and Project Performance: An Investigation into the Role of Gatekeepers." *Management Science* 26 (11): 1071–85.

UNESCO (United Nations Educational, Scientific and Cultural Organization). 2019. *Regional Guidelines on Innovative Financing Mechanisms and Partnership for Early Childhood Care and Education (ECCE)*. Paris: UNESCO Publishing.

UNICEF (United Nations Children's Fund). 2019. *A World Ready to Learn: Prioritizing Quality Early Childhood Education*. New York: UNICEF.

Urban, M., M. Vandenbroeck, K. Van Laere, A. Lazzari, and J. Peeters. 2012. "Towards Competent Systems in Early Childhood Education and Care. Implications for Policy and Practice." *European Journal of Education* 47 (4): 508–26.

US Department of Health and Human Services. 2010. *Head Start Impact Study: Final Report, January 2010*. Washington, DC: Administration for Children and Families, Office of Planning, Research and Evaluation. https://www.acf.hhs .gov/sites/default/files/documents/opre/executive_summary_final_508.pdf.

van Huizen, T., and J. Plantenga. 2018. "Do Children Benefit from Universal Early Childhood Education and Care? A Meta-Analysis of Evidence from Natural Experiments." *Economics of Education Review* 66: 206–22.

Vargas-Barón, E. 2013. "Building and Strengthening National Systems for Early Childhood Development." In *Handbook of Early Childhood Development Research and Its Impact on Global Policy*, edited by P. R. Britto. P. L. Engle, and C. M. Super, 443–66. Oxford: Oxford University Press.

Vargas-Barón, E. 2015. "Policies on Early Childhood Care and Education: Their Evolution and Some Impacts." Paper commissioned for the *EFA Global Monitoring Report 2015*. Paris: UNESCO Publishing.

Vargas-Barón, E., J. Small, D. Wertlieb, H. Hix-Small, R. Gómez Botero, K. Dieh, P. Vergara, and P. Lynch. 2019. *Global Survey of Inclusive Early Childhood Development and Early Childhood Intervention Programs*. Washington, DC: Rise Institute.

von Bertalanffy, L. 1950. "The Theory of Open Systems in Physics and Biology." *Science* 111 (2872): 23–29.

Wagner, T. 1994. *How Schools Change.* Boston: Beacon Press.

Watson, J. 2012. "Starting Well: Benchmarking Early Education across the World." The Economist Intelligence Unit, London.

Weiland, C., and H. Yoshikawa. 2013. "Impacts of a Prekindergarten Program on Children's Mathematics, Language, Literacy, Executive Function, and Emotional Skills." *Child Development* 84 (6): 2112–30.

Whitehurst, G. R. 2018. "Does State Pre-K Improve Children's Achievement?" *Evidence Speaks Reports* 2 (59). Brookings Institution, Washington, DC.

World Bank. 2018. "Republic of Azerbaijan Early Childhood Development SABER Country Report." World Bank, Washington, DC.

Yoshikawa, H., A. J. Wuermli, A. Raikes, S. Kim, and S. B. Kabay. 2018. "Toward High Quality Early Childhood Development Programs and Policies at National Scale: Directions for Research in Global Contexts." *Social Policy Report* 31 (1): 1–36.

www.ingramcontent.com/pod-product-compliance
Lightning Source LLC
Chambersburg PA
CBHW041303210326
41598CB00005B/10